1000
Best Courses
in Britain and Ireland

Foreword by Ronan Rafferty

AURUM PRESS

First published in Great Britain 1999
by Aurum Press Ltd, 25 Bedford Avenue, London WC1B 3AT

A catalogue record for this book is available from the British Library.

ISBN 1 85410 623 6

Text compiled and written by Jim Humberstone
Design by Don Macpherson
Typeset by Action Publishing Technology Ltd, Gloucester
Printed and bound by in Great Britain by
CPD Group, Wales

Contents

Foreword

Enjoyment from playing golf means different things to different people. For some, it is friendly competition that brings the enjoyment. For others, the enjoyment comes from attaining mastery of the game. For the majority, however, it derives from the diverse and beautiful locations in which the game is played. While a tennis court is defined by the same white lines from Wimbledon to Flushing Meadow, and a football pitch conforms to roughly the same dimensions from Wembley to the Bernabeu, golf courses differ in design and type throughout the world. The constraints imposed on many games simply do not apply to golf.

Despite having played over 400 courses in Britain and Ireland, it still amazes me the different locations in which golf is played on these isles. Just when you think you have seen it all, and finalised your own personal-favourites list, a course or a particular hole comes along that completely changes your mind, or your concept of what makes a great golf course. That feeling of discovery is what keeps golfers in love with the game, just waiting to play the next outstanding course and have the next great experience.

Of course, it doesn't take too long for them to come along, because Britain and Ireland are blessed with some of the greatest and most natural golf courses in the world. From the historic links courses that dot every stretch of coastline, to the heather and heath courses of southern England, to the moorland courses of the North, the travelling golfer is faced with an embarrassment of riches unrivalled anywhere in the world.

Personal favourites for me include Royal County Down, Royal West Norfolk and Woodhall Spa, but they change all the time depending on recent experiences. What never changes, whether as a professional player or playing in one's spare time, is the thrill of standing on the 1st tee at places like St Andrews, Prestwick and Machrihanish, with all those uncharted waters ahead.

Golf has been very kind to me in my career. My enthusiasm for the professional circuit is certainly matched by my love of courses, in both an aesthetic and design sense. I certainly hope the readers of this book use it as a passport to a wider love of the game. Within these 1000 courses there are a host of well-known, established layouts that offer a great golfing day out. But there are also courses that have been forgotten over the years, like Silloth-on-Solway, Burnham and Berrow and Prince's, which deserve to be rediscovered. Search them out – my experience is that you will not be disappointed.

Ronan Rafferty

Preface

Welcome to *Golf World's 1000 Best Courses in Britain and Ireland*, a book I hope you will keep as a invaluable guide for many years to come. For golfers who love to visit new courses, this book is an exciting introduction to the best on offer and will ensure that you do not waste your time or money on a course that simply does not come up to scratch. On the following pages you will be guided to the best value golf courses, sure in the knowledge that these have been rated individually by readers and experienced *Golf World* staff.

This book is about making judgements about courses, so that you know that the places you are going to visit already have our own special approval. Some are better than others, and our course rating obviously reflects individual standards as we examine the total golf experience – the quality of welcome, the course itself, the catering and the overall value for money.

Golf World, Europe's top-selling monthly golf magazine, is proud of the accolades it receives for its biennial rankings of the Top 100 courses in the British Isles. This book takes those rankings further to include more courses, many of which are more accessible and affordable than the original Top 100 listings.

Whether you wish to visit some of the courses featured with a friend or as part of a society, this book will help you decide where to go. The book is divided into counties to make your search easier. Separate listings have also been given for the most friendly clubs, the best value clubs, and for each county we spotlight the favourite course for the area.

Discovering new courses that offer a wonderful day's golf is one of the biggest appeals of the game. We trust that, with our help, you will enjoy many special days in the years to come.

Good golfing.

David Clarke
Editor, *Golf World*

Introduction

Golf World launched its first nationwide survey of golf courses in October 1998. Through our readers, we aimed to produce the first independent, authoritative guide to the best golf courses to play in Britain and Ireland. The rankings and ratings contained in this book completely reflect the thoughts and experiences of ordinary golfers.

Lists of the best places to play are typically selected by professionals, course designers and figures of authority within the golfing industry. Unlike the golfing cognoscenti, who are not out there playing courses day in day out, the green-fee-paying golfer is, and is often better placed to identify the strengths and weaknesses of the top courses.

Upon this premise, we asked our readers to evaluate 1000 pre-selected courses in eight different categories: value for money, course presentation, course difficulty, quality of food and drink, quality of pro shop, quality of practice facilities and the quality of welcome. Finally, they were asked to give an overall rating that accurately reflected the quality of the golf experience.

By ranking the courses in these categories, we aimed to answer questions that the typical golfer might ask before visiting a new course: Is it worth the money? Is the course too hard for a player of my standard? Where will I be made welcome? We also wanted to know what, in the opinion of the grass-roots golfers, were the best courses in Britain and Ireland.

While the ratings and rankings achieved the purpose of grading each course, we also wanted golfers' comments about them. At the foot of each entry in this guide you will find individual comments about the 1000 courses from the people who have played them – in many cases the comments are as illuminating as the ratings.

Any guide that attempts to grade courses is open to criticism. People like different courses for different reasons, just as people enjoy playing golf for different reasons. We are acutely aware of this fact and have tried to balance the ratings and comments to achieve a fair, rational view. Hopefully you will agree. If not, it should cause a lively debate in the club bar, and we welcome any views or comments you should have about this guide.

How to use this guide

The book is split into three sections. In the first section are the rankings of the Top 100 Courses, the 50 Best Value Courses, the 20 Most Difficult Courses and the Top 10 Courses for Welcome in Britain and Ireland. In the second section are the star ratings for all 1000 courses, rated from five star to one star as follows:

★★★★★   – Exceptional. The best.
★★★★   – Excellent. An outstanding day's golf.
★★★   – Very good.
★★   – Good, but not great.
★   – Standard. Nothing special.

The third section is the main part of the book, listing all 1000 courses. Here you will find all the information you need to organise a game. The listing starts county by county with England, then Scotland, Wales and Ireland. The division of courses in Scotland and Wales has been chosen for simplicity rather than to adhere to the new county boundaries. A review of *Golf World*'s favourite course (or courses) in the area appears at the beginning of each county listing (with the exceptions of Middlesex, West Midlands, Tyne & Wear and East Yorkshire).

This is a typical entry:

North Foreland Golf Club   ★★★★

Convent Road, Thanet, CT10 3PU
Nearest main town: Broadstairs

Secretary:	Mr B. Preston	Tel: 01843 862140
		Fax: 01843 862663
Professional:	Mr N. Hanson	Tel: 01843 604471

Playing: Midweek: round £27.50; day £37.50. Weekend: round £37.50; day n/a. Handicap certificate required.

Facilities: Bar: 11am–11pm. Food: Breakfast, lunch and dinner from 9am–6pm. Bar snacks.

Comments: Very exposed and bracing ... Very few hazards and yet it's so difficult ... Played it in a gale – super ... Real triumph for the designers ... Not in great condition but that's how it is supposed to be.

– The information listed is accurate at the time of going to press. The bar and catering times given are expected opening times during the summer. In many cases during the winter, bar and catering times are likely to be shorter due to the early close of play.

– There are four possible green fee prices for weekday round/day and weekends round/day. Where there is no price next to an entry, it means that price is not available at the club.

Advice for Visitors

It often feels like you need a special handshake to get into some golf courses. Clubs tend to be protective of their courses, much as a child guards his or her favourite toy. Provided you have a handicap and are clear on golf etiquette, there are just a few simple rules to smooth the way.

The majority of the courses listed in the book require visitors to contact the club in advance and be able to produce a handicap certificate on the day of play. That is normally sufficient. When approaching some of the more exclusive courses, it is recommended that you write a letter of introduction direct to the secretary or organise a letter of introduction from your own club secretary.

With the exception of a very few clubs, there is nothing to stop you playing the best courses in the country, provided you follow these basic introductions. If you do not have a handicap, then the best advice is to follow the normal procedures and hope for the best – you may be asked to prove your ability when you arrive at the club.

Clubs have many competition and society days during the year, so find out the best days for visitors before you go. If you turn up on the door, you may be disappointed. Also, remember to pack a jacket and tie as many clubs have a dress code in the bar and dining room.

Good golfing!

TOP 100 COURSES

1. Royal County Down	45. Burnham and Berrow
2. Woodhall Spa	46. Formby
3. Royal Portrush (Dunluce)	47. Gullane (No. 1)
4. Gleneagles (Kings)	48. Ballyliffin (Glashedy)
5. Royal Birkdale	49. East Sussex National
6. Muirfield	50. Boat of Garten
7. Chart Hills	51. The Berkshire (Red)
8. Royal Dornoch	52. Killarney (Kileen)
9. Carnoustie	53. Blairgowrie (Rosemount)
10. Ballybunion (Old)	54. Carden Park
11. Turnberry (Ailsa)	55. The Berkshire (Blue)
12. Cruden Bay	56. Slaley Hall
13. Silloth-on-Solway	57. Hanbury Manor
14. Royal Lytham & St Annes	58. Glasson
15. Mount Juliet	59. Dunbar
16. The Alwoodley	60. Skibo
17. St George's Hill	61. Tenby
18. Lahinch (Old)	62. Stoke Poges
19. Sunningdale (Old)	63. St Andrews (Jubilee)
20. Royal St George's	64. Nefyn and District
21. St Andrews (Old)	65. Royal Liverpool
22. Portmarnock (Old)	66. West Sussex
23. Hillside	67. Mannings Heath (Waterfall)
24. Ladybank	68. Nairn
25. Royal Porthcawl	69. Beau Desert
26. Hankley Common	70. St Andrews (New)
27. Royal Troon	71. Machrihanish
28. County Sligo (Rosses Point)	72. Portstewart (Strand)
29. Crieff	73. Waterville
30. Ballybunion (Cashen)	74. Killarney (Mahoney's Point)
31. St Enodoc	75. Isle of Purbeck
32. Tralee	76. Brancepeth Castle
33. Woburn (Dukes)	77. Hunstanton
34. Royal St David's	78. Dalmahoy
35. Portmarnock Links	79. North Berwick
36. West Lancashire	80. Dooks
37. Glasgow Gailes	81. Prince's
38. Montrose Links Trust	82. County Tipperary
39. Old Head of Kinsale	83. The European Club
40. Western Gailes	84. St Mellion (Nicklaus)
41. Walton Heath (Old)	85. Downfield
42. Southerness	86. Berwick-on-Tweed
43. Ganton	87. Forest of Arden
44. Saunton (East)	88. Sunningdale (New)

89. Perranporth
90. Dartmouth
91. Ferndown
92. Edzell
93. Crail
94. Portsalon

95. Notts
96. Lundin
97. Powfoot
98. Trevose
99. Royal West Norfolk
100. Ballyliffin (Old)

50 BEST VALUE COURSES

1. Silloth-on-Solway
2. Perranporth
3. Boat of Garten
4. Tenby
5. Isle of Purbeck
6. Southerness
7. Kingussie
8. Machrie Hotel
9. Burnham and Berrow
10. Royal St David's
11. Dooks
12. Hayling Island
13. Llanymynech
14. Borth and Ynyslas
15. Carlow
16. Nefyn and District
17. St Enodoc
18. Tilgate Forest
19. Dunbar
20. Glasson
21. Cruden Bay
22. Machrihanish
23. Aberdovey
24. York
25. Stoneham
26. Belleisle
27. County Sligo (Rosses Point)
28. Tralee
29. St Andrews (New)
30. Connemara
31. Woodhall Spa
32. Barton-on-Sea
33. Hankley Common
34. Prince's
35. Tramore
36. Crieff
37. Nairn
38. The Hertfordshire
39. Thorpe Wood
40. Saunton (East)
41. La Moye
42. Broadstone
43. Hillside
44. Royal West Norfolk
45. Westport
46. Headport
47. Crowborough Beacon
48. Ladybank
49. Pennard
50. Pyle and Kenfig

20 MOST DIFFICULT COURSES

1. Carnoustie
2. Royal Portrush (Dunluce)
3. Woodhall Spa
4. Turnberry (Ailsa)
5. Royal County Down
6. The Alwoodley
7. Royal St David's
8. Royal Lytham and St Annes
9. Muirfield
10. St Mellion (Nicklaus)
11. Royal Birkdale
12. Silloth-on-Solway
13. Royal Troon
14. Royal St George's
15. Western Gailes
16. Burnham and Berrow
17. Royal Dornoch
18. Waterville
19. Moortown
20. St Andrews (Jubilee)

TOP 10 COURSES FOR WELCOME

1. East Sussex National
2. Portstewart (Strand)
3. The European Club
4. Duff House Royal
5. Royal Dornoch
6. Forest Pines
7. Carden Park
8. Tralee
9. Mount Juliet
10. County Sligo

STAR RATINGS

★★★★★

Ballybunion (Old)
Ballybunion (Cashen)
Ballyliffin (Glashedy)
Boat of Garten
Burnham and Berrow
Carnoustie
Chart Hills
County Sligo (Rosses Point)
Crieff
Cruden Bay
East Sussex National
Formby
Ganton
Glasgow Gailes
Gleneagles (Kings)
Gullane (No. 1)
Hankley Common
Hillside
Ladybank
Lahinch (Old)
Montrose Links Trust
Mount Juliet
Muirfield
Old Head of Kinsale
Portmarnock (Old)

Portmarnock Links
Royal Birkdale
Royal County Down
Royal Dornoch
Royal Lytham & St Annes
Royal Porthcawl
Royal Portrush (Dunluce)
Royal St David's
Royal St George's
Royal Troon
St Andrews (Old)
St Enodoc
St George's Hill
Saunton (East)
Silloth-on-Solway
Southerness
Sunningdale (Old)
The Alwoodley
Tralee
Turnberry (Ailsa)
Walton Heath (Old)
West Lancashire
Western Gailes
Woburn (Dukes)
Woodhall Spa

★★★★

Aberdovey
Adare Manor
Aldeburgh
Ashburnham
Ashridge
Aspley Guise and Woburn Sands
Balbirnie Park
Ballykisteen
Ballyliffin (Old)
Bamburgh Castle
Barton-on-Sea

Bearwood Lakes
Beau Desert
Beaufort
Belleisle
Belvoir Park
Berwick-on-Tweed
Bingley St Ives
Blackmoor
Blairgowrie (Rosemount)
Bolton Old Links
Borth and Ynyslas

Bowood
Brampton
Brancepeth Castle
Broadstone
Brookmans Park
Carden Park
Carlow
Carlyon Bay
Castlerock
Castletown
Cavendish
Ceann Sibeal (Dingle)
Celtic Manor (Roman Road)
Collingtree Park
Connemara
Conwy
Cork
County Louth
County Tipperary
Crail
Cumberwell Park
Dalmahoy
Dartmouth
Delamere Forest
Donegal
Dooks
Downfield
Druids Glen
Duff House Royal
Dunbar
East Berkshire
East Dorset
Edzell
Enniscrone
Ferndown
Forest of Arden
Forest Pines
Foxhills
Frilford Heath (Red)
Fulford
Fulford Heath
Gainsborough (Karsten)
Galway
Glasson
Gleneagles (Monarchs)
Gleneagles (Queens)

Gog Magog
Goring and Streatley
Hadley Wood
Hanbury Manor
Harrogate
Hawkstone Park Hotel
Hayling Island
Hesketh
Hindhead
Hunstanton
Ilkley
Irvine (Bogside)
Isle of Purbeck
John O'Gaunt (Main)
K-Club
Killarney (Kileen)
Killarney (Mahoney's Point)
Kilmarnock (Barrassie)
Kingussie
La Moye
Lahinch (Castle)
Lanhydrock
Leven
Lindrick
Liphook
Little Aston
Littlestone
Llanymynech
Loch Lomond
Longcliffe
Luffness New
Lundin
Lytham Green Drive
Machrie Hotel
Machrihanish
Manchester
Mannings Heath (Waterfall)
Manor House
Monifieth (Medal)
Moor Allerton
Moor Park (High)
Moortown
Moray (Old)
Nairn
Nefyn and District
Nizels

North Berwick
North Foreland
North Hants
Northamptonshire County
Notts
Pennard
Perranporth
Piltdown
Portpatrick (Dunskey)
Portsalon
Portstewart (Strand)
Powfoot
Prestwick
Prince's
Pyle and Kenfig
Rathsallagh
Rosapenna
Ross-on-Wye
Rotherham
Royal Aberdeen
Royal Ashdown Forest (Old)
Royal Dublin
Royal Jersey
Royal Liverpool
Royal Musselburgh
Royal North Devon
Royal Portrush (Valley)
Royal West Norfolk
Royal Worlington and Newmarket
St Andrews (Dukes)
St Andrews (Eden)
St Andrews (Jubilee)
St Andrews (New)
St Margaret's
St Mellion (Nicklaus)
St Pierre
Sand Moor
Sandiway
Scarcroft
Scotscraig
Seacroft
Seaford
Shanklin and Shandown
Skibo

Slaley Hall
Southerndown
Southport and Ainsdale
Stoke Poges
Stoneham
Sunningdale (New)
Tadmarton Heath
Tain
Tandridge
Tenby
The Addington
The Belfry (Brabazon)
The Berkshire (Blue)
The Berkshire (Red)
The Buckinghamshire
The European Club
The Glen
The Heswall
The Island
The Kendleshire
The London Club (Heritage)
The Roxburghe
Thorpeness
Thurlestone
Tilgate Forest
Tramore
Trevose
Tytherington
Wallasey
Waterville
Welcombe Hotel
Wellingborough
Wentworth (East)
West Cornwall
West Derby
West Hill
West Surrey
West Sussex
Westport
Woburn (Duchess)
Woking
Worksop
Worplesdon
York

★★★

Aberdour
Abridge
Alderney
Alloa
Alyth
Ardglass
Army
Ashdown Forest (Old)
Athlone
Auchterarder
Badgemore Park
Ballybofey and Stranorlar
Ballycastle
Balmoral
Bangor
Barnard Castle
Bath
Beaconsfield
Bedford and County
Belmont Lodge
Belton Woods Hotel
Berkhamstead
Bigbury
Birchwood
Braemar
Brampton Park
Branston
Bristol and Clifton
Broadway
Brockenhurst Manor
Brocton Hall
Brora
Bruntsfield Links
Buchanan Castle
Bude and North Cornwall
Bundoran
Burhill
Burnham Beeches
Bury St Edmunds
Cairndhu
Callander
Camberley Heath
Came Down
Carlisle

Castletroy
Cathkin Braes
Charlesland
Charleville
Chesterfield
Chiltern Forest
China Fleet
Chorlton-cum-Hardy
Church Stretton
Churston
Clandeboye (Ava)
Clandeboye (Dufferin)
Clevedon
Clitheroe
Cooden Beach
Coombe Hill
Copthorne
Corhampton
Courtown
Coventry
Coxmoor
Cradoc
Crowborough Beacon
Deer Park
Deeside
Denham
Drift
Dromoland Castle
Duddingston
Dumfries and County
Dummer
Dundalk
Dungannon
Dunstable Downs
Eaglescliffe
East Devon
East Renfrewshire
Eaton
Eden
Edgbaston
Effingham
Elgin
Ellesborough
Enville (Highgate)

Enville (Lodge)
Exeter
Fairhaven
Faithlegg House
Farrington (Main)
Faversham
Felixstowe Ferry
Five Lakes (Lakes)
Fleetwood
Forfar
Forres
Fortrose and Rosemarkie
Freshwater Bay
Frilford Heath (Blue)
Frodsham
Fulwell
Galway Bay
Garforth
Gerrards Cross
Glasgow
Golf House Club
Golspie
Grange Park
Grantown-on-Spey
Great Yarmouth and Caister
Guildford
Gullane (No. 2)
Gullane (No. 3)
Haggs Castle
Halifax
Hallamshire
Harleyford
Hartlepool
Headfort
Hellidon Lakes
Henley
Hermitage
Hever
High Post
Hill Valley (Emerald)
Hillsborough
Hilton Park
Hockley
Holyhead
Hopeman
Horsley Lodge

Huddersfield
Huntercombe
Ilfracombe
Inverness
Ipswich (Purdis Heath)
Isle of Wedmore
Kedleston Park
Kenmare
Keswick
Kilkenny
Killorgin
Kilmacolm
Kilspindie
Kilworth Springs
Kings Lynn
Kings Norton
Kington
Kirkbymoorside
Kirkcaldy
Kirkistown Castle
Knock
Knole Park
Lakeside Lodge
Lancaster
Langdon Hills
Langley Park
Lee Valley
Letham Grange (Old)
Limerick County
Linden Hall
Littlehampton
Llandudno
London Club (International)
Long Ashton
Longniddry
Luffenham Heath
Luttrellstown Castle
Lyneham
Malone
Mannings Heath (Kingfisher)
Massereene
Mendip Springs (Brinsea)
Meon Valley
Mere
Merrist Wood
Mill Ride

Millbrook
Millport
Moffat
Monifieth (Ashludie)
Moray (New)
Mottram Hall
Mount Temple
Murcar
Murrayshall
Musselburgh
Nairn Dunbar
Narin and Portnoo
Nevill
New Zealand
Newburgh-on-Ythan
Newbury and Crookham
Newmachar (Hawkshill)
Newmachar (Swailend)
Newport
North Shore Hotel
Northcliffe
Northop
Oake Manor
Old Thorns
Orchardleigh
Ormskirk
Panmure
Pannal
Parknasilla
Parkstone
Penrith
Peterborough Milton
Belfry (PGA National)
Pitlochry
Portal (Championship)
Portal (Premier)
Porters Park
Porthmadog
Portlethen
Powerscourt
Prestbury
Prestwick St Cuthberts
Pyrford
Raddison Roe Park
Reading
Reddish Vale

Redlibbets
Rolls of Monmouth
Romanby
Romford
Roserrow
Rosslare
Rowlands Castle
Royal Blackheath
Royal Burgess
Royal Cinque Ports
Royal Cromer
Royal Eastbourne
Royal Epping Forest
Royal Guernsey
Royal Mid-Surrey
Royal Norwich
Royal Winchester
Rudding Park
Rushmere
Rye
St Annes Old Links
St Augustines
Salisbury and South Wilts
Sandford Springs
Saunton (West)
Scarborough North Cliff
Scarborough South Cliff
Seahouses
Seascale
Seaton Carew
Seckford
Selsdon Park Hotel
Shannon
Shaw Hill
Sherborne
Sheringham
Sherwood Forest
Shifnal
Shipley
Shiskine
Silecroft
Slieve Russell
South Herts
South Winchester
Southfield
Southport Old Links

Standish Court
Stock Brook Manor
Stockley Park
Stockport
Stocks Hotel
Stoke-by-Nayland
  (Gainsborough)
Stonehaven
Stratford-upon-Avon
Strathhaven
Sundridge Park (East)
Sundridge Park (West)
Sutton Coldfield
Swindon
Temple
The Childwall
The Lambourne
The Oxfordshire
The Shropshire
The Suffolk
The Warwickshire (SE)
The Wisley
Thetford
Thorpe Wood
Three Rivers (Kings)
Tidworth Garrison
Torquay

Troon Portland
Tullamore
Turnberry (Arran)
Ulverston
Verulam
Wakefield
Walton Heath (New)
Waterlooville
West Berks
West Byfleet
West Essex
West Waterford
Whitekirk
Whittington Heath
Wildwood
Windlesham
Windyhill
Wollaton Park
Woodbrige
Woodbrook
Woodbury Park
Woodenbridge
Woodhall Spa (Bracken)
Workington
Worthing
Yeovil

★★

Abbotsley (Abbotsley)
Aberystwyth
Aboyne
Aldenham (Old)
Alnmouth
Appleby
Austin Lodge
Aylesbury Vale
Ballochmyle
Barrow
Basingstoke
Beadlow Manor (Baroness)
Beamish Park
Bellingham
Belton Park

Beverley and East Riding
Birch Hall
Black Bush
Blairgowrie (Lansdowne)
Bognor Regis
Boldon
Bolton
Braehead
Braintree
Bramshaw (Manor)
Breadsall Priory (Moor)
Brunston Castle
Bull Bay
Buxton and High Peak
Caerphilly

Calcot Park
Caldy
Cams Hall (Creek)
Canterbury
Castle Eden
Castle Royle
Castlehume
Cathcart Castle
Celtic Manor (Coldra Woods)
Chapel-en-le-Frith
Chelmsford
Cherry Lodge
Chesfield Downs
Chichester (Cathedral)
Chichester (Tower)
Chigwell
Chipping Sodbury
Chorley
Cleve Hill
Cleveland
Cocksford
Cold Ashby
Copt Heath
Cotgrave Place
County Cavan
Cruit Island
Cullen
Dainton Park
Dean Wood
Dinsdale Spa
Doncaster
Downshire
Drayton Park
Druids Heath
Dudsbury
Dukes Dene
Dunfermline
Dungarvan
Dunham Forest
Dunmurry
Dunstanburgh Castle
Eastbourne Downs
East Herts
Eaton
Elton Furze
Epsom

Falmouth
Farnham
Farnham Park
Five Lakes (Links)
Flackwell Heath
Forest Park (Old Foss)
Frilford Heath (Green)
Frinton (Long)
Furness
Garesfield
Gatton Manor
George Washington Hotel
Girton
Goodwood
Gorleston
Gourock
Great Hadham
Greenore
Greetham Valley
Hallowes
Harewood Downs
Haydock Park
Headingley
Henbury
Herons Reach
Hexham
Heyrose
Hollywood Lakes
Hornsea
Hoylake (Municipal)
Isle of Wedmore
Jarvis Gloucester Hotel
John O'Gaunt (Carthagena)
Keighley
Kemnay
Kendal
Kilkeel
Killeen
Kilworth Springs
Kings Norton
Kintore
Kirkby Lonsdale
Kirriemuir
Knockanally
Knowle
Lanark

Largs
Launceston
Leeds
Leek
Leigh
Leighton Buzzard
Letchworth
Lisburn
Littlehampton
Llandrindod Wells
Longridge
Looe
Loudoun Gawf
Lullingstone Park
Lurgan
Mahee Island
Maidenhead
Malahide
Mallow
Malton and Norton
Mapperley
Market Harborough
Marlborough
Mentmore
Mid Sussex
Milngavie
Minchinhampton (Avening)
Minchinhampton (Cherington)
Minehead and West Somerset
Moatlands
Mortonhall
Mount Murray
Mount Wolsley
Mullingar
Mullion
Newark
Newmachar (Swailend)
North Middlesex
Northenden
North Wilts
Nuremore
Oakdale
Oakridge
Orsett
Paisley
Panshanger

Patshull Park
Penrhos
Peterculter
Prestwick St Nicholas
Puckrup Hall
Pype Hayes
Ramsdale Park (High)
Ramside Hall
Reigate Heath
Robin Hood
Rochester and Cobham
Royal Belfast
Royal Tarlair
Royal Wimbledon
Ruddington Grange
Rufford Park
St Austell
St David's
St Helen's Bay
St Mellons
Sandwell Park
Sandy Lodge
Seaford Head
Sedlescombe
Seedy Mill
Shirley Park
Shrigley Hall
Sickleholme
Sonning
South Beds
South Kyme
South Moor
Southampton
Spalding
Staddon Heights
Stapleford Abbots
Staverton Park
Stinchcombe Hill
Stoke-by-Nayland (Constable)
Swinton Park
Tavistock
Teignmouth
Telford
Tewkesbury Park
The Burstead
The Essex

The Warwickshire (NW)
The Wrekin
Theydon Bois
Tiverton
Tracy Park
Traigh
Trent Park
Tudor Park Hotel
Ufford Park Hotel
Ullesthorpe
Upavon
Upminster
Walmer and Kingsdown
Warrenpoint
Waterford
Waterford Castle
Waterstock
Wearside
Wensum Valley (Valley)
West Byfleet
West Herts
West Hove
West Kilbride
West Park
West Wilts

Western
Westerwood
Weston Turville
Weston-super-Mare
Westwood (Leek)
Weymouth
Wharton Park
Whipsnade Park
Whitefield
Wick
Wicklow
Wilmslow
Wiltshire
Windermere
Winter Hill
Woodham
Woodlands
Woodlands Manor
Woodsome Hall
Woodspring
Worcester
Wrangaton
Wyboston Lakes
Yelverton

★

Abbotsley (Cromwell)
Allendale
Arscott
Bank House
Barnham Broom Hotel
Bawburgh
Beacon Park
Bedlingtonshire
Bidford Grange
Bishop Auckland
Blackburn
Bondhay
Boston
Botley Park
Braid Hills
Brailes
Breadsall Priory (Priory)

Brett Vale
Bridgnorth
Bridlington
Bridport and West Dorset
Broome Park
Burghill Valley
Burton-on-Trent
Cambridge Meridian
Cambridgeshire Moat Hotel
Cape Cornwall
Carholme
Carradale
Carrickfergus
Castlewarden
Catterick
Cave Castle
Chalgrave Manor

Channels
Chesterton
Chipping Norton
Chirk
Churchill and Blakedown
Clonmel
Clontarf
Cockermouth
Colmworth
Cosby
Cottesmore (Griffin)
Cowglen
Cranbrook
Delvin Castle
Disley
Dullatur
Duns
Dunscar
Dyke
Edmondstown
Elderslie
Ennis
Farthingstone
Filton
Flamborough Head
Forest Hills
Gainsborough (Thonock)
Glamorganshire
Glencruitten
Gort
Grange Fell
Grange-over-Sands
Hagley
Halifax Bradley Hall
Hastings
Hayston
Hennerton
Herefordshire
Hintelsham Hall
Kilkea Castle
Killeline
Kingsthorpe
Kirkhill
Leamington and County
Leominster
Letterkenney

Liberton
Limerick
Lochranza
Lochwinnoch
Lothianburn
Loughrea
Lydd
Magdalene Fields
Manor of Groves
Mendip
Mid Kent
Mid Yorkshire
Mile End
Mill Green
Monkstown
Monmouthshire
Morecambe
Morlais Castle
Moseley
Mountrath
Muir of Ord
Muskerry
New Forest
Newbiggin-by-the-Sea
Newquay
North West
North Worcesterhire
Northumberland
Northwood
Oakmere Park
Ogbourne Downs
Old Conna
Otley
Oundle
Park Hill
Parklands
Penwortham
Peterhead
Pleasington
Pontypridd
Port Glasgow
Portadown
Pwllheli
Pyecombe
Radyr
Ranfurly Castle

Reigate Hill
Reymerston
Richmond
Richmond Park
Romiley
Roscommon
Royal Belfast
Rush
Shirehampton Park
Shirland
Silkstone
Singing Hills
Slinford Park
South Shields
Stand
Stirling
Strandhill
Strathlene
Tankersley Park
Test Valley

The Heath
Trentham Park
Vale
Vale of Leven
Warren
Weald of Kent
West Bowling
West Monmouthshire
West Park
Whitefields Hotel
Whitley Bay
Whitsand Bay
Wimbledon Common
Windmill Village
Windwhistle
Woodlands
Wooler
Worfield
Worsley

ENGLAND

Bedfordshire

John O'Gaunt Golf Club (Main) ★★★★

Sutton Park, Sandy, Biggleswade, SG17 2LY
Nearest main town: Biggleswade

Fred Hawtree is primarily known in the British Isles for his work on Hillside, the less illustrious but gorgeous neighbour of Royal Birkdale in Southport. One of the lesser works on his CV is the Main course at John O'Gaunt, a course located not far outside Biggleswade in Bedfordshire. Cut through parkland, it is a course with a wonderfully British feel and design.

British golfers generally have a preference for links, heathland and woodland (in roughly that order) golf, so it comes as no surprise that John O'Gaunt is never too busy and can, as a result, usually be found in exceptional condition. It is by far the best course in the county, and as a result holds all the important county and regional competitions.

In truth, it is part woodland and part parkland, but the trees rarely interfere with your line of sight and merely provide the backdrop for the course. That's not to say it is not difficult, indeed as a par-71 with only two par-5s and three par-3s, it is long at around 6,500 yards. There are a number of par-4s of over 400 yards, the pick being a 472-yard par-4 that the members grudgingly approach as if it were a par-5. Two of the finest holes on the course are the 10th, a par-3 where trouble lurks all around, and the 17th, where the green is located on an old castle mound.

With the fairways cut to curb aggression, and the greens small and well-protected, John O'Gaunt could be labelled unfair. You may even feel that there are not enough par-5s and par-3s to break the monotony of the 13 par-4s. But you're unlikely to come away from John O'Gaunt being anything but impressed with its condition and certain that there is nothing to beat it in the area.

Secretary:	Mr J. Keight	Tel: 01767 260360
		Fax: 01767 262834
Professional:	Mr P. Round	Tel: 01767 260094
		Fax: 01767 261381
Playing:	Midweek: round £45.00; day £45.00. Weekend: round £50.00; day £50.00. Handicap certificate required.	

Facilities: Bar: 11am–11pm. Food: Breakfast, lunch and dinner from 9am–9pm. Bar snacks.

Comments: Can be unwelcoming for non-members ... Challenging with delightful, changing views ... A very natural course with a river influencing play on four holes ... Far better than the Carthagena ... Very exciting ... Wonderful feel to this club.

Aspley Guise & Woburn Sands Golf Club   ★★★★

West Hill, Aspley Guise, Milton Keynes, MK17 8DX
Nearest main town: Milton Keynes

Secretary: Mr B. Hunt   Tel: 01908 583596
Fax: 01908 582974
Professional: Mr D. Marsden   Tel: 01908 582974
Fax: 01908 582974

Playing: Midweek: round £23.00; day £29.00. Weekend: round n/a; day n/a. Handicap certificate required.

Facilities: Bar: 11.30am–10.30pm. Food: Lunch and dinner from 11am–11pm. Bar snacks.

Comments: This course just makes you feel good – enough said ... Heavenly greens, accuracy at a premium ... Play the percentages here as there are plenty of big trees ... Undulating heathland with silver birch ... Make your score on the front nine ... Heathland beauty in area bereft of good golf.

Aylesbury Vale Golf Club   ★★

Wing, LU7 0UJ
Nearest main town: Leighton Buzzard

Secretary: Mr C. Wright   Tel: 01525 240196
Fax: 01525 240848
Professional: Mr C. Skeet   Tel: 01525 240197

Playing: Midweek: round £12.00; day £18.00. Weekend: round £21.00; day £26.00.

Facilities: Bar: 11am–11pm. Food: Lunch and dinner from 12pm–6pm. Bar snacks.

Comments: Very good for a young course (just eight years old) and fine value ... Needs 10 years to fully mature ... Good value and fun course where water is often in play ... Highlight is the 13th, a real cracker.

Beadlow Manor Hotel Golf and Country Club

Beadlow, Shefford, SG17 5PH
Nearest main town: Shefford

Secretary:	Mr R. Tommey	Tel: 01525 860800
		Fax: 01525 861345
Professional:	Mr P. Hetherington	Tel: 01525 861292

Playing: Midweek: round £22.00; day £22.00. Weekend: round £33.00; day £33.00. Handicap certificate required.

Facilities: Bar: 11am–11pm. Food: Lunch and dinner from 11am–11pm. Bar snacks.

Comments: Excellent facilities at this parkland course ... Condition varies but nice amateur course ... 36-hole complex with little to choose between the two courses ... US-style layout with plenty of water hazards ... Courses could be better given the standard of facilities ... Fair value.

Bedford & County Golf Club   ★★★

Green Lane, Clapham, MK41 6ET
Nearest main town: Bedford

Secretary:	Mr R. P. Walker	Tel: 01234 352617
		Fax: 01234 357195
Professional:	Mr R. Tattersall	Tel: 01234 359189

Playing: Midweek: round £24.00; day £30.00. Weekend: round n/a; day n/a. Handicap certificate required.

Facilities: Bar: 11am–10pm. Food: Lunch from 11am–6pm. Bar snacks.

Comments: Pleasing, straightforward parkland course ... Mature layout which can play long at times ... 15th the highlight of this cheerful course ... Quiet club in quiet golfing region.

Chalgrave Manor Golf Club

Dunstable Road, Chalgrave, Toddington, LU5 6JN
Nearest main town: Dunstable

Secretary:	Mr S. Rumball	Tel: 01525 876556
		Fax: 01525 876556
Professional:	Mr M. Brewer	Tel: 01525 876554

Playing: Midweek: round £15.00; day £25.00. Weekend: round £30.00; day £45.00.

Facilities: Bar: 11am–10pm. Food: Bar snacks.

Comments: New course with prospects ... Fun starts on the back nine ... Average condition ... Simple with plenty of birdie chances ... Adequate facilities.

Colmworth Golf Club ★

New Road, Colmworth, MK44 2NV
Nearest main town: Bedford

Secretary:	Mr P. Watmough	Tel: 01234 378181
		Fax: 01234 376235
Professional:	Mr A. Clifford	Tel: 01234 378181
		Fax: 01234 376235

Playing: Midweek: round £10.00; day £16.00. Weekend: round £17.00; day £26.00.

Facilities: Bar: 8am–10pm. Food: Breakfast, lunch and dinner from 8am–10pm. Bar snacks.

Comments: Poor condition ... A 'second shot' course ... Just about worth it for the weekday rate ... Very friendly club.

Dunstable Downs Golf Club

Whipsnade Road, Dunstable, LU6 2NB
Nearest main town: Dunstable

Secretary:	Mr D. Mear	Tel: 01582 604472
		Fax: 01582 478700
Professional:	Mr M. Weldon	Tel: 01582 478700
		Fax: 01582 478700

Playing: Midweek: round £20.00; day £30.00. Weekend: round n/a; day n/a. Handicap certificate required.

Facilities: Bar: Members only. Food: Members only.

Comments: Dramatic course with elevated tees above sweeping fair-ways ... Consistently surprising and interesting down-land/parkland course ... Few memorable holes with the exception of the 9th ... Edged out by John O'Gaunt as best Beds course.

John O'Gaunt Golf Club (Carthagena)   ★★

Sutton Park, Sandy, Biggleswade, SG17 2LY
Nearest main town: Biggleswade

Secretary: Mr J. Keight   Tel: 01767 260360
                                      Fax: 01767 262834
Professional: Mr P. Round   Tel: 01767 260094
                                      Fax: 01767 261381

Playing: Midweek: round £45.00; day £45.00. Weekend: round £50.00; day £50.00. Handicap certificate required.

Facilities: Bar: 11am–11pm. Food: Breakfast, lunch and dinner from 9am–9pm. Bar snacks.

Comments: Not as mature or natural as the main course ... Very challenging holes ... Shorter than main course and short on challenge ... If you're in the area, play the main course.

Leighton Buzzard Golf Club   ★★

Plantation Road, Leighton Buzzard, LU7 7JF
Nearest main town: Leighton Buzzard

Secretary: Mr J. Burchell   Tel: 01525 244800
                                      Fax: 01525 244801
Professional: Mr L. Scarbrow   Tel: 01525 244815
                                      Fax: 01525 244801

Playing: Midweek: round £20.00; day £27.00. Weekend: round n/a; day n/a. Handicap certificate required.

Facilities: Bar: 11am–11pm. Food: Lunch from 11.30am–2.30pm. Dinner from 5pm–8.30pm.

Comments: Tree-lined, mature course ... Can be very busy ... Members a little protective ... Overshadowed by nearby Woburn ... Great finish.

Mentmore Golf & Country Club ★★

Mentmore, Leighton Buzzard, LU7 OUA
Nearest main town: Leighton Buzzard

Secretary:	Mr M. Fallows	Tel: 01296 662020
		Fax: 01296 662592
Professional:	Mr P. Elson	Tel: 01296 662020

Playing: Midweek: round £30.00; day £50.00. Weekend: round £30.00; day £50.00.

Facilities: Bar: 11am–11pm. Food: Lunch on Sundays only from 12am–4pm. Dinner bookings for Friday and Saturday from 7pm–10pm.

Comments: For all the grace and splendour of the main building, the course has a long way to go ... Not much between the two 18-hole courses, but both short of highest order ... Good day out with all the facilities.

Millbrook Golf Club ★★★

Millbrook Village, Ampthill, MK45 2JB
Nearest main town: Ampthill

Secretary:	Mr D. Cook	Tel: 01525 840252
		Fax: 01525 406249
Professional:	Mr D. Armor	Tel: 01525 402269

Playing: Midweek: round £18.00; day £25.00. Weekend: round £30.00; day n/a. Handicap certificate required.

Facilities: Bar: 11am–9pm. Food: Bar snacks.

Comments: You need to be fit to play here ... Quite challenging ... Long course through woodland on rolling hills ... Good value ... Playable most of the year ... Progressive club ... Value golf.

South Bedfordshire Golf Club ★★

Warden Hill Road, Luton, LU2 7AA
Nearest main town: Luton

Secretary:	Mr C. Guyford	Tel: 01582 591500
		Fax: 01582 495381
Professional:	Mr E. Cogle	Tel: 01582 591209

Playing: Midweek: round £19.00; day £29.00. Weekend: round £25.00; day £36.50. Handicap certificate required.

Facilities: Bar: 11.30am–11pm. Food: Lunch and dinner from 11.30am–11pm. Bar snacks.

Comments: Plenty of holes (27), but all of average quality ... Normally in good condition ... Very busy ... Worth a try once ... Downland course with some dramatic holes.

Wyboston Lakes Golf Club   ★★

Wyboston Lakes, Wyboston, MK44 3AL
Nearest main town: St Neots

Secretary: Mr B. Chinn   Tel: 01480 223004
                                       Fax: 01480 407330
Professional: Mr P. Ashwell   Tel: 01480 223004
                                       Fax: 01480 407330

Playing: Midweek: round £11.00; day £22.00. Weekend: round £15.00; day £30.00.

Facilities: Bar: 11.30am–11pm. Food: Lunch and dinner from 11.30am–10pm. Bar snacks.

Comments: Beginner's course ... Terrific facilities and a worthy challenge ... A cheap course, not far behind some of the better ones in Beds ... Practice areas high class.

Berkshire

The Berkshire Golf Club (Red and Blue) ★★★★

Swinley Road, Ascot, SL5 8AY
Nearest main town: Ascot

Some golfers swear that the perfect golfing day out is to be had not on the links courses of Britain and Ireland but just off the M3 near Bracknell. Thirty-six holes of golf, playing the Red and Blue courses at the Berkshire, one either side of lunch, is, they say, sheer golfing heaven and a wonderful escape from the outside world.

The peace and tranquillity that can be found on these fairways, carved out of pine, chestnut and birch forest, is truly intoxicating. Not even the great heath and heather courses of nearby Surrey have quite the same feel as a late afternoon in the forest at the Berkshire. Which course you play matters little, as there is no general consensus as to which is the best, and no one knows which one the designer, Herbert Fowler (he of Walton Heath and Saunton fame), preferred.

The Red Course is certainly more interesting, mixing six par-3, six par-4s and six par-5s, a very modern blend of holes that many players wish they could have more of. The par-5s are really needed because of the depth and difficulty of the par-3s, many of which require long irons to tiny greens, protected on all sides. The 221-yard 16th, where the plateau green can only be held with a shot to the centre, is a good example. Indeed, it is a very tough track where, even if you do manage to keep out of the trees, you are still likely to get tangled up in heather.

For a more traditional round, the Blue Course may appeal more. The hazards are essentially the same as the Red with a stream coming into play on several fairways. It is shorter and perhaps a little easier than the Red, although the bunkering appears to be more precise and more thought is needed when you are standing on the tee.

Some say when you make a composite course of the two, as they do for competitions, you have the perfect golf course. Play this course on a crisp autumn or spring day, and you won't disagree.

Secretary:	Col J. Hunt	Tel: 01344 621496
		Fax: 01344 873090
Professional:	Mr P. Anderson	Tel: 01344 622351
Playing:	Prices on application.	

Facilities: Bar: Members only. Food: Members only.

Comments: It just gets tougher and tougher – a wonderful design ...
Attractive heather ... Both courses are what golf is all
about ... Stuffy atmosphere, but who cares when the
golf is this good ... Classic heathland course where you
can contemplate amongst the trees ... Everything you
would expect from an inland woodland course ... Can I
take this course home with me? ... Unusual, unique and
unchanged ... The best 36 holes (Blue and Red) in the
UK, without question.

Bearwood Lakes Golf Club   ★★★★

Bearwood Road, Sindlesham, RG41 4SJ
Nearest main town: Wokingham

Secretary: Miss J. Cobban   Tel: 0118 979 7900
                                         Fax: 0118 979 2911
Professional: Mr E. Inglis   Tel: 0118 978 3030

Playing: Prices on application.

Facilities: Bar: Members only. Food: Members only.

Comments: Modern design ... No two holes are the same ... One
of the best new courses around ... Very helpful pro shop
... Parkland course with a smattering of water ... Best
holes on the back nine around the lake.

Calcot Park Golf Club   ★★

Bath Road, Calcot, RG31 7RN
Nearest main town: Reading

Secretary: To be appointed.   Tel: 0118 9427124
                                         Fax: 0118 9453373
Professional: Mr I. Campbell   Tel: 0118 9427797

Playing: Midweek: round £36.00; day £36.00. Weekend: round
n/a; day n/a. Handicap certificate required.

Facilities: Bar: 11am–11pm. Food: Lunch and dinner from
11am–9pm. Bar snacks.

Comments: Undulating, open fairways ... Get out the driver ... 6th worth looking out for ... Interesting water features ... Company helped me enjoy this tough, changing track ... Fun to play with friends.

Castle Royle Golf Club   ★★

Bath Road, Knowl Hill, Reading, RG10 9XA
Nearest main town: Reading

Secretary: Mr M. Warne   Tel: 01628 829252
                                         Fax: 01628 825442
Professional: Mr P. Stanwick   Tel: 01628 825442

Playing: Midweek: round £35.00; day £50.00. Weekend: round £45.00; day n/a. Handicap certificate required.

Facilities: Bar: 7.30am–10.30pm. Food: Breakfast, lunch and dinner from 7.30am–8pm. Bar snacks.

Comments: Fairly unremarkable land for a golf course ... Way too pricey ... Neil Coles did a good job with raw materials ... Plenty of water ... Too expensive ... Views of Windsor Castle.

Downshire Golf Club   ★★

Easthampstead Park, Wokingham, RG11 3DH
Nearest main town: Wokingham

Secretary: Mr D. M. Coles   Tel: 01344 302030
                                         Fax: 01344 301020
Professional: Mr W. Owers   Tel: 01344 302030

Playing: Midweek: round £13.50; day n/a, Weekend: round £16.50; day n/a.

Facilities: Bar: 11am–11pm. Food: Breakfast and lunch from 7am–4pm. Dinner by arrangement.

Comments: Course catering for all standards ... Extremely good pay-and-play ... Mature public parkland course, hard to beat for municipal golf ... 7th and 15th stand out here ... Well done Downshire, best municipal in the land!

East Berkshire Golf Club ★★★★

Ravenswood Avenue, Crowthorne, RG45 6BD
Nearest main town: Crowthorne

Secretary:	Mr J. Stocker	Tel: 01344 772041
		Fax: 01344 7773378
Professional:	Mr A. Roe	Tel: 01344 774112

Playing: Midweek: round £37.00; day £37.00. Weekend: round £37.00; day £37.00. Handicap certificate required.

Facilities: Bar: 11am–8pm. Food: Lunch from 11am–5pm. Bar snacks.

Comments: Not far behind The Berkshire ... Very easy on the eye ... First rate course in heavenly countryside ... The smell of heather and pine simply intoxicating ... Not as hilly as other nearby courses ... A picture ... Heather makes life very tough.

Goring & Streatley Golf Club ★★★★

Rectory Road, Streatley-on-Thames, RG8 9QA
Nearest main town: Streatley-on-Thames

Secretary:	Mr I. McCall	Tel: 01491 872688
		Fax: 01491 875224
Professional:	Mr R. Mason	Tel: 01491 873715

Playing: Midweek: round £22.00; day £30.00. Weekend: round £22.00; day £30.00. Handicap certificate required.

Facilities: Bar: 10.30am–11pm. Food: Lunch and dinner from 11am–8pm. Bar snacks.

Comments: Hilly course ... Sloping lies and high scores ... Wonderful views of the River Thames ... Very friendly club – wish you could say the same about the course ... Views of the Ridgeway on this up-and-down course.

Hennerton Golf Club ★

Crazies Hill Road, Wargrave, RG10 8LT
Nearest main town: Wargrave

Secretary:	Mrs S. Dean	Tel: 0118 9401000
Professional:	Mr W. Farrow	Tel: 0118 9404778

Playing: Midweek: round £15.00; day n/a. Weekend: round
£18.00; day n/a.

Facilities: Bar: 11am–11pm. Food: Lunch and dinner from
10am–8pm. Bar snacks.

Comments: Not many nine-holers in the area but this is the best ...
Very natural ... Good value for nine holes ... Good for
anyone who can't cope with a full round ... Fun for
beginners, swerve it if you know the game.

Maidenhead Golf Club   ★★

Shoppenhangers Road, Maidenhead, SL6 2PZ
Nearest main town: Maidenhead

Secretary: Mr T. Jackson   Tel: 01628 624693
                                          Fax: 01628 780758
Professional: Mr S. Geary   Tel: 01628 624067

Playing: Midweek: round £27.00; day £35.00. Weekend: round
£35.00; day n/a. Handicap certificate required.

Facilities: Bar: 11am–10pm. Food: Lunch from 11am–6pm. Bar
snacks.

Comments: Par-3s really stand out ... Very flat and fairly simple ...
Good short holes ... Parkland course, but there is better
in Berkshire.

Mill Ride Golf Club   ★★★

Mill Ride, Ascot, SL5 8LT
Nearest main town: Ascot

Secretary: Mr G. Irvine   Tel: 01344 886777
                                          Fax: 01344 886820
Professional: Mr M. Palmer   Tel: 01344 886777

Playing: Midweek: round £40.00; day £60.00. Weekend: round
£60.00; day n/a. Handicap certificate required.

Facilities: Bar: 7.30am–11pm. Food: Breakfast and lunch from
7.30am–6pm.

Comments: New course with plenty of character ... A little expensive
... Best yet to come ... Very challenging ... Overpriced,
like all the courses in this area.

Newbury & Crookham Golf Club ★★★

Burys Bank Road, Greenham, Newbury, RG19 8BZ
Nearest main town: Newbury

Secretary: Mrs J. L. Hearsey   Tel: 01635 40035
                                          Fax: 01635 40045
Professional: Mr D. W. Harris   Tel: 01635 31201

Playing: Midweek: round £20.00; day £30.00. Weekend: round n/a; day n/a. Handicap certificate required.

Facilities: Bar: 11am–11pm. Food: Lunch from 11am–2pm. Bar snacks. Dinner by arrangement.

Comments: Decent value for a hugely underrated course ... Interesting parkland ... Think carefully around this strategic track ... Trees seemingly in the way all the time ... Good value ... Condition varies and facilities a little poor ... Best course for miles around.

Reading Golf Club ★★★

17 Kidmore End Road, Emmer Green, Reading, RG4 8SG
Nearest main town: Reading

Secretary: Mr R. J. Harris   Tel: 0118 947 2909
Professional: Mr A. R. Wild   Tel: 0118 947 6115

Playing: Midweek: round £30.00; day £30.00. Weekend: round n/a; day n/a. Handicap certificate required.

Facilities: Bar: 11am–11pm. Food: Bar snacks.

Comments: Very friendly and simple club ... Par-5 the highlight ... Not much to get excited about.

Sonning Golf Club ★★

Duffield Road, Sonning, Reading, RG4 6GJ
Nearest main town: Reading

Secretary: Mr P. F. Williams   Tel: 0118 9693332
                                          Fax: 0118 9448409
Professional: Mr R. T. McDougall   Tel: 0118 9692910

Playing: Midweek: round £25.00; day £35.00. Weekend: round n/a; day n/a. Handicap certificate required.

Facilities: Bar: 11am–11pm. Food: Lunch from 12pm–2pm. Dinner from 6pm–9pm.

Comments: Flat, but long and hard course ... Fairly flat and dull ... Key is driving the ball well ... Pretty straightforward and open – just how I like it ... By no means in the top echelon in Berkshire, but lovely feel to this club ... Clubhouse recently improved, much overdue.

Temple Golf Club   ★★★

Henley Road, Hurley, SL6 5LH
Nearest main town: Maidenhead

Secretary: Mr K. G. M. Adderley   Tel: 01628 824795
                                       Fax: 01628 828119
Professional: Mr J. Whiteley   Tel: 01628 824254

Playing: Midweek: round £30.00; day £45.00. Weekend: round £35.00; day £50.00. Handicap certificate required.

Facilities: Bar: 11am–10pm. Food: Bar snacks. Dinner by arrangement.

Comments: Nobble your opening tee shot and the ball just scampers down the hill ... Great variety at this exclusive bolt-hole near Marlow ... The punchbowl green at the 12th throws out the rulebook ... Some monster par-4s with long iron approaches ... A fine parkland course with great values and service ... Lovely autumn course when the colours are so bold ... 11th is the toughest hole here.

West Berkshire Golf Club   ★★★

Chaddleworth, Newbury, RG16 0HS
Nearest main town: Newbury

Secretary: Mrs C. M. Clayton   Tel: 01488 638574
                                    Fax: 01488 638781
Professional: Mr P. Simpson   Tel: 01488 638851

Playing: Midweek: round £18.00; day £26.00. Weekend: round £22.00; day n/a.

Facilities: Bar: 11am–11pm. Food: Lunch from 9am–4.30pm. Bar snacks.

Comments: Goes on forever ... Decent value ... Long and not that interesting ... Expected heath and heather but got a flattish, nondescript course ... Not blessed with area's fine scenery ... Good value ... Easy walking for a long course ... Par-5 5th is one of longest in England at over 600 yards ... Get a buggy ... Long par-5 is just a joke.

Winter Hill Golf Club ★★

Grange Lane, Cookham, SL6 9RP
Nearest main town: Maidenhead

Secretary:	Mr J. E. Hoskings	Tel: 01628 527613
		Fax: 01628 527613
Professional:	Mr R. Frost	Tel: 01628 527610

Playing: Midweek: round £18.00; day £25.00. Weekend: round n/a; day n/a.

Facilities: Bar: 11.30am–9.30pm. Food: Bar snacks from 11.30am–5pm.

Comments: Views overlooking the River Thames towards Cliveden don't disguise how average this course is ... Straightforward course with many uninteresting holes ... Very open, bad shots not always punished ... Not on my list in Berkshire.

Buckinghamshire

Woburn Golf Club (Dukes)   ★★★★★

Bow Brickhill, Milton Keynes, MK17 9LJ
Nearest main town: Milton Keynes

One of the best known and most popular courses in England, Woburn consistently justifies its position as a favourite among discerning golfers. Few other courses in the country have as much appeal as Woburn, a feeling that was perpetuated by the flattering TV pictures of the course when the British Masters was held here on a regular basis. Although it no longer hosts top tournaments, the condition of the course is always good and provides a quality golfing day out, particularly for golf societies that aspire to deliver a quality course for their members at reasonable rates. As a consequence, the course can get busy and it's worth checking out when to play in advance. The Woburn experience is not something that you can keep to yourself.

The course is certainly demanding, and is not recommended for the inexperienced, who will find it a long slog and a hopeless criss-cross across the fairways to find the ball in woods. Woburn is essentially a driver's course, and the player who can hit it long and straight invariably can score well as there are few dangers around the greens. Most of the fairways are bordered by magnificent pines, so there is no real need for any rough at Woburn, except on some of the more exposed holes around the turn. One of the hardest shots you will have to master here is how to play your ball off pine needles, which really need to be nipped off a tight lie. This is particularly the case at the 4th, a wonderful dogleg played through a funnel of pines, and the 17th and 18th, two similar right-hand doglegs where you must place your tee shot with great accuracy. The best stretch of holes is from the 13th onwards.

Practice facilities here are some of the best in Europe, while the club lunch is legendary. No one who plays at Woburn should leave without dining here. The advice is not to have something too big at breakfast as portions over lunch are more than generous. You'll enjoy the quality of the food as much as you will the course. And that goes for the Duchess Course as well.

Secretary: Mrs G. Beasley   Tel: 01908 370756
                                            Fax: 01908 378436
Professional: Mr L. Blacklock   Tel: 01908 647987

Playing:	Midweek: round £44.00; day £81.00. Weekend: round n/a; day n/a. Handicap certificate required.
Facilities:	Bar: 12am–8pm. Food: Lunch from 12pm–2pm.
Comments:	Just a fine golfing experience – perfect ... Fantastic day's golf ... Cut out of a forest, this course is simply superb ... Outstanding day out spoilt by the cost of play ... Most imaginatively designed course in the south of England ... Quality course demanding quality golf ... Bad press undeserved ... Woburn is still the one to beat.

Beaconsfield Golf Club   ★★★

Seer Green, Beaconsfield, HP9 2UR
Nearest main town: Beaconsfield

Secretary:	Mr R. E. Thomas	Tel: 01494 676545 Fax: 01494 681148
Professional:	Mr M. Brothers	Tel: 01494 676616
Playing:	Midweek: round £30.00; day £40.00. Weekend: round n/a; day n/a. Handicap certificate required.	
Facilities:	Bar: 11am–9.30pm. Food: Breakfast and lunch from 9am–5pm. Dinner by arrangement.	
Comments:	Played here in abysmal weather but not one blade of grass was out of place ... Good, interesting parkland course requiring a subtle short game to score well ... Much improved over the last two years ... Not particularly welcoming but the course makes up for it ... Cracking clubhouse and the course, well, I didn't want to leave ... Arresting course that never takes the driver out of your hands ... Better than Stoke Poges and more homely for the visitor ... Could not wait to play after glimpsing it from the railway ... Super finish to elegant course.	

Burnham Beeches Golf Club   ★★★

Green Lane, Burnham, SL1 8EG
Nearest main town: Slough

Secretary:	Mr A. J. Buckner	Tel: 01628 661448 Fax: 01628 668968
Professional:	Mr R. Bolton	Tel: 01628 661661

Playing: Midweek: round £30.00; day £45.00. Weekend: round n/a; day n/a. Handicap certificate required.

Facilities: Bar: 11am–10pm. Food: Lunch and dinner from 10am–8pm.

Comments: Traditional parkland golf ... Value given its proximity to some pricey courses ... Continues to be a proper golf club ... Almost as good as nearby Stoke Poges ... If you go, take time to enjoy the woods ... Surprisingly open, welcoming club – usually quiet.

Chiltern Forest Golf Club ★★★

Aston Hill, Halton, HP22 5NQ
Nearest main town: Aylesbury

Secretary: Mr S. Thornton   Tel: 01296 631267
                                  Fax: 01296 631267
Professional: Mr C. Skeet   Tel: 01296 631817

Playing: Midweek: round n/a, day £18.00. Weekend: round n/a; day n/a.

Facilities: Bar: 11am–11pm. Food: Lunch and dinner from 12pm–6pm. Bar snacks.

Comments: Very underrated ... Scenic but don't be fooled by the course ... Danger everywhere you look ... Great-looker but not that difficult.

Denham Golf Club ★★★

Tilehouse Lane, Denham, UB9 5DE
Nearest main town: Denham

Secretary: Mr M. J. Miller   Tel: 01895 832002
                                   Fax: 01895 835340
Professional: Mr S. Campbell   Tel: 01895 832801

Playing: Midweek: round £35.00; day £53.00. Weekend: round n/a; day n/a. Handicap certificate required.

Facilities: Bar: 11am–8pm. Food: Lunch from 11am–4pm. Bar snacks.

Comments: Dropped in by chance and felt thoroughly welcome ... So nice, so close to London ... Its difficulty is somewhat reliant on the weather ... Beguiling parkland/heathland ... Top of the tree in Bucks ... Hilly, but you don't mind here.

Ellesborough Golf Club ★★★

Butlers Cross, Aylesbury, HP17 OTZ
Nearest main town: Aylesbury

Secretary:	Mr P. M. J. York	Tel: 01296 622114
		Fax: 01296 622114
Professional:	Mr M. Squire	Tel: 01296 623126

Playing: Midweek: round £30.00; day £40.00. Weekend: round n/a; day n/a. Handicap certificate required.

Facilities: Bar: 11am–11pm. Food: Breakfast and lunch from 11am–7pm.

Comments: Interesting course with scenery to match ... Not too difficult to master and excellent facilities ... Too hilly to be considered top class ... Dreary downland track.

Farnham Park Golf Club ★★

Park Road, Stoke Poges, SL2 4PJ
Nearest main town: Stoke Poges

Secretary:	Mrs M. Brooker	Tel: 01753 647065
Professional:	Mr P. Warner	Tel: 01753 643332

Playing: Midweek: round £9.00; day n/a. Weekend: round £12.00; day n/a.

Facilities: Bar: 11am–11pm. Food: Lunch and dinner from 11am–11pm. Bar snacks.

Comments: Pay-and-play that is consistently good ... A quality pay-and-play ... Mix of bland and interesting holes ... 9th is particular good driving over the corner of a lake ... Some class holes on the front nine ... Condition not great but well worth it for the price ... Can get a bit boggy.

Flackwell Heath Golf Club ★★

Treadaway Road, Flackwell Heath, High Wycombe, HP10 9PE
Nearest main town: High Wycombe

Secretary:	Mr M. Lowry	Tel: 01628 520027
		Fax: 01628 530040
Professional:	Mr P. Watson	Tel: 01628 523017

Playing: Midweek: round £20.00; day £30.00. Weekend: round n/a; day n/a. Handicap certificate required.

Facilities: Bar: 11am–8pm. Food: Lunch from 12am–2pm. Bar snacks. Dinner from 6pm–9pm.

Comments: Clip on the crampons ... Very hilly with good par-3s ... Long 7th next to the M40 is a very unattractive hole ... 15th is a cracker ... Short front nine consistently interesting, although a little easy ... Not the best in Bucks.

Gerrards Cross Golf Club ★★★

Chalfont Park, Gerrards Cross, SL9 0QA
Nearest main town: Gerrards Cross

Secretary:	Mrs I. Perkins	Tel: 01753 883263
		Fax: 01753 883593
Professional:	Mr M. Barr	Tel: 01753 885300

Playing: Midweek: round £32.50; day £40.00. Weekend: round n/a; day n/a. Handicap certificate required.

Facilities: Bar: 11am–11pm. Food: Breakfast, lunch and dinner available 8am–10pm. Bar snacks.

Comments: Sensational unknown course that never fails to surprise ... Nice doglegs and straightaway holes ... Par-3s are the highlight of this well-prepared and exclusive course ... This and Beaconsfield are superb to play and just sublime on warm summer evenings ... Can't pick between this and Beaconsfield.

Harewood Downs Golf Club ★★

Cokes Lane, Chalfont St Giles, HP8 4TA
Nearest main town: Amersham

Secretary:	Wg Cdr M. R. Cannon	Tel: 01494 762184
		Fax: 01494 766869

Professional: Mr G. C. Morris   Tel: 01494 764102

Playing: Midweek: round £25.00; day n/a. Weekend: round £30.00; day n/a. Handicap certificate required.

Facilities: Bar: 11am–10pm. Food: Lunch from 12am–2pm.

Comments: Exhausting and interesting course with some nice par-5s, particularly the 2nd ... Nice members' course with warm, open clubhouse ... A little up-and-down with enjoyable plunging approach shots on many holes ... Let me play here all the time, please ... Short but not particularly sweet.

Harleyford Golf Club   ★★★

Harleyford Estate, Henley Road, Marlow, SL7 2SP
Nearest main town: Marlow

Secretary: Mr R. Eades (Manager)   Tel: 01628 402338
                                       Fax: 01628 478434
Professional: Mr A. Barr   Tel: 01628 402300

Playing: Midweek: round £40.00; day £40.00. Weekend: round £60.00; day £60.00. Handicap certificate required.

Facilities: Bar: 11am–11pm. Food: Lunch and dinner from 10am–9pm. Bar snacks.

Comments: Very British feel to this new course ... Rich countryside in affluent area ... Very mature woodland site ... Grass bunkers give an old-fashioned feel ... Feels like a country retreat ... Holes wind their way down to the Thames ... Watch out for the chalk pit on the 12th ... Fine new course.

Stoke Poges Golf Club   ★★★★

Park Road, Stoke Poges, SL2 4PG
Nearest main town: Stoke Poges

Secretary: Mr R. C. Pickering   Tel: 01753 717162
                                      Fax: 01753 717181
Professional: Mr D. Woodward   Tel: 01753 717170

Playing: Midweek: round £60.00; day £90.00. Weekend: round £125.00; day n/a. Handicap certificate required.

Facilities: Bar: 11am–9pm. Food: Lunch and dinner from 11am–9pm. Bar snacks.

Comments: A tough course that can be a long slog at times ... The clubhouse is almost a palace – a gorgeous course ... Well presented and always in cream condition ... Clever bunkering ... Once one of my favourite old-fashioned clubs, now a vulgar country club (but the condition's better) ... Superbly restored clubhouse and the course is becoming a real complement ... Follow in the footsteps of James Bond.

The Buckinghamshire Golf Club   ★★★★

Denham Court, Denham Court Drive, Denham, UB9 5BG
Nearest main town: Uxbridge

Secretary: Mr W. Kirby   Tel: 01895 835777
                                        Fax: 01895 835210
Professional: Mr J. O'Leary

Playing: Midweek: round £70.00; day n/a. Weekend: round £80.00; day n/a. Handicap certificate required.

Facilities: Bar: 11am–11pm. Food: Lunch from 12pm–2pm. Dinner from 7pm–9pm.

Comments: Greens the best all year ... A real pleasure to play ... Greens just perfect ... Super greens – slick but holding ... A good test in unrivalled atmosphere ... Best course in the UK, fantastic practice facilities and excellent clubhouse ... A new course that feels as if it's been around for years ... Don't miss it.

The Lambourne Golf Club   ★★★

Dropmore Road, Burnham, SL1 8NF
Nearest main town: Burnham

Secretary: Mr W. Sheffield   Tel: 01628 666755
                  (General Manager)   Fax: 01628 663301
Professional: Mr D. T. Hart   Tel: 01628 662936

Playing: Midweek: round £36.00; day £45.00. Weekend: round £36.00; day £45.00. Handicap certificate required.

Facilities: Bar: 11am–11pm. Food: Lunch and dinner from 10am–9pm. Bar snacks.

Comments: A new course in a perfect location ... Well worth visiting and some cracking courses nearby ... A new course with big ambition ... Championship feel here and close to Burnham Beeches.

Weston Turville Golf Club ★★

New Road, Weston Turville, Aylesbury, HP22 5QT
Nearest main town: Aylesbury

Secretary:	Mr B. J. Hill	Tel: 01296 424084
		Fax: 01296 395376
Professional:	Mr G. George	Tel: 01296 425949

Playing: Midweek: round £20.00; day £25.00. Weekend: round £25.00; day n/a.

Facilities: Bar: 10am–9pm. Food: Bar snacks.

Comments: Easy walking ... Nothing special here ... Some interesting, natural holes ... Good value for a well-conditioned course ... Flat course with little definition ... Pretty good value for money.

Woburn Golf Club (Duchess) ★★★★

Bow Brickhill, Milton Keynes, MK17 9LJ
Nearest main town: Milton Keynes

Secretary:	Mrs G. Beasley	Tel: 01908 370756
		Fax: 01908 378436
Professional:	Mr L. Blacklock	Tel: 01908 370756

Playing: Midweek: round £44.00; day £81.00. Weekend: round n/a; day n/a. Handicap certificate required.

Facilities: Bar: 11am–8pm. Food: Lunch from 12pm–2pm.

Comments: Looks great ... Excellent carvery meal ... Super day out ... Slightly easier than the Dukes but first class in its own right ... Give me the Duchess over the Dukes anyday ... Can't wait for the third course at Woburn, but how can they beat the delightful Duchess!

Cambridgeshire

The Gog Magog Golf Club ★★★★

Shelford Bottom, Cambridge, CB2 4AB
Nearest main town: Cambridge

With a name like Gog Magog, you certainly expect something different from this course. In fact, it is very traditional and English, a hillside/parkland layout which has not changed much since its creation almost a hundred years ago.

Just three and a half miles south-west of the university town of Cambridge, Gog Magog is accustomed to entertaining some of the best amateur golfers in the country. The famous Lagonda Trophy has been played here many times and even the best amateurs have struggled to humiliate a course that celebrates its centenary in 2001.

Gog Magog is hilly in terms of Cambridgeshire's general relief, with the first two holes rising away and the last two holes descending to the clubhouse. In between you will find punishing rough, deep pot bunkers, hard and fast greens, and a mix of winds that makes it increasingly difficult throughout the round to stay on the straight and narrow.

It is a fine challenge for a par-70 and the members will tell you that the front nine, 330 yards shorter than the back, is the place to make your score. Certainly the 1st is as gentle an opening hole as you find anywhere and the 2nd, despite sounding intimidating with an old quarry in front of the tee box, is anything but, and can be a fair birdie opportunity. Out in the open country the course gets progressively flatter and more straightforward. Protecting your score is dependent on accurate driving and scoring well on the simple holes.

The finishing trio of holes is tough. The 449-yard 16th is regarded as the signature hole with heavy-handed fairway bunkering, while the 17th is a tricky downhill par-3 of 165 yards with a difficult-to-hold green. As a finishing hole, the 18th is a cracker, a par-4 of 446 yards running downhill to a green that runs away from you.

Secretary:	Mr I. Skellern	Tel: 01223 247626
		Fax: 01223 414990
Professional:	Mr I. Bamborough	Tel: 01223 246058
Playing:		Midweek: round £30.00; day £37.50. Weekend: round n/a; day n/a. Handicap certificate required.

Facilities: Bar: 11am–11pm. Food: Lunch and dinner from 10am–9pm.

Comments: Challenging, hilly course that leaves you wanting more ... Forget the Wandlebury, the one you want is the Old Course ... Improves all the time ... Well maintained pro shop ... The finest course in Cambridgeshire ... A must play for the traditionalist.

Abbotsley Golf Club & Hotel (Main) ★★

Eynesbury, Hardwicke, St Neots, PE19 4XN
Nearest main town: Cambridge

Secretary: Mr R. Jessop   Tel: 01480 474000
    Fax: 01480 471018
Professional: Mrs V. Saunders   Tel: 01480 474000

Playing: Midweek: round £25.00; day £30.00. Weekend: round £36.00; day n/a. Handicap certificate required.

Facilities: Bar: 10am–12pm. Food: Bar snacks. Dinner from 7.30pm–9.30pm.

Comments: Value for the money ... Mature parkland with numerous water hazards ... In design terms, way ahead of the Cromwell ... Tough finish ... Course surrounds a moated country house.

Abbotsley Golf Club & Hotel (Cromwell) ★

Eynesbury, Hardwicke, St Neots, PE19 4XN
Nearest main town: Cambridge

Secretary: Mr R. Jessop   Tel: 01480 215153
    Fax: 01480 403280
Professional: Mrs V. Saunders   Tel: 01480 215153

Playing: Midweek: round £11.00; day £18.00. Weekend: round £15.00; day £28.00.

Facilities: Bar: 11am–11pm. Food: Bar snacks.

Comments: Very simple ... Less taxing than the main course ... Nice course to learn the game ... Average condition and challenge.

Brampton Park Golf Club ★★★

Buckden Road, Brampton, Huntingdon, CB4 5DR
Nearest main town: Huntingdon

Secretary:	Mr M. N. Staveley	Tel: 01480 434700
		Fax: 01480 411145
Professional:	Mr A. Currie	Tel: 01480 434705

Playing: Midweek: round £25.00; day £25.00. Weekend: round £35.00; day £35.00.

Facilities: Bar: 11am–11pm. Food: Bar snacks.

Comments: Island green at the 4th ... Nice touches on this attractive course ... Solid club, very welcoming ... Good value for the area.

Cambridge Meridian Golf Club ★

Comberton Road, Toft, Cambridge, CB3 8EU
Nearest main town: Cambridge

Secretary:	Mr K. Brothwell	Tel: 01223 264700
		Fax: 01223 264701
Professional:	Mr M. Clemons	Tel: 01223 264702

Playing: Midweek: round £25.00; day £35.00. Weekend: round £30.00; day £45.00.

Facilities: Bar: 10.30am–9pm. Food: Bar snacks.

Comments: Can think of better places to be ... Very long ... A little unnatural ... Bold, sweeping parkland.

Cambridgeshire Moat House Golf Club ★

Bar Hill, Cambridge, CB3 8EU
Nearest main town: Cambridge

Secretary:	Mr D. Vernon	Tel: 01954 780555
		Fax: 01954 780010
Professional:	Mr D. Vernon	Tel: 01954 780098

Playing: Midweek: round £22.00; day £27.00. Weekend: round £30.00; day n/a.

Facilities: Bar: 11am–11pm. Food: Breakfast, lunch and dinner from 7am–10pm.

Comments: Goes on and on ... Lakes and natural water hazards ... Parkland ... Pretty ordinary.

Elton Furze Golf Club

Bullock Road, Haddon, Peterborough, PE7 3TT
Nearest main town: Peterborough

Secretary:	Mrs A. Hyde	Tel: 01832 280189
		Fax: 01832 280299
Professional:	Mr F. Kiddie	Tel: 01832 280614

Playing: Midweek: round £22.00; day £30.00. Weekend: round £32.00; day n/a. Handicap certificate required.

Facilities: Bar: 11am–11pm. Food: Lunch from 12.30pm–2pm. Bar snacks. Dinner from 6pm–8.45pm.

Comments: Can only get better ... Not one for the notebook ... Parkland without much character.

Girton Golf Club

Dodford Lane, Girton, CB3 0QE
Nearest main town: Cambridge

Secretary:	Miss V. Webb	Tel: 01223 276169
		Fax: 01223 277150
Professional:	Mr S. Thomson	Tel: 01223 276991

Playing: Midweek: round £16.00; day £16.00. Weekend: round n/a; day n/a.

Facilities: Bar: 11am–11pm. Food: Lunch and dinner from 11am–8pm, except Mondays.

Comments: Exceptional value ... Very flat and open ... Not visually attractive but a good technical challenge ... Enjoyed my society day here immensely ... Rather bleak and can get wet.

Lakeside Lodge Golf Club

Fen Road, Pidley, Huntingdon, PE17 3DD
Nearest main town: Huntingdon

Secretary:	Mrs J. Hopkins	Tel: 01487 740540
		Fax: 01487 740852
Professional:	Mr S. Waterman	Tel: 01487 741541

Playing: Midweek: round £10.00; day n/a. Weekend: round £16.00; day n/a.

Facilities: Bar: 11am–11pm. Food: Lunch and dinner from 12pm–9pm. Closed Monday and Tuesday evenings.

Comments: Pay-and-play with excellent practice facilities ... Training ground for new players – can't be bettered in its field ... Open, kind course ... 9th and 18th around the lake are the best holes.

Peterborough Milton Golf Club   ★★★

Milton Ferry, Peterborough, PE6 7AG
Nearest main town: Peterborough

Secretary:	Mrs D. Adams	Tel: 01733 380204
		Fax: 01733 332774
Professional:	Mr D. Gallagher	Tel: 01733 380793

Playing: Midweek: round £20.00; day £25.00. Weekend: round £25.00; day n/a. Handicap certificate required.

Facilities: Bar: 11am–11pm. Food: Bar snacks.

Comments: Friendly private club ... Best in Peterborough ... A little over-priced.

Thorpe Wood Golf Club   ★★★

Nene Parkway, Peterborough, PE3 7AG
Nearest main town: Peterborough

Secretary:	Mr R. Palmer	Tel: 01733 267701
		Fax: 01733 332774
Professional:	Mr D. Fitton	Tel: 01733 380793

Playing: Midweek: round £20.00; day £25.00. Weekend: round £25.00; day n/a. Handicap certificate required.

Facilities: Bar: 11am–11pm. Food: Lunch and dinner from 10am–9pm.

Comments: Excellent greens and layout for a municipal ...
Alliss/Thomas turn their hands to municipals ... Over
7,000 yards, so best value for money in the country ...
Well presented, an absolute pleasure to play whatever
your handicap ... Superb municipal with excellent
service.

Channel Islands

Royal Jersey Golf Club ★★★★

Grouville, JE3 9BD
Nearest main town: St Helier

There is some great golf to have on the Channel Islands, but the best golf is on Jersey, where there are two cracking links, the Royal course and La Moye. Royal Jersey is a flat links that runs at sea level along the exposed links turf of Grouville Bay. The bay was such a favourite with Queen Victoria that she insisted it be called the Royal Bay of Grouville. Close by is the little fishing village of Gorey, and above on the headland is a thirteenth-century fortress known as Mont Orgueil, which commands attention from every corner of the course.

The opening hole at Royal Jersey is one of the toughest in the British Isles. Fresh from the changing rooms, you are asked to thread your new ball on this 468-yard monster between the old remains of Fort Henry and two German pill-boxes (the Germans occupied the Channel Islands for five years from 1939–1944). Any slight push on any part of the hole goes over the wall, on to the sand and – depending on the tides which vary hugely from day to day – into the sea.

The first nine holes run alongside the shore, while the second nine has a more inland feel, with more evidence of bracken and gorse. The layout actually takes up a remarkably small plot of land and it has been tweaked over the years, in order to ease congestion and improve safety. Plateau greens are a feature, not least at the finish, where the 15th, 16th and 17th are notoriously slippery to stay on.

Harry Vardon, the greatest British golfer of all time who won the Open six times, was born just a duffed chip away from the 12th and his spirit lives on here. In his prime, he is said to have never missed a fairway in a two-year spell. During the same period, stories tell of him driving in his afternoon round into the divot marks he had made in the morning.

The demand for golf on the Channel Islands well outstrips supply, so if you want to play Royal Jersey in the summer be prepared for a crowded course.

Secretary: Mr R. C. Leader Tel: 01534 854416
Fax: 01534 854684
Professional: Mr T. Horton Tel: 01534 852234

Playing: Midweek: round £40.00; day n/a. Weekend: round £40.00; day n/a. Handicap certificate required.

Facilities: Bar: 8am–midnight. Food: Breakfast, lunch and dinner from 8am–9pm. Bar snacks.

Comments: Harry Vardon was born here ... Short course but you always need to be good off the tee ... Seaside links on blessed piece of land ... Old club, a pleasure to play.

Alderney Golf Club ★★★

Route des Carrieres, Alderney, GY9 3YD
Nearest main town: St Anne's

Secretary: Mr D. Thornburgh   Tel: 01481 822835
                                          Fax: 01481 823609

Professional: None.

Playing: Midweek: round n/a, day £15.00. Weekend: round n/a; day £20.00. Handicap certificate required.

Facilities: Bar: 8.30am–7pm. Food: Bar snacks.

Comments: Up in the clouds ... Nine holes at this neat seaside course ... Views are what makes it ... Come here for the views, not the golf.

La Moye Golf Club ★★★★

St Brelade, Jersey, JE3 8FL
Nearest main town: St Helier

Secretary: Mr C. H. M. Greetham   Tel: 01534 43401
                                          Fax: 01534 47289
Professional: Mr M. Deeley   Tel: 01534 43130

Playing: Midweek: round £40.00; day n/a. Weekend: round £45.00; day n/a. Handicap certificate required.

Facilities: Bar: 10am–11pm. Food: Lunch from 12pm–2pm. Dinner from 7pm–8pm. Booking essential.

Comments: Stunning location ... Incredibly natural terrain ... Exciting blind shots ... You need years to understand this course ... Many memorable summer evenings here ... Cold and windy ... Wonderfully natural with dunes and gulleys.

Royal Guernsey Golf Club   ★★★

L'Ancresse, Guernsey,
Nearest main town: St Peter's Port

Secretary: Mr M. de Laune   Tel: 01481 46523
                                          Fax: 01481 43960
Professional: Mr N. Wood   Tel: 01481 45070

Playing: Midweek: round n/a, day £34.00. Weekend: round n/a;
                  day £34.00. Handicap certificate required.

Facilities: Bar: 9.30am–11pm. Food: Lunch from 12pm–1.45pm.
                  Dinner from 7pm–9.30pm.

Comments: Can get very busy ... Impossible when the wind gets up
                  ... Use your imagination ... You'll never play another
                  like it ... Very unfair in the summer ... In the summer it's
                  like playing pinball ... Gets very busy ... Location
                  superb ... Riveting course.

Cheshire

Carden Park Golf Club

Carden, Broxton, Chester, CH3 9DQ
Nearest main town: Chester

Carden Park is a new member of the Jack Nicklaus design stable and is also the first co-design in Britain with his son, Steve. Just a few miles from Chester, this course made it into *Golf World*'s 10 Best New Developments as the part of the magazine's biennial ratings last year and is a course with an exciting future.

The first course at Carden Park has been open since 1993, but the addition of a Nicklaus course is set to make it a popular venue for visitors and societies. Essentially, this is a one-stop shop for golfers with the Nicklaus teaching facility, one of the best pro shops in the country, an excellent driving range and a luxury hotel.

But Carden Park has essentially received the accolades on account of the course, an innovative, imaginative layout, demanding the best from players, whether you're a scratch golfer or a high handicapper. Even though it can be a relatively short off the front tees, the tiger tees transform the challenge to 7,010 yards.

The course embodies the ethos of Nicklaus design – golf should be fun, challenging and fair (some say this means easy). Everything is in front of the player with no blind shots, hidden obstacles or surprises. Two holes, the 7th and 15th, embody the characteristic Nicklaus double-fairway option with the emphasis purely on risk and reward.

An elevated tree with a dramatic drop to a fairway bordered by trees on the left is the start of the Nicklaus experience. Immediately from the 450-yard, par-4 1st, the emphasis is put on length and accuracy, qualities the Golden Bear had perhaps more than anyone.

After the short par-4 2nd, you face up to one of a tough selection of par-3s, the 205-yard 3rd is perhaps the pick. The 12th is another strong par-3 at 231 yards with water on the right and a well-guarded green. Two par-5s on the back nine at the 13th and 18th make a tough closing loop, but those who can drive the ball far will really enjoy the test.

Secretary: Mr D. Nutter   Tel: 01829 731600
                                  Fax: 01829 731636
Professional: Mr D. Llewellyn   Tel: 01829 731600

Playing: Midweek: round £30.00; day n/a. Weekend: round
                   £30.00; day n/a.

Facilities: Bar: 11am–11pm. Food: Bar snacks.

Comments: Beautifully presented course with excellent facilities ...
                   Fair to all handicaps ... Young course but a club with the
                   right attitude ... Best course played since St Andrews ...
                   Top class practice facilities and can't wait for the second
                   course to be built ... Very good driving range for practice
                   ... Canteen good for food and drink ... Nicklaus boys
                   have excelled themselves ... Progressive club going the
                   right way with this parkland layout – keep it up.

Birchwood Golf Club   ★★★

Kelvin Close, Birchwood, Warrington, WA3 7PB
Nearest main town: Warrington

Secretary: Mrs A. Harper   Tel: 01925 818819
                                          Fax: 01925 822403
Professional: Mr P. McEwan   Tel: 01925 816574
                                          Fax: 01925 816574

Playing: Midweek: round £18.00; day £26.00. Weekend: round
                   £34.00; day £34.00.

Facilities: Bar: 11am–11pm. Food: Lunch and dinner from
                   12pm–6pm. Bar snacks.

Comments: Excellent facilities all round ... Just under 7,000 yards
                   but a still a fair test ... Moorland marvel ... 612-yard
                   par-5 a novelty ... Bit of everything on this underrated,
                   undulating layout ... Not as good as Castletown, but
                   don't visit the Isle of Man without popping in.

Delamere Forest Golf Club   ★★★★

Station Road, Delamere, CW8 2JE
Nearest main town: Northwich

Secretary: Mr T. G. Owen   Tel: 01606 883264
                                          Fax: 01606 883800
Professional: Mr E. G. Jones   Tel: 01606 883307

Playing: Midweek: round £30.00; day £40.00. Weekend: round
                   £35.00; day n/a.

Facilities: Bar: 11am–11pm. Food: Bar snacks.

Comments: One of England's hidden gems – a Herbert Fowler layout with excellent long par-4s ... Take advantage of the day rate – exceptional value ... Challenging, well presented and scenic ... Undulating heathland, something different for Cheshire ... Heathland, then pine forests – what a course!

Disley Golf Club   ★

Stanley Hall Lane, Disley, Stockport, SK12 2JX
Nearest main town: Stockport

Secretary: Mr D. English   Tel: 01663 762071
Professional: Mr A. G. Esplin   Tel: 01663 762884

Playing: Midweek: round £25.00; day £25.00. Weekend: round £30.00; day £30.00. Handicap certificate required.

Facilities: Bar: 12am–11pm. Food: Lunch from 12pm–2pm. Bar snacks. Dinner from 7pm–9.30pm. Closed on Mondays.

Comments: Worth seeking out ... Cheap golf on refined course ... Moorland/parkland combination ... Sloping lies and high winds make this a challenge ... Cracking value.

Dunham Forest Golf & Country Club   ★★

Oldfield Lane, Altrincham, WA14 4TY
Nearest main town: Altrincham

Secretary: Mrs S. Klaus   Tel: 0161 928 2605
                                          Fax: 0161 929 8975
Professional: Mr I. Wrigley   Tel: 0161 928 2727

Playing: Midweek: round £40.00; day £45.00. Weekend: round £45.00; day n/a. Handicap certificate required.

Facilities: Bar: 11am–11pm. Food: Lunch from 12pm–2.30pm.

Comments: Fine woodland course ... Invariably well presented ... Facilities don't cater for visitors ... Magnificent beech trees frame this clever track ... Unknown outside Manchester ... Very long and penal.

Eaton Golf Club ★★

Guy Lane, Chester, Chester, CH3 7PH
Nearest main town: Chester

Secretary:	Mr G. C. Parry	Tel: 01244 335885
		Fax: 01244 335782
Professional:	Mr N. Dunroe	Tel: 01244 335826

Playing: Midweek: round £25.00; day £25.00. Weekend: round £30.00; day n/a. Handicap certificate required.

Facilities: Bar: 11am–11pm. Food: Lunch and dinner from 10am–9pm. Bar snacks.

Comments: Long new course with plenty going for it ... Mature trees give this new course an established feel ... Not as gaudy as many new clubs ... Preferred the old venue ... Better value than some of the new clubs in Cheshire.

Frodsham Golf Club ★★★

Simons Lane, Frodsham, WA6 6HE
Nearest main town: Cheshire

Secretary:	Mr E. I. Roylance	Tel: 01928 732159
		Fax: 01928 734070
Professional:	Mr G. Tonge	Tel: 01928 739442

Playing: Midweek: round £30.00; day n/a. Weekend: round n/a; day n/a.

Facilities: Bar: 11am–11pm. Food: Lunch and dinner from 11am–9pm. Bar snacks.

Comments: Very picturesque and in fair condition ... A tough nut to crack but not impossible ... Top condition on each visit ... Parkland course with few significant characteristics ... There's a lot better in Cheshire.

Heyrose Golf Club ★★

Budworth Road, Tabley, Knutsford, WA16 0HY
Nearest main town: Knutsford

Secretary:	Mr C. Stewart	Tel: 01565 733664
		Fax: 01565 733664
Professional:	Mr M. Redrup	Tel: 01565 734267

Playing: Midweek: round £19.00; day £24.00. Weekend: round £24.00; day £29.00.

Facilities: Bar: 12pm–10.30pm. Food: Lunch and dinner from 12pm–10.30pm. Bar snacks.

Comments: Attractive club in wooded valley ... Quaint course ... A little overlong for some ... Nice welcome from the pro ... Very relaxed feel to this parkland course.

Leigh Golf Club   ★★

Kenyon Hall, Culcheth, Warrington, WA3 4BG
Nearest main town: Warrington

Secretary: Mr P. F. Saunders   Tel: 01925 762943
                                         Fax: 01925 765097
Professional: Mr A. Baguley   Tel: 01925 762013

Playing: Midweek: round £26.00; day n/a. Weekend: round £33.00; day n/a.

Facilities: Bar: 12pm–10.30pm. Food: Lunch and dinner from 12pm–8.30pm. Bar snacks.

Comments: Well regarded in Cheshire ... Doesn't live up to its billing – too short ... Short but undeniably sweet ... Nice woodland gives boring design a lift ... Something a bit different for the area.

Mere Golf and Country Club

Chester Road, Mere, WA16 6LJ
Nearest main town: Knutsford

Secretary: Mr W. G. Squires   Tel: 01565 830155
                                         Fax: 01565 830713
Professional: Mr P. Eyre   Tel: 01565 830219

Playing: Midweek: round n/a, day £50.00. Weekend: round n/a; day n/a.

Facilities: Bar: 11am–11pm. Food: Breakfast, lunch and dinner from 9am–11pm. Bar snacks

Comments: Gorgeous parkland course ... Very friendly to visitors ... Great water hazards at the 7th and 8th ... Multi-tiered greens protected by deep bunkers ... Modern feel.

Mottram Hall Golf Centre   ★★★

Wilmslow Road, Mottram St Andrews, Prestbury, SK10 4QT
Nearest main town: Prestbury

Secretary:	Mr D. Goodwin	Tel: 01625 828135
		Fax: 01625 829284
Professional:	Mr T. Rastall	Tel: 01625 820064

Playing: Midweek: round £39.00; day n/a. Weekend: round
£44.00; day n/a. Handicap certificate required.

Facilities: Bar: 7am–10pm. Food: Bar snacks.

Comments: Decent challenge although greens poor on visit ...
Condition not what you would expect for hotel course ...
Not up to its five-star rating ... Flat, meadowland course
with few distinguishing features.

Portal Golf & Country Club   ★★★

Cobblers Cross Lane, Tarporley, CW6 ODJ
Nearest main town: Chester

Secretary:	Mr D. Wills	Tel: 01829 733933
		Fax: 01829 733928
Professional:	Mr M. Slater	Tel: 01829 733933

Playing: Midweek: round £40.00; day £50.00. Weekend: round
£40.00; day £50.00. Handicap certificate required.

Facilities: Bar: 12am–11pm. Food: Lunch from 12pm–2.30pm.
Dinner from 6pm–9pm.

Comments: Very hilly, take a buggy if you can ... Exhilarating course
with plunging approaches ... Amazing construction on
the side of a hill ... Heady golf ... An epic encounter
with Donald Steel ... Facilities some of the best in
country.

Portal Premier   ★★★

Forest Road, Tarporley, CW6 OJA
Nearest main town: Chester

Secretary:	Mrs J. Kite	Tel: 01829 733884
		Fax: 01829 733666
Professional:	Miss J. Statham	Tel: 01829 733884

Playing: Midweek: round £30.00; day £45.00. Weekend: round
£35.00; day n/a. Handicap certificate required.

Facilities: Bar: 11am–11pm. Food: Lunch and dinner from
11.30am–9.30pm. Closed Sunday and Monday
evenings.

Comments: Not far behind the main course ... Prefer it to the overlong Championship course ... Difficult for high
handicappers.

Prestbury Golf Club   ★★★

Macclesfield Road, Prestbury, CH3 8NL
Nearest main town: Macclesfield

Secretary: Mrs D. Bradley   Tel: 01625 829388
Fax: 01625 828241
Professional: Mr N. Summerfield   Tel: 01625 828242

Playing: Midweek: round £38.00; day £38.00. Weekend: round
n/a; day n/a. Handicap certificate required.

Facilities: Bar: 12pm–2pm & 4pm–10.30pm. Food: Lunch from
11.30am–2.30pm. Dinner from 5pm–9pm.

Comments: In good condition with challenging holes ... Lovely clubhouse ... Looked after by a Master Greenkeeper ...
Real slog, so many undulations ... I thought you didn't
get fit playing golf?

Reddish Vale Golf Club   ★★★

Southcliffe Road, Reddish, Stockport, SK5 7EE
Nearest main town: Stockport

Secretary: Mr R. G. Dean   Tel: 0161 480 2359
Fax: 0161 477 8242
Professional: Mr B. Freeman   Tel: 0161 480 3824

Playing: Midweek: round n/a, day £23.00. Weekend: round n/a;
day n/a. Handicap certificate required.

Facilities: Bar: 11am–11pm. Food: Lunch from 12pm–2.30pm.
Dinner by arrangement.

Comments: An Alister Mackenzie gem of a course in the least fashionable part of Stockport – great value for money ...
Situated in the River Tame valley ... One of the best
examples of heathland golf around.

Romiley Golf Club ★

Goosehouse Green, Romiley, SK6 4LJ
Nearest main town: Stockport

Secretary: Mr B. Lindley   Tel: 0161 430 2392
                                        Fax: 0161 430 7258
Professional: Mr G. Butler   Tel: 0161 430 7122

Playing: Midweek: round £30.00; day £40.00. Weekend: round
                  £40.00; day £50.00. Handicap certificate required.

Facilities: Bar: 11am–11pm. Food: Lunch and dinner from
                  10am–8pm. Bar snacks.

Comments: Some nice individual holes ... Overall a bit of a disap-
                  pointment ... Nestles at the foot of the Derbyshire Hills
                  ... Liked the back nine ... Not in the top rank in the
                  area.

Sandiway Golf Club ★★★★

Chester Road, Sandiway, CW8 2DJ
Nearest main town: Chester

Secretary: Mr M. C. Gilyeat   Tel: 01606 883247
                                        Fax: 01606 888548
Professional: Mr W. Laird   Tel: 01606 883180
                                        Fax: 01606 889562

Playing: Midweek: round £35.00; day £40.00. Weekend: round
                  £40.00; day £45.00. Handicap certificate required.

Facilities: Bar: 11am–11pm. Food: Breakfast and lunch from
                  9am–3pm. Dinner by arrangement.

Comments: Strong, beautiful amateur course that deserves more
                  recognition ... Par-3 finish lets down an otherwise pleas-
                  ant experience ... Classic design that has no tricks or
                  twists ... Very pretty parkland ... Too many sloping lies
                  ... Clear strategy needed here ... Fell in love with it.

Shrigley Hall Hotel Golf Club ★★

Shrigley Park, Port Shrigley, Macclesfield, SK10 5SB
Nearest main town: Macclesfield

Secretary:	Miss J. Parkin	Tel: 01625 575757
		Fax: 01625 573323
Professional:	Mr G. A. Ogden	Tel: 01625 575626

Playing: Midweek: round £28.00; day £35.00. Weekend: round £35.00; day n/a. Handicap certificate required.

Facilities: Bar: 8am–8.30pm. Food: Breakfast and lunch served from 8am–6pm.

Comments: Undulating and very enjoyable ... Another Donald Steel disappointment ... Views over Peak District make up for what course lacks ... Preferred the hotel to the course.

Stockport Golf Club ★★★

Offerton Road, Offerton, Stockport, SK2 5HL
Nearest main town: Stockport

Secretary:	Mr J. E. Flanagan	Tel: 0161 427 8369
		Fax: 0161 449 8293
Professional:	Mr M. Peel	Tel: 0161 427 2421

Playing: Midweek: round £35.00; day n/a. Weekend: round £45.00; day n/a. Handicap certificate required.

Facilities: Bar: 11am–9pm. Food: Bar snacks. Lunch and dinner by arrangement.

Comments: Superb greens ... Bites you if you stop concentrating ... Open course of little standing ... Tough opener that really sets the standard on this parkland treasure.

The Tytherington Club ★★★★

Macclesfield, SK10 2JP
Nearest main town: Macclesfield

Secretary:	Mr D. Young	Tel: 01625 434562
		Fax: 01625 430882
Professional:	Mr M. McCleod	Tel: 01625 434562

Playing: Midweek: round £28.00; day £45.00. Weekend: round £34.00; day £68.00. Handicap certificate required.

Facilities: Bar: 8am–11pm. Food: Lunch from 12pm–2.30pm. Dinner from 6.30pm–10pm. Closed Sunday and Monday.

Comments: Excellent off-course facilities ... Course requires pure, strong hitting ... Good quality mature parkland course that plays tough and fair ... Always have good offers on ... Can get very busy ... Improving and a variety of holes ... Exceptional clubhouse and food ... Excellent course spoilt by too many society days ... Signature hole is the 12th, a genuine three-shotter par-5.

Wilmslow Golf Club   ★★

Great Warford, Mobberley, Knutsford, WA16 7AY
Nearest main town: Wilmslow

Secretary: Mrs M. I. Padfield   Tel: 01565 872148
                                       Fax: 01565 872172
Professional: Mr J. Nowicki   Tel: 01565 873620
                                       Fax: 01565 873620

Playing: Midweek: round £40.00; day £50.00. Weekend: round £50.00; day £60.00.

Facilities: Bar: 12pm–2pm & 4.30pm–10pm. Food: Lunch from 12pm–2pm. Bar snacks. Dinner from 5pm–8.30pm.

Comments: Far better than nearby Mottram Hall ... Nice condition ... Long parkland course with much character ... Very expensive but worth it ... Gulped at the price ... Perfect condition ... Never a bad lie.

Cornwall

St Enodoc Golf Club ★★★★★

Rock, Wadebridge, PL27 6LD
Nearest main town: Wadebridge

Like so much of the natural beauty adorning the rugged coastline of Cornwall, the small yachting village of Rock and the nearby golf course at St Enodoc are little known north of the border, or, as the Cornish would say, in England. But to the many discerning golfers of this proud county, the stretch of links that separates the Camel Estuary with Daymer Bay is the finest natural golf they know.

In his introduction to the official handbook on the history of St Enodoc, the late poet laureate, Sir John Betjeman, who lived at Trebetherick and died there in 1984, wrote that 'golf is a solitary game even if you are playing in a foursome. It makes you aware of the lie of the land, of the hills, outline, grass, flowers and sky.' At St Enodoc, you have it all.

It is by no means a long course – measuring 6,207 yards – but its skilful design dictates that it will not surrender easily to just a brash, powerful game. Nowhere is this more apparent than at the 1st hole, a rolling 518-yard par-5 with a fairway of erratic folds and undulations. Your drive and lay-up are not threatened, but the green is set on a natural plateau, curved at the edges, and frustrating to hit no matter how short your third shot is.

Very few golf courses can shock you visually, but at the 6th you will be. Known as the 'Himalayas' hole, what is believed to be the largest sandhill on any course in Britain rises some 80 feet above the fairway, totally eclipsing your view of the green, which lies amid dunes about 100 yards beyond. And at the 10th you encounter a little church dug out of the sand sixty years ago, which stands as the centrepiece for a magnificent stretch of holes that ends at the 15th.

You'll spend plenty of time in the dunes at St Enodoc, and you'll probably have more than a few encounters with the thick rough. Throw in an overgrown marsh, blind greens and a pond, and you'll come away from St Enodoc wanting to play again.

Secretary: Col L. Guy OBE   Tel: 01208 863216
    Fax: 01208 862976
Professional: Mr N. J. Williams   Tel: 01208 862402

Playing: Midweek: round £35.00; day £50.00. Weekend: round £40.00; day £55.00. Handicap certificate required.

Facilities: Bar: 8am–11pm. Food: Lunch and dinner from 11.30am–10pm. Bar snacks.

Comments: Unmissable course for the serious golfer ... Not for the beginner ... Great fun – some very unusual holes and bizarre challenges ... Good variety of holes and superb facilities ... 10th hole is a beauty ... Marvellous surroundings and variety on this unforgettable links ... Could play every day and not get bored ... Last three holes give a great finish ... Sand dunes like ocean liners and the one on the 6th like the Titanic ... A super course but spoilt by the attitude of some of the members.

Bude & North Cornwall Golf Club   ★★★

Burn View, Bude, EX23 8DA
Nearest main town: Bude

Secretary: Mr P. K. Brown   Tel: 01288 352006
                                          Fax: 01288 356855
Professional: Mr J. Yeo   Tel: 01288 352006

Playing: Midweek: round £20.00; day £28.00. Weekend: round £30.00; day n/a. Handicap certificate required.

Facilities: Bar: 11am–8.30pm. Food: Bar snacks.

Comments: Course looks bad, but is welcoming inside ... Natural links, a little shabby around the edges ... Not the best example of a natural links ... Top-class local course.

Cape Cornwall Golf & Country Club   ★

St Just, Penzance, TR19 7NL
Nearest main town: Penzance

Secretary: Mr M. Waters   Tel: 01736 788611
                                          Fax: 01736 788611
Professional: None.

Playing: Midweek: round £20.00; day £25.00. Weekend: round £20.00; day £25.00.

Facilities: Bar: 11am–11pm. Food: Lunch from 10am–5pm.

Comments: Very scenic but poor condition ... Natural course with walls part of the old design ... Superb facilities overshadow the course ... Not your average country club ... Course rather out of place with spanking new country club ... Good value for a very natural game.

Carlyon Bay Golf Club   ★★★★

Carlyon Bay, St Austell, PL25 6LJ
Nearest main town: St Austell

Secretary: Mr Y. Lister   Tel: 01726 814250
                                         Fax: 01726 814250
Professional: Mr M. Rowe   Tel: 01726 814228

Playing: Midweek: round £28.00; day £35.00. Weekend: round £28.00; day £35.00. Handicap certificate required.

Facilities: Bar: 9am–11pm. Food: Lunch and dinner from 10am–9pm. Bar snacks.

Comments: Fair course for holiday golf ... A real slog ... Don't send your worst enemy there ... Prevailing wind makes course so tough ... Much improved due to excellent hotel ... With the hotel, this is a good package.

China Fleet Country Club   ★★★

Saltash, PL12 6LJ
Nearest main town: Plymouth

Secretary: Mr D. W. O'Sullivan   Tel: 01752 848668
                                         Fax: 01752 848456
Professional: Mr R. A. Moore   Tel: 01752 848668

Playing: Midweek: round £22.50; day n/a. Weekend: round £27.50; day n/a. Handicap certificate required.

Facilities: Bar: 11am–11pm. Food: Bar snacks all day. Dinner from 7pm–9pm.

Comments: Course and greens good ... Basic country club facilities ... Not the best course in Cornwall, but nice atttitude.

Falmouth Golf Club   ★★

Swanpool Road, Falmouth, TR11 5BQ
Nearest main town: Falmouth

Secretary: Mr R. Wooldridge   Tel: 01326 311262
                                        Fax: 01326 317783
Professional: Mr B. Patterson   Tel: 01326 311262

Playing: Midweek: round £20.00; day £27.00. Weekend: round
                  £20.00; day £27.00. Handicap certificate required.

Facilities: Bar: 11am–11pm. Food: Lunch from 11am–5pm.
                  Dinner by arrangement.

Comments: Outstanding coastal views ... Beautiful course over-
                  looking the harbour ... Well bunkered and can be a
                  tough challenge ... Anyone know of a better practice
                  ground? I mean, five acres.

Lanhydrock Golf Club   ★★★★

Lostwithiel Road, Bodmin, PL30 5AQ
Nearest main town: Bodmin

Secretary: Mr G. Bond   Tel: 01208 73600
                                        Fax: 01208 77325
Professional: Mr J. Broadway   Tel: 01208 77325

Playing: Midweek: round £26.00; day £34.00. Weekend: round
                  £26.00; day £34.00. Handicap certificate required.

Facilities: Bar: 11am–9pm. Food: Lunch and dinner from
                  8am–9pm. Bar snacks.

Comments: The real beast of Bodmin ... Scenic course in wooded
                  valley ... A real pleasure to play ... Understated and
                  underrated.

Launceston Golf Club   ★★

St Stephens, Launceston, PL15 8HF
Nearest main town: Bude

Secretary: Mr B. J. Grant   Tel: 01566 773442
                                        Fax: 01566 777506
Professional: Mr J. Tozer   Tel: 01566 775359

Playing: Midweek: round £20.00; day £24.00. Weekend: round
                  n/a; day n/a. Handicap certificate required.

Facilities: Bar: 11.30am–11pm. Food: Members only.

Comments: Great cardiac-arrest course ... Excellent facilities and
friendly members ... Undulating with four greens sitting
on a hill ... Is this really how the game was meant to be
played?

Looe Golf Club   ★★

Bin Down, Looe, PL13 1PX
Nearest main town: Looe

Secretary:	Mr P. Street	Tel: 01503 240239
		Fax: 01503 240864
Professional:	Mr A. MacDonald	Tel: 01503 240239

Playing: Midweek: round £20.00; day £26.00. Weekend: round
£20.00; day £26.00. Handicap certificate required.

Facilities: Bar: 10.30am–11pm. Food: Lunch from 11am–6pm.
Bar snacks.

Comments: Proud club ... Views of the Cornwall coast ...
Established course and excellent design ... Not the best
condition ... Views more impressive than the course ...
Holiday golf at fair price.

Mullion Golf Club   ★★

Cury, Helston, TR12 7BP
Nearest main town: Helston

Secretary:	Mr G. Fitter	Tel: 01326 240685
		Fax: 01326 240685
Professional:	Mr P. Blundell	Tel: 01326 241176

Playing: Midweek: round £20.00; day £20.00. Weekend: round
£20.00; day £20.00. Handicap certificate required.

Facilities: Bar: 12pm–11pm. Food: Lunch from 12pm–3pm. Bar
snacks. Dinner from 6pm–9.30pm.

Comments: Catches the spirit of golf in Cornwall ... Spectacular
setting ... Perching on a cliff top, this is a treat ...
Special and exhilarating ... Not as famous as St Enodoc
but gives the player a real rush.

Newquay Golf Club

Tower Road, Newquay, TR7 1LT
Nearest main town: Newquay

Secretary: Mr G. Binney   Tel: 01637 874354
                                      Fax: 01637 874066
Professional: To be appointed.   Tel: 01637 874830

Playing: Midweek: round £23.00; day £28.00. Weekend: round £23.00; day £28.00. Handicap certificate required.

Facilities: Bar: 11am–11pm. Food: Lunch and dinner from 11am–11pm. Bar snacks.

Comments: Exciting course to play ... Exposed layout, not well known, but value nonetheless ... One of my favourite courses in Cornwall.

Perranporth Golf Club ★★★★

Budnic Hill, Perranporth, TR6 0AB
Nearest main town: Perranporth

Secretary: Mr S. Brooking   Tel: 01872 573701
                                        Fax: 01872 573701
Professional: Mr D. C. Mitchell   Tel: 01872 572317

Playing: Midweek: round £20.00; day £20.00. Weekend: round £25.00; day £25.00. Handicap certificate required.

Facilities: Bar: 11.30am–11pm. Food: Breakfast, lunch and dinner from 7.30am–10pm. Bar snacks.

Comments: A brilliant layout, hardly ever talked about or advertised ... You have to feel very strong for this course ... Par-5s make this one.

Roserrow Golf & Country Club

Roserrow, St Miniver, PL27 6QT
Nearest main town: St Miniver

Secretary: Mr J. Blewitt   Tel: 01208 863000
                                       Fax: 01208 863002
Professional: Mr A. Cullen

Playing: Midweek: round £24.00; day £30.00. Weekend: round £24.00; day £30.00.

Facilities: Bar: 11am–11pm. Food: Lunch and dinner from 10am–9pm. Bar snacks.

Comments: New course but already well established with excellent facilities ... Seems as though it has been around for years ... Facilities overshadow the course ... An excellent addition to golf in Cornwall ... Another bloody country club.

St Austell Golf Club   ★★

Tregongeeves, St Austell, PL26 7DS
Nearest main town: St Austell

Secretary: Mr K. Trahair   Tel: 01726 74756
                                        Fax: 01726 74756

Professional: Mr T. Pitts   Tel: 01726 68621

Playing: Midweek: round £18.00; day £18.00. Weekend: round n/a; day n/a. Handicap certificate required.

Facilities: Bar: 11.30am–11pm. Food: Lunch from 12pm–2.30pm. Dinner from 6pm–8.30pm. Bar snacks.

Comments: What views! ... Fairly unknown course and good value ... Very interesting and fun ... Would come again.

St Mellion Hotel Golf & Country Club   ★★★★

St Mellion, Saltash, PL12 6SD
Nearest main town: Saltash

Secretary: Mr R. Brewer   Tel: 01579 351351
                                        Fax: 01579 350537

Professional: Mr A. Milton

Playing: Prices on application.

Facilities: Bar: 11am–11pm. Food: Breakfast, lunch and dinner from 7am–9pm. Bar snacks.

Comments: Green fees on application...Very testing and in excellent condition ... Course gets very boggy after a little rain ... Difficult tee shots with trouble seemingly everywhere ... Too long for the average player ... A real masterpiece of design ... Tough and exhilarating ... The toughest course in the country ... Rather hilly so consider a buggy.

Trevose Golf Club   ★★★★

Constantine Bay, Padstow, PL28 8JB
Nearest main town: Padstow

Secretary:	Mr P. W. O'Shea	Tel: 01841 520208
		Fax: 01841 521057
Professional:	Mr G. Aliss	Tel: 01841 520261
		Fax: 01841 520261

Playing: Midweek: round £28.00; day £28.00. Weekend: round £28.00; day £28.00. Handicap certificate required.

Facilities: Bar: 11am–11pm. Food: Lunch and dinner from 10am–9pm. Bar snacks.

Comments: Excellent links and friendly club ... Exhilarating links ... Brilliant links course in fantastic setting ... Trevose or St Enodoc? – I can't decide ... Wonderful golf on a links of real mystery and excitement ... A memorable afternoon ... Links legend that just gets better and better.

West Cornwall Golf Club   ★★★★

Lelant, St Ives, TR26 3DZ
Nearest main town: St Ives

Secretary:	Mr M. C. Lack	Tel: 01736 753401
Professional:	Mr P. Atherton	Tel: 01736 753177

Playing: Midweek: round £20.50; day n/a. Weekend: round £25.00; day n/a. Handicap certificate required.

Facilities: Bar: 11am–11pm. Food: Bar snacks.

Comments: Overlooked by many ... One of Cornwall's best but few go here ... Great 'Calamity Corner' from the 5th–7th ... A little exposed ... Great thought in the design ... A short course that has never been mastered ... Can be unfair with sloping fairways ... Recommended ... Include it with St Enodoc, Trevose and Perranporth in a golfing break – can't be bettered.

Whitsand Bay Hotel Golf Club   ★

Portwrinkle, Torpoint, PL11 3BU
Nearest main town: Plymouth

Secretary: Mr G. G. Dyer   Tel: 01503 230470
                                      Fax: 01503 230329

Professional: Mr S. Poole   Tel: 01503 230778

Playing: Midweek: round £17.50; day n/a. Weekend: round £20.00; day n/a. Handicap certificate required.

Facilities: Bar: 11am–11pm. Food: Bar snacks. Dinner from 7.30pm–8.15pm.

Comments: Interesting cliff-top course linked to country club ... Unusual par-3s ... Facilities poor for country club ... Very bracing.

Cumbria

Silloth-on-Solway Golf Club

Silloth, Carlisle, CA5 4BL
Nearest main town: Carlisle

Silloth-on-Solway's isolated location on the north-west coast of England has been a boon for the golfers of Cumbria for many years. The presence of such a magnificent links in an industrial and soulless area of England has meant empty fairways and time to get to understand and appreciate the intricacies of this form of undiluted golf.

The benefits have also been felt in the condition of the course, which is consistently excellent, the fairways like silk, accentuating every natural contour of the land. The greens, too, have a wonderful feel, the ball clinging to the subtle borrows of each and every putting surface. Silloth-on-Solway is that rare beast – an outstanding course that no one knows about.

It is a very flat, exposed course. The wind is not tunnelled through dunes like many links, rather it belligerently rushes in from the south west and the holes rarely change character, which is a blessing because otherwise Silloth would be as stern a test of golf as you will find. The problems start off the tee where the ball must be placed on delicate contoured fairways, which run off in places or channel your ball into depressions. From there, normally a sloping lie, you are invariably asked to find tight greens with very small approach areas. Silloth's individuality is further enhanced by the fact that the fairway bunkers have been replaced with wiry gorse and heather.

The attraction of Silloth, ignoring the obvious, such as the condition of the course and its peace and tranquillity, is its price. In a period when green fees are rising all the time, you will not find better value anywhere in Britain and Ireland.

Secretary:	Mr J. G. Proundlock	Tel: 016973 31304
		Fax: 016973 31782
Professional:	None.	Tel: 016973 32404
Playing:	Midweek: round n/a, day £25.00. Weekend: round £30.00; day n/a. Handicap certificate required.	
Facilities:	Bar: 12pm–11pm. Food: Bar snacks.	

Comments: Tremendous links course – everything as it should be ... Good, contrasting nines ... Championship links that is tough in wind ... A fabulous links in tip-top condition ... An under-valued and underused course ... Fantastic links.

Appleby Golf Club

Brackenber Moor, Appleby, CA16 6LP
Nearest main town: Appleby

Secretary: Mr D. Metcalfe   Tel: 017683 51432
Professional: Mr P. Jenkinson   Tel: 017683 51432

Playing: Midweek: round £14.00; day £14.00. Weekend: round £18.00; day £18.00.

Facilities: Bar: 7.45am–11pm. Food: Breakfast, lunch and dinner from 7.45am–7.30pm. Closed for dinner on Tuesdays.

Comments: One of the best value courses in the country ... Very remote ... Fine heather and moorland at sale prices ... Cracking welcome ... Great golf at a snip ... Really strong course at crazy price.

Barrow Golf Club

Rakesmoor Lane, Hawcoat, Barrow-in-Furness, LA14 4QB
Nearest main town: Barrow-in-Furness

Secretary: Mr J. Slater   Tel: 01229 825444
Professional: Mr J. McLeod   Tel: 01229 832121

Playing: Midweek: round £15.00; day £15.00. Weekend: round £15.00; day £15.00. Handicap certificate required.

Facilities: Bar: 4pm–11pm (weekends 12am–11pm). Food: Bar snacks.

Comments: On a wet, windy day it can feel very lonely here ... Views of Lakeland fells ... Wonderful on a tortured, windswept day ... A real test in this bleak landscape.

Brampton Golf Club ★★★★

Brampton, CA8 1HN
Nearest main town: Brampton

Secretary:	Mr I. J. Meldrum	Tel: 016977 2255
		Fax: 016977 41487
Professional:	Mr S. Harrison	Tel: 016977 2000
		Fax: 016977 41487

Playing: Midweek: round n/a, day £22.00. Weekend: round n/a; day £28.00.

Facilities: Bar: 11am–11pm. Food: Bar snacks.

Comments: Pleasant but tricky ... Has propensity to get wet underfoot ... Fell country course that plays long ... Course rarely dries out.

Carlisle Golf Club   ★★★

Aglionby, CA4 8AG
Nearest main town: Carlisle

Secretary:	Mr C. Ward	Tel: 01228 513303
		Fax: 01228 513303
Professional:	Mr J. S. More	Tel: 01228 513241

Playing: Midweek: round £22.00; day £33.00. Weekend: round £40.00; day n/a. Handicap certificate required.

Facilities: Bar: 11am–11pm. Food: Lunch and dinner from 11am–11pm. Bar snacks.

Comments: Superb course, great facilities ... A very well-respected and friendly club ... Good location and some tricky holes ... Stands out in an otherwise barren corner of golfing country ... Parkland course with fine turf that hosts Open qualifying.

Cockermouth Golf Club   ★

Embleton, Cockermouth, CA13 9SG
Nearest main town: Cockermouth

Secretary:	Mr R. D. Pollard	Tel: 017687 76223
		Fax: 017687 76941
Professional:	None.	

Playing: Midweek: round n/a, day £15.00. Weekend: round n/a; day £20.00.

Facilities: Bar: 12pm–2pm & 4pm–8pm.

Comments: Too hilly ... As much a fitness test as a round of golf ...
Gets better each year ... Very typical Cumbria course ...
Fell walking ... Not great in winter.

Eden Golf Club ★★★

Crosby-on-Eden, Carlisle, CA6 4RA
Nearest main town: Carlisle

Secretary: Mr T. Smith Tel: 01228 573003
Fax: 01228 818435
Professional: Mr S. Harrison Tel: 01228 573003

Playing: Midweek: round £18.00; day £23.00. Weekend: round
£23.00; day £28.00.

Facilities: Bar: 9.30am–11pm. Food: Breakfast, lunch and dinner
from 9.30am–9pm. Bar snacks.

Comments: Nice little course, very pretty and good fun ... Club
facilities are rather better than the course ... Boring
parkland course that offers few exciting challenges.

Furness Golf Club ★★

Walney Island, Barrow-in-Furness, LA14 6HB
Nearest main town: Barrow-in-Furness

Secretary: Mr W. T. French Tel: 01229 471232
Professional: Mr A. G. Crook

Playing: Midweek: round £17.00; day £17.00. Weekend: round
£17.00; day £17.00.

Facilities: Bar: 12pm–11pm. Food: Lunch from 12pm–3pm.

Comments: One of the better courses in Cumbria ... Housing estate
makes some holes unattractive ... Unusual links ...
Rugged second nine ... Links of indefinable character
... Fairly isolated.

Grange Fell Golf Club ★

Fell Road, Grange-over-Sands, LA11 6HB
Nearest main town: Grange-over-Sands

Secretary: Mr J. S. Asplin Tel: 015395 32536

Professional: None.

Playing: Midweek: round n/a, day £12.00. Weekend: round n/a; day £17.00. Handicap certificate required.

Facilities: Bar: 11am–11pm.

Comments: Great, fun holiday golf, but it's not in the league of other courses in the area ... Hard work, not for the over 50s ... Good par-5 8th with terrific views ... Hillside course with outstanding views on a clear day.

Grange-over-Sands Golf Club   ★

Meathop Road, Grange-over-Sands, LA11 6QX
Nearest main town: Grange-over-Sands

Secretary: Mr J. R. Green   Tel: 015395 33180
                                       Fax: 015395 33754
Professional: Mr S. Summer-Roberts Tel: 015395 35937

Playing: Midweek: round £18.00; day £24.00. Weekend: round £24.00; day £28.00. Handicap certificate required.

Facilities: Bar: 11am–11pm. Food: Lunch from 11am–5pm.

Comments: Not up to much ... Can be fun on a warm day ... Nothing you haven't seen before ... Poor condition ... Not worth the effort ... Pleasant enough parkland course.

Kendal Golf Club   ★★

The Heights, Kendal, LA9 4PQ
Nearest main town: Kendal

Secretary: Mr I. Grant   Tel: 01539 724079
Professional: Mr D. Turner   Tel: 01539 723499
                                        Fax: 01539 723499

Playing: Midweek: round £20.00; day £20.00. Weekend: round £25.00; day £25.00. Handicap certificate required.

Facilities: Bar: 11.30am–11pm. Food: Breakfast, lunch and dinner from 9am–9pm. Bar snacks.

Comments: Go here for the views, not much else ... Fell golf ... Have done well with what they have got ... Nice example of a fell-land course ... Not highly rated by pros in the area.

Keswick Golf Club ★★★

Threlkeldd Hall, Keswick, CA12 4SX
Nearest main town: Keswick

Secretary:	Mr J. V. Simpson	Tel: 017687 79324
Professional:	Mr C. Hamilton	Tel: 017687 79010

Playing: Midweek: round £17.00; day n/a. Weekend: round £22.00; day n/a. Handicap certificate required.

Facilities: Bar: 11am–11pm.

Comments: Pray for a dry day because it can get depressing out there ... Set in the magnificent scenery of the Lake District ... Challenging.

Kirkby Lonsdale Golf Club ★★

Scalebar Lane, Barbon, Camforth, LA6 2LE
Nearest main town: Camforth

Secretary:	Mr G. Hall	Tel: 015242 76365
Professional:	Mr C. Barrett	Tel: 015242 76366
		Fax: 015242 763666

Playing: Midweek: round £20.00; day n/a. Weekend: round £25.00; day n/a.

Facilities: Bar: 11am–11pm. Food: Lunch from 11am–6pm. Dinner by arrangement.

Comments: Cheap course that does everything well ... Very natural ... Water hazards cleverly placed ... A fine, unpretentious layout.

Penrith Golf Club ★★★

Salkeld Road, Penrith, CA11 8SG
Nearest main town: Penrith

Secretary:	Mr D. Noble	Tel: 01768 891919
		Fax: 01768 891919
Professional:	Mr G. Key	Tel: 01768 891919

Playing: Midweek: round £20.00; day £25.00. Weekend: round £25.00; day £30.00. Handicap certificate required.

Facilities: Bar: 11am–11pm. Food: Breakfast and lunch from 8am–6pm.

Comments: Spectacular views on the edge of the Lake District ... Good course, views and welcome ... Short track on rolling moorland ... Good condition and one of the better cheaper courses in Cumbria.

Seascale Golf Club   ★★★

Seascale, CA20 1QL
Nearest main town: Whitehaven

Secretary: Mr C. Taylor   Tel: 019467 28202
                                              Fax: 019467 28202
Professional: Mr J. Graham   Tel:

Playing: Midweek: round £20.00; day £25.00. Weekend: round £25.00; day £30.00.

Facilities: Bar: 11am–11pm. Food: Bar snacks.

Comments: A real test of golf to be enjoyed by all handicaps ... Course quality matches quality of the views over the Irish Sea ... Old-fashioned golf in unfettered club environment ... Refreshing, simple course ... Clear your mind at Seascale.

Silecroft Golf Club   ★★★

Silecroft, Millom, LA18 4AG
Nearest main town: Millom

Secretary: Mr D. L. A. MacLardie   Tel: 01229 774250
Professional: None.

Playing: Midweek: round £15.00; day £15.00. Weekend: round £15.00; day £15.00.

Facilities: Bar: 11am–9pm.

Comments: Just nine holes but nine excellent links holes ... Best greens in county ... Better links course nearby – and with 18 holes ... Nothing manufactured here, just nine natural golf holes ... Very basic ... Not exactly great holiday golf.

Ulverston Golf Club   ★★★

Bardsea Park, Ulverston, LA12 9QJ
Nearest main town: Ulverston

Secretary:	Mr J. Wood	Tel: 01229 582584
Professional:	Mr M. R. Smith	Tel: 01229 582806

Playing: Midweek: round £25.00; day £30.00. Weekend: round £30.00; day £35.00. Handicap certificate required.

Facilities: Bar: 11am–11pm. Food: Lunch and dinner from 11am–9pm.

Comments: Inhaler was required for the 17th ... Beautiful part of the country ... Excellent course but hilly ... Great course in lovely part of the world.

Windermere Golf Club   ★★

Cleabarrow, Windermere, LA23 3NB
Nearest main town: Windermere

Secretary:	Mr K. R. Moffat	Tel: 015394 43123
		Fax: 015394 43123
Professional:	Mr W. S. M. Rooke	Tel: 015394 43550

Playing: Midweek: round £23.00; day £23.00. Weekend: round £28.00; day £28.00. Handicap certificate required.

Facilities: Bar: 11am–11pm. Food: Lunch from 12pm–2pm. Dinner from 6pm–9pm. Bar snacks.

Comments: Play here and die ... Everything about this place is excellent ... Short and very sweet ... Stupendous scenery ... Blind shots to narrow landings among heather – just perfect.

Workington Golf Club   ★★★

Branthwaite Road, Workington, CA14 4SS
Nearest main town: Workington

Secretary:	Mr T. Stout	Tel: 01900 603460
Professional:	Mr A. Drabble	Tel: 01900 67828
		Fax: 01900 67828

Playing: Midweek: round £15.00; day £19.00. Weekend: round £18.00; day £25.00. Handicap certificate required.

Facilities: Bar: 11am–11pm. Food: Lunch and dinner from 11am–9pm. Bar snacks.

Comments: Nice condition ... Ordinary setting ... Kept in good condition ... Not championship stuff ... Parkland/ meadowland ... Back nine can put the wind up you.

Derbyshire

Cavendish Golf Club ★★★★

Gadley Lane, Buxton, SK17 6XD
Nearest main town: Buxton

Alister Mackenzie's influence on golf in England is often underrated, much like Cavendish, one of his designs set in the heart of Derbyshire. From the man who crafted Augusta, the home of the Masters, this is England's answer to the 'Cathedral in the Pines'.

No one would ever claim that Cavendish, near Buxton, is as immaculately kept as its Georgia counterpart, but its prime condition and the quality of its High Peak turf is impressive. This parkland/downland course is also exceptional value for money. Founded in 1925, it has become a firm favourite among golfers in the area, and at 5,800-plus yards, it presents a challenge that is not too daunting for the average player. It is one of those courses that you would be happy to recommend to anyone who enjoys fair golf in a wonderful setting.

The hallmarks of Mackenzie design are evident wherever you look – huge swales in front of the greens, tees set in shoots of trees and putting surfaces that meander and dip with a vengeance worthy of its American sister. It is a generous course like Augusta in that the fairways are accommodating and there is no punishing rough. It gets its own back by placing a premium on shotmaking – land in the wrong part of the fairway and the shot to the green is always tough, but get the tee shot right and you are presented with a birdie opportunity.

The course really begins to bite at the 8th, the start of a loop of five holes which are seen by members as the biggest card-wreckers – three of the par-4s in this stretch are over 400 yards long and the 9th is a tricky par-3 with a small green.

An added bonus at Cavendish is that for visitors to the Peak District, it is particularly well placed, especially if you are staying in Buxton, less than a mile away.

Secretary: Mr J. Rushden   Tel: 01298 234949
   Fax: 01298 23494
Professional: Mr P. Hunstone   Tel: 01298 25052
Playing: Midweek: round £26.00; day n/a. Weekend: round £35.00; day n/a.

Facilities: Bar: 11am–11pm. Food: Lunch and dinner from 12pm–9pm. Bar snacks.

Comments: You really need a short game on these greens ... Friendly atmosphere at this parkland/moorland course ... Fantastic day, fantastic course ... Subtle greens – a tribute to Alastair Mackenzie.

Birch Hall Golf Club   ★★

Dronsfield, S41 9EN
Nearest main town: Chesterfield

Secretary: Mr B. Hubbard   Tel: 01246 291979
Professional: Mr P. Ball

Playing: Midweek: round £10.00; day £15.00. Weekend: round £10.00; day £15.00.

Facilities: Bar: 11am–11pm. Food: Lunch and dinner from 12pm–9pm. Bar snacks.

Comments: For the price, this is good stuff ... Poor facilities for the visitor ... Can't fault the value ... Really nasty and challenging ... Rough, raw and ready.

Bondhay Golf Club   ★

Bondhay Lane, Whitwell, Worksop, S80 3EH
Nearest main town: Worksop

Secretary: Mr H. Hardisty   Tel: 01909 723608
                                         Fax: 01909 720226
Professional: Mr M. Bell

Playing: Midweek: round £17.50; day £30.00. Weekend: round £22.50; day £40.00.

Facilities: Bar: 11am–11pm. Food: Lunch and dinner from 11am–9pm. Bar snacks.

Comments: New course with basic facilities you would expect ... Course caters for all players – not a compliment ... What I'd call an early learning centre for golfers ... Some exciting water holes but not much substance ... Kept in good order despite popularity.

Breadsall Priory Hotel Golf & Country Club (Priory)   ★★

Moor Road, Morley, Derby, DE7 6DL
Nearest main town: Derby

Secretary:	Mr C. Anderson	Tel: 01332 832235
		Fax: 01332 833509
Professional:	Mr A. Smith	Tel: 01332 834425

Playing: Midweek: round £40.00; day £55.00. Weekend: round £45.00; day n/a. Handicap certificate required.

Facilities: Bar: 11am–11pm. Food: Breakfast, lunch and dinner from 9am–9pm. Bar snacks.

Comments: Overpriced for standard of course ... Looks great ... Staff too stuffy and food could improve ... Overpriced for reasonable course.

Breadsall Priory Hotel Golf & Country Club (Moor)   ★★

Moor Road, Morley, Derby, DE7 6DL
Nearest main town: Derby

Secretary:	Mr C. Anderson	Tel: 01332 832235
		Fax: 01332 833509
Professional:	Mr A. Smith	Tel: 01332 834425

Playing: Midweek: round £35.00; day £55.00. Weekend: round £40.00; day n/a. Handicap certificate required.

Facilities: Bar: 11am–11pm. Food: Breakfast, lunch and dinner from 9am–9pm. Bar snacks.

Comments: Still fairly new and can be difficult if the wind blows ... Slightly overpriced ... A little too easy, needs tightening up ... Like the Priory course, a little overpriced.

Burton-on-Trent Golf Club   ★

43 Ashby Road East, Burton-on-Trent, DE15 OPS
Nearest main town: Burton

Secretary:	Mr D. Hartley	Tel: 01283 544551
		Fax: 01283 544551
Professional:	Mr G. Stafford	Tel: 01283 562240

Playing: Midweek: round £27.00; day £32.00. Weekend: round £30.00; day £35.00. Handicap certificate required.

Facilities: Bar: 11am–11pm. Food: Lunch and dinner from 11am–9pm. Bar snacks.

Comments: Long and tiring ... Improves on the back nine ... Well worth the money ... Very long and difficult.

Buxton & High Peak Golf Club   ★★

Townsend, Buxton, SK17 7EN
Nearest main town: Derby

Secretary: Mr J. W. Critchlow   Tel: 01298 23453
                                       Fax: 01298 26333
Professional: Mr G. Brown   Tel: 01298 23112

Playing: Midweek: round £20.00; day £25.00. Weekend: round £25.00; day £30.00. Handicap certificate required.

Facilities: Bar: 11am–11pm. Food: Lunch from 11am–6pm. Bar snacks. Dinner by arrangement.

Comments: As tough as they come ... Course can eat you alive ... Blind shots to small undulating greens – enough said ... If you forget the condition, this is great fun ... Highest course in Derbyshire ... Plenty of blind driving and second shots.

Chapel-en-le-Frith Golf Club   ★★

The Cockyard, Manchester Road, Chapel-en-le-Frith, SK23 9UH
Nearest main town: Stockport

Secretary: Mr J. Hilton   Tel: 01298 813943
                                   Fax: 01298 813943
Professional: Mr D. J. Cullen   Tel: 01298 812118

Playing: Midweek: round £22.00; day £22.00. Weekend: round £30.00; day £30.00.

Facilities: Bar: 11am–11pm. Food: Lunch and dinner served from 11am–9pm. Bar snacks.

Comments: Value for money here ... Design a little lacking but scenery exceptional ... Easy on your pocket ... Very scenic ... Views best in the area.

Chesterfield Golf Club ★★★

Walton, Chesterfield, S42 7LA
Nearest main town: Chesterfield

Secretary:	Mr D. A. Peacock	Tel: 01246 279256
		Fax: 01246 276622
Professional:	Mr M. McLean	Tel: 01246 276297

Playing: Midweek: round £25.00; day £34.00. Weekend: round n/a; day n/a. Handicap certificate required.

Facilities: Bar: 11am–11pm. Food: Lunch from 12pm–2pm. Dinner from 7pm–9pm. Bookings required.

Comments: Traditional club, one of the best in Derbyshire … Pleasant parkland golf with good 19th … Nice reception … Course not known for its condition.

Horsley Lodge Golf Club ★★★

Smalley Mill Road, Horsley, DE21 5BL
Nearest main town: Derby

Secretary:	Mr G. Johnson	Tel: 01332 780838
		Fax: 01332 781118
Professional:	Mr P. Kent	Tel: 01332 780838

Playing: Midweek: round £25.00; day £37.00. Weekend: round £25.00; day £37.00. Handicap certificate required.

Facilities: Bar: 11am–11pm. Food: Lunch from 12pm–3pm. Dinner from 6pm–9pm. Bar snacks.

Comments: First-class driving range … Good place to practise … Very open … Tasty food … Quality new facility.

Kedleston Park Golf Club ★★★

Kedleston, Quarndon, DE22 5JD
Nearest main town: Derby

Secretary:	Mr K. Wilson	Tel: 01332 840035
		Fax: 01332 842329
Professional:	Mr D. J. Russell	Tel: 01332 841685

Playing: Midweek: round £28.00; day £35.00. Weekend: round £28.00; day £35.00.

Facilities: Bar: 11am–11pm. Food: Lunch and dinner from 11am–11pm.

Comments: New clubhouse a vast improvement ... Fine course with views of Kedleston Hall ... Condition not what it should be ... Course management severely tested.

Shirland Golf Club ★

Lower Delves, Shirland, DE5 6AU
Nearest main town: Alfreton

Secretary: Mr G. Brassington   Tel: 01773 834935
Professional: Mr N B. Hallam   Tel: 01773 834935

Playing: Midweek: round £15.00; day £25.00. Weekend: round £20.00; day £30.00.

Facilities: Bar: 10am–11pm. Food: Lunch and dinner from 10am–9pm. Bar snacks.

Comments: Parkland course with good welcome ... Fairly open with little definition ... Always very welcoming.

Sickleholme Golf Club ★★

Bamford, Sheffield, S33 OBH
Nearest main town: Sheffield

Secretary: Mr P. H. Taylor   Tel: 01433 651306
                                   Fax: 01433 651306
Professional: Mr P. H. Taylor   Tel: 01433 651306

Playing: Midweek: round £27.00; day £27.00. Weekend: round £30.00; day £30.00. Handicap certificate required.

Facilities: Bar: 10am–11pm. Food: Lunch and dinner from 10am–9pm. Bar snacks.

Comments: Right in the middle of the Peak District ... Very rough and rugged ... You can get lost out there ... Deep ravines and outstanding views ... Very pure, clean air.

Devon

Saunton Golf Club (East)   ★★★★★

Braunton, EX33 1LG
Nearest main town: Barnstaple

It has been said that if ever the Open Championship had to be staged in the West Country, the East Course at Saunton would be the only true candidate. Indeed, The Royal and Ancient, alive to the importance of expanding the list of Open venues from the present number, are currently in the process of examining its claims. Its feasibility would surely not be dependent on the quality of the course, but rather the land available to house all the tents and corporate trappings of such a big event.

The course is set amid a sea of sand dunes on the northern crest of Devon's engaging Bideford Bay, almost directly opposite the famous links at Westward Ho!, and quite frankly, links golf does not come much better than this. It charms and captures you with a surreal, mystical ambience. Each and every fairway winds its way about what can only be described as God-given property, and once you set off, you're rarely aware of anything but the hole at hand, locked in a natural tunnel of dunes.

Saunton, designed by the great Herbert Fowler who crafted The Berkshire and Walton Heath, but only worked on one other links course, Royal Lytham and St Annes, is a wonderfully balanced course, with survival the name of the game for the first four and final four holes. Players who know the East Course will temper their games to fit this design, taking caution early on before opening their shoulders and being a little more aggressive around the turn. Unlike a lot of links courses, this policy is not so dependent on the wind because each hole at Saunton is well protected and the greens nestle in the bosoms of the dunes. There are exceptions, of course, like the 5th where you could be hitting a wedge or a long iron depending on the wind.

Saunton may not have the exhilarating nature of other links courses, where the wind burns your cheeks and shots are played across bays or rocks, but it has its own discreet nature, and if you're greedy, it will turn the screw on you.

Secretary: Mr T. C. Reynolds   Tel: 01271 812436
                                      Fax: 01271 814241
Professional: Mr A. T. Mackenzie   Tel: 01271 812013

Playing: Midweek: round £30.00; day £45.00. Weekend: round £40.00; day £55.00. Handicap certificate required.

Facilities: Bar: 11am–10.30pm. Food: Breakfast, lunch and dinner 11am–9pm. Bar snacks.

Comments: Quite simply, the best in the West ... A course worthy of the Open at half the price ... Golf in traditional links setting ... True raw links ... Not cheap, but a superior course ... Great golf club, course and facilities first class ... Great welcome, fascinating course – well worth the drive ... Encompasses all that is best about links golf ... An Open venue in the making surely ... If you want a new Open course, try here ... An absolute belter!

Bigbury Golf Club   ★★★

Bigbury on Sea, Kingsbridge, TQ7 4BB
Nearest main town: Plymouth

Secretary: Mr B. J. Perry   Tel: 01548 810557
Professional: Mr S. Lloyd   Tel: 01548 810412

Playing: Midweek: round £24.00; day £24.00. Weekend: round £26.00; day £26.00. Handicap certificate required.

Facilities: Bar: 11am–11pm. Food: Breakfast and lunch from 9am–6pm.

Comments: Beautiful coastal course that proves a friendly day out ... Views over the River Avon ... Impressive setting for short, tricky course ... Something a little bit different.

Churston Golf Club   ★★★

Churston, Brixham, TQ5 0LA
Nearest main town: Brixham

Secretary: Mr K. P. Loosemore   Tel: 01803 842751
                                          Fax: 01803 845738
Professional: Mr N. Holman   Tel: 01803 843442

Playing: Midweek: round £22.50; day £25.50. Weekend: round £27.50; day £30.50. Handicap certificate required.

Facilities: Bar: 11am–11pm. Food: Breakfast, lunch and dinner from 8am–7pm. Bar snacks.

Comments: Excellent new clubhouse ... Cliff-top course that needs all the shots ... Course that hugs the cliff tops ... Real cliffhanger ... Tangly gorse.

Dainton Park Golf Club   ★★

Totnes Road, Ipplepen, Newton Abbot, TQ12 5TN
Nearest main town: Newton Abbot

Secretary: Mr M. Pembleton   Tel: 01803 813812
                                         Fax: 01803 813390
Professional: Mr M. Tyson   Tel: 01803 813812

Playing: Midweek: round £14.50; day £20.00. Weekend: round £17.00; day £24.00. Handicap certificate required.

Facilities: Bar: 11am–11pm. Food: Bar snacks.

Comments: Up-and-coming club ... Course can get heavy underfoot, so watch out ... New course but well thought out ... Blind shots make for accurate club selection ... Interesting course that gets better each year ... Great par-3s ... Cracking value in the Devon countryside ... Never heard of it but well worth the money.

Dartmouth Golf & Country Club   ★★★★

Blackawton, Totnes, TQ9 7DE
Nearest main town: Totnes

Secretary: Mr S. Bawden   Tel: 01803 712686
                                         Fax: 01803 716628
Professional: Mr S. Dougan   Tel: 01803 712650

Playing: Midweek: round £27.00; day n/a. Weekend: round £37.00; day n/a.

Facilities: Bar: 11am–11pm. Food: Breakfast, lunch and dinner from 7.30am–9.30pm. Bar snacks.

Comments: Best to have a buggy ... No two holes the same on this thinking man's golf course ... Very difficult, excellent course ... Difficult but satisfying course ... 4th hole sums up everything about Dartmouth ... No bailing out on this tough-as-old-boots layout ... West Country woe on this parkland monster.

East Devon   ★★★

North View Road, Budleigh Salterton, EX9 6DQ
Nearest main town: Budleigh Salterton

Secretary:	Mr R. Burley	Tel: 01395 442018
		Fax: 01395 445547
Professional:	Mr T. Underwood	Tel: 01395 445195
		Fax: 01395 445195

Playing: Midweek: round £27.00; day £35.00. Weekend: round £35.00; day £42.00.

Facilities: Bar: 11am–7pm. Food: Bar snacks.

Comments: Best in the area without doubt ... Very fair test of golf on attractive downland turf ... Need high levels of skill ... Cliff top beauty ... On a clear day so refreshing.

Exeter Golf & Country Club   ★★★

Countess Wear, Exeter, EX2 7AE
Nearest main town: Exeter

Secretary:	Mr K. J. Ham	Tel: 01392 874139
		Fax: 01392 874139
Professional:	Mr M. Rowett	Tel: 01392 875028

Playing: Midweek: round £26.00; day £26.00. Weekend: round £26.00; day £26.00. Handicap certificate required.

Facilities: Bar: 11am–11pm. Food: Lunch and dinner served from 10am–9pm. Bar snacks.

Comments: Very flat ... Popular layout that can get busy ... Basic country club course ... Mature and full of character.

Ferndown Golf Club   ★★★★

119 Golf Links Road, Ferndown, BH22 8BU
Nearest main town: Ferndown

Secretary:	Mr E. Robertson	Tel: 01202 874602
		Fax: 01202 873926
Professional:	Mr I. A. B. Parker	Tel: 01202 873825

Playing: Midweek: round £42.00; day £52.00. Weekend: round £50.00; day £60.00. Handicap certificate required.

Facilities: Bar: 11am–10pm. Food: Lunch from 10am–5pm. Dinner by arrangement.

Comments: Best course in Dorset and splendid, friendly clubhouse ... Gorse, pine trees, numerous doglegs ... One of the most interesting courses around ... Solid reputation and wasn't disappointed ... Matches some of the best inland courses in Surrey ... One of the best kept courses in the country ... In fine nick but a rather boring layout that is vastly overrated ... Views across the Isle of Wight ... I wish I knew a member!

Ilfracombe Golf Club ★★★

Hele Bay, Ilfracombe, EX34 9RT
Nearest main town: Ilfracombe

Secretary: Mr A. Keyworth Tel: 01271 862176
Fax: 01271 867731
Professional: Mr D. Hoare Tel: 01271 863328

Playing: Midweek: round £19.00; day £19.00. Weekend: round £22.00; day £22.00.

Facilities: Bar: 11am–11pm. Food: Breakfast, lunch and dinner from 9am–9pm. Bar snacks.

Comments: Unusual, breathtaking views and great welcome ... Bristol Channel the backdrop for this supreme test ... Devon delight in heathland setting.

Royal North Devon Golf Club ★★★★

Golf Links Road, Westward Ho!, EX39 1HD
Nearest main town: Bideford

Secretary: Mr R. F. Fallow Tel: 01237 473817
Fax: 01237 423456
Professional: Mr I. Higgins Tel: 01237 477598

Playing: Midweek: round £28.00; day £34.00. Weekend: round £30.00; day £36.00. Handicap certificate required.

Facilities: Bar: 11am–11pm. Food: Breakfast, lunch and dinner from 9am–7pm. Bar snacks.

Comments: A unique golf experience ... From the 3rd things get very interesting ... No better place to play ... Links legend that never fails to surprise or disappoint ... What golf is all about ... Heavenly links that catches spirit of bygone days.

Saunton Golf Club (West)   ★★★

Saunton, EX33 1LG
Nearest main town: Barnstaple

Secretary: Mr T. C. Reynolds   Tel: 01271 812436
                                          Fax: 01271 814241
Professional: Mr A. T. Mackenzie   Tel: 01271 812013

Playing: Midweek: round £30.00; day £45.00. Weekend: round £40.00; day £55.00. Handicap certificate required.

Facilities: Bar: 11am–10.30pm. Food: Lunch and dinner from 11am–9pm. Bar snacks.

Comments: Wonderful links (although not as good as the East) with outstanding practice facilities ... Great test for all abilities ... I don't know which I prefer ... Shorter than the East but more interesting ... What lucky members to have two such sublime links.

Staddon Heights Golf Club   ★★

Plystock, Plymouth, PL9 9SP
Nearest main town: Plymouth

Secretary: Mr K. Bravant   Tel: 01752 402475
                                          Fax: 01752 401998
Professional: Mr I. Marshall   Tel: 01752 492630

Playing: Midweek: round £18.00; day £18.00. Weekend: round £22.00; day £22.00. Handicap certificate required.

Facilities: Bar: 11am–11pm. Food: Lunch and dinner from 11am–7pm. Bar snacks.

Comments: Unique layout with one par-3 over a road ... Worth seeking out ... Not the best condition ... Keep on the straight and narrow ... A value course for visitors.

Tavistock Golf Club ★★

Down Road, Tavistock, PL19 9AQ
Nearest main town: Tavistock

Secretary: Mr R. Vandenbergh   Tel: 01822 612344
                                          Fax: 01822 612344
Professional: Mr D. Rehaag   Tel: 01822 612316

Playing: Midweek: round £20.00; day £20.00. Weekend: round £25.00; day £25.00.

Facilities: Bar: 11am–11pm. Food: Lunch and dinner from 10am–9pm. Bar snacks.

Comments: The better of the two courses in Tavistock ... Superb setting ... Springy turf ... Rarified atmosphere here ... Don't let your guard down.

Teignmouth Golf Club ★★

Exeter Road, Teignmouth, TQ14 9NY
Nearest main town: Teignmouth

Secretary: Mr D. Holloway   Tel: 01626 777070
                                          Fax: 01626 777070
Professional: Mr P. Ward   Tel: 01626 772894

Playing: Midweek: round £22.50; day £22.50. Weekend: round £25.50; day n/a. Handicap certificate required.

Facilities: Bar: Members only. Food: Members only.

Comments: Good, tough course ... Windswept ... Good challenge for low handicaps ... Greens excellent ... The day spoiled by reception at this exclusive club ... Holiday golf but without the welcome ... Heathland course spoilt by club's exclusivity.

Thurlestone Golf Club ★★★★

Thurlestone, Kingsbridge, TQ7 3NZ
Nearest main town: Kingsbridge

Secretary: Mr R. Marston   Tel: 01548 560405
                                        Fax: 01548 560405
Professional: Mr P. Laugher   Tel: 01548 560715
                                        Fax: 01548 560715

Playing: Midweek: round £26.00; day £26.00. Weekend: round £26.00; day £26.00.

Facilities: Bar: 11.15am–2.15pm & 5pm–7.30pm. Food: Lunch from 10am–5.30pm. Bar snacks.

Comments: Lovely links course ... Presentation without fault all year round ... Harsh test of golf ... Fine finish to this cliffhanger ... Downland course on edge of cliffs ... Typical Devon course and always in fine nick.

Tiverton Golf Club   ★★

Post Hill, Tiverton, EX16 4NE
Nearest main town: Tiverton

Secretary: Mrs R. Perry   Tel: 01884 252187
                                      Fax: 01884 252187
Professional: Mr D. Sheppard   Tel: 01884 254836

Playing: Midweek: round £25.50; day £25.50. Weekend: round £33.00; day £33.00. Handicap certificate required.

Facilities: Bar: 11am–11pm. Food: Lunch and dinner from 10.30am–9pm. Bar snacks.

Comments: Excellent condition ... Fairways always finely cut ... Diverse parkland ... Not that exciting ... A slightly unusual Devon course ... Always well kept.

Torquay Golf Club   ★★★

Petitor Road, St Marychurch, Torquay, TQ1 4QF
Nearest main town: Torquay

Secretary: Mr B. G. Long   Tel: 01803 314591
                                      Fax: 01803 316116
Professional: Mr M. Ruth   Tel: 01803 329113

Playing: Midweek: round £24.00; day £24.00. Weekend: round £28.00; day £28.00. Handicap certificate required.

Facilities: Bar: 11am–11pm. Food: Lunch and dinner from 10am–9pm. Bar snacks.

Comments: Well-laid-out course with a few difficult holes ... Views over Dartmoor best part of otherwise taciturn course.

Warren Golf Club ★

Dawlish Warren, EX7 0NF
Nearest main town: Dawlish

Secretary:	Mr D. Daniell	Tel: 01626 862255
		Fax: 01626 888005
Professional:	Mr A. J. Naldrett	Tel: 01626 864002

Playing: Midweek: round £21.50; day £21.50. Weekend: round £24.50; day £24.50. Handicap certificate required.

Facilities: Bar: 11am–11pm. Food: Lunch from 10.30am–4pm. Dinner from 5.30–7.30pm. Bar snacks.

Comments: Links with much personality ... Treasured location ... Cute links on Exe estuary ... Railway runs along 18th ... Located on a spit between estuary and sea ... A little bleak and exposed ... Condition lets it down.

Woodbury Park Golf Club ★★★

Woodbury Castle, Woodbury, EX5 1JJ
Nearest main town: Exmouth

Secretary:	Mr P. J. Flavin	Tel: 01395 233382
		Fax: 01395 233384
Professional:	Mr A. Richards	Tel: 01395 233382

Playing: Midweek: round £35.00; day n/a. Weekend: round £45.00; day n/a.

Facilities: Bar: 11am–11pm. Food: Breakfast, lunch and dinner from 9am–11pm. Bar snacks.

Comments: Progressive club with nice attitude ... Nicely balanced course with woodland and parkland ... Great variety with beautiful woodland ... Super resort course ... Crater-sized bunkers make life a misery ... A US-style course that blends with the countryside ... An excellent addition to golf in Devon ... Will improve with age.

Wrangaton Golf Club ★★

Golf Links Road, Wrangaton, South Brent, PL20 6BN
Nearest main town: Ivybridge

Secretary:	Mr G. Williams	Tel: 01364 73229
		Fax: 01364 73229

Professional: Mr A. Whitehead   Tel: 01364 72161

Playing: Midweek: round £17.00; day £17.00. Weekend: round £23.00; day £23.00. Handicap certificate required.

Facilities: Bar: 11am–11pm. Food: Lunch and dinner from 11am–10pm. Bar snacks.

Comments: Like much of Devon golf, greens in excellent condition ... Course in so-so nick despite the sheep and fences ... Set in Dartmoor National Park ... If you want sheep and ponies as immovable obstructions, try here ... Won't be going there again.

Yelverton Golf Club   ★★

Golf Links Road, Yelverton, PL20 6BN
Nearest main town: Plymouth

Secretary: Mr H. S. Fleming   Tel: 01822 852824
                                            Fax: 01822 852824
Professional: Mr T. McSherry   Tel: 01822 853593

Playing: Midweek: round £30.00; day £30.00. Weekend: round £40.00; day £40.00. Handicap certificate required.

Facilities: Bar: 11am–11pm. Food: Lunch from 11pm–5pm. Bar snacks.

Comments: Welcoming, good food and excellent value for money ... Another typical Devon course with good welcome ... Will be back again for the views and quality back nine ... Well worth the money for interesting golf in pleasant atmosphere.

Dorset

Isle of Purbeck Golf Club ★★★★

Studland, BH19 3AB
Nearest main town: Studland

Bournemouth is traditionally a popular stopping-off point for golfers, housing four magnificent courses including Ferndown, Broadstone, Parkstone and Isle of Purbeck. Although it may not be as technically gifted as the others, Isle of Purbeck holds a special place in the hearts of golfers for the sheer majesty of its views.

Set on high ground with views across Studland Bay to Poole and Bournemouth, Purbeck is an enchanting place to play golf, completely isolated on a verdant plateau. The impression of peace and tranquillity is unrivalled, but don't expect to find your karma when the wind is blowing, which can be vicious and will unsettle you as you stand over the ball.

Spread all before you are heather and gorse, eating into the fairways and affording the golfer a clear understanding of where is safe to play and where is dangerous. On the edge of the course, as if Purbeck was not afforded enough choice scenery, is a nature reserve for plant and bird-lovers.

Although the course has a links feel, it is not officially one, its character entirely defined by the heather. That's not to say you won't have to employ links-type shots, the bump-and-run an important weapon in the armoury, as the fairways at Purbeck can get dry and dusty in the summer.

A wonderful course, well worth seeking out.

Secretary:	Mrs J. Robinson	Tel: 01929 450361
		Fax: 01929 450354
Professional:	Mr I. Brake	Tel: 01929 450354
Playing:	Midweek: round £26.00; day £35.00. Weekend: round £32.00; day £40.00. Handicap certificate required.	
Facilities:	Bar: 11am–10pm. Food: Lunch from 12.30pm–5.30pm except Mondays.	

Comments: Views. Oh, what views! ... Play Purbeck and die a happy man ... Set on the Purbeck Hills ... Gorse and heather everywhere ... The natural selection ... Most spectacular views anywhere in Britain ... Best in the county and in fantastic, natural condition ... Wonderful turf and views ... Simply unique.

Bridport & West Dorset Golf Club ★

East Cliff, West Bay, Bridport, DT6 4EP
Nearest main town: Bridport

Secretary: Mr P. J. Ridler   Tel: 01308 422597
                                  Fax: 01308 421095
Professional: Mr D. Parsons   Tel: 01308 421491

Playing: Midweek: round £22.00; day n/a. Weekend: round £22.00; day n/a. Handicap certificate required.

Facilities: Bar: 11am–11pm. Food: Lunch and dinner from 11am–10pm. Bar snacks.

Comments: Typical cliff top course ... Very in tune with natural surroundings ... Clever design for this subtle course ... Par-3 14th an instant classic.

Broadstone Golf Club

Wentworth Drive, Broadstone, BH18 8DQ
Nearest main town: Poole

Secretary: Mr C. Robinson   Tel: 01202 692595
                                 Fax: 01202 692595
Professional: Mr N. Tokely   Tel: 01202 692835

Playing: Midweek: round £28.00; day £37.00. Weekend: round £40.00; day n/a. Handicap certificate required.

Facilities: Bar: 11am–11pm. Food: Lunch and dinner from 11am–9pm. Bar snacks.

Comments: Tight and difficult course in excellent condition ... Certainly in the top three in Dorset, but not for welcome ... Good clubhouse but members don't exactly welcome you with open arms ... Value, quality course although there's better in Dorset ... A peach of a golf experience – will be back ... Heathland heaven for us links haters.

Came Down Golf Club ★★★

Came Down, Dorchester, DT2 8NR
Nearest main town: Dorchester

Secretary:	Mr D. E. Matthews	Tel: 01305 813494
		Fax: 01305 813494
Professional:	Mr D. Holmes	Tel: 01305 812670

Playing: Midweek: round £22.00; day £22.00. Weekend: round £27.50; day £27.50. Handicap certificate required.

Facilities: Bar: 11am–11pm. Food: Lunch from 10am–6pm. Bar snacks.

Comments: Venue for many local championships ... Honest and tough ... Exceptional value ... Wonderful downland course with lush feel ... Best value for money in Dorset.

Dudsbury Golf Club ★★

Christchurch Road, Ferndown, BH22 8ST
Nearest main town: Bournemouth

Secretary:	Mr G. H. Legg	Tel: 01202 593499
		Fax: 01202 594555
Professional:	Mr R. Tuddenham	Tel: 01202 594488

Playing: Midweek: round £30.00; day £35.00. Weekend: round £35.00; day £40.00. Handicap certificate required.

Facilities: Bar: 11am–11pm. Food: Lunch and dinner from 10am–9pm. Bar snacks.

Comments: Well presented but can be a brutal course in the winter ... Not as busy as some of the clubs in Devon and well worth the trip.

East Dorset Golf Club ★★★★

Bere Regis, Wareham, BH20 7NT
Nearest main town: Wool

Secretary:	Mr B. R. Lee	Tel: 01929 472244
		Fax: 01929 471294
Professional:	Mr D. Honan	Tel: 01929 472244

Playing: Midweek: round £27.00; day £32.00. Weekend: round £32.00; day £37.00. Handicap certificate required.

Facilities: Bar: 11am–11pm. Food: Lunch from 11.30am–2.30pm. Dinner from 6pm–9.30pm.

Comments: Underrated course and improving all time ... Presentation could not be faulted ... Established course with decent practice facilities ... Nice attitude at this parkland pearl ... Keep up the good work East Dorset ... Standard scratch of 73 says it all.

Parkstone Golf Club ★★★

Links Road, Parkstone, BH14 9QS
Nearest main town: Bournemouth

Secretary: Mr A. Peach Tel: 01202 707138
Fax: 01202 706027
Professional: Mr M. Thomas Tel: 01202 708092

Playing: Midweek: round £30.00; day £40.00. Weekend: round £40.00; day £50.00. Handicap certificate required.

Facilities: Bar: 11am–11pm. Food: Lunch from 11am–5.30pm. Bar snacks. Dinner on Fridays only from 8pm–10pm.

Comments: Golf in its purest and finest form ... Old club with set-in-stone attitude ... Not as good as Purbeck or Ferndown but a good third string ... Heathland master-piece that I can't help going back to again and again ... Mesmerising course.

Sherborne Golf Club ★★★

Clatcombe, Sherborne, DT9 4RN
Nearest main town: Sherborone

Secretary: Mrs J. M. C. Guy Tel: 01935 814431
Fax: 01935 814218
Professional: Mr S. Wright Tel: 01935 812274

Playing: Midweek: round £30.00; day £40.00. Weekend: round £30.00; day £40.00. Handicap certificate required.

Facilities: Bar: 11am–10.30pm. Food: Lunch and dinner from 10am–8pm except Mondays. Bar snacks.

Comments: Delightful part of the country ... Don't want to really let this cat out of the bag ... Natural course relying on slope of the land for its defence ... You can never really fully understand the greens ... Protected greens ... One of the best parkland courses in Dorset ... Charming course and same goes for nearby village.

Weymouth Golf Club   ★★

Links Road, Weymouth, DT4 0PF
Nearest main town: Weymouth

Secretary: Mr B. R. Chatham   Tel: 01305 773981
                                      Fax: 01305 788029
Professional: Mr D. Lochrie   Tel: 01305 773997

Playing: Midweek: round n/a, day £22.00. Weekend: round n/a; day £28.00. Handicap certificate required.

Facilities: Bar: 11am–7pm. Food: Breakfast and lunch from 9.30am–5pm. Bar snacks.

Comments: Pleasing course near the seaside ... Not much style here ... Fairly straightforward and simple ... Cheap holiday golf.

County Durham

Brancepeth Castle Golf Club ★★★★

Brancepeth Village, Durham, DH7 8EA
Nearest main town: Durham

Brancepeth Castle is tucked away in the Durham countryside down a leafy lane from Brancepeth village, a former best-kept village in England. It is also a best-kept secret, never too crowded and usually in good condition.

This parkland course is very exposed and is apt to be very windy, even to the admission of a linksman. You will find that it is essentially a strategic course with the exception of some of the closing holes, and the bunkering will generally direct you in the right areas to find the one line for the approach shot. Your strategy will also be directed by the mature trees that have separated themselves from the wooded surrounds.

The course's architect, Harry Colt, was not a man impressed with immaculately kept courses, and for him a nasty lie now and again was to be accepted with a rueful smile rather than an expletive directed at the greenkeeper. Consequently, in keeping with Colt's philosophy, the fairways are rippled, a drainage effect, and you should be prepared to hit approach shots off downslopes. The greens are also humpy, true and very quick, and they peak in mid-summer, the best time to visit the club.

Much of the enjoyment of playing Brancepeth Castle is not from the beauty of the parkland, but the historic surrounds that include the twelfth-century castle and the church of St Brandon which flanks the castle and sits behind the 18th green. There's also a deep ravine that has to be crossed three times over a wobbling bridge constructed by the Royal Engineers.

The drive at the 18th is straight over the ravine and it requires a solid strike if you don't want to be delving for more balls. Spanning the chasm is a metal bridge and if you are of a nervous disposition then don't look down. The best hole, though, is probably the 9th, a par-3 through a chute of trees and it's all carry to a small green that drops sharply away to the right and rises equally sharply to the left. The green is positioned at the foot of the castle, but only a monstrous hook will cause damage.

Secretary: Mr B. Cullen   Tel: 0191 378 0075
Fax: 0191 378 3835
Professional: Mr D. Howden   Tel: 0191 378 0183

Playing: Midweek: round £29.00; day £29.00. Weekend: round £35.00; day £35.00. Handicap certificate required.

Facilities: Bar: 11am–11pm. Food: Lunch and dinner from 11am–9.30pm. Bar snacks.

Comments: Rolling fairways in parkland setting ... Great selection of par-3s ... Difficult par-3s ... What do you expect from the man who designed Pine Valley? ... Cracking 1st hole and doesn't let up ... Colourful club with proud tradition ... Best par-3s on any course plus splendid views ... Always a great challenge and in excellent condition.

Barnard Castle Golf Club   ★★★

Harmire Road, Barnard Castle, DL12 8QN
Nearest main town: Barnard Castle

Secretary: Mr W. C. Raine   Tel: 01833 638355
                                     Fax: 01833 638355
Professional: Mr D. Pearce   Tel: 01883 631980

Playing: Midweek: round £18.00; day £26.00. Weekend: round £25.00; day £32.00. Handicap certificate required.

Facilities: Bar: 11am–11pm. Food: Lunch and dinner from 11am–10.30pm. Bar snacks.

Comments: Improved since the course was extended in mid-90s ... Full of character ... Enjoyable, simple course ... Views up Teesdale ... Water in play on almost all the holes with natural becks.

Beamish Park Golf Club   ★★

Beamish, DH9 0RH
Nearest main town: Stanley

Secretary: Mr B. Bradley   Tel: 0191 370 1382
                                     Fax: 0191 370 2937
Professional: Mr C. Cole   Tel: 0191 370 1984

Playing: Midweek: round £16.00; day £20.00. Weekend: round £24.00; day £30.00.

Facilities: Bar: 11am–11pm. Food: Lunch and dinner from 10am–9pm. Bar snacks.

Comments: Parkland course with value food and drink ... Henry Cotton design ... Nice club attitude, but course average.

Bishop Auckland Golf Club   ★

High Plains, Durham Road, Bishop Auckland, DL14 8DL
Nearest main town: Bishop Auckland

Secretary: Mr G. Thatcher   Tel: 01388 602198
                                        Fax: 01388 607005
Professional: Mr D. Skiffington   Tel: 01388 661618

Playing: Midweek: round £20.00; day £24.00. Weekend: round £26.00; day n/a. Handicap certificate required.

Facilities: Bar: 11am–11pm. Food: Lunch and dinner from 11am–10pm. Bar snacks.

Comments: In good condition and clubhouse lacks nothing ... Pleasant parkland, manicured fairways and fast greens ... Views over the Wear Valley ... Only two par-4s in first 12 holes ... Club that bleeds tradition ... 7th hole is the highlight.

Castle Eden & Peterlee Golf Club   ★★

Castle Eden, Hartlepool, TS27 4SS
Nearest main town: Peterlee

Secretary: Mr D. Livingston   Tel: 01429 836510
                                        Fax: 01429 836510
Professional: Mr G. Laidlaw   Tel: 01429 836510

Playing: Midweek: round £18.00; day £22.00. Weekend: round £30.00; day £30.00. Handicap certificate required.

Facilities: Bar: 11am–11pm. Food: Lunch and dinner (booking recommended) from 11am–9.30pm. Bar snacks.

Comments: Site of Cotton's infamous 620-yard par-5, now thankfully shortened ... Dogged opening with three killer par-4s ... Charming course, so testing ... Attractive course with little spinneys ... One of the best in the area, give it a go ... Easy walking.

Dinsdale Spa Golf Club ★★

Middleton St George, Darlington, DL12 1DW
Nearest main town: Darlington

Secretary:	Mr D. W. Corcoran	Tel: 01325 332222
		Fax: 01325 332222
Professional:	Mr C. Imlah	Tel: 01325 332515

Playing: Midweek: round £20.00; day £20.00. Weekend: round n/a; day n/a.

Facilities: Bar: 11am–11pm. Food: Breakfast, lunch and dinner from 8am–9pm.

Comments: A bit straightforward for the demanding player ... Gentle course but fairly bland ... Bleak, short course ... Toughest stretch from the start ... Fair condition through the year.

Eaglescliffe Golf Club ★★★

Yarn Road, Eaglescliffe, Stockton-on-Tees, TS16 0DQ
Nearest main town: Stockton-on-Tees

Secretary:	Mr A. H. Painter	Tel: 01642 780238
		Fax: 01642 780238
Professional:	Mr P. Bradley	Tel: 01642 790122

Playing: Midweek: round n/a, day £24.00. Weekend: round n/a; day £30.00.

Facilities: Bar: 11am–11pm. Food: Lunch and dinner from 11am–9pm. Bar snacks.

Comments: Club that enjoys having visitors ... Club's history lends the club a rather noble air ... Super par-5 14th ... Endless fun on this cheery course ... Not much better in the area ... Hilly course with views to the Cleveland Hills.

Hartlepool Golf Club ★★★

Hart Warren, Hartlepool, TS24 9QF
Nearest main town: Hartlepool

Secretary:	Mr L. G. Gordon	Tel: 01429 274398
		Fax: 01429 274129

Professional: Mr M. E. Cole   Tel: 01429 267473

Playing: Midweek: round n/a; day £20.00. Weekend: round n/a; day £30.00. Handicap certificate required.

Facilities: Bar: 11am–11pm. Food: Lunch from 12pm–2.30pm. Dinner from 6pm–9pm.

Comments: Better than Seaton Carew ... Underrated ... Links for which you need a strong heart ... Refined club with course to match ... Highlight of the back nine is the par-3 11th ... Unique links played along the North Sea ... Not a classic design but a raw test ... Highly recommended by those in the area.

Ramside Hall Golf Club   ★★

Ramside Hall Hotel, Carville, Durham, DH1 1TD
Nearest main town: Durham

Secretary: Mr T. I. Flowers   Tel: 0191 386 9514
                                         Fax: 0191 386 9519
Professional: Mr R. Lister   Tel: 0191 386 9514

Playing: Midweek: round £27.00; day £33.00. Weekend: round £33.00; day £40.00.

Facilities: Bar: 11am–11pm. Food: Lunch from 12pm–2.30pm. Bar snacks. Dinner from 7pm–9.30pm. Bar snacks.

Comments: Average facilities and greens could be better ... Recently opened 'super-course' with three nines ... Golf academy and driving range ... Courses don't match the facilities or hotel.

Seaton Carew Golf Club   ★★★

Tees Road, Hartlepool, TS25 1DE
Nearest main town: Hartlepool

Secretary: Mr P. R. Wilson   Tel: 01429 261473
                                         Fax: 01429 261040
Professional: Mr W. Hector   Tel: 01429 890660

Playing: Midweek: round n/a; day £29.00. Weekend: round n/a; day £40.00. Handicap certificate required.

Facilities: Bar: 11am–11pm. Food: Lunch and dinner from 10am–9pm. Bar snacks.

Comments: Links test of all the shots ... Most enjoyable day out ...
Dignified club, surely underrated ... This wild, tortured
links is always in good condition ... Exposed with unappealing views, but what a sensual feast.

South Moor Golf Club   ★★

The Middles, Craghead, Stanley, DH9 6AG
Nearest main town: Durham

Secretary: Mr B. Davison   Tel: 01207 232848
                                          Fax: 01207 284616
Professional: Mr S. Cowell   Tel: 01207 283525

Playing: Midweek: round £15.00; day £22.00. Weekend: round
£26.00; day £26.00.

Facilities: Bar: 11am–11pm. Food: Lunch and dinner from
11am–9pm. Bar snacks.

Comments: Testing course and superb welcome in the clubhouse ...
Fair test of golf on well-presented course ... Moor and
heathland which never lets up ... Golfing outpost that
like many courses in area feels exposed ... 12th a
terrific hole ... Open course that complements many
courses in the area.

Woodham Golf & Country Club   ★★

Burnhill Way, Newton Aycliffe, DH5 4PM
Nearest main town: Newton Aycliffe

Secretary: Mr J. D. Jenkinson   Tel: 01325 320574
                                          Fax: 01325 315254
Professional: Mr E. Wilson   Tel: 01325 315257

Playing: Midweek: round £15.00; day £20.00. Weekend: round
£24.00; day n/a.

Facilities: Bar: 11am–11pm. Food: Lunch from 12pm–2.30pm.
Dinner from 7pm–9.30pm.

Comments: Brute of a course ... Fairly unnatural ... Easily missable
... Very tough for the beginner ... Nice facilities but
course lacks character.

Essex

Thorndon Park Golf Club   ★★★

Ingrave, Brentwood, CM13 3RH
Nearest main town: Brentwood

If anyone refers to Essex as a golfing wasteland, don't take a blind bit of notice. Londoners head in all directions but east to find golfing fulfilment, which is a pity because they are missing out on courses of the pedigree of Thorndon Park. Set in the grounds of a former hunting estate, dominated by an impressive neo-classical mansion, Thorndon Park is a charming course.

Designed by Harry Colt, who counts on his CV courses like Royal Portrush and The Alwoodley, Thorndon Park is ostensibly a members' club, and the benefits of not being overplayed are very clear. The condition of fairways and greens is consistently excellent, and even the wilder parts of the course on the front nine are still well manicured.

The contrast between the two nines is subtle but influences the way you play the course. The front nine is more open and in the summer has a baked appearance, requiring thought and planning to cope with the variable bounces. But as you make the turn, the course, running through tall stands of mature trees, has a lush appearance and rewards strong, accurate hitting. Indeed, as you walk down to the lowest part of the course, it is so well watered that it has a continental appearance.

This variety is traditionally the hallmark of a great course and provides much entertainment in planning and executing shots. Of course, you would be hard pressed to agree after playing the 1st, a wishy-washy par-4 where you can hit an enormous hook off the tee and still be well placed to reach the green. But don't give up – it gets better.

There's an enormous lake to carry at the 3rd, a short par-4 over a gully at the 4th and a brutish par-4 at the 6th. On the back nine, fine holes include the huge dogleg at the par-4 11th and a par-4 over the corner of the lake at the 17th. In between, you can get up to all sorts of scrapes escaping from the trees. Thorndon Park is a quality layout that constantly challenges you visually and technically.

Secretary:	Mr J. Leggitt	Tel: 01277 810345
		Fax: 01277 810645
Professional:	Mr B. V. White	Tel: 01277 810736

Playing: Midweek: round £35.00; day n/a. Weekend: round n/a; day n/a. Handicap certificate required.

Facilities: Bar: 11am–7pm. Food: Lunch from 11am–2pm. Bar snacks.

Comments: The 3rd over the lake is a joy ... Beautiful course – greens exceptional ... Value for money not bad ... Expensive, but in superb condition, especially the greens ... Difficult-to-judge approach shots make this a difficult course ... Lovely variety of holes with no holes running in the same direction ... Unknown club that manages to feel unstuffy and welcoming ... Weak 1st hole but it just gets better and better ... Clever course with interesting selection of holes.

Abridge Golf & Country Club ★★★

Epping Lane, Stapleford Tawney, RW14 1ST
Nearest main town: Romford

Secretary: Mr G. Winckless   Tel: 01708 688396
                                         Fax: 01708 688550
Professional: Mr S. Layton   Tel: 01708 688333

Playing: Midweek: round £30.00; day £40.00. Weekend: round n/a; day n/a. Handicap certificate required.

Facilities: Bar: 11am–11pm. Food: Lunch from 11am–5pm.

Comments: Very good facilities ... Many holes crossing valleys ... Mature and very challenging ... Can play very long ... A monster off the back tees ... Strong par-4s ... First rate par-4s ... Genuine par-4s.

Braintree Golf Club ★★

Kings Lane, Stisted, Braintree, CM7 8DA
Nearest main town: Braintree

Secretary: Mr M. N. D. Robinson   Tel: 01376 346079
                                         Fax: 01376 331216
Professional: Mr T. Parcell   Tel: 01376 343465

Playing: Midweek: round £18.00; day £25.00. Weekend: round n/a; day £40.00. Handicap certificate required.

Facilities: Bar: 11am–11pm. Food: Lunch from 12pm–2.30pm. Dinner from 7pm–9.30pm on Friday and Saturday only.

Comments: 17th plays right next to a church ... Not the best condition ... Heavily bunkered ... Condition variable ... Decent design ... A bit flat.

Channels Golf Club   ★

Belsteads Farm Lane, Little Waltham, Chelmsford, CM3 3PT
Nearest main town: Chelmsford

Secretary:	Mr A. M. Squire	Tel: 01245 440005
		Fax: 01245 442032
Professional:	Mr I. B. Sinclair	Tel: 01245 441056

Playing: Midweek: round £25.00; day £35.00. Weekend: round n/a; day n/a. Handicap certificate required.

Facilities: Bar: 11am–11pm. Food: Lunch and dinner from 11am–10pm. Bar snacks.

Comments: Old gravel works makes maximum use of lakes and mounds ... Lush rough with undulating fairways ... Unfamiliar, unfashionable course that asks a lot of questions from the player ... Flattish, exciting course.

Chelmsford Golf Club

Widford, Chelmsford, CM2 9AP
Nearest main town: Chelmsford

Secretary:	Mr A. Johnson	Tel: 01245 250555
		Fax: 01245 256483
Professional:	Mr G. D. Bailey	Tel: 01245 257079

Playing: Midweek: round £27.00; day £36.00. Weekend: round n/a; day n/a. Handicap certificate required.

Facilities: Bar: 11am–9pm. Food: Lunch from 11am–6pm. Bar snacks.

Comments: Club with a colourful history ... Very good condition ... Very taxing par-68 ... Never had a bad time here ... Good value ... A little short ... Facilities a little substandard.

Chigwell Golf Club ★★

High Road, Chigwell, IG7 5BH
Nearest main town: London

Secretary:	Mr R. H. Danzey	Tel: 0181 500 2059
		Fax: 0181 501 3410
Professional:	Mr R. Beard	Tel: 0181 500 2384

Playing: Midweek: round £20.00; day £20.00. Weekend: round n/a; day n/a. Handicap certificate required.

Facilities: Bar: 11am–11pm. Food: Lunch from 11am–5pm. Bar snacks.

Comments: A good course, tucked away in sparse golfing country ... Quality greens on visit ... Surprisingly undulating for Essex ... Meadowland but don't let that put you off.

Essex Golf & Country Club ★★

Earls Colne, Colchester, CO6 2NS
Nearest main town: Colchester

Secretary:	Mr D. J. Clark	Tel: 01787 224466
		Fax: 01787 224410
Professional:	Mr M. Spooner	

Playing: Midweek: round £20.00; day £27.00. Weekend: round £25.00; day £35.00.

Facilities: Bar: 11am–11pm. Food: Lunch and dinner from 10am–9pm. Bar snacks.

Comments: Premier new course in Essex ... Target golf ... US-style course with water everywhere ... A course for the average punter ... Too long ... Huge complex bringing golf to the masses ... Go there to practise, not play ... Practise there all the time ... Overblown ... Exciting.

Five Lakes Hotel Golf & Country Club (Links) ★★

Colchester Road, Tolleshunt Knights, Maldon, CM9 8HX
Nearest main town: Colchester

Secretary:	Mr M. Tucker	Tel: 01621 868888
		Fax: 01621 869696
Professional:	Mr G. Carter	Tel: 01621 862326
		Fax: 01621 862320

Playing: Midweek: round £18.00; day £25.00. Weekend: round £25.00; day £33.00. Handicap certificate required.

Facilities: Bar: 11am–11pm. Food: Lunch from 12pm–2.30pm. Dinner from 7pm–10pm. Bar snacks.

Comments: Not as good as the Lakes course ... Preferred the Lakes ... Very flat and boring ... Not a patch on the Lakes ... As far from a links as you could get ... Facilities good but poor course.

Five Lakes Hotel Golf & Country Club (Lakes)   ★★★

Colchester Road, Tolleshunt Knights, Maldon, CM9 8HX
Nearest main town: Colchester

Secretary:	Mr M. Tucker	Tel: 01621 868888
		Fax: 01621 869696
Professional:	Mr G. Carter	Tel: 01621 862326
		Fax: 01621 862320

Playing: Midweek: round £25.00; day £37.50. Weekend: round £33.00; day £44.00. Handicap certificate required.

Facilities: Bar: 11am–11pm. Food: Lunch from 12pm–2.30pm. Dinner from 7pm–10pm. Bar snacks.

Comments: Out in the wilds ... Plenty of other things to do at this country club ... US-style course, very unnatural with lakes and huge moundings ... There's better in Essex, believe me ... Good for the beginner.

Frinton Golf Club   ★★

1 The Esplanade, Frinton-on-Sea, CO13 9EP
Nearest main town: Colchester

Secretary:	Lt Col R. W. Attrill	Tel: 01255 674618
		Fax: 01255 674618
Professional:	Mr P. Taggart	Tel: 01255 671618

Playing: Midweek: round £25.00; day £25.00. Weekend: round £25.00; day £25.00. Handicap certificate required.

Facilities: Bar: 11am–11pm. Food: Lunch and dinner from 11am–10pm. Bar snacks.

Comments: The only true links in Essex ... Interesting Zulu hut by the 10th ... Condition variable ... Nice design but not blessed with great land ... Very generous fairways and greens ... Wide fairways as rough can get very unruly ... The only links in Essex – thank goodness!

Langdon Hills Golf Centre   ★★★

Lower Dunton Road, Bulphan, RM14 3TY
Nearest main town: Basildon

Secretary: Mr B. Hardie   Tel: 01268 548444
                                        Fax: 01268 490084
Professional: Mr T. Moncur   Tel: 01268 544300

Playing: Midweek: round £11.45; day £19.50. Weekend: round £14.75; day £19.50.

Facilities: Bar: 11am–11pm. Food: Lunch and dinner from 11am–9.30pm. Bar snacks.

Comments: Great value-for-money for course in good condition ... Three nines of varying standard ... Nice practice facilities for beginner ... A bit of a donkey track ... Fun golf with friends.

Orsett Golf Club   ★★

Brentwood Road, Orsett, RM16 3DS
Nearest main town: Orsett

Secretary: Mr Y. N. Collingwood Tel: 01375 891352
                                        Fax: 01375 892471
Professional: Mr P. Joiner   Tel: 01375 891797

Playing: Midweek: round n/a; day £32.50. Weekend: round n/a; day n/a. Handicap certificate required.

Facilities: Bar: 11am–variable. Food: Bar snacks from 11am–2pm.

Comments: One of the best in Essex ... Regional Open qualifying course ... Lovely pines, silver birch and hawthorn ... Really natural with plenty of gorse and hawthorn ... Undoubtedly one of the top dogs in Essex ... Be accurate ... Quality par-4s ... Nice variety of long and short par-4s.

Romford Golf Club   ★★★

Heath Drive, Gidea Park, Romford, RM2 5QB
Nearest main town: Romford

Secretary:	Mrs H. Robinson	Tel: 01708 740986
		Fax: 01708 752157
Professional:	Mr H. Flatman	Tel: 01708 749393

Playing: Midweek: round £25.00; day £35.00. Weekend: round n/a; day n/a. Handicap certificate required.

Facilities: Bar: 11am–11pm. Food: Lunch from 10am–5pm.

Comments: Historic course ... Wasn't looking forward to playing but loved it ... Loads of sand ... Almost has a 'Surrey' feel to it ... Perhaps the best in Essex ... Top notch.

Royal Epping Forest Golf Club   ★★★

Forest Approach, Chingford, London, E4 7AZ
Nearest main town: London

Secretary:	Mrs P. Runciman	Tel: 0181 529 2195
		Fax: 0181 559 4664
Professional:	Mr J. Francis	Tel: 0181 529 5708

Playing: Midweek: round £10.10; day n/a. Weekend: round £13.80; day n/a.

Facilities: Bar: 11am–11pm. Food: Bar snacks.

Comments: The course where you must wear red clothes ... Eccentric club ... Not a great course but an interesting one that has to be played ... Loved it ... Unusual ... Very cheap.

Stapleford Abbotts Golf Club   ★★

Horseman's Side, Tysea Hill, Stapleford Abbotts, RM4 1JU
Nearest main town: Romford

Secretary:	None.
Professional:	Mr D. Eagle Tel: 01708 381278

Playing: Prices on application. Handicap certificate required.

Facilities: Bar: 11am–11pm. Food: Lunch and dinner from 11am–10pm. Bar snacks.

Comments: Green fees on application ... 47 holes at this fair golf centre ... Getting better but still not in top condition ... Abbotts is best of three courses ... Great facilities for beginner.

Stock Brook Manor Golf Club   ★★★

Queen's Park Avenue, Billericay, CM12 OSP
Nearest main town: Chelmsford

Secretary:	Mr K. Roe Tel: 01277 653616
	Fax: 01277 633063
Professional:	Mr K. Merry Tel: 01277 653616

Playing: Midweek: round n/a; day £25.00. Weekend: round n/a; day £30.00. Handicap certificate required.

Facilities: Bar: 11am–11pm. Food: Lunch and dinner from 11am–10pm. Bar snacks.

Comments: First-class clubhouse ... Magnificent clubhouse ... Really treat the visitor well here ... Impressive society day ... Good for beginners with training holes ... Treats everyone well ... Par-5 9th has two lakes ... Exciting holes for the novice.

Stoke-by-Nayland Golf Club (Constable)   ★★

Keepers Lane, Leavenheath, Colchester, CO6 4PZ
Nearest main town: Colchester

Secretary:	Mr D. Howell Tel: 01206 262836
	Fax: 01206 263356
Professional:	Mr K. Lovelock Tel: 01206 262769

Playing: Midweek: round £22.00; day £35.00. Weekend: round £27.50; day n/a. Handicap certificate required.

Facilities: Bar: 11am–11pm. Food: Bar snacks.

Comments: Just shorter than the Gainsborough but just as good ...
Not great condition but fun ... Very similar to the
Gainsborough ... Parkland of very little character.

Stoke-by-Nayland Golf Club (Gainsborough)   ★★★

Keepers Lane, Leavenheath, Colchester, CO6 4PZ
Nearest main town: Colchester

Secretary: Mr D. Howell   Tel: 01206 262836
                                          Fax: 01206 263356
Professional: Mr K. Lovelock   Tel: 01206 262769

Playing: Midweek: round £22.00; day £35.00. Weekend: round
£27.50; day n/a. Handicap certificate required.

Facilities: Bar: 11am–11pm. Food: Bar snacks.

Comments: Playing both courses in a day gives better value ...
Great value for societies ... It's got everything for a
day's golf including the best value ... Undulating course
with water and plenty of natural hazards ... Not bad for
a golf centre.

The Burstead Golf Club   ★★

Tye Common Road, Little Burstead, Billericay, CM12 9SS
Nearest main town: Billericay

Secretary: Mr L. Mence   Tel: 01277 631171
                                          Fax: 01277 632766
Professional: Mr K. Bridges   Tel: 01277 631171

Playing: Midweek: round £19.00; day £25.00. Weekend: round
n/a; day n/a.

Facilities: Bar: 11am–11pm. Food: Bar snacks. Dinner from
7pm–9.30pm on Thursday, Friday and Saturday.

Comments: Food first class ... If only the course was as good as the
food ... Welcoming clubhouse ... Better courses to be
had in Essex ... Very fair ... Not particularly difficult.

Theydon Bois Golf Club   ★★

Theydon Bois, Epping, CM16 4EH
Nearest main town: Epping

Secretary:	Mr R. S. Blower Tel: 01992 813054
	Fax: 01992 813054
Professional:	Mr R. J. Hall Tel: 01992 812460

Playing: Midweek: round n/a; day £32.00. Weekend: round n/a; day n/a. Handicap certificate required.

Facilities: Bar: 11am–11pm. Food: Lunch from 12pm–2.30pm.

Comments: Testing golf at an affordable price ... Original nine holes in Epping Forest a treat ... Club with good tradition and nice welcome.

Three Rivers Golf Club   ★★★

Stow Road, Purleigh, Chelmsford, CM3 6RR
Nearest main town: Maldon

Secretary:	Mr J. Johnson Tel: 01621 828631
	Fax: 01621 828060
Professional:	Mr P. O'Connor Tel: 01621 829781

Playing: Midweek: round £20.00; day £25.00. Weekend: round £25.00; day £35.00.

Facilities: Bar: 11am–11pm. Food: Lunch and dinner from 10am–9pm. Bar snacks.

Comments: You would have to go a long way to find a more enjoyable course ... Clubhouse is second to none ... Good challenge ... Interesting course with ponds, doglegs and natural hazards ... Wooded parkland ... Value for money.

Upminster Golf Club

114 Hall Lane, Upminster, RM14 1AU
Nearest main town: Upminster

Secretary:	Mr W. J. Collantine Tel: 01708 222788
	Fax: 01708 222788
Professional:	Mr N. Carr Tel: 01708 220000

Playing: Midweek: round £25.00; day £30.00. Weekend: round n/a; day n/a. Handicap certificate required.

Facilities: Bar: 11am–11pm. Food: Lunch from 12pm–2.30pm.

Comments: Very attractive clubhouse ... A bit of old world charm ...
Liked it ... Riverside course ... Best holes probably the
6th and 11th ... Greens consistently good.

West Essex Golf Club   ★★★

Bury Road, Sewardstonebury, London, E4 7QL
Nearest main town: Chingford

Secretary:	Mr D. Wilson	Tel: 0181 529 7558
		Fax: 0181 524 7870
Professional:	Mr R. Joyce	Tel: 0181 529 4367
		Fax: 0181 529 4367

Playing: Midweek: round £28.00; day £35.00. Weekend: round
n/a; day n/a. Handicap certificate required.

Facilities: Bar: 11am–11pm. Food: Lunch from 12pm–3pm.

Comments: Very admirable course ... Epping Forest setting ... Too
hilly ... Tiring in sections ... Hogs-back fairways, pulpit
greens, rich forest – not too shabby ... A diverse challenge ... Real variety ... Club that really tries hard ...
Club very proud of its course.

Gloucestershire

Long Ashton Golf Club ★★★

Clarken Coombe, Long Ashton, BS17 2TG
Nearest main town: Bristol

Gloucestershire is not renowned for the depth and variety of its courses, and any discussion of the best course would not find universal agreement. One of the contenders, situated on the western outskirts of Bristol, would surely be Long Ashton, a wooded parkland course that you'll generally find in excellent order.

Long Ashton is a very traditional course bar one welcome eccentricity – a par-3, played over a road to a green nestled in an old quarry. It's worth the price of admission alone. But Long Ashton has more to offer than just its signature hole: two very distinctive nines that will test your patience and only reward good golf.

The preferred nine is on the front side, with the holes sweeping along a plateau with views of Bristol at the eastern extent of the course (if you're lucky, hot air balloons take off from Ashton Park through the year and soar above the course). The fairways hug every contour of the land and taper towards fairly open, but subtle undulating greens. The back nine is flatter, with a few holes you would willingly chuck out. It is here that you make your score, with the par-4s fairly short and the par-3 without much trouble.

Long Ashton is unusual for an old, provincial course in that it houses a practice range worthy of an Open venue.

Secretary: Mr B. J. G. Manning Tel: 01275 392229
                                    Fax: 01275 394395
Professional: Mr D. Scanlan Tel: 01275 391165

Playing: Midweek: round £28.00; day £32.00. Weekend: round £35.00; day n/a. Handicap certificate required.

Facilities: Bar: 11am–11pm. Food: Breakfast and lunch from 9.30am–6pm. Bar snacks.

Comments: Fascinating par-3 over the road marks this out as something special ... A little exposed in places although the course makes good use of the land ... Nice selection of secluded and open holes at this friendly club ... Value golf and excellent practice ground.

Bristol & Clifton Golf Club   ★★★

Beggar Bush Lane, Failand, Bristol, Bristol, BS8 3TH
Nearest main town: Bristol

Secretary:	Mr R. C. Bennett	Tel: 01275 393474
		Fax: 01275 394611
Professional:	Mr P. Mawson	Tel: 01275 393031
		Fax: 01275 393031

Playing: Midweek: round n/a; day £35.00. Weekend: round n/a; day £40.00. Handicap certificate required.

Facilities: Bar: 11am–11pm. Food: Breakfast and lunch from 8am–6pm. Bar snacks.

Comments: Setting what makes this course ... Rather ungroomed ... Make a beeline for this one ... Stand-out par-3s ... Make sure you don't miss it.

Broadway Golf Club   ★★★

Willersey Hill, Broadway, WR12 7LG
Nearest main town: Broadway

Secretary:	Mr B. Carnie	Tel: 01386 853683
		Fax: 01386 858643
Professional:	Mr M. Freeman	Tel: 01386 853275

Playing: Midweek: round £27.00; day £33.00. Weekend: round £35.00; day £35.00. Handicap certificate required.

Facilities: Bar: 11am–11pm. Food: Lunch and dinner from 11am–9pm. Bar snacks.

Comments: Interesting course with views over the Vale of Evesham ... 800ft above sea level – not worth the climb! ... For a downland course, fairly unnatural.

Chipping Sodbury Golf Club   ★★

Chipping Sodbury, BS17 6PU
Nearest main town: Bristol

Secretary:	Mr D. Bird	Tel: 01454 319042
		Fax: 01454 319042
Professional:	Mr M. Watts	Tel: 01454 314087

Playing: Midweek: round £22.00; day £27.00. Weekend: round £25.00; day £30.00. Handicap certificate required.

Facilities: Bar: 11am–11pm. Food: Lunch and dinner from 11am–7pm.

Comments: After major surgery, this course is easily the best presented in the Bristol area ... Much improved and a nice challenge ... Drainage dyke the main hazard ... Changes are best decision the club ever made.

Cleeve Hill Golf Club ★★

Cleeve Hill, Cheltenham, GL52 3PW
Nearest main town: Cheltenham

Secretary: Mr S. Gilman Tel: 01242 672025
Fax: 01242 672025
Professional: Mr S. Usher Tel: 01242 672592
Fax: 01242 672592

Playing: Midweek: round £10.00; day £18.00. Weekend: round £12.00; day £20.00.

Facilities: Bar: 11am–11pm. Food: Lunch and dinner from 11am–9pm. Bar snacks.

Comments: Course deficiencies nullified by fine views ... Great day out ... Inland course with spectacular views.

Filton Golf Club ★

Golf Course Lane, Bristol, BS34 7QS
Nearest main town: Bristol

Secretary: Mr M. Burns Tel: 0117 969 4169
Fax: 0117 931 4359
Professional: Mr J. C. N. Lumb Tel: 0117 969 4158

Playing: Midweek: round £20.00; day £25.00. Weekend: round n/a; day n/a. Handicap certificate required.

Facilities: Bar: 11am–11pm. Food: Lunch from 11am–6pm. Bar snacks.

Comments: One of the weaker courses in Bristol ... On a clear day look for the Brecon Beacons ... Very challenging.

Forest Hills Golf Club ★

Mile End Road, Coleford, GL16 7BY
Nearest main town: Coleford

Secretary:	Mr P. Burston	Tel: 01594 810620
Professional:	Mr J. Nicol	Tel: 01594 810620

Playing: Midweek: round £13.00; day £18.00. Weekend: round £15.00; day £20.00. Handicap certificate required.

Facilities: Bar: 11am–11pm. Food: Lunch from 11am–6pm. Bar snacks.

Comments: Unimaginative ... Spectacular finish ... One of the cheapest courses around ... Good facilities for visitors.

Henbury Golf Club

Westbury-on-Trym, Bristol, BS10 7QB
Nearest main town: Bristol

Secretary:	Mr R. H. White	Tel: 0117 950 0044
		Fax: 0117 959 1928
Professional:	Mr N. Riley	Tel: 0117 950 2121

Playing: Midweek: round £21.00; day £28.00. Weekend: round £21.00; day £28.00. Handicap certificate required.

Facilities: Bar: 11am–11pm. Food: Lunch and dinner from 11am–9pm. Bar snacks.

Comments: Much improved now alterations complete ... Best to have a member as guide ... Parkland course with attractive woodland ... Short track but good value.

Jarvis Gloucester Hotel Golf Club

Matson Lane, Gloucester, GL4 9EA
Nearest main town: Gloucester

Secretary:	Mr P. Darnell	Tel: 01452 411311
Professional:	Mr P. Darnell	Tel: 01425 411311

Playing: Midweek: round £19.00; day n/a. Weekend: round £25.00; day n/a. Handicap certificate required.

Facilities: Bar: 11am–11pm. Food: Breakfast, lunch and dinner from 7am–10pm.

Comments: Sheer value for money and very accommodating to large groups ... Two very different nines, one very flat, one very undulating ... Pro shop extremely well informed and helpful ... One hole named Coronary Hill – enough said ... Undulating with vistas to the Cotswolds.

Knowle Golf Club   ★★

Fairway, West Town Lane, Brislington, BS4 5DF
Nearest main town: Bristol

Secretary: Mrs J. D. King   Tel: 0117 977 0660
                                     Fax: 0117 972 0615
Professional: Mr G. M. Brand   Tel: 0117 977 9193

Playing: Midweek: round £22.00; day £27.00. Weekend: round £27.00; day £32.00. Handicap certificate required.

Facilities: Bar: 11am–11pm. Food: Lunch from 12pm–2pm. Bar snacks.

Comments: Lovely greens ... Interesting par-3s ... Don't be put off by the strenous start – it gets easier ... Attractive course, if a little easy.

Minchinhampton Golf Club (Avening)   ★★

Minchinhampton, Stroud, GL6 9BE
Nearest main town: Stroud

Secretary: Mr D. T. Calvert   Tel: 01453 833866
                                      Fax: 01453 835703
Professional: Mr C. Steele   Tel: 01453 833860

Playing: Midweek: round n/a; day £25.00. Weekend: round n/a; day £30.00. Handicap certificate required.

Facilities: Bar: 11am–11pm. Food: Lunch from 11am–6pm. Dinner by arrangement.

Comments: A well-kept straightforward course with a variety of pleasant holes ... Excellent catering ... Cotswold views ... Better than the Cherington and unbeatable value.

Minchinhampton Golf Club (Cherington)   ★★

Minchinhampton, Stroud, GL6 9BE
Nearest main town: Stroud

Secretary:	Mr D. T. Calvert	Tel: 01453 833866
		Fax: 01453 835703
Professional:	Mr C. Steele	Tel: 01453 833860

Playing: Midweek: round n/a; day £25.00. Weekend: round n/a; day £30.00. Handicap certificate required.

Facilities: Bar: 11am–11pm. Food: Lunch from 11am–6pm. Dinner by arrangement.

Comments: Fairly new course on plateau with excellent clubhouse ... Exciting course with plenty of startling features ... Pot bunkers, sloping greens – great test for a new course.

Shirehampton Park Golf Club   ★

Park Hill, Shirehampton, Bristol, BS11 0UL
Nearest main town: Bristol

Secretary:	Mr G. W. Rees	Tel: 0117 982 2083
		Fax: 0117 982 2083
Professional:	Mr B. Ellis	Tel: 0117 982 2488

Playing: Midweek: round £18.00; day £18.00. Weekend: round n/a; day n/a. Handicap certificate required.

Facilities: Bar: 11am–11pm. Food: Lunch from 12pm–2.30pm. Dinner from 5pm–8pm.

Comments: Weak for the Bristol area ... Don't slice it at the 1st! ... Some attractive features but overall poor ... Could be better.

Stakis Puckrup Hall Hotel Golf Club   ★★

Puckrup, Tewkesbury, GL20 6EL
Nearest main town: Tewkesbury

Secretary:	Mrs C. Sandyford-Sykes	Tel: 01684 296200
		Fax: 01684 850788
Professional:	Mr K. Pickett	Tel: 01684 271591

Playing: Midweek: round £20.00; day £25.00. Weekend: round £25.00; day £30.00.

Facilities: Bar: 11am–11pm. Food: Breakfast, lunch and dinner from 7am–10pm. Bar snacks.

Comments: Expensive food and drink ... A little over-priced for standard of course ... Undulating parkland layout which makes good use of land ... Nice course with good back-up facilities – will go again.

Stinchcombe Hill Golf Club ★★

Stinchcombe Hill, Dursley, GL11 6AQ
Nearest main town: Dursley

Secretary: Mr G. L. Davies   Tel: 01453 542015
                               Fax: 01453 549545
Professional: Mr P. Bushell   Tel: 01453 543878

Playing: Midweek: round £13.00; day £25.00. Weekend: round £20.00; day £25.00.

Facilities: Bar: 11am–11pm. Food: Lunch from 10am–6pm. Bar snacks.

Comments: Lofty location ... Looks out over the Cotswolds ... Views make it ... At its best when the wind is up ... Downland course with personality.

Tewkesbury Park Hotel Golf Club ★★

Lincoln Green Lane, Tewkesbury, GL20 7DN
Nearest main town: Tewkesbury

Secretary: Mr R. S. Nichol   Tel: 01684 299452
                               Fax: 01684 292386
Professional: Mr R. Taylor   Tel: 01684 294892

Playing: Midweek: round £15.00; day n/a. Weekend: round £20.00; day n/a.

Facilities: Bar: 11am–11pm. Food: Lunch from 12pm–2.30pm. Dinner from 6pm–9.30pm.

Comments: Peaceful course with good greens and lovely views ... Can feel pretty depressing on a wet day ... Best holes are on the back nine ... In variable condition but hotel makes up for it ... Good, open course that lends itself to practice before tackling better courses ... Open, bleak course on undulating ground that did nothing for me ... Good value for standard of facilities.

The Kendleshire Golf Club   ★★★★

Henfield Road, Coalpit Heath, Bristol, BS17 2TG
Nearest main town: Bristol

Secretary:	Mr P. Murphy	Tel: 0117 956 7007
		Fax: 0117 957 3433
Professional:	Mr P. Barrington	Tel: 0117 956 7000
		Fax: 0117 956 6191

Playing: Midweek: round £20.00; day £40.00. Weekend: round £40.00; day n/a.

Facilities: Bar: 11am–11pm. Food: Lunch and dinner from 12pm–9pm. Bar snacks.

Comments: A fun course ... Very welcoming ... Water hazards intelligently used ... 10 hazards on 18 holes is too much ... Island green 11th a dead-ringer for Sawgrass ... For learners a very exciting course ... Never played anything like it ... Target golf but well thought out and planned.

Tracy Park Golf Club   ★★

Tracy Park, Bath Road, Wick, BS15 5RN
Nearest main town: Bath

Secretary:	Mr S. Taylor	Tel: 0117 937 2251
		Fax: 0117 937 4288
Professional:	Mr R. Berry	Tel: 0117 937 3521

Playing: Midweek: round £24.00; day £30.00. Weekend: round £30.00; day £35.00.

Facilities: Bar: 1am–11pm. Food: Lunch and dinner from 10am–9.30pm.

Comments: Clubhouse the best part about this club ... 17th-century clubhouse ... Quite natural ... Condition needs improving ... Couldn't call it value for money ... Condition poor on last visit ... 27 holes of fairly average golf.

Woodlands Golf Club   ★★

Woodlands Lane, Almondsbury, Bristol, BS12 4JZ
Nearest main town: Bristol

Secretary: Mr J. Seymour   Tel: 01454 619319
                                         Fax: 01454 619397

Professional: None.

Playing: Midweek: round £11.00; day £18.00. Weekend: round
                  £15.00; day n/a.

Facilities: Bar: 11am–11pm. Food: Bar snacks.

Comments: In good condition even during the winter months ... Five
                  par-3s set around lakes are best feature of otherwise
                  bland course ... Classic case of overuse of water ...
                  Good value for interesting course.

Woodspring Golf Club   ★★

Woodlands Lane, Almondsbury, BS18 9LR
Nearest main town: Bristol

Secretary: Mr M. Pierce   Tel: 01275 394378
                                         Fax: 01275 394473

Professional: Mr N. Beer

Playing: Midweek: round £20.00; day £20.00. Weekend: round
                  £28.50; day £28.50. Handicap certificate required.

Facilities: Bar: 11am–11pm. Food: Lunch and dinner from
                  12am–9pm. Bar snacks.

Comments: Superb site for a new course ... Heathland setting ...
                  Will get better with time ... Natural new course by
                  Alliss/Clark ... Very tough.

Greater Manchester

Manchester Golf Club

Hopwood Cottage, Rochdale Road, Manchester, M24 2QP
Nearest main town: Manchester

Unlike London, which has many fine courses in its suburbs, Manchester
is not well blessed, and its best courses are located to the north of the
city, where the moorland landscape provides excellent drainage. For
many, the best in the area is Bolton Old Links, a venerable course set
on the side of the hill with ravines and grand trees. Others choose
Manchester, a fine parkland/moorland course located just ten miles
north of the city centre.

Manchester is a very user-friendly course as it is never too busy
(peculiar for a course next to such a large urban centre) and has excellent practice facilities. Once you tee-off, it won't take you long to realise
that the course is not so accommodating, with the wind whipping across
the rugged moorland landscape and accentuating badly struck shots,
particularly so with the proliferation of sloping lies you can get on these
undulating fairways.

Despite the temptation to try and overwhelm the course with brute
strength, Manchester embraces intelligent play, and the members
generally cite the 12th as a good example. At this par-4 a driver off the
tee will leave you with a short iron off a sloping lie, while an iron off the
tee will leave you a longer approach shot but a flat lie. These trade-offs
are classic Colt design traits and if you bear this in mind throughout you
should have few problems with the course.

As you would expect in this area of the country, the reception at the
club is always first class and you always feel as if you are a member of
the club, if only for a day. Recommended.

Secretary:	Mr K. G. Flett	Tel: 0161 643 3202
		Fax: 0161 643 9174
Professional:	Mr B. Connor	Tel: 0161 643 2638
Playing:	Midweek: round £30.00; day £40.00. Weekend: round £45.00; day n/a. Handicap certificate required.	
Facilities:	Bar: 11am–11pm. Food: Lunch from 12pm–2.30pm. Dinner by arrangement.	

Comments: A course that puts golfers first and not profit ... High-class moorland golf at an affordable price ... Characters at this club make it a pleasure to play ... Good finish.

Chorlton-cum-Hardy Golf Club   ★★★

Barlow Hall, Barlow Hall Road, Manchester, M21 7JJ
Nearest main town: Manchester

Secretary: Mrs K. Poole   Tel: 0161 881 5830
                                    Fax: 0161 881 5830
Professional: Mr D. Screeton   Tel: 0161 881 9911

Playing: Midweek: round n/a; day £22.00. Weekend: round n/a; day £27.00.

Facilities: Bar: 12pm–11pm. Food: Lunch and dinner from 11am–9pm. Bar snacks.

Comments: Average meadowland course ... Keep clear of the streams and ditches ... Fair condition but nothing special ... Good matchplay course.

Northenden Golf Club   ★★

Palatine Road, Manchester, M22 4FR
Nearest main town: Manchester

Secretary: Mr R. Kemp   Tel: 0161 998 4738
                                   Fax: 0161 945 5592
Professional: Mr P. Scott   Tel: 0161 945 3386

Playing: Midweek: round n/a; day £27.00. Weekend: round n/a; day £30.00.

Facilities: Bar: 11am–11pm. Food: Bar snacks. Lunch and dinner by arrangement.

Comments: Parkland course next to the River Mersey ... Cheap, fun golf on a championship-length course ... Nothing special ... Not great value for money.

Stand Golf Club   ★

The Dales, Ashbourne Grove, Manchester, M45 7NL
Nearest main town: Manchester

Secretary:	Mr E. B. Taylor	Tel: 0161 766 3197
		Fax: 0161 796 3234
Professional:	Mr M. Dance	Tel: 0161 766 2214

Playing: Midweek: round £25.50; day £25.50. Weekend: round £30.50; day £30.50.

Facilities: Bar: 11am–11pm. Food: Lunch and dinner from 10am–9pm. Bar snacks.

Comments: It's all about the finish here ... Devilish climax to a fairly average layout ... Parkland/moorland ... Reasonable value.

Swinton Park Golf Club   ★★

East Lancashire Road, Swinton, M27 5LX
Nearest main town: Manchester

Secretary:	Mr A. Bowden	Tel: 0161 794 0861
Professional:	Mr J. Wilson	Tel: 0161 793 8077

Playing: Midweek: round £25.00; day £25.00. Weekend: round n/a; day n/a. Handicap certificate required.

Facilities: Bar: 11am–11pm. Food: Lunch from 12pm–6pm.

Comments: Fascinating course ... Bit of a trek ... One of the longest in Lancashire ... Recent improvements have really picked up the course ... Worth a long, lingering look.

Whitefield Golf Club   ★★

Higher Lane, Whitefield, M45 7EZ
Nearest main town: Manchester

Secretary:	Mrs A. Scorfield	Tel: 0161 766 2904
		Fax: 0161 767 9502
Professional:	Mr P. Reeves	Tel: 0161 766 3096

Playing: Midweek: round £25.00; day £25.00. Weekend: round £35.00; day n/a.

Facilities: Bar: 12pm–3pm. Food: Lunch and dinner from 12pm–2.30pm. Dinner on Tuesday and Thursday by arrangement.

Comments: Fantastic landscape ... Unbelievable par-3s ... Sporting, welcoming course ... Golf without the snobbery of a member's club ... Never had a bad experience here.

Worsley Golf Club ★

Stableford Avenue, Monton Green, Eccles, M30 8AP
Nearest main town: Manchester

Secretary: Mr R. Pizzey MBE   Tel: 0161 789 4202
    Fax: 0161 789 3200
Professional: Mr C. Cousins   Tel: 0161 789 4202

Playing: Midweek: round £20.00; day £25.00. Weekend: round £30.00; day n/a. Handicap certificate required.

Facilities: Bar: 11am–11pm. Food: Lunch and dinner from 10am–6pm. Bar snacks.

Comments: Open woodland track ... Plenty of birdie chances ... Woodland but enough room for wayward shots ... Good value for money.

Hampshire

North Hants Golf Club ★★★★

Minley Road, Fleet, GU13 8RE
Nearest main town: Farnborough

North Hants' star has recently risen with the emergence of one of its favourite sons, Justin Rose, the amateur who threatened to win the Open Championship at Royal Birkdale last year. There is no greater testament to a course than the player it breeds, and on that basis North Hants is very good, although a little uncultured around the edges.

Rose's proficiency in the wind at Birkdale suggested a lifetime's playing on an exposed course. But, ironically, North Hants is a very protected course, designed intelligently through dense woods where you will find it very easy to concentrate on your game. The most difficult part of the course is the tee-shots, which have to be cleverly placed to facilitate an easy line into the flag. The greens are generally large and approach shots tend to hold the ball well. Indeed, the condition of the course is a tribute to the greenkeeping staff.

Like The Berkshire, located close by, North Hants is heathland in type, and like that gem it has a great variety of holes that keeps the player consistently interested. There are blind shots which make club selection exceptionally difficult at times and holes where the shape of the fairways dictates the flight of shot you should hit. It is perhaps not a course to experiment on, however, as the trees, heather and gorse gobble up anything off line.

Golfers in Hampshire are spoilt for choice and there are those that prefer the nearby charms of Blackmoor and Liphook. But for the welcome and experience, North Hants is hard to beat, as a visit will testify.

Secretary: Mr I. R. Goodliffe   Tel: 01252 616443
                                     Fax: 01252 811627
Professional: Mr S. Porter   Tel: 01252 61655

Playing: Midweek: round £30.00; day £37.00. Weekend: round £35.00; day £45.00. Handicap certificate required.

Facilities: Bar: 11am–11pm. Food: Bar snacks.

Comments: Super course and obviously a good training ground for Justin Rose ... Blind holes, undulating ground ... Tough task to select clubs with confidence ... Tree-lined course, a real marvel.

Army Golf Club

Laffans Road, Aldershot, GU11 2HF
Nearest main town: Aldershot

Secretary: Maj J. W. G. Douglas   Tel: 01252 337272
                                         Fax: 01252 337562

Professional: Mr G. Cowley   Tel: 01252 336722

Playing: Midweek: round £24.00; day £36.00. Weekend: round n/a; day n/a. Handicap certificate required.

Facilities: Bar: 11am–11pm. Food: Lunch from 11.30am–7pm.

Comments: Respected club ... Very traditional ... One of the oldest in the area ... Nice touches on this subtle course ... Plenty of room for expression ... Not very welcoming.

Barton-on-Sea Golf Club

Miford Lane, New Milton, BH25 5PP
Nearest main town: New Milton

Secretary: Mr N. Hallam-Jones   Tel: 01425 615308
                                         Fax: 01425 621457

Professional: Mr P. Coombs   Tel: 01425 611210

Playing: Midweek: round n/a; day £27.50. Weekend: round n/a; day £32.50. Handicap certificate required.

Facilities: Bar: 11am–11pm. Food: Lunch from 12pm–2pm. Dinner by arrangement.

Comments: Welcoming and friendly links golf ... Excellent course, very friendly and food superb ... Good day out with three nines ... Good golfing experience ... Provided a fabulous day out with tasty bar snacks ... Golf slightly pricey.

Basingstoke Golf Club   ★★

Kempshott Park, Basingstoke, RG23 7LL
Nearest main town: Basingstoke

Secretary:	Mr W. A. Jefford	Tel: 01256 465990
		Fax: 01256 331793
Professional:	Mr I. Hayes	Tel: 01256 51332

Playing: Midweek: round £25.00; day £35.00. Weekend: round n/a; day n/a. Handicap certificate required.

Facilities: Bar: 11am–11pm. Food: Lunch and dinner from 11am–7pm.

Comments: Challenging, well presented and good value ... Attractive course in rolling countryside ... Scenic and a round to savour.

Blackmoor Golf Club   ★★★★

Whitehill, Borden, GU35 9EH
Nearest main town: Borden

Secretary:	Miss C. Hayllar	Tel: 01420 472775
		Fax: 01420 487666
Professional:	Mr S. Clay	Tel: 01420 472345

Playing: Midweek: round n/a; day £40.00. Weekend: round n/a; day n/a. Handicap certificate required.

Facilities: Bar: 11am–11pm. Food: Lunch from 11am–6pm. Bar snacks.

Comments: Very attractive, some great holes and good greens ... A real gem ... A smaller Wentworth West course ... Snobby clubhouse but good society venue.

Botley Park Hotel Golf & Country Club   ★

Winchester Road, Boorley Green, Botley, SO3 2UA
Nearest main town: Southampton

Secretary:	Miss M. Johnstone	Tel: 01489 780888
		Fax: 01489 789242
Professional:	Mr T. Barter	Tel: 01489 789771

Playing: Midweek: round £30.00; day £45.00. Weekend: round £30.00; day £45.00. Handicap certificate required.

Facilities: Bar: 11am–11pm. Food: Breakfast, lunch and dinner from 7am–10pm.

Comments: Attractive course, although not in same echelon as many of its neighbours ... Typical country club where the course isn't the star.

Bramshaw Golf Club ★★

Brook, Lyndhurst, SO43 7HE
Nearest main town: Southampton

Secretary:	Mr R. D. Tingey	Tel: 01703 813433
		Fax: 01703 813958
Professional:	Mr C. Bonner	Tel: 01703 813434

Playing: Midweek: round £27.00; day £40.00. Weekend: round n/a; day n/a. Handicap certificate required.

Facilities: Bar: 11am–11pm. Food: Breakfast, lunch and dinner from 7am–10pm. Bar snacks.

Comments: Why can't all courses be as natural as this? ... Mature trees and greens at this lovely course.

Brockenhurst Manor Golf Club ★★★

Sawy Road, Brockenhurst, SO42 7SG
Nearest main town: Brockenhurst

Secretary:	Mr P. E. Clifford	Tel: 01590 623332
		Fax: 01590 624140
Professional:	Mr J. Lovell	Tel: 01590 623092

Playing: Midweek: round £30.00; day £40.00. Weekend: round n/a; day £55.00. Handicap certificate required.

Facilities: Bar: 11am–9pm. Food: Bar snacks.

Comments: Nice course in summer with much game in residence ... Very friendly club and course ... Food and drink very good ... Prime location on the edge of the New Forest ... A new, intriguing challenge at every turn.

Cams Hall Estate Golf Club ★★

Portchester Road, Fareham, PO16 8UP
Nearest main town: Portsmouth

Secretary:	Mr R. Griffiths	Tel: 01329 827222
		Fax: 01329 827111

Professional: Mr J. Neve   Tel: 01329 827732

Playing: Midweek: round £19.00; day £25.00. Weekend: round £25.00; day £30.00. Handicap certificate required.

Facilities: Bar: 11am–11pm. Food: Lunch and dinner by arrangement.

Comments: Modern club with course to match ... Manufactured course with some idiosyncrasies ... Plenty of lakes and mounding ... One of the best new courses in Hampshire ... Excellent ... Fair value.

Corhampton Golf Club   ★★★

Sheep's Pond Lane, Corhampton, SO32 3LP
Nearest main town: Winchester

Secretary: Mr R. E. Jones   Tel: 01489 877279
                                       Fax: 01489 877680
Professional: Mr I. Roper   Tel: 01489 877638

Playing: Midweek: round £20.00; day £30.00. Weekend: round n/a; day n/a.

Facilities: Bar: 11am–11pm. Food: Lunch from 10am–3pm. Dinner by arrangement.

Comments: Very picturesque ... Downland course that makes you think ... Fine setting in the Meon Valley.

Dummer Golf Club   ★★★

Dummer, RG25 2AR
Nearest main town: Basingstoke

Secretary: Mr R. Watson   Tel: 01256 397888
                                       Fax: 01256 397889
Professional: Mr G. Stubbington   Tel: 01256 397950

Playing: Midweek: round £30.00; day £40.00. Weekend: round n/a; day n/a. Handicap certificate required.

Facilities: Bar: 11am–11pm. Food: Lunch and dinner from 12pm–8pm. Bar snacks.

Comments: The 10th is a superb design ... Alliss/Clark course of variable quality ... Two 9-hole loops of character.

Freshwater Bay Golf Club ★★★

Afton Down, Freshwater, Isle of Wight, PO40 9TZ
Nearest main town: Freshwater

Secretary: Mr J. Copleston   Tel: 01983 752955
                                            Fax: 01983 756704

Professional: None.

Playing: Midweek: round n/a; day £20.00. Weekend: round n/a;
                    day £24.00. Handicap certificate required.

Facilities: Bar: 11am–11pm. Food: Lunch and dinner served from
                    9am–9pm. Bar snacks.

Comments: Well-named club ... You feel so fresh and alive here ...
                    Views all around of the English Channel ... Glorious air
                    here.

Hayling Golf Club ★★★★

Links Lane, Hayling Island, PO11 OBX
Nearest main town: Havant

Secretary: Mr C. J. Cavill   Tel: 01705 464446
                                            Fax: 01705 464446
Professional: Mr R. Gadd   Tel: 01705 464491
                                            Fax: 01705 464491

Playing: Midweek: round £27.00; day £33.00. Weekend: round
                    £35.00; day £44.00. Handicap certificate required.

Facilities: Bar: 11am–11pm. Food: Breakfast, lunch and dinner
                    from 8am–9pm. Bar snacks.

Comments: A joy to play ... Lovely springy turf ... When the wind
                    blows this is proper golf ... .Excellent value, very friendly
                    and links golf to boot ... Views to the Isle of Wight mark
                    this out as special ... Most interesting course in Hants.

Hockley Golf Club ★★★

Twyford, Winchester, SO21 1PL
Nearest main town: Winchester

Secretary: Mrs L. Dyer   Tel: 01962 713165
                                            Fax: 01962 713612
Professional: Mr T. Lane   Tel: 01962 713678

Playing: Midweek: round £25.00; day £35.00. Weekend: round £25.00; day £35.00. Handicap certificate required.

Facilities: Bar: 11am–11pm. Food: Breakfast, lunch and dinner from 9am–9pm. Bar snacks.

Comments: High quality downland course ... One of the best in Hampshire ... Excellent views.

Liphook Golf Club   ★★★★

Liphook, GU30 7EH
Nearest main town: Petersfield

Secretary: Maj J. B. Morgan MBE   Tel: 01428 723785
                                       Fax: 01428 724853
Professional: Mr I. Large   Tel: 01428 723271

Playing: Midweek: round £30.00; day £40.00. Weekend: round £40.00; day £50.00. Handicap certificate required.

Facilities: Bar: 11am–11pm. Food: Bar snacks.

Comments: An ideal course for the middle-handicapper ... Heather plays its part ... Course has got everything in a beautifully understated way ... Made to feel very welcome ... Easy heathland course in class golfing country.

Marriott Meon Valley Hotel Golf Club   ★★★

Sandy Lane, Shedfield, Southampton, SO32 2HQ
Nearest main town: Southampton

Secretary: Mr G. McMenemy   Tel: 01329 833455
                                 Fax: 01329 834411
Professional: Mr J. O'Malley Tel: 01329 832184

Playing: Midweek: round £30.00; day £45.00. Weekend: round £40.00; day n/a. Handicap certificate required.

Facilities: Bar: 11am–11pm. Food: Breakfast, lunch and dinner from 7am–10pm.

Comments: Well-known course connected to country club ... Feels as though its been around for years ... Exciting ... Well presented ... No complaints ... Lovely design making full use of parkland.

New Forest Golf Club ★

Southampton Road, Lyndhurst, SO43 7BU
Nearest main town: Southampton

Secretary: Mrs B. Shaw   Tel: 01703 282752
                                    Fax: 01703 282484

Professional: Mr D. Harris

Playing: Midweek: round £12.00; day £16.00. Weekend: round £12.00; day £16.00. Handicap certificate required.

Facilities: Bar: 11am–11pm. Food: Lunch from 11am–3.30pm. Bar snacks.

Comments: Heathland setting ... Something of a mixed bag ... High class feel ... A little short ... You don't need to be a big hitter ... Tricky.

Old Thorns Golf Club ★★

Longmoor Road, Griggs Green, Liphook, GU30 7PE
Nearest main town: Petersfield

Secretary: Mr G. M. Jones   Tel: 01428 724555
                                    Fax: 01428 725036

Professional: Mr P. Loxley

Playing: Midweek: round £35.00; day £50.00. Weekend: round £45.00; day £65.00.

Facilities: Bar: 11am–11pm. Food: Dinner from 6.30pm–9pm. Bar snacks.

Comments: Very expensive ... Great facilities for non-golfer ... Course not worthy of its high prices ... Condition good, but it should be at that price ... Sumptuous setting.

Rowlands Castle Golf Club ★★

31 Links Lane, Rowlands Castle, PO9 6AE
Nearest main town: Petersfield

Secretary: Mr K. D. Fisher   Tel: 01705 412784
                                    Fax: 01705 413649
Professional: Mr P. Klepacz   Tel: 01705 412785

Playing: Midweek: round n/a; day £25.00. Weekend: round £30.00; day n/a. Handicap certificate required.

Facilities: Bar: 11am–11pm. Food: Bar snacks.

Comments: Excellent clubhouse and well-tended course ... Armchair green at the 7th ... Open all year round for fine golf ... Not the most well-known course in Hants – keep it that way ... Doglegs the course's primary protection.

Royal Winchester Golf Club   ★★★

Sarum Road, Winchester, SO22 5QE
Nearest main town: Winchester

Secretary: Mr D. Thomson   Tel: 01962 852462
                                      Fax: 01962 865048
Professional: Mr S. Hunter   Tel: 01962 862473

Playing: Midweek: round £28.00; day £35.00. Weekend: round n/a; day n/a. Handicap certificate required.

Facilities: Bar: 12pm–8pm. Food: Lunch from 11am–5pm. Bar snacks.

Comments: Friendly course with beautiful vistas ... Surprising course with handful of fine, attractive holes ... Can be tough at times although the finish is a little weak ... Nice opening nine but tails off towards the end ... Was getting a little bored near the death ... Be on your game quick here or you will never get your score back.

Sandford Springs Golf Club   ★★★

Wolverton, Tadley, RG26 5RT
Nearest main town: Basingstoke

Secretary: Mr G. Tipple   Tel: 01635 297881
                                      Fax: 01635 298065
Professional: Mr G. Edmunds   Tel: 01635 297883

Playing: Midweek: round £23.00; day £29.00. Weekend: round n/a; day n/a. Handicap certificate required.

Facilities: Bar: 11am–11pm. Food: Bar snacks.

Comments: Three loops of nine for what is a memorable day's golf ... Take lots of balls ... Great views from highest point ... Something for every player here ... Consistently surprising course.

Shanklin & Sandown Golf Club ★★★★

Fairway Lake, Sandown, Isle of Wight, PO36 9PR
Nearest main town: Sandown

Secretary:	Mr A. J. Messing	Tel: 01983 403217
		Fax: 01983 403217
Professional:	Mr P. Hammond	Tel: 01983 404424
		Fax: 01983 404424

Playing: Midweek: round £22.00; day £22.00. Weekend: round £25.00; day £25.00. Handicap certificate required.

Facilities: Bar: 11am–11pm. Food: Lunch and dinner from 10am–6pm. Bar snacks.

Comments: A very good feel to the whole club, welcoming, relaxing and appealing ... Always interesting course ... Heathland in jaw-dropping location ... Simply superb day's golf ... Will be going again.

South Winchester Golf Club ★★★

Romsey Road, Pitt, Winchester, SO22 5QW
Nearest main town: Winchester

Secretary:	Mr S. Wright	Tel: 01962 877800
		Fax: 01962 877900
Professional:	Mr R. Adams	Tel: 01962 840469

Playing: Midweek: round n/a; day £20.00. Weekend: round n/a; day £26.00.

Facilities: Bar: Members only. Food: Members only.

Comments: Fair condition and enjoyable to play ... Should mature into a great test of golf ... Excellent par-5s ... Carved from ancient woodland, this is an exercise in ball placement ... Young course – one to play in the millennium.

Southampton Golf Club ★★

Golf Course Road, Bassett, Southampton, SO16 7AY
Nearest main town: Southampton

Secretary:	Mr B. Gibson	Tel: 01703 760546
		Fax: 01703 760412
Professional:	Mr J. Waring	Tel: 01703 768407

Playing: Midweek: round £8.60; day n/a. Weekend: round £11.90; day n/a.

Facilities: Bar: 6am–10pm. Food: Breakfast, lunch and dinner from 6am–10pm. Bar snacks

Comments: One of the best municipals in the country ... Exceptional muni where you feel very welcome ... Knocks spots off many private clubs ... A real people's course ... Value all the way.

Stoneham Golf Club   ★★★★

Monks Wood Close, Bassett, Southampton, SO16 3TT
Nearest main town: Southampton

Secretary: Mr A. Bray   Tel: 01703 769272
                                       Fax: 01703 766320
Professional: Mr I. Young   Tel: 01703 768397

Playing: Midweek: round £29.00; day £36.00. Weekend: round £40.00; day £40.00. Handicap certificate required.

Facilities: Bar: 11am–11pm. Food: Lunch from 11am–5pm. Bar snacks.

Comments: Excellent greens ... Always a rewarding challenge ... Always made very welcome ... Excellent, hilly course with sprinkling of heather ... Cross bunkers can make life difficult.

Test Valley Golf Club   ★

Micheldever Road, Overton, RG25 3DS
Nearest main town: Basingstoke

Secretary: Mr A. Briggs   Tel: 01256 770916
                                       Fax: 01256 771153
Professional: Mr A. Briggs   Tel: 01256 771737

Playing: Midweek: round £16.00; day £24.00. Weekend: round £22.00; day £34.00.

Facilities: Bar: 11am–11pm. Food: Breakfast, lunch and dinner from 9am–9pm. Bar snacks.

Comments: Hosted many events but can't see why ... Extremely long ... Highly rated in the area ... Found it in poor condition ... Wasn't that impressed ... Fun for the high handicapper with lakes and prominent bunkers.

Waterlooville Golf Club   ★★★

Cherry Tree Avenue, Cowplain, Waterlooville, PO8 8AP
Nearest main town: Portsmouth

Secretary: Mr D. Nairne   Tel: 01705 263388
                                         Fax: 01705 347513
Professional: Mr J. Hay   Tel: 01705 256911
                                         Fax: 01705 256911

Playing: Midweek: round £25.00; day £30.00. Weekend: round n/a; day n/a. Handicap certificate required.

Facilities: Bar: 11am–11pm. Food: Lunch from 11am–5pm. Bar snacks.

Comments: Highly thought of in the area ... Excellent variety ... Very challenging ... Par-5s genuine three-shotters.

Hereford & Worcester

Ross-on-Wye Golf Club ★★★★

Two Park, Gorsley, Ross-on-Wye, HR9 7UT
Nearest main town: Ross-on-Wye

Just before you enter the grey, industrial corridor of south Wales where golfers head to play some great links courses, travellers from the north pass through the beautiful Wye Valley. The only stop-off point for golfers here is Ross-on-Wye, a fairly new course that is cut through a verdant forest and provides some exciting golf.

Keeping the ball in play is the secret at Ross-on-Wye, although if you do land in the trees, there is always an escape route – the greenkeepers are instructed to keep the undergrowth at a minimum. The course's other protection are the bunkers which have been reconstructed in the last 12 months and have added a new dimension to the course.

Some golfers find this sort of golf unappealing, but it is not all a matter of accurate hitting. Indeed, at the 5th and 6th, you are faced with consecutive par-5s where the trees open out and the player is allowed to hit freely. There's also a strong selection of par-3s, including the 9th and the 12th, a par-3 played over a pond, the only one on the course.

With a standard scratch score of 73, there is no denying that Ross-on-Wye is hard, but the number of societies that are booked in for the coming year, and the steady stream of visitors, suggests its difficulty does not take away from the experience. Off-course the feel is good also, with a lively bar and genial atmosphere bleeding through the club.

Secretary:	Mr N. G. Ovens	Tel: 01989 720267
		Fax: 01989 720212
Professional:	Mr N. Catchpole	Tel: 01989 720439

Playing: Midweek: round £30.00; day £40.00. Weekend: round £30.00; day £40.00. Handicap certificate required.

Facilities: Bar: 11am–11pm. Food: Lunch from 11am–5pm. Bar snacks. Dinner by arrangement.

Comments: Gracious members and well-kept course ... Tree-lined, you really need to know where to drive ... Undulating parkland through silver birch forest – fine stuff ... Greens always good.

Bank House Hotel Golf & Country Club   ★

Bransford, Worcester, WR6 5JD
Nearest main town: Worcester

Secretary: Mr P. A. D. Holmes   Tel: 01886 833551
                                          Fax: 01886 832545
Professional: Mr C. George   Tel: 01886 833621

Playing: Midweek: round £15.00; day £25.00. Weekend: round
                  £25.00; day n/a.

Facilities: Bar: 11am–11pm. Food: Breakfast, lunch and dinner
                  from 7am–10pm.

Comments: American-style course with lots of water and tough
                  finishing holes ... Enjoyable day out ... Poor use of
                  water hazards ... Very unnatural use of water ... Island
                  greens and sculptured fairways.

Belmont Lodge and Golf Club   ★★★

Belmont House, Belmont, Hereford, HR2 9SA
Nearest main town: Hereford

Secretary: Mr T. Thomas   Tel: 01432 352666
                                          Fax: 01432 358090
Professional: Mr M. Walsh   Tel: 01432 352717

Playing: Midweek: round £10.00; day n/a. Weekend: round
                  £16.00; day n/a.

Facilities: Bar: 11am–11pm. Food: Lunch and dinner from
                  11am–11pm. Bar snacks.

Comments: Nice variety ... Two nines with a very different flavour ...
                  Outstanding views over Herefordshire ... Best holes run
                  alongside the River Wye ... Felt very contented walking
                  off the 18th.

Burghill Valley Golf Club   ★★

Tillington Road, Burghill, HR4 7RW
Nearest main town: Hereford

Secretary: Mr K. Smith   Tel: 01432 760456
                                          Fax: 01432 761654
Professional: Mr N. Clarke   Tel: 01432 760808

Playing: Midweek: round £17.00; day £25.00. Weekend: round £25.00; day n/a.

Facilities: Bar: 11am–11pm. Food: Lunch and dinner from 10am–10pm. Bar snacks.

Comments: Fairly unoriginal ... Very easy walking ... Condition not in the top bracket ... Cuts through a cider orchard at one point ... A course that suits all standards ... Not on my 'wish' list.

Churchill & Blakedown Golf Club   ★

Churchill Lane, Blakedown, DY10 3NB
Nearest main town: Kidderminster

Secretary: Mr J. G. Guest   Tel: 01562 700018
Professional: Mr K. Wheeler   Tel: 01562 700454

Playing: Midweek: round £17.50; day n/a. Weekend: round n/a; day n/a.

Facilities: Bar: 11am–11pm. Food: Lunch and dinner from 11am–9pm. Bar snacks.

Comments: Nine-hole hilltop course ... Nothing special apart from views ... Nine-holer with character ... Condition not great.

Fulford Heath Golf Club   ★★★★

Tanners Green Lane, Wythall, B47 6BH
Nearest main town: Birmingham

Secretary: Mrs M. A. Tuckett   Tel: 01564 824758
                                        Fax: 01564 822629
Professional: Mr D. Down   Tel: 01564 822930

Playing: Midweek: round £32.50; day £32.50. Weekend: round n/a; day n/a. Handicap certificate required.

Facilities: Bar: 11am–2pm & 6pm–10pm. Food: Lunch from 12am–2pm. Dinner from 6pm–9pm.

Comments: Such magnificent condition, every hole is just so different ... Imaginative course, still a pleasure to play ... Mature parkland ... Two stunning par-3s.

Hagley Country Club ★

Wassell Grove, Hagley, Stourbridge, DY9 9JW
Nearest main town: Birmingham

Secretary:	Mr G. F. Yardley	Tel: 01562 883701
		Fax: 01562 887518
Professional:	Mr I. Clark	Tel: 01562 883852

Playing: Midweek: round £22.00; day £28.00. Weekend: round n/a; day n/a. Handicap certificate required.

Facilities: Bar: 11am–11pm. Food: Lunch from 12pm–3pm. Dinner from 6pm–9pm. Food not served on Mondays.

Comments: Very good value ... Course nothing special but good value ... Thoroughly enjoyed this undulating course ... Value.

Herefordshire Golf Club ★

Raven's Causeway, Wormsley, Hereford, HR4 8LY
Nearest main town: Hereford

Secretary:	Mr R. W. Dando	Tel: 01432 830219
Professional:	Mr D. Hemming	Tel: 01432 830465

Playing: Midweek: round £17.00; day £22.00. Weekend: round £20.00; day £28.00.

Facilities: Bar: 11am–11pm. Food: Bar snacks.

Comments: Parkland of variable character ... Plenty of birdie chances ... Course gives you a clear strategy ... Average condition.

Kings Norton Golf Club ★★

Brockhill Lane, Weatheroak, Alvechurch, B48 7ED
Nearest main town: Birmingham

Secretary:	Mrs S. Weatherhead	Tel: 01564 826789
		Fax: 01564 826955
Professional:	Mr K. Hayward	Tel: 01564 822635

Playing: Midweek: round £30.00; day £35.00. Weekend: round n/a; day n/a. Handicap certificate required.

Facilities: Bar: 11am–11pm. Food: Lunch and dinner from 12am–9pm. Bar snacks.

Comments: Traditional design ... Condition not what it used to be ... Respected course ... Long and exacting ... If you like a challenge ... One for the big hitters ... Need to bomb it off the tee ... Don't be put off by the length.

Kington Golf Club   ★★★

Bradnor Hill, Kington, HR5 3RE
Nearest main town: Kington

Secretary: Mr G. R. Wictome   Tel: 01544 340270
                                      Fax: 01544 340270
Professional: Mr D. Oliver   Tel: 01544 231320

Playing: Midweek: round £14.00; day £18.00. Weekend: round £18.00; day £22.00. Handicap certificate required.

Facilities: Bar: 11am–11pm. Food: Lunch from 11am–4pm. Dinner by arrangement.

Comments: Links-type course ... Difficult to master in the wind ... Highest 18-hole course in England and worth the climb ... Natural course with no bunkers ... Fascinating course that plays very tough despite lack of man-made hazards.

Leominster Golf Club   ★

Ford Bridge, Leominster, HR6 OLE
Nearest main town: Leominster

Secretary: Mr J. A. Ashcroft   Tel: 01568 610055
                                       Fax: 01568 610055
Professional: Mr A. Ferriday   Tel: 01568 611402

Playing: Midweek: round £14.50; day £18.00. Weekend: round £21.00; day £21.00.

Facilities: Bar: 11am–11pm. Food: Lunch from 11.30am–2pm. Dinner from 6pm–9pm.

Comments: Short and hilly, not everyone's choice ... A day you won't forget and you can fish too ... Best holes run alongside the River Lugg ... Exceptional value and fun as well.

Moseley Golf Club   ★

Springfield Road, Kings Heath, Birmingham, B14 7DX
Nearest main town: South Birmingham

Secretary:	Mr R. A. Jowle	Tel: 0121 444 4957
		Fax: 0121 441 4662
Professional:	Mr G. Edge	Tel: 0121 444 2063

Playing: Midweek: round £37.00; day £37.00. Weekend: round n/a; day n/a. Handicap certificate required.

Facilities: Bar: 11am–11pm. Food: Lunch and dinner from 11am–9pm. Bar snacks.

Comments: Didn't do it for me ... Welcome and facilities a little lacking ... Not the best in the area ... Couple of nice holes ... Wasn't bowled over.

North Worcestershire Golf Club   ★

Frankley Beeches Road, Northfield, Birmingham, B31 5LP
Nearest main town: Birmingham

Secretary:	Mr D. Wilson	Tel: 0121 475 1047
		Fax: 0121 476 8681
Professional:	Mr F. Clark	Tel: 0121 475 1047

Playing: Midweek: round £18.50; day £27.50. Weekend: round n/a; day n/a. Handicap certificate required.

Facilities: Bar: 11am–11pm. Food: Lunch and dinner from 11am–9pm. Bar snacks.

Comments: Well worth a visit ... Old established course with very fair standards ... Well-designed, testing course ... Obviously a well-run club and greens were first rate.

The Vale Golf & Country Club   ★

Bishampton, Pershore, WR10 2LZ
Nearest main town: Evesham

Secretary:	Mr D. Cudmore	Tel: 01386 462781
		Fax: 01386 462597
Professional:	Mrs C. Griffiths	Tel: 01386 462520

Playing: Midweek: round £20.00; day £30.00. Weekend: round £25.00; day n/a. Handicap certificate required.

Facilities: Bar: 11am–11pm.

Comments: Young course ... Extensive practice facilities ... American-style course – fairly unimaginative ... Big greens look receptive, but are protected by lots of water and sand ... Good society venue.

Wharton Park Golf Club   ★★

Long Bank, Bewdley, DY12 2QW
Nearest main town: Bewdley

Secretary: Mr P. Wild   Tel: 01299 405222
                                         Fax: 01299 405121
Professional: Mr A. Hoare   Tel: 01299 405163

Playing: Midweek: round £20.00; day n/a. Weekend: round £25.00; day n/a. Handicap certificate required.

Facilities: Bar: 11am–11pm. Food: Bar snacks.

Comments: Protected by its length ... Long and tiring ... Par-73 that plays every inch ... Genuine three shot par-5s ... Overrated in the area ... Can try the patience ... Wide open ... Predominantly a driver's course.

Worcester Golf & Country Club

Boughton Park, Worcester, WR2 4EZ
Nearest main town: Worcester

Secretary: Mr D. G. Bettsworth   Tel: 01905 422555
                                         Fax: 01905 749090
Professional: Mr C. Colenso   Tel: 01905 422044

Playing: Midweek: round £25.00; day £25.00. Weekend: round n/a; day n/a. Handicap certificate required.

Facilities: Bar: 11am–11pm. Food: Bar snacks. Dinner from 7pm–9pm.

Comments: Pretty tough ... A stern test ... Doesn't look too tricky ... Country club course that has retained an identity ... Get to know it ... Mature parkland ... Views of the Malvern Hills ... A stiff challenge.

Hertfordshire

Hanbury Manor Golf Club ★★★★

Funridge, Ware, SG12 OSD
Nearest main town: Ware

Creating the perfect country house retreat is a tricky business. Sometimes the quest for authenticity clouds the issue and often does the opposite, making for a feeling of falseness – almost a film-set atmosphere rather than the real thing.

Hanbury Manor was an ambitious project, turning a former convent into a luxury hotel with a championship golf course in its grounds, but it has been more successful than most.

There is no doubting the expertise that has shaped the golf course. It may not have been Jack Nicklaus himself that crafted the beautifully lush and intriguing holes, but his son Jack Jr has done an excellent job, under the guidance of the great man. It is tough, uncompromising yet picturesque, mixing an open and undulating front nine played on the edge of a valley, with a wooded and winding back half. Its conditioning is first class, far superior to a glut of excellent new courses nearby including Hadley Wood and The Hertfordshire.

The tone for the round is set at the 1st, a driveable par-4, protected by a ravine in front of the green. There are plenty of other do-or-die holes on the layout, and some excellent par-5s, specifically the 9th, a long three-shotter that snakes up to the clubhouse and the 17th, where you must be careful of the lake for your approach to the green.

Hanbury Manor has an excellent reputation, having hosted the English Open in the past, and the hotel more than matches it – an exquisite restaurant and superb off-course facilities.

It is probably Hanbury's stone's-throw location from London that keeps the cost on the highish side, but if you do have the clout, you can not deny that a lot of life's pleasures are here to be indulged in and thoroughly indulged.

Secretary:	Mr M. Newey	Tel: 01920 487722
		Fax: 01920 487692
Professional:	Mr P. Blaze	Tel: 01920 463474
Playing:	Prices on application.	
Facilities:	Bar: Hotel guests & members only. Food: Hotel guests and members only.	

Comments: Not as good value for money as you would expect ... Fantastic around the English Open ... Two contrasting nines ... Beautifully manicured course ... Fairways better than some club greens ... Great course in a lovely setting ... Five holes with water and two with greens on the edge of water ... Refreshment at halfway was welcome ... Jack Nicklaus II design of great character ... Some holes based on original Harry Vardon design ... Book a room at the hotel to play this course ... Greens fast and true each time I go back.

Aldenham Golf Club   ★★

Church Lane, Aldenham, WD2 8AL
Nearest main town: Watford

Secretary:	Mrs J. Phillips	Tel: 01923 853929
		Fax: 01923 858472
Professional:	Mr P. Winston	Tel: 01923 857889

Playing: Midweek: round £22.00; day £32.00. Weekend: round £30.00; day n/a.

Facilities: Bar: 11am–11pm. Food: Bar snacks. Sunday lunch by arrangement.

Comments: The 13th should be a par-6 – I'd hate to play it from the back tees ... Facilities for visitors are a little basic ... Parkland course but there are better examples around.

Ashridge Golf Club   ★★★★

Little Gaddesden, Berkhamsted, HP4 1LY
Nearest main town: Berkhamsted

Secretary:	Mr M. S. Silver	Tel: 01442 842244
		Fax: 01442 843770
Professional:	Mr A. Ainsworth	Tel: 01442 842307

Playing: Midweek: round £43.00; day £60.00. Weekend: round n/a; day n/a. Handicap certificate required.

Facilities: Bar: 11am–11pm. Food: Lunch from 12pm–2pm. Bar snacks.

Comments: Where Henry Cotton used to be club professional ...
Fairly straightforward course with rough the primary
defence ... A real good-looker ... Very captivating ...
Relaxing venue ... You feel completely untroubled on
this little beauty ... Keep it straight.

Berkhamsted Golf Club   ★★★

The Common, Berkhamsted, HP4 2QB
Nearest main town: Berkhamsted

Secretary: Mr C. D. Hextall   Tel: 01442 865832
                                           Fax: 01442 863730
Professional: Mr B J. Proundfoot   Tel: 01442 865851

Playing: Midweek: round £25.00; day £35.00. Weekend: round
                   £35.00; day £35.00. Handicap certificate required.

Facilities: Bar: 11am–11pm. Food: Lunch from 11am–2.30pm.
                   Dinner by arrangement.

Comments: Still fairly unknown, thank goodness ... High quality golf
                   in nice surroundings ... Some long carries over heather
                   ... No bunkers ... Bunkers – who needs them when it's
                   this tough ... Would willingly trade my membership for
                   this club.

Brookmans Park Golf Club   ★★★★

Brookmans Park, Hatfield, AL9 7AT
Nearest main town: Hatfield

Secretary: Mr P. A. Gill   Tel: 01707 652468
                                           Fax: 01707 661851
Professional: Mr I. Jelley   Tel: 01707 652468

Playing: Midweek: round £28.00; day £36.00. Weekend: round
                   n/a; day n/a. Handicap certificate required.

Facilities: Bar: 11am–11pm. Food: Bar snacks.

Comments: Generally kept in fine condition ... Clever, tricky holes
                   ... Value in buckets ... Makes the visitor welcome ...
                   Can play long depending on tees ... Not too intimidat-
                   ing.

Chesfield Downs Golf Club ★★★

Jack's Hill, Graveley, SG4 7EQ
Nearest main town: Graveley

Secretary:	Mr D. Burridge	Tel: 01462 482929
		Fax: 01462 482930
Professional:	Ms J. Fernley	Tel: 01462 482929

Playing: Midweek: round £14.75; day £20.00. Weekend: round £21.00; day £30.00.

Facilities: Bar: 11am–11pm. Food: Breakfast, lunch and dinner from 8am–10pm. Bar snacks.

Comments: Course that is aimed at beginners ... Nice place to learn the game ... Facilities second to none ... Excellent golf centre catering to learners ... Natural downland ... Couldn't get excited about this rather bleak course.

East Herts Golf Club ★★

Hamels Park, Buntingford, SG9 9NA
Nearest main town: Puckeridge

Secretary:	Mr C. Wilkinson	Tel: 01920 821978
		Fax: 01920 823700
Professional:	Mr S. M. Bryan	Tel: 01920 821922

Playing: Midweek: round £26.00; day £33.00. Weekend: round n/a; day n/a. Handicap certificate required.

Facilities: Bar: 11am–11pm. Food: Lunch from 12pm–2.30pm. Dinner by arrangement.

Comments: A beautiful parkland course, unfortunately greens were poor on visit ... Worth a visit but not the best in Herts by any measure ... Fair value for course in good condition.

Great Hadham Golf Club ★★

Great Hadham Road, Bishop's Stortford, SG10 6JE
Nearest main town: Bishop's Stortford

Secretary:	Mr C. Day	Tel: 01279 843558
		Fax: 01279 842122
Professional:	Mr K. Lunt	Tel: 01279 843888

Playing: Midweek: round £16.00; day £28.00. Weekend: round £23.00; day n/a.

Facilities: Bar: 11am–11pm. Food: Lunch from 12pm–2.30pm. Dinner by arrangement.

Comments: Bent over backwards to make sure you enjoyed yourself ... Open course with varying difficulty of holes ... Undulating meadowland/links with fair facilities and welcome.

Hadley Wood Golf Club ★★★★

Beech Hill, Hadley Wood, Barnet, EN4 OJJ
Nearest main town: Barnet

Secretary: Mr C. Shilcox   Tel: 0181 449 4328
                                   Fax: 0181 364 8633
Professional: Mr P. Jones   Tel: 0181 449 3285

Playing: Midweek: round £36.00; day £48.00. Weekend: round n/a; day n/a. Handicap certificate required.

Facilities: Bar: 11am–11pm. Food: Bar snacks. Dinner by arrangement.

Comments: An absolute gem ... Food is fabulous ... Appealing course for big hitter although there is severe rough ... As golf should be played ... Many nice features at this progressive club ... Give me the keys to the club ... Everything right about this attractive club.

Letchworth Golf Club ★★

Letchworth Lane, Letchworth, SG6 3NQ
Nearest main town: Letchworth

Secretary: Mr A. R. Bailey   Tel: 01462 683203
                                    Fax: 01462 484567
Professional: Mr S. J. Mutimer   Tel: 01462 682713

Playing: Midweek: round £24.00; day £33.00. Weekend: round n/a; day n/a. Handicap certificate required.

Facilities: Bar: 11am–11pm. Food: Lunch from 11am–2pm. Dinner from 6pm–9pm. Bar snacks.

Comments: Mixed course with good and bad holes ... Wouldn't rank it that highly ... Peaceful ... Tranquil setting but golf rather weak ... Had many great rounds here ... Tough par-70 ... Doesn't give you birdies.

Manor of Groves Golf Club   ★

High Wych, Sawbridgeworth, CM21 0LA
Nearest main town: Harlow

Secretary: Mrs S. Hughes   Tel: 01279 722333
                                          Fax: 01279 726972
Professional: Mr C. Laurence   Tel: 01279 721986

Playing: Midweek: round £20.00; day £30.00. Weekend: round £25.00; day n/a. Handicap certificate required.

Facilities: Bar: 11am–11pm. Food: Lunch from 11.30am–2pm. Dinner from 6pm–10pm. Bar snacks.

Comments: Varied holes in wood/farmland setting ... Interesting course ... Average quality all round ... Fair value for unimposing course.

Mill Green Golf Club   ★

Gypsy Lane, Mill Green, Welwyn Garden City, AL7 4TY
Nearest main town: Welwyn Garden City

Secretary: Mr J. Tubb   Tel: 01707 276900
                                          Fax: 01707 276898
Professional: Mr A. Hall   Tel: 01707 270542

Playing: Midweek: round £19.00; day £29.00. Weekend: round £25.00; day £45.00.

Facilities: Bar: 11am–11pm. Food: Breakfast, lunch and dinner from 10am–9pm. Bar snacks.

Comments: What you'd expect from an Alliss/Clark creation ... New course for all levels ... One of a good collection of courses in Welwyn Garden City ... Won't produce a Nick Faldo ... Wooded holes better than the meadowland section.

Moor Park Golf Club   ★★★★

Rickmansworth, WD3 1QN
Nearest main town: Rickmansworth

Secretary:	Mr J. A. Davies	Tel: 01923 773146
		Fax: 01923 777109
Professional:	Mr L. Farmer	Tel: 01923 774113

Playing: Midweek: round £50.00; day £80.00. Weekend: round n/a; day n/a. Handicap certificate required.

Facilities: Bar: 11am–11pm. Food: Lunch from 12pm–2.30pm.

Comments: Attractive, well-kept course although very expensive ... Surprisingly friendly and good golf facilities ... High course is far superior to the West ... Well worth the rather pricey green fee.

Panshanger Golf Complex   ★★

Old Herns Lane, Welwyn Garden City, AL7 2ED
Nearest main town: Welwyn Garden City

Secretary:	Mrs S. Ryan	Tel: 01707 333312
		Fax: 01707 390010
Professional:	Mr B. Lewis	Tel: 01707 333312

Playing: Midweek: round £11.50; day n/a. Weekend: round £15.70; day n/a.

Facilities: Bar: 11am–11pm. Food: Lunch and dinner from 11am–11pm. Bar snacks.

Comments: A real value course ... If you object to high green fees, this is the one for you ... Recommended to all.

Porters Park Golf Club   ★★★

Shenley Hill, Radlett, WD7 7AZ
Nearest main town: Radlett

Secretary:	Mr P. Phillips	Tel: 01923 854127
		Fax: 01923 575992
Professional:	Mr D. Gleeson	Tel: 01923 854366

Playing: Midweek: round £29.00; day £44.00. Weekend: round n/a; day n/a. Handicap certificate required.

Facilities: Bar: Members only. Food: Members only.

Comments: Rather exclusive club ... Well worth the money ... Fantastic presentation ... Benefits from restricted play ... Excellent condition ... A real good-looker ... Very lush ... Can't go in the bar but you only come here for the course ... Super layout ... Very difficult to get to know.

Sandy Lodge Golf Club   ★★

Sandy Lodge Lane, Northwood, HA6 2JD
Nearest main town: Northwood

Secretary: Mrs H. Inman   Tel: 01923 825429
                                       Fax: 01923 824319
Professional: Mr J. Pinsent   Tel: 01923 825321

Playing: Midweek: round £31.00; day £41.00. Weekend: round n/a; day n/a. Handicap certificate required.

Facilities: Bar: 11am–11pm. Food: Bar snacks.

Comments: Sandy soil perfect for golf ... Heathland-type course – not out of place ... Very enjoyable ... Linksy feel.

South Herts Golf Club   ★★★

Links Drive, Totteridge, London, HR9 7UA
Nearest main town: London

Secretary: Mr P. Wise   Tel: 0181 445 2035
                                       Fax: 0181 445 7569
Professional: Mr P. Y. Mitchell   Tel: 0181 445 4637

Playing: Midweek: round £25.00; day £35.00. Weekend: round n/a; day n/a.

Facilities: Bar: 11am–11pm. Food: Lunch from 11am–4pm. Bar snacks.

Comments: Harry Vardon and Dai Rees were professionals here ... Well worth the visit ... One of the best in London ... Would go again ... Greens exceptional ... Find time to play here.

Stocks Hotel Golf Club ★★★

Stocks Road, Aldbury, Tring, HP23 5RX
Nearest main town: Tring

Secretary:	Mr S. Phillips	Tel: 01442 851341
		Fax: 01442 851253
Professional:	Mr P. R. Lane	Tel: 01442 851491

Playing: Midweek: round £30.00; day n/a. Weekend: round £40.00; day n/a. Handicap certificate required.

Facilities: Bar: 11am–11pm. Food: Breakfast, lunch and dinner from 7am–10pm.

Comments: Well-managed course and country club ... How a resort course should be ... First-class facilities and course ... Not a 'name' course but well worth playing ... Really tries hard ... Very difficult (standard scratch 73) ... They treat you well here.

Verulam Golf Club ★★★

London Road, St Albans, AL1 1JG
Nearest main town: St Albans

Secretary:	Mr A. R. Crichton-Smith	Tel: 01727 853327
		Fax: 01727 812201
Professional:	Mr N. Burch	Tel: 01727 861401

Playing: Midweek: round £25.00; day £35.00. Weekend: round n/a; day n/a.

Facilities: Bar: 11am–11pm. Food: Lunch and dinner from 10am–9pm. Bar snacks.

Comments: Home of Sam Ryder ... Greens are not so hot but course is a spirited test of any player ... Course could be better maintained and welcome not so good ... 14 holes with out of bounds ... Good stretch of holes near the turn.

West Herts Golf Club ★★

Cassiobury Park, Watford, WD1 7SL
Nearest main town: Watford

Secretary:	Mr C. C. Dodman	Tel: 01923 236484
		Fax: 01923 222300

Professional: Mr C. S. Gough   Tel: 01923 220352

Playing: Midweek: round £20.00; day £30.00. Weekend: round £30.00; day n/a.

Facilities: Bar: 11am–11pm. Food: Breakfast, lunch and dinner from 7.30am–6pm. Bar snacks.

Comments: A welcome smile whether in the pro shop or at the bar ... Open all year round ... Rarely gets boggy ... Well established club with mind-boggling tradition ... Go play, it's a treat ... A memorable round in the late afternoon sun.

Whipsnade Park Golf Club   ★★

Studham Lane, Dagnall, HP4 1RH
Nearest main town: Hemel Hempstead

Secretary: Mr D. Whalley   Tel: 01442 842330
                                        Fax: 01442 842090
Professional: Mr M. Lewendon   Tel: 01442 842310
                                        Fax: 01442 842090

Playing: Midweek: round £24.00; day £34.00. Weekend: round £35.00; day n/a.

Facilities: Bar: 12am–9pm. Food: Lunch from 12pm–3pm.

Comments: Very long track right near the zoo ... Poor facilities for visitors ... Not value for money ... Bit of a bore ... Nice views ... Average course in the Chilterns.

Isle of Man

Castletown Golf Links Club ★★★★

Fort Island, Derbyhaven, IM9 1UA
Nearest main town: Castletown

Step outside the front of the Links Hotel and you are straight on the 1st tee at Castletown – but just pray the wind is not blowing too hard.

The Castletown Links is set on a rocky peninsula on the south of the Isle of Man and, as such, is completely exposed. When squalls race in off the Irish Sea, players rush in all directions for shelter as the course is just too difficult to play – as you hit, you feel as if the ball is going to come back over your head. It is an extremely elemental golf experience – rocks jut out from the fairway as natural hazards and you must drive over the Irish Sea itself (the 17th), certainly the highlight of any round.

There are other high points too, particularly the challenging 5th that the hotel manager is always happy to have a bet with you about. The wager is straightforward: a bottle of champagne for anyone who pars the hole, and if you fail, you buy the champagne for the manager. He says he has rarely lost his money at this hole that has a habit of enticing a push or a slice. When Greg Norman played here he managed a par but not many do, especially when the wind is up. Tug your tee shot left and you hit a rugged bank.

As befits a links, the wind will always play a pivotal role on a layout that offers an intriguing mix of long and short holes. The course can look deceptively easy as it not a monster in length, but be prepared to be surprised. The course is undoubtedly the best on the island and there are no shortage of competitions. Those in the know always make sure to visit during a quiet period when Castletown is at its toughest and most satisfying.

Secretary:	Mr R. Griffiths	Tel: 01624 822201
		Fax: 01624 824633
Professional:	Mr M. Crowe	Tel: 01624 822211
Playing:	Midweek: round £25.00; day £25.00. Weekend: round £30.00; day £30.00.	
Facilities:	Bar: 10am–11pm. Food: Lunch from 12pm–2pm. Bar snacks. Dinner from 7pm–10pm.	

Comments: A very tricky course on the Langness Peninsula ... Plenty of Manx charm here ... Sea covers the course on three sides ... So tough, so beautiful, so wild ... Hard to master even in calm conditions.

Mount Murray Golf & Country Club   ★★

Santon, IM4 2HT
Nearest main town: Douglas

Secretary:	Mr A. D. Dyson	Tel: 01624 661111
		Fax: 01624 611116
Professional:	Mr A. D. Dyson	Tel: 01624 661111

Playing: Midweek: round £18.00; day £18.00. Weekend: round £24.00; day £24.00.

Facilities: Bar: 11am–11pm. Food: Breakfast, lunch and dinner from 8am–11pm. Bar snacks.

Comments: Really underrated ... Views out of this world ... Lovely outlook over the Isle of Man ... Moorland beauty ... Very exposed on moorland outcrop ... Massive par-5s ... A real behemoth of a course at 6,600+ yards.

Kent

Chart Hills Golf Club ★★★★★

Weeks Lane, Biddenden, TN27 8JX
Nearest main town: Ashford

First and foremost, Chart Hills is famed for its association with Nick Faldo. His first course design in England, Chart Hills has been under the microscope ever since Faldo committed himself to the project in 1993. On the whole, the course has been received well, and the opinion of club players has, at times, verged on blatant hero worship.

Chart Hills has proved a particular favourite with golf societies. In many ways, it is an exciting and simple course for a first-time visitor to enjoy – you can see where you are going, with everything laid out clearly in front of you, and in no place is it tricked-up. Although it is not the cheapest place to play, it is considered to be good value.

One of the first things that you notice about Chart Hills is Faldo's inventive use of bunkers. Faldo has to some extent followed modern design principles in emphasising the use of water, but at Chart Hills, he chose to implement extensive bunkering. On some holes they seem to take up complete fairways, and such is their intricate design, you can almost believe Faldo would have sat there carving them himself in his own fastidious style.

The start is impressive – a 599-yard par-5 from an elevated tee to a wide, meandering fairway. Going off line does not punish you severely here unless you find a water hazard, and there are quite a few dotted about on the course, including an island-style green on the 17th – a great short hole just as you think you have cracked the course.

Chart Hills was designed to get people around. There are not too many places where you can lose your ball, the greens are always of a high standard and when the putter is on song, a good score is definitely on the cards. Off the back tees, the course stretches to over 7,000 yards but visitors will normally play off the front tees which reduces the length of the course to a manageable challenge for the average player: 5,841 yards off the yellows.

The members of this exclusive club are rightly proud of its course and particularly the clubhouse that offers splendid views over the course. The standard of service is always high and the menu top quality. Well worth a visit.

Secretary:	Mr R. Hyder	Tel: 01580 292222
	(Manager)	Fax: 01580 292233
Professional:	Mr D. French	Tel: 01580 292148

Playing: Midweek: round £60.00; day n/a. Weekend: round £70.00; day n/a. Handicap certificate required.

Facilities: Bar: 11am–11pm. Food: Lunch and dinner by arrangement.

Comments: Daunting first impression ... Need a good short game ... A golfer's dream ... Immaculate, class shows from arrival to the moment the last putt drops ... Best food ever tasted at a golf club ... Par-4s and 5s well designed, shame about the 3s ... Top notch venue, though expensive worth every penny ... Unusual course with challenging tee shots ... If God played golf he would play here ... Fabulous test and for a young course it is an instant classic ... A fantastic course but overpriced ... Take advantage of the twilight fees ... Designed by Nick Faldo ... Knockout ... Unbeatable.

Austin Lodge Golf Club   ★★

Eynsford, Swanley, DA4 OHU
Nearest main town: Swanley

Secretary: Mr S. Bevan   Tel: 01322 863000
                                   Fax: 01322 862406

Professional: Mr P. Edwards

Playing: Midweek: round £16.00; day £28.00. Weekend: round £25.00; day n/a.

Facilities: Bar: 11am–11pm. Food: Breakfast, lunch and dinner from 7am–7pm. Bar snacks.

Comments: Long and hilly, a buggy may be required ... Idyllic setting ... Well drained ... Very challenging and quite difficult ... Demanding course in a tranquil setting, requiring all the shots ... Picturesque surroundings, very challenging ... Quiet, long course offering value and interest ... Good welcome.

Broome Park Golf Club   ★

Broome Park Estate, Barham, Canterbury, CT4 6QX
Nearest main town: Canterbury

Secretary:	Mr R. C. Cheeseworth	Tel: 01227 831701
		Fax: 01227 831973
Professional:	Mr T. Britz	Tel: 01227 831126
		Fax: 01227 831972

Playing: Midweek: round £28.00; day £32.00. Weekend: round £32.00; day £37.00. Handicap certificate required.

Facilities: Bar: 11am–11pm. Food: Breakfast, lunch and dinner from 7am–10pm.

Comments: Nice parkland course ... Kitchener's House makes a fabulous clubhouse ... Absolutely wonderful setting ... Championship course I'll visit again.

Canterbury Golf Club ★★

Scotland Hills, Littlebourne Road, Canterbury, CT1 1TW
Nearest main town: Canterbury

Secretary:	Mrs P. Bates	Tel: 01227 453532
		Fax: 01227 784277
Professional:	Mr P. Everard	Tel: 01227 462865

Playing: Midweek: round £27.00; day £36.00. Weekend: round £27.00; day £36.00. Handicap certificate required.

Facilities: Bar: 11am–11pm. Food: Lunch and dinner from 11am–9pm. Bar snacks.

Comments: All the trouble is off the tee ... Heavily wooded ... Peace and seclusion ... Very tight driving ... You need a game plan.

Cherry Lodge Golf Club ★★

Jail Lane, Biggin Hill, Westerham, TN16 3AX
Nearest main town: Bromley

Secretary:	Mr C. F. Smith	Tel: 01959 572250
		Fax: 01959 540672
Professional:	Mr N. Child	Tel: 01959 572989

Playing: Midweek: round £25.00; day £35.00. Weekend: round n/a; day n/a. Handicap certificate required.

Facilities: Bar: 11am–11pm. Food: Lunch from 10am–6pm. Bar snacks.

Comments: High up with strong winds a persistent factor ... Presentation always first class ... Greens consistently good ... Looks good ... Not everyone's favourite.

Executive Golf Club of Cranbrook

Golford Road, Cranbrook, TN17 4AL
Nearest main town: Tunbridge Wells

Secretary:	Mr C. Cooper	Tel: 01580 712833
		Fax: 01580 714274
Professional:	Mr A. Gillard	

Playing: Midweek: round £23.00; day n/a. Weekend: round £30.00; day n/a.

Facilities: Bar: 11am–11pm. Food: Bar snacks.

Comments: Well thought of in Kent ... Keeps you interested ... Wonderful countryside ... Not well known but great test of golf ... Make sure to make a visit.

Faversham Golf Club

Belmont Park, Faversham, ME13 OHB
Nearest main town: Faversham

Secretary:	Mr J. Edgington	Tel: 01795 890561
		Fax: 01795 890760
Professional:	Mr S. Rokes	Tel: 01795 890275

Playing: Midweek: round £26.00; day £30.00. Weekend: round n/a; day n/a. Handicap certificate required.

Facilities: Bar: 10.30am–11pm. Food: Lunch and dinner from 11am–7pm. Bar snacks.

Comments: A testing course with fastish greens ... Could have had a better welcome ... Inland masterpiece ... Go find your game on this straightforward and welcoming course.

Hever Golf Club ★★★

Hever, TN8 7NG
Nearest main town: Edenbridge

Secretary:	Mr A. Chase	Tel: 01732 700711
		Fax: 01732 700711
Professional:	Mr R. Tinworth	Tel: 01732 700711

Playing: Midweek: round £35.00; day £42.00. Weekend: round £55.00; day £69.00. Handicap certificate required.

Facilities: Bar: 7am–11pm. Food: Breakfast, lunch and dinner from 7am–9pm. Bar snacks.

Comments: Pricey but well-run club ... Very modern and very long ... One of the best new courses in Britain ... Bit of a monster ... Has a wonderful feel ... American style new course ... Worth the wait.

Knole Park Golf Club   ★★★

Seal Hollow Road, Sevenoaks, TN15 OHJ
Nearest main town: Sevenoaks

Secretary:	Mr P. F. Lamb	Tel: 01732 452150
		Fax: 01732 463159
Professional:	Mr P. E. Gill	Tel: 01732 451740

Playing: Midweek: round £32.00; day £42.00. Weekend: round n/a; day n/a. Handicap certificate required.

Facilities: Bar: 11am–11pm. Food: Lunch and dinner from 10am–6pm. Bar snacks.

Comments: Beautiful parkland course with some tricky holes – mind the deer! ... Deer running loose ... Well kept with views of the North Downs ... Greens to putt on all year ... Superb greens ... Exclusive feel to this welcoming club.

Langley Park Golf Club   ★★★

Barnfield Wood Road, Beckenham, BR3 6SZ
Nearest main town: Bromley

Secretary:	Mr R. Oakes	Tel: 0181 658 6849
		Fax: 0181 658 6310
Professional:	Mr C. Staff	Tel: 0181 650 1663

Playing: Midweek: round £35.00; day £35.00. Weekend: round n/a; day n/a.

Facilities: Bar: 11am–11pm. Food: Lunch from 12pm–2.30pm. Dinner from 7pm–9.30pm.

Comments: Well wooded ... Cracking finishing hole ... One of the best in the area ... Tough, long par-4s ... Always a pleasure to play here ... Regional Open qualifying course ... Never get bored of it.

Littlestone Golf Club   ★★★★

St Andrews Road, Littlestone, New Romney, TN28 8RB
Nearest main town: New Romney

Secretary: Col C. Moorhouse   Tel: 01797 363355
                                      Fax: 01797 362740
Professional: Mr S. Watkins   Tel: 01797 362231

Playing: Midweek: round £30.00; day £42.00. Weekend: round £45.00; day £50.00. Handicap certificate required.

Facilities: Bar: 11am–11pm. Food: Lunch from 12pm–2.30pm. Bar snacks.

Comments: Fantastic links with immaculate greens ... An absolute classic ... Design-wise there is very little to touch it ... Located on Romney Marshes ... Exceptional, interesting course ... Now for something a little bit different.

Lullingstone Park Golf Club   ★★

Parkgate Road, Chelsfield, Orpington, BR6 7PX
Nearest main town: Orpington

Secretary: Mr M. Watt   Tel: 01959 533793
                                      Fax: 01959 533795
Professional: Mr M. Watt   Tel: 01959 533794

Playing: Midweek: round £10.00; day n/a. Weekend: round £15.00; day n/a.

Facilities: Bar: 11am–11pm. Food: Lunch from 10am–4pm. Bar snacks.

Comments: Very welcoming ... For price, you won't get a better round of golf – superb ... Popular course and rightly so with facilities ... Good set-up.

Lydd Golf Club   ★

Romney Road, Lydd, Romney Marsh, TN29 9LS
Nearest main town: Ashford

| **Secretary:** | Mr B. M. Evans | Tel: 01797 320808 |
| | | Fax: 01797 321482 |

Professional: Mr G. Richie

Playing: Midweek: round £15.00; day £26.00. Weekend: round £20.00; day £35.00.

Facilities: Bar: 11am–11pm. Food: Lunch from 12pm–3pm. Dinner by arrangement.

Comments: Links-style course ... Wide open linksy course ... Not strictly a links but many of its features ... Golfer's course ... Course that is fair to all categories of player.

Mid Kent Golf Club ★

Singlewell Road, Gravesend, DA11 7RB
Nearest main town: Gravesend

| **Secretary:** | Mr A. McCririck | Tel: 01474 568035 |
| | | Fax: 01474 564218 |

Professional: Mr M. Foreman   Tel: 01474 332810

Playing: Midweek: round £20.00; day £30.00. Weekend: round n/a; day n/a. Handicap certificate required.

Facilities: Bar: 11am–11pm. Food: Lunch and dinner from 11am–8pm. Bar snacks.

Comments: Stiff opening stretch but gets easier ... Popular course in fair condition ... Downland with plenty of challenge ... Well established.

Moatlands Golf Club ★★

Watermans Lane, Brenchley, Tonbridge, TN12 6ND
Nearest main town: Matfield

| **Secretary:** | Mr K. Wiley | Tel: 01892 724400 |
| | | Fax: 01892 723300 |

Professional: Mr S. Wood   Tel: 01892 724252

Playing: Midweek: round £29.00; day £45.00. Weekend: round £39.00; day £55.00. Handicap certificate required.

Facilities: Bar: 11am–11pm. Food: Bar snacks. Dinner from 6pm–9.30pm on Thursday–Saturday.

Comments: Built to high standards ... Lovely clubhouse ... Friendly club with special off-course facilities ... Watch out for the Victorian bath-house on the back nine ... Long course making clever use of natural setting ... Rolling parkland course.

Nizels Golf Club   ★★★★

Nizels Lane, Hildenborough, Tonbridge, TN11 8NX
Nearest main town: Tonbridge

Secretary: Mr D. Bonser   Tel: 01732 833138
                                        Fax: 01732 833764
Professional: Mr B. Wynne   Tel: 01732 838926

Playing: Midweek: round £30.00; day £40.00. Weekend: round £35.00; day n/a.

Facilities: Bar: 11am–11pm. Food: Lunch and dinner from 11am–9pm.

Comments: Water features and natural landscape are sources of interest and challenge ... Unusually named club and course ... Fascinating woodland course ... One for the notebook ... Outstanding wildlife and nature's blessing makes this a course to treasure.

North Foreland Golf Club   ★★★★

Convent Road, Thanet, CT10 3PU
Nearest main town: Broadstairs

Secretary: Mr B. Preston   Tel: 01843 862140
                                        Fax: 01843 862663
Professional: Mr N. Hanson   Tel: 01843 604471

Playing: Midweek: round £27.50; day £37.50. Weekend: round £37.50; day n/a. Handicap certificate required.

Facilities: Bar: 11am–11pm. Food: Breakfast, lunch and dinner from 9am–6pm. Bar snacks.

Comments: Very exposed and bracing ... Very few hazards and yet it's so difficult ... Played it in a gale – super ... Real triumph for the designers ... Not in great condition but that's how it is supposed to be.

Prince's Golf Club   ★★★★

Sandwich Bay, Sandwich, CT13 9QB
Nearest main town: Sandwich Bay

Secretary: Mr W. M. Howie   Tel: 01304 611118
                                      Fax: 01304 612000
Professional: To be appointed.

Playing: Midweek: round £40.00; day £45.00. Weekend: round
                  £42.00; day £51.00. Handicap certificate required.

Facilities: Bar: 11am–11pm. Food: Lunch and dinner from
                  11am–9pm. Bar snacks.

Comments: Everyone here makes you feel so welcome … Friendly
                  classic links in tremendous location … Great day out
                  on a championship links … Refreshing links golf …
                  Sea breezes can mean changing your driver for a
                  wedge … Worth travelling to from afar … Always a
                  great welcome for visitors … Fabulous in every respect
                  … Watch out for chapping on this exposed links …
                  A natural beauty.

Redlibbets Golf Club   ★★★

Manor Lane, West Yoke, Nr Sevenoaks, TN15 7HT
Nearest main town: Sevenoaks

Secretary: Mr J. Potter   Tel: 01474 879190
                                      Fax: 01474 879290
Professional: Mr R. Taylor   Tel: 01474 872278

Playing: Midweek: round £27.50; day n/a. Weekend: round
                  £40.00; day n/a. Handicap certificate required.

Facilities: Bar: 11am–11pm. Food: Lunch and dinner from
                  10am–6pm. Dinner by arrangement.

Comments: Fine new course … Shot-maker's course … Take your
                  time to plot your way around this course … Condition
                  excellent … This course's stock is set to rise.

Rochester & Cobham Park Golf Club   ★★

Park Pale, Rochester, ME2 3UL
Nearest main town: Gravesend

Secretary: Maj J. W. Irvine   Tel: 01474 823411
                                           Fax: 01474 824446
Professional: Mr J. Blair   Tel: 01474 823658

Playing: Midweek: round £26.00; day £36.00. Weekend: round
                   n/a; day n/a. Handicap certificate required.

Facilities: Bar: 11am–11pm. Food: Lunch and dinner from
                   10.30am–6.30pm. Bar snacks.

Comments: Long and difficult ... Very narrow so watch your driving
                   ... Keep it straight, John ... Very varied and interesting
                   ... Excellent value for such a fascinating course.

Royal Blackheath Golf Club   ★★★

Court Road, London, SE9 5AF
Nearest main town: London

Secretary: Mr A. Dunlop   Tel: 0181 850 1795
                                          Fax: 0181 859 0150
Professional: Mr I. McGregor   Tel: 0181 850 1763

Playing: Midweek: round £30.00; day £40.00. Weekend: round
                   n/a; day n/a. Handicap certificate required.

Facilities: Bar: 11am–11pm. Food: Lunch and dinner from
                   11am–9pm.

Comments: Steeped in history and just a few miles from Marble Arch
                   ... A club bathed in history and tradition ... The best
                   trophy room in golf? ... Parkland golf at its best.

Royal Cinque Ports Golf Club   ★★★

Golf Road, Deal, CT14 6RF
Nearest main town: Deal

Secretary: Mr C. C. Hammond   Tel: 01304 374007
                                          Fax: 01304 379530
Professional: Mr A. Reynolds   Tel: 01304 374170
                                          Fax: 01304 374170

Playing: Midweek: round £60.00; day £60.00. Weekend: round
                   £70.00; day £70.00. Handicap certificate required.

Facilities: Bar: 11am–8pm. Food: Bar snacks. Dinner by arrange-
                   ment.

Comments: Friendly staff and members ... Never had so much fun
             playing golf ... Really tough course ... 16th is a classic
             ... Refreshingly warm welcome ... Blustery course but
             easy on your legs ... One of the Top 100 in the British
             Isles ... So many stories and memories ... Nothing but
             the best here.

Royal St George's Golf Club   ★★★★★

Sandwich, CT13 9PB
Nearest main town: Sandwich

Secretary: Mr G. E. Watts   Tel: 01304 613090
                                       Fax: 01304 611245
Professional: Mr A. Brooks   Tel: 01304 615236
                                       Fax: 01304 615236

Playing: Midweek: round £60.00; day £85.00. Weekend: round
               n/a; day n/a. Handicap certificate required.

Facilities: Bar: 11am–11pm. Food: Lunch from 12pm–2.30pm.
               Dinner from 7pm–9.30pm.

Comments: Probably the best in the world ... Don't forget your
               bucket and spade – you can get lost in the bunkers ...
               In the footsteps of heroes – what a course ... History,
               tradition, windy, interesting and the chance to pretend
               you are playing in the Open ... Always enjoy tackling
               this giant ... Untouched by human hands, the natural
               way to play golf ... Open venue at reasonable price – if
               only they were all like this ... Warmth of welcome unsur-
               passed ... Didn't want to leave.

St Augustines Golf Club   ★★

Cottington Road, Cliffsend, Ramsgate, CT12 5JN
Nearest main town: Ramsgate

Secretary: Mr L. P. Dyke   Tel: 01843 590333
                                       Fax: 01843 590444
Professional: Mr D. B. Scott   Tel: 01843 590222

Playing: Midweek: round £21.50; day £21.50. Weekend: round
               £23.50; day £23.50. Handicap certificate required.

Facilities: Bar: 11am–11pm. Food: Lunch from 11am–4pm.

Comments: Close to some more illustrious neighbours ... Too short
to take seriously ... Very short but it's good ... Very low
standard scratch ... Play it for fun.

Sundridge Park Golf Club (East)   ★★★

Garden Road, Bromley, BR1 3NE
Nearest main town: Bromley

Secretary:	Mr R. Burden	Tel: 0181 460 0278
		Fax: 0181 289 3050
Professional:	Mr B. Cameron	Tel: 0181 460 5540

Playing: Midweek: round n/a; day £40.00. Weekend: round n/a;
day n/a. Handicap certificate required.

Facilities: Bar: 11am–11pm. Food: Lunch from 12pm–2.30pm.

Comments: Open qualifying course ... Test of genuine quality ...
Tough finish ... Many holes played through a valley ...
16th weakest hole on the course ... 18th is a cracking
finish with massive elevated tee on long dogleg right.

Sundridge Park Golf Club (West)   ★★★

Garden Road, Bromley, BR1 3NE
Nearest main town: Bromley

Secretary:	Mr R. Burden	Tel: 0181 460 0278
		Fax: 0181 289 3050
Professional:	Mr B. Cameron	Tel: 0181 460 5540

Playing: Midweek: round n/a; day £40.00. Weekend: round n/a;
day n/a. Handicap certificate required.

Facilities: Bar: 11am–11pm. Food: Lunch from 12pm–2.30pm.

Comments: Pleasant woodland ... 4th is a bit of a joke ... Easy
finish with driveable par-4 and simple par-5 ... Views
over London.

The London Golf Club (Heritage)   ★★★★

South Ash Manor Estate, Ash, Sevenoaks, TN15 7EN
Nearest main town: Sevenoaks

Secretary:	Mr J. Paulin	Tel: 01474 879899
		Fax: 01474 879912

Professional: Mr K. Ryan

Playing: Prices on application.

Facilities: Bar: Members only. Food: Members only

Comments: More than you should pay but worth double ... Can only play with a member ... Outstanding condition ... A very unnatural course, not for links lovers ... Had a great time, but couldn't wait to get away ... Conditioning second to none ... Not Nicklaus' finest moment.

The London Golf Club (International) ★★★

South Ash Manor Estate, Ash, Sevenoaks, TN15 7EN
Nearest main town: Sevenoaks

Secretary: Mr J. Paulin   Tel: 01474 879899
                                   Fax: 01474 879912

Professional: Mr K. Ryan

Playing: Prices on application.

Facilities: Bar: Members only. Food: Members only

Comments: Still the best greens around ... Find a member and play it ... Little to choose between two courses ... Lakes and generous fairways – designed for all standards but no-one can play it ... Delight to play, but club lacks character.

Tudor Park Hotel Golf Club ★★

Ashford Road, Bearstead, Maidstone, ME14 4NQ
Nearest main town: Maidstone

Secretary: Mr J. Ladbrook   Tel: 01622 734334
                                    Fax: 01622 735360
Professional: Mr N. MacNally   Tel: 01622 739412

Playing: Midweek: round £25.00; day £30.00. Weekend: round £35.00; day n/a.

Facilities: Bar: 11am–11pm. Food: Breakfast, lunch and dinner served from 7am–10pm. Bar snacks.

Comments: Great facilities – should do more with the course ... A little overplayed but facilities are first class ... Little ragged around the edges but a nice day out ... Good society venue ... Undulating course but not particularly challenging between the ears.

Walmer & Kingsdown Golf Club   ★★

The Leas, Kingsdown, Deal, CT14 8EP
Nearest main town: Deal

Secretary: Mr J. P. Morgan   Tel: 01304 373256
                                          Fax: 01304 382336
Professional: Mr M. Paget   Tel: 01304 363017

Playing: Midweek: round £22.00; day £28.00. Weekend: round
                  £24.00; day £30.00. Handicap certificate required.

Facilities: Bar: 11am–11pm. Food: Breakfast, lunch and dinner
                  from 7.30am–9pm. Bar snacks.

Comments: Cliff-top thrills ... A real adventure ... Not given recog-
                  nition it deserves ... Views of the North Sea ... Nicely
                  presented ... Facilities lacking ... Overall very good
                  scenic course.

Weald of Kent Golf Club   ★

Maidstone Road, Headcorn, TN27 9PT
Nearest main town: Maidstone

Secretary: Mr S. Doran   Tel: 01622 891671
                                          Fax: 01622 891793
Professional: None.

Playing: Midweek: round £15.50; day £30.00. Weekend: round
                  £19.00; day £37.00. Handicap certificate required.

Facilities: Bar: 11am–11pm. Food: Lunch and dinner from
                  11am–9pm.

Comments: Good value ... For the money, very reasonable ...
                  Course uses natural defences ... Parkland ... Lots of
                  streams and ditches.

Woodlands Manor Golf Club   ★★

Woodlands, Tinkerpot Lane, Sevenoaks, TN15 6AB
Nearest main town: Sevenoaks

Secretary: Mr E. F. Newman   Tel: 01959 523806
Professional: Mr P. Womack   Tel: 01959 524161

Playing: Midweek: round £18.00; day £28.50. Weekend: round
                  £24.00; day n/a. Handicap certificate required.

Facilities: Bar: 11am–11pm. Food: Lunch and dinner from 10am–10pm.

Comments: Facile parkland course ... One of the cheaper quality courses in Kent ... Progressive club ... Always turned out well.

Lancashire

Royal Lytham & St Annes Golf Club ★★★★★

Links Gate, Lytham St Annes, FY8 3LQ
Nearest main town: St Annes

Royal Lytham and St Annes is a different breed to most links, set in an urban landscape and lacking most of the distinguishing features of that type of course – no sandhills between fairways and no dramatic landscapes. Neither is there any sign that the course, situated just south of the gaudy holiday town of Blackpool, is near the sea.

This confusing picture does not make it one of the favoured Open Championship courses with amateurs, but it is still highly rated for the diversity of the holes, achieved on a rather unremarkable piece of land. It is also liked for the difficulty of its finish, certainly on a level with the finish at Royal Troon – the back nine has, in the past, played four shots harder than the front nine in the same weather conditions for players in the Open.

The great golf writer, Bernard Darwin, once described some of the closing holes as 'unpleasantly difficult'. Jack Nicklaus was more straightforward, describing the 15th as one of the hardest holes he had ever played when, in the 1974 Open Championship, the average score for this 468-yard monster was an almost unprecedented stroke average of a full shot over par.

The 11th is the only par-5 coming back, but, at 542 yards, it is normally out of reach in two shots. Meanwhile, the lone par-3 on the back nine, the 12th, is equally uncompromising. With its shallow, narrow green, protected by six bunkers and unkempt grassy ridges (not forgetting the out-of-bounds perilously close down the right) and you have the most exacting shot of the whole round. Seve Ballesteros voted this hole the best par-3 in the British Isles in a *Golf World* survey, while Tom Watson was similarly full of praise.

The prevailing wind is from the north-west at Royal Lytham which helps most of the way on the outward nine. It is here that the course has more of a links feel; the dunes are wild and owe nothing to any sculpting or moulding. The 8th green is a superb example, an exposed target from the fairway below, as is the 9th, a pure target nestling among bunkers.

The 18th is a short finishing hole and not exactly the climax you expect. The only problems come from overclubbing when you might find yourself hitting your recovery shot backhanded like Gary Player from the walls of the magnificent red-bricked Victorian clubhouse.

Secretary:	Mr L. B. Goodwin	Tel: 01253 724206
		Fax: 01253 780946
Professional:	Mr E. Birchenough	Tel: 01253 720094

Playing: Midweek: round £80.00; day n/a. Weekend: round n/a; day n/a. Handicap certificate required.

Facilities: Bar: 11am–11pm. Food: Breakfast, lunch and dinner from 7am–10pm. Bar snacks.

Comments: Worth playing at least once ... Good value for an Open course ... So many memorable holes ... Great atmosphere ... Back nine is outstanding ... Extremely trying on the patience ... Apart from the course, very poor and disappointing ... Great experience for the traditionalist ... A must for links lovers ... Never liked a par-3 start – like it even less now ... One of the worst Open courses ... Lacks atmosphere ... Worthy Open venue and the best attitude towards visitors.

Beacon Park Golf Club ★

Beacon Lane, Up Holland, WN8 7RU
Nearest main town: Dalton

Secretary:	Mr T. Harris	Tel: 01695 627500
		Fax: 01695 633066
Professional:	Mr R. Peters	Tel: 01695 622700

Playing: Midweek: round £6.50; day n/a. Weekend: round £9.00; day n/a.

Facilities: Bar: 11am–11pm. Food: Lunch from 11.30am–2.30pm.

Comments: Outstanding practice facilities ... Topography not ideal for beginners ... Very hilly ... Condition not great ... Everything you need to practise with purpose.

Blackburn Golf Club ★

Beardwood Brow, Blackburn, BB2 7AX
Nearest main town: Blackburn

Secretary:	Mr P. D. Haydock	Tel: 01254 51122
		Fax: 01254 665578
Professional:	Mr A. Rodwell	Tel: 01254 55942

Playing: Midweek: round £24.00; day £24.00. Weekend: round £28.00; day £28.00. Handicap certificate required.

Facilities: Bar: 11am–11pm. Food: Breakfast, lunch and dinner from 7am–9pm. Bar snacks.

Comments: Looking out over the Pennines ... Set on a plateau ... Not the best condition ... High up and exposed.

Bolton Golf Club ★★

Lostock Park, Bolton, BL6 4AJ
Nearest main town: Bolton

Secretary: Mrs H. M. Stuart   Tel: 01204 843067
                                      Fax: 01204 843067
Professional: Mr R. Longworth   Tel: 01204 843073

Playing: Midweek: round £29.00; day £36.00. Weekend: round £33.00; day £40.00. Handicap certificate required.

Facilities: Bar: 11am–11pm. Food: Bar snacks. Dinner from 6pm–9.30pm Thursday–Saturday.

Comments: Overshadowed by the Old Links ... Heathland ... Not always in top condition ... A brutal finish to a traditional course ... If you're in the area, pop in.

Bolton Old Links Golf Club ★★★★

Chorley Old Road, Montserrat, Bolton, BL1 5SU
Nearest main town: Bolton

Secretary: Mr A. W. Turner   Tel: 01204 840050
                                      Fax: 01204 842307
Professional: Mr P. Horridge   Tel: 01204 843089
                                      Fax: 01204 843089

Playing: Midweek: round £27.00; day £27.00. Weekend: round £45.00; day £45.00.

Facilities: Bar: 11am–11pm. Food: Breakfast, lunch and dinner from 9.30am–9pm.

Comments: Certainly worth a visit but not in the winter ... Moorland course with great character and history.

Chorley Golf Club ★★

Hall o' th' Hill, Heath Charnock, Chorley, PR6 9HX
Nearest main town: Chorley

Secretary:	Mrs A. Allan	Tel: 01257 480263
		Fax: 01257 480722
Professional:	Mr G. P. Mutch	Tel: 01257 481245

Playing: Midweek: round £27.00; day £27.00. Weekend: round £40.00; day £40.00.

Facilities: Bar: 11am–9pm. Food: Lunch from 11.30am–2.30pm.

Comments: Good condition for moorland ... Clean air and well-kept course – perfect ... As nature intended ... Very amiable members ... Worth the drive.

Clitheroe Golf Club ★★★

Whalley Road, Clitheroe, BB7 1PP
Nearest main town: Clitheroe

Secretary:	Mr G. Roberts JP	Tel: 01200 422292
		Fax: 01200 422292
Professional:	Mr J. Twissell	Tel: 01200 424242

Playing: Midweek: round £33.00; day £33.00. Weekend: round £39.00; day £39.00. Handicap certificate required.

Facilities: Bar: 11am–11pm. Food: Lunch from 11am–5pm. Bar snacks. Dinner by arrangement.

Comments: Worth the visit ... A thinking course demanding different shots ... Excellent course with friendly atmosphere and good welcome ... Unknown course that must be one of the finest inland tracks in the country ... Absolute delight ... Not a name course, but who cares if it keeps the visitors down?

Dean Wood Golf Club ★★

Lafford Lane, Up Holland, Skelmersdale, WN8 0QZ
Nearest main town: Wigan

Secretary:	Mr A. McGregor	Tel: 01695 622219
		Fax: 01695 622245
Professional:	Mr A. B. Coop	Tel: 01695 622980

Playing: Midweek: round £27.00; day £27.00. Weekend: round £30.00; day £30.00. Handicap certificate required.

Facilities: Bar: 12pm–11pm. Food: Lunch and dinner from 10.30am–9.30pm.

Comments: Nice condition, fairly unremarkable course ... Front nine boring but back nine spices it up ... Two courses in one ... Good greenkeeping ... Condition usually good ... Challenging holes on back nine.

Dunscar Golf Club   ★

Longworth Lane, Bromley Cross, Bolton, BL7 9QY
Nearest main town: Bolton

Secretary: Mr J. W. Jennings   Tel: 01204 303321
Professional: Mr G. Threadgold   Tel: 01204 592992

Playing: Midweek: round n/a; day £20.00. Weekend: round n/a; day £30.00. Handicap certificate required.

Facilities: Bar: 11am–11pm. Food: Lunch from 12pm–2.30pm. Dinner from 7pm–9pm.

Comments: Fine value at this picturesque moorland course ... Many good days golfing here ... Presentation sometimes lacking ... Conditioning not perfect ... Very natural and not for moaners.

Fairhaven Golf Club

Lytham Hall Park, Ansdell, Lytham St Annes, FY8 4JU
Nearest main town: St Annes

Secretary: Mr H. Fielding   Tel: 01253 736741
                                 Fax: 01253 731461
Professional: Mr B. Blucknett   Tel: 01253 736976

Playing: Midweek: round £33.00; day n/a. Weekend: round £40.00; day n/a. Handicap certificate required.

Facilities: Bar: 11am–11pm. Food: Lunch and dinner from 11am–9pm. Bar snacks.

Comments: Memorable holes and bunkers ... Lovely parkland course ... Long and hard with lots of bunkers ... Very long and difficult ... One bunker for every day of the year here ... Good facilities and particularly liked the reading room.

Fleetwood Golf Club   ★★★

Golf House, Princes Way, Fleetwood, FY7 8AF
Nearest main town: Fleetwood

Secretary: Mr R. Yates   Tel: 01253 773573
                                           Fax: 01253 773573
Professional: Mr S. McLaughlin   Tel: 01253 873661

Playing: Midweek: round £24.00; day £24.00. Weekend: round
                  £30.00; day £30.00. Handicap certificate required.

Facilities: Bar: 11am–11pm. Food: Lunch and dinner from
                  10am–9pm. Bar snacks.

Comments: Wind makes it very difficult ... Wind dictates how the
                  course plays ... An interesting course that is made
                  wonderful by strong winds ... Flat, long track but a
                  place to enjoy and contemplate ... Good food ... Nice
                  unpretentious club.

Herons Reach Hotel & Golf Club   ★★

East Park Drive, Blackpool, FY3 8LL
Nearest main town: Blackpool

Secretary: Mr T. Honeysett   Tel: 01253 838866
                                           Fax: 01253 798800
Professional: Mr D. Naughton   Tel: 01253 766156

Playing: Midweek: round £30.00; day n/a. Weekend: round
                  £35.00; day n/a. Handicap certificate required.

Facilities: Bar: 11am–11pm. Food: Breakfast, lunch and dinner
                  from 7am–10pm. Bar snacks.

Comments: Tough course with greens extremely hard to read ...
                  Difficult due to the water ... Not set up for the high handi-
                  capper ... Very difficult course with greens tricky to judge.

Lancaster Golf Club   ★★★

Ashton Hall, Ashton-with-Stoddary, Lancaster, LA2 0AJ
Nearest main town: Lancaster

Secretary: Mr K. E. Butcher   Tel: 01524 751247
                                           Fax: 01524 752742
Professional: Mr D. E. Sutcliffe   Tel: 01524 751802

Playing: Midweek: round n/a; day £32.00. Weekend: round n/a; day n/a. Handicap certificate required.

Facilities: Bar: 11am–11pm. Food: Lunch and dinner from 10am–10pm. Bar snacks.

Comments: An attractively set course – well worth playing ... Extremely friendly, helpful staff with a superb course ... Situated on the Lune Estuary ... Old club with grand tradition ... Welcoming club ... Flattish course, not difficult by any yardstick.

Longridge Golf Club   ★★

Fell Barn, Jeffrey Hill, Preston,
Nearest main town: Preston

Secretary: Mr D. C. Wensley   Tel: 01772 783291
Professional: Mr S. Taylor   Tel: 01722 783291

Playing: Midweek: round £15.00; day £20.00. Weekend: round £25.00; day £25.00.

Facilities: Bar: 11am–11pm. Food: Lunch and dinner served from 11am–9pm. Bar snacks.

Comments: Old course that's seen better days ... Moorland walking ... Views can't be bettered in Lancashire ... Variable condition.

Lytham Green Drive Golf Club   ★★★★

Ballam Road, Lytham, FY8 4LE
Nearest main town: Lytham St Annes

Secretary: Mr R. Kershaw   Tel: 01253 737390
                                   Fax: 01253 731350
Professional: Mr A. Lancaster Tel: 01253 737379

Playing: Midweek: round £25.00; day £35.00. Weekend: round £35.00; day £45.00. Handicap certificate required.

Facilities: Bar: 11am–11pm. Food: Lunch and dinner served from 11am–8pm. Bar snacks.

Comments: A joy to play and captain made a point of welcoming us ... Nice, true greens ... Holiday parkland course, nothing serious ... If you find yourself here, you're at the wrong Lytham.

Morecambe Golf Club ★

Bare, Morecambe, LA4 6AJ
Nearest main town: Morecambe

Secretary: Mrs J. Atkinson   Tel: 01524 412841
Fax: 01524 412841
Professional: Mr S. Fletcher   Tel: 01524 415596

Playing: Midweek: round £22.00; day £27.00. Weekend: round £27.00; day £32.00. Handicap certificate required.

Facilities: Bar: 11am–11pm. Food: Lunch from 10am–4pm. Dinner by arrangement.

Comments: Holiday course ... Best course for miles around ... Very welcoming to holiday golfers ... Go there every year ... Very fair seaside parkland course.

Ormskirk Golf Club ★★★

Cranes Lane, Lathom, Ormskirk, L40 5UJ
Nearest main town: Ormskirk

Secretary: Mr R. D. J. Lawrence   Tel: 01695 572112
Fax: 01695 572227
Professional: Mr J. Hammond   Tel: 01695 572074

Playing: Midweek: round £30.00; day n/a. Weekend: round £35.00; day n/a. Handicap certificate required.

Facilities: Bar: 11.30am–11pm. Food: Bar snacks. Dinner from 6pm–8.30pm.

Comments: In immaculate condition and secretary's welcome very pleasing ... Flat, parkland course – like many in the area ... Welcoming sort of club ... Easy course ... Worth a detour for 18 peaceful holes.

Penwortham Golf Club ★

Blundell Lane, Penwortham, Preston, PR1 OAX
Nearest main town: Preston

Secretary: Mr J. Parkinson   Tel: 01772 744630
Fax: 01772 744630
Professional: Mr N. Marshall   Tel: 01772 742345

Playing: Midweek: round £22.00; day £25.00. Weekend: round £28.00; day £28.00.

Facilities: Bar: 11am–11pm. Food: Lunch and dinner served from 11am–8pm.

Comments: Reasonable value ... Poor by Lancashire standards ... Tree-lined fairways ... Good individual holes ... Very fair but not the best.

Pleasington Golf Club   ★

Pleasington, Blackburn, BB2 5JF
Nearest main town: Blackburn

Secretary: Mr M. Trickett   Tel: 01254 202177
                                  Fax: 01254 201028
Professional: Mr G. J. Furey   Tel: 01254 201630

Playing: Midweek: round £36.00; day £36.00. Weekend: round £42.00; day £42.00. Handicap certificate required.

Facilities: Bar: 11am–11pm. Food: Lunch and dinner served from 11am–9pm.

Comments: Not for the faint-hearted ... Good clubhouse and tasty food ... Demanding but enjoyable course ... Always well presented and beautifully scenic ... Please, please let me play ... The pleasure was all mine at this up-and-down moorland masterpiece ... Back nine is where it all starts happening.

Shaw Hill Hotel Golf & Country Club   ★★★

Preston Road, Whittle-le-Woods, Chorley, PR6 7PP
Nearest main town: Chorley

Secretary: Mr D. Dimsdale   Tel: 01257 269221
                                  Fax: 01257 261223
Professional: Mr D. Clarke   Tel: 01257 279222

Playing: Midweek: round £30.00; day n/a. Weekend: round £40.00; day n/a.

Facilities: Bar: 11am–11pm. Food: Lunch from 12pm–2.30pm. Dinner from 7pm–9.30pm. Bar snacks.

Comments: Poor condition of tees and greens ... Great layout in scenic location ... Watery graves lurk everywhere ... Peaceful and scenic ... Fairly simple course but nice tranquil atmosphere.

St Annes Old Links Golf Club   ★★★

Highbury Road, Lytham St Annes, FY8 2LD
Nearest main town: Blackpool

Secretary:	Mr P. W. Ray	Tel: 01253 723597
		Fax: 01253 781506
Professional:	Mr G. G. Hardiman	Tel: 01253 722432

Playing: Midweek: round £35.00; day £35.00. Weekend: round £45.00; day £45.00. Handicap certificate required.

Facilities: Bar: 11am–11pm. Food: Breakfast and lunch from 9am–5pm.

Comments: Open qualifying course of some repute ... Extremely long and tiring ... Memorable links ... Par-3 9th a legend in these parts ... Worth it just for the 9th ... An unknown links that deserves more acclaim ... Real test if you want to make it to the Open.

Standish Court Golf Club   ★★★

Rectory Lane, Standish, WN6 OXD
Nearest main town: Wigan

Secretary:	Mr S. T. Dawson	Tel: 01257 425777
		Fax: 01257 425888
Professional:	Mr T. Kershaw	Tel: 01257 425777

Playing: Midweek: round £11.00; day £20.00. Weekend: round £16.00; day £30.00.

Facilities: Bar: 11am–11pm. Food: Lunch and dinner from 11am–9pm. Bar snacks.

Comments: Short but well worth a look ... Back nine cuts through woodland ... Much admired little course ... Very popular in the area ... Basic facilities but course makes up for it.

Leicestershire

Longcliffe Golf Club

Snells Nook Lane, Nanpantan, Loughborough, LE11 3YA
Nearest main town: Loughborough

To be fair, Longcliffe suffers from a little bit of an identity problem. It is labelled a heathland course but over the years the heather has receded and you have to be incredibly unlucky nowadays to find your ball buried in heather. It now resembles parkland, but do not be put off into thinking that it is in any way dull. Longcliffe is a refreshing course that constantly surprises.

Indeed, almost every hole here is tree-lined, which gives the course a splendid isolated feel. Along each avenue of trees the fairways undulate gently, and as you would expect, placement of your tee shot is the first and most important thing you need to do here to score well. Go off line, and you are likely to run up a big score once in the trees.

The course's feature hole is probably the 15th, a par-3 played from an elevated tee to a green surrounded by a pond and dangerous bunkers. It's a gamble to go for the flag but there are a lot of such dilemmas at Longcliffe.

Much of the pleasure of playing here is the atmosphere created by the members, which is always jolly and rings of laughter can often be heard on different holes as you pass through the avenues of tree. They are an active bunch and it really does give the course a very homely feel.

In the pecking order of courses in Leicestershire, there are plenty to rival Longcliffe, and many think that nearby Luffenham Heath is a better test. Maybe, but you certainly won't feel as welcome there as you do here.

Secretary:	Mr G. Harle	Tel: 01509 239129
Professional:	Mr I. Bailey	Tel: 01509 231450

Playing: Midweek: round £25.00; day £32.00. Weekend: round n/a; day n/a. Handicap certificate required.

Facilities: Bar: 11am–11pm. Food: Lunch and dinner from 11.30am–8.45pm. Bar snacks.

Comments: Absolute blinder ... Trouble everywhere with granite outcrops, heather and tangly gorse ... Real test of man versus course ... Could not ask for more, especially at the bargain price ... A perfect golf experience.

Cosby Golf Club   ★

Chapel Lane, Broughton Road, Cosby, LE9 1RG
Nearest main town: Leicester

Secretary: Mr G. T. Kirkpatrick   Tel: 0116 286 4759
                                             Fax: 0116 286 4484
Professional: Mr M. Wing   Tel: 0116 284 8275

Playing: Midweek: round £16.00; day £26.00. Weekend: round
                   n/a; day n/a. Handicap certificate required.

Facilities: Bar: 11am–11pm. Food: Bar snacks.

Comments: Friendly welcome and good value for visitors ... Narrow
                   course but little trouble around the greens ... Best value
                   golf in Leicestershire ... Parkland course with right atti-
                   tude.

Greetham Valley Golf Club   ★★

Greetham, Oakham, LE15 7NP
Nearest main town: Oakham

Secretary: Mr F. E. Hinch   Tel: 01780 460004
                                             Fax: 01780 460623
Professional: Mr J. Pengelly   Tel: 01780 460666

Playing: Midweek: round £22.00; day £26.00. Weekend: round
                   £25.00; day £30.00. Handicap certificate required.

Facilities: Bar: 11am–11pm. Food: Lunch from 12pm–4pm.
                   Dinner by arrangment.

Comments: Mixture of good and bad holes ... Fairly new golf centre
                   with good facilities ... Condition variable.

Kilworth Springs Golf Club   ★★

South Kilworth Road, North Kilworth, Lutterworth, LE17 6HJ
Nearest main town: Lutterworth

Secretary: Mrs A. Vickers   Tel: 01858 575082
                                             Fax: 01858 575078
Professional: Mr N. Melvin   Tel: 01858 575082

Playing: Midweek: round £17.00; day £30.00. Weekend: round
                   £21.00; day £30.00.

Facilities: Bar: 7.30am–10pm. Food: Breakfast, lunch and dinner from 7.30am–8pm. Bar snacks.

Comments: Always open for play ... Two contrasting nines ... Fair course but low down the pecking order in the county rankings.

Market Harborough Golf Club   ★★

Great Oxendon Road, Market Harborough, LE16 8NF
Nearest main town: Market Harborough

Secretary: Mr J. R. Ingleby   Tel: 01858 525688
                                      Fax: 01858 525688
Professional: Mr F. J. Baxter   Tel: 01858 463684

Playing: Midweek: round £20.00; day £25.00. Weekend: round n/a; day n/a. Handicap certificate required.

Facilities: Bar: 11am–11pm. Food: Lunch and dinner from 11am–9pm. Bar snacks.

Comments: Not in the same league as others in the county ... Club with welcoming attitude ... Best holes towards the end ... Average greens and condition ... Numerous lakes and streams.

Park Hill Golf Club

Park Hill, Seagrave, LE12 7NG
Nearest main town: Leicester

Secretary: Mrs S. L. Hardy   Tel: 01509 815454
                                      Fax: 01509 816062
Professional: Mr D. C. Mee   Tel: 01509 815775

Playing: Midweek: round £20.00; day £28.00. Weekend: round £24.00; day £36.00. Handicap certificate required.

Facilities: Bar: 11am–11pm. Food: Bar snacks.

Comments: Fairly new course but getting better all the time ... Views over Charnwood Forest ... Unusual finish with two par-5s ... Over 7,000 yards of parkland golf.

Ullesthorpe Court Hotel Golf Club

Frolesworth Road, Ullesthorpe, LE17 5BZ
Nearest main town: Lutterworth

Secretary:	Mr P. E. Woolley	Tel: 01455 209023
		Fax: 01455 202537
Professional:	Mr D. Bowring	Tel: 01455 209150

Playing: Midweek: round £15.50; day £26.00. Weekend: round n/a; day n/a.

Facilities: Bar: 11am–11pm. Food: Breakfast, lunch and dinner from 7am–10pm.

Comments: Tricky course but they are forgiven because of the best BLT in golf ... Parkland course set around 17th-century manor house ... A lovely place to spend three or four days golfing.

Western Park Golf Club ★★

Scudamore Road, Leicester, LE3 1UQ
Nearest main town: Leicester

Secretary:	Mr I. A. Nicholson	Tel: 0116 287 2339
		Fax: 0116 287 2339
Professional:	Mr D. E. Butler	Tel: 0116 287 2339

Playing: Midweek: round £8.75; day n/a. Weekend: round £10.25; day n/a.

Facilities: Bar: 11am–11pm. Food: Lunch and dinner from 11am–10pm. Bar snacks.

Comments: Quite simple parkland course ... Small club with decent facilities ... Nothing striking ... Fair upkeep ... Not one to go out of your way for.

Lincolnshire

Woodhall Spa Golf Club ★★★★★

Woodhall Spa, Woodhall Spa, LN10 0DD
Nearest main town: Woodhall Spa

It is hard to dislike Woodhall Spa. There's something particularly beguiling about its setting in the heart of Lincolnshire and a fresh, welcoming feel about the club, far detached from the frosty reception you can receive at other courses of repute. It surely ranks as one of the best inland courses in the world, and yet there's no preciousness or crowing on the part of its members. Woodhall Spa is truly a 'must' play for golfers.

Not only is the layout challenging but traditional, the condition of the course is rarely anything but superb. However, you must be on your game to get the most out of it. Woodhall Spa is a punishing course if you cannot stay on the fairway, and the greens are some of the fastest to be found in England. Off the tee, the course generally plays pretty tight, and if you do go off line there is dense woodland, acres of heather and gorse and some large bunkers, for which the course is famed.

Four classic par-4s make a tough start with some remission at the par-3 5th, although it is brutally bunkered. The par-3 treatment is repeated at the well-bunkered 8th, played to a plateau green, and the 12th, slightly shorter but no less difficult. One of the best holes on the course is the 550-yard 9th, where cross bunkers at 340 yards off the tee mean you must carry them with your second shot if you are to have any chance of getting on in three.

The back nine has just one short hole and overall is a few yards longer than the outward nine, but the variety of holes is no less enchanting. The par-4 13th can often take two woods to get on and the 14th normally plays very long, too. The next three holes, although shorter, are extremely penal, with the penultimate 17th renowned for its punishment of pushed or sliced shots with woods running along the length of the right side.

Woodhall Spa is home to the English Golf Union and recently opened a second course, the Bracken, which was voted one of the Top Ten New Developments in *Golf World*'s biennial course rankings in 1998.

Secretary: Mr B. H. Fawcett   Tel: 01526 352511
                                        Fax: 01526 352778
Professional: Mr C. C. Elliot   Tel: 01526 353229

Playing: Midweek: round £40.00; day £65.00. Weekend: round
                  £40.00; day £65.00. Handicap certificate required.

Facilities: Bar: 11am–11pm. Food: Lunch from 10am–6pm. Bar
                  snacks.

Comments: Very fair course and well worth the journey ... Very hard
                  and demanding ... You really want to play here – then
                  go round again ... Exceptional value with an EGU
                  discount ... Tremendous condition and facilities since
                  EGU took over – sensational now ... Very challenging
                  with good bunkering ... Very high standard club without
                  airs and graces ... Wish it was easier to get there ...
                  UK's finest inland course.

Belton Park Golf Club   ★★

Belton Lane, Londonthorpe Road, Grantham, NG31 9SH
Nearest main town: Grantham

Secretary: Mr T. Ireland   Tel: 01476 567399
                                             Fax: 01476 592078
Professional: Mr B. McKee   Tel: 01476 563911

Playing: Midweek: round £26.00; day £32.00. Weekend: round
                  £32.00; day £38.00. Handicap certificate required.

Facilities: Bar: 11am–11pm. Food: Lunch and dinner from
                  11am–9pm.

Comments: Well-established, difficult-to-master course ... Three
                  loops of nine at this undulating parkland venue ... In
                  poor condition on last visit ... Progressive club, well
                  worth the visit ... Mature parkland course.

Belton Woods Hotel Golf Club   ★★★

Belton, Grantham, NG32 2LN
Nearest main town: Grantham

Secretary: Mr T. Roberts   Tel: 01476 593200
                                             Fax: 01476 574547
Professional: Mr T. Roberts   Tel: 01476 514332

Playing: Midweek: round £27.00; day £40.00. Weekend: round
                  £30.00; day £50.00. Handicap certificate required.

Facilities: Bar: 11am–11pm. Food: Breakfast, lunch and dinner
                  from 7am–10pm. Bar snacks.

Comments: Testing course in spacious surroundings ... Course okay but condition subject to weather ... Spike bar is excellent although food and drink is a little overpriced ... Needs to mature ... Two 18-hole courses and knockout practice facilities ... Very user-friendly club ... Woodside course has third longest hole in Europe – a whopping 613 yards.

Boston Golf Club   ★

Cowbridge, Horncastle Road, Boston, PE22 7EL
Nearest main town: Boston

Secretary:	Mr D. E. Smith	Tel: 01205 350589
		Fax: 01205 350589
Professional:	Mr T. R. Squires	Tel: 01205 362306

Playing: Midweek: round £18.00; day £24.00. Weekend: round £24.00; day £30.00. Handicap certificate required.

Facilities: Bar: 11am–11pm. Food: Lunch from 12pm–2.30pm. Dinner from 7pm–9pm.

Comments: Plenty of watery graves ... Unimaginative ... Always a great welcome ... Very welcoming ... Course not great but plenty of fun to be had.

Carholme Golf Club   ★

Carholme Road, Lincoln, LN1 1SE
Nearest main town: Lincoln

Secretary:	Mr R. D. Motts	Tel: 01522 523725
		Fax: 01522 533733
Professional:	Mr G. Leslie	Tel: 01522 536811

Playing: Midweek: round £14.00; day £18.00. Weekend: round £17.00; day n/a.

Facilities: Bar: 11am–11pm. Food: Lunch from 12pm–2pm. Dinner from 6pm–9pm.

Comments: Adequate condition ... Played better for the money ... Fairly dour parkland course.

Forest Pines Golf Club ★★★★

Ermine Street, Brigg, DN20 OAQ
Nearest main town: Scunthorpe

Secretary:	Mr D. Edwards	Tel: 01652 650756
		Fax: 01652 650495
Professional:	Mr D. Edwards	

Playing: Midweek: round £30.00; day £35.00. Weekend: round £30.00; day £35.00. Handicap certificate required.

Facilities: Bar: 11am–11pm. Food: Bar snacks.

Comments: Swarming with visitors from Yorkshire ... Good new course with friendly welcome ... Extremely good greens and fairways ... Great facilities ... Course very well laid out ... New, emerging course that deserves its plaudits ... It really is good ... Attractive new course undoubtedly going the right way ... Parkland/heathland mix of subtle, intriguing holes ... One for the notebook if you're in the area.

Gainsborough Golf Club (Karsten) ★★★★

Thonock, Gainsborough, DN21 1PZ
Nearest main town: Gainsborough

Secretary:	Mr D. Bowers	Tel: 01427 613088
		Fax: 01427 810172
Professional:	Mr S. Cooper	

Playing: Midweek: round £25.00; day £35.00. Weekend: round n/a; day n/a.

Facilities: Bar: Members only. Food: Lunch from 12pm–2.30pm.

Comments: Loads of water and trees – very interesting ... One of the best clubhouses in the country ... Club owned by Ping ... Off the back tees this is a monster ... Facilities first class ... Not for the faint hearted.

Gainsborough Golf Club (Thonock) ★

Thonock, Gainsborough, DN21 1PZ
Nearest main town: Gainsborough

Secretary:	Mr D. Bowers	Tel: 01427 613088
		Fax: 01427 810172
Professional:	Mr S. Cooper	

Playing: Midweek: round £18.00; day £35.00. Weekend: round n/a; day n/a.

Facilities: Bar: Members only. Food: Lunch from 12pm–2.30pm.

Comments: Less of a challenge than Karsten Lakes ... Shorter than the Lakes and far less impressive ... Not as good as the Lakes but facilities still the best around.

Luffenham Heath Golf Club   ★★★

Ketton, Stamford, PE9 3UU
Nearest main town: Stamford

Secretary: Mr I. F. Davenport   Tel: 01780 720205
Professional: Mr I. Burnett   Tel: 01780 720298

Playing: Midweek: round £35.00; day £35.00. Weekend: round £40.00; day £40.00. Handicap certificate required.

Facilities: Bar: 11am–11pm. Food: Lunch and dinner from 11am–9pm. Bar snacks.

Comments: Very enchanting ... Gripping stuff ... In good condition ... No manicuring here, just fine golf in scenic surroundings ... One of the county best.

North Shore Hotel Golf Club   ★★★

North Shore Road, Skegness, PE25 1DN
Nearest main town: Skegness

Secretary: Mr B. Howard   Tel: 01754 763298
                                       Fax: 01754 761902
Professional: Mr J. Cornelius   Tel: 01754 764822

Playing: Midweek: round £19.00; day £29.00. Weekend: round £29.00; day £39.00. Handicap certificate required.

Facilities: Bar: 11am–11pm. Food: Lunch from 12pm–2.30pm. Bar snacks. Dinner from 6pm–9.30pm.

Comments: Wonderful combination of links and parkland ... Rip-roaring value on reasonable course with sea views ... Most welcoming ... Visited twice and first class in nearly all respects – going back next year! ... James Braid bruiser – well worth the drive ... Had never heard of it, but can't get it out my head now ... Links/parkland hybrid – and pulls it off ... Unfashionable course but we don't mind.

Seacroft Golf Club   ★★★★

Seacroft, Skegness, PE25 3AU
Nearest main town: Skegness

Secretary:	Mr F. A. Williams	Tel: 01754 763020
		Fax: 01754 763020
Professional:	Mr R. Lawie	Tel: 01754 769624

Playing: Midweek: round £25.00; day £35.00. Weekend: round £30.00; day £40.00. Handicap certificate required.

Facilities: Bar: 11am–11pm. Food: Lunch and dinner from 10am–9pm. Bar snacks.

Comments: Very good links – deserves a major! ... Flat links, nothing to get excited about ... Nothing brash about this club, just good, honest golf ... Reading the subtle undulations is the key to good scoring.

South Kyme Golf Club   ★★

Skinners Lane, South Kyme, Lincoln, LN4 4AT
Nearest main town: Lincoln

Secretary:	Mr B. Overton	Tel: 01526 861113
		Fax: 01526 861113
Professional:	Mr P. Chamberlain	Tel: 01526 861113

Playing: Midweek: round £12.00; day £18.00. Weekend: round £14.00; day £20.00.

Facilities: Bar: 11am–11pm (weekends only). Food: Bar snacks.

Comments: Only seven years old but the course is exceptional value ... Hospitality second to none ... Course is difficult due to the wind ... Improving ... Food very cheap and good value ... Unheralded course which does everything the right way ... Don't shout too loud about this one – it's our secret ... Fenland course.

Spalding Golf Club   ★★

Surfleet, Spalding, PE11 4EA
Nearest main town: Spalding

Secretary:	Mr B. W. Walker	Tel: 01775 680386
		Fax: 01775 680988

Professional: Mr J. Spencer   Tel: 01775 680474
                                         Fax: 01775 680474

Playing: Midweek: round £25.00; day £25.00. Weekend: round £30.00; day £30.00. Handicap certificate required.

Facilities: Bar: 11am–11pm. Food: Lunch from 11am–2pm. Dinner from 5pm–9pm. Closed on Tuesdays.

Comments: All sorts of rivers, lakes and ponds here ... Fairly one-dimensional course but good value ... Bundles of fun ... Very long and very stern.

Woodhall Spa Golf Club (Bracken)   ★★★

Woodhall Spa, LN10 6PU
Nearest main town: Woodhall Spa

Secretary: Mr B. H. Fawcett   Tel: 01526 352511
                                          Fax: 01526 352778
Professional: Mr C. C. Elliot   Tel: 01526 353229

Playing: Midweek: round £40.00; day £65.00. Weekend: round £40.00; day £65.00. Handicap certificate required.

Facilities: Bar: 11am–11pm. Food: Lunch and dinner from 10am–6pm. Bar snacks.

Comments: A serious disappointment given the EGU's unlimited budget for the course ... Only two memorable holes on what could have been a great course ... Very good when a bit more mature.

Merseyside

Royal Birkdale Golf Club

Waterloo Road, Birkdale, Southport, PR8 2LX
Nearest main town: Southport

Royal Birkdale was recently voted the No. 1 course in the British Isles by *Golf World*. For an Open Championship venue, it could be considered a fairly unremarkable achievement. But if you consider that only seven years ago the world's top players were slating Birkdale for the quality of its greens, suddenly it becomes quite a feat.

Birkdale has always been regarded as a pure example of links golf, but now it is even better. Massive improvements were made prior to the 1998 Open that have given the course some solid foundations for the future.

Five years ago the club decided to take serious action in the battle against meadow grass, thatching and compaction on the greens that caused uproar at the Open. They removed the surfaces, replaced the sub-soil with one that encouraged a deeper root base and then replaced the turf. Greens were overseeded with fescue grass and some of them were re-contoured. The result: greens that were regarded as some of best ever for an Open Championship.

Other major changes have been the felling of 20 acres of silver birch trees which had begun to encroach on the course, with the effect of making the layout more exposed and more of an authentic links. But all the work certainly did not make it easier.

Birkdale is very tough to master. From the 1st it demands the very best of all that play here. Your game must be plotted from tee to green, and as you would expect the wind plays a major part in how you score, particularly as the dunes which follow the fairways protect the player from it – you'll find that distances are very difficult to judge here.

Holes to watch out for are the 6th, a dogleg right to a green protected in the sandhills, the 12th, one of the finest par-3s in the country and the 17th, a par-5 where the drive must be threaded through a gap in the sandhills.

It's a tough start and a tough finish with not too many forgiving holes in between. Cherish the moment when you stand on the 18th tee – this is a wonderful vista after what should be a memorable round. If you get time, take tea in the clubhouse and you can sit down by the massive windows and look out on the 18th green and this wonderful, evocative place to play golf.

Secretary:	Mr N. T. Crewe	Tel: 01704 567920
		Fax: 01704 562327
Professional:	Mr R. N. Bradbeer	Tel: 01704 568857
		Fax: 01704 562615

Playing: Midweek: round £90.00; day £110.00. Weekend: round £110.00; day n/a. Handicap certificate required.

Facilities: Bar: 11am–11pm. Food: Breakfast, lunch and dinner from 8am–9pm. Bar snacks. Green fee price includes lunch.

Comments: Excellent, if a little expensive ... Excellent – the best Merseyside course ... Best course in England, very hard to beat ... Terrific spectator viewing for the Open – even better from the fairways ... Played one month after the Open and brilliant all-round ... I agree – the No. 1 in the British Isles ... A cracking course with so much history ... Wonderful, the time of my life.

Caldy Golf Club ★★

Links Hay Road, Caldy, Wirral, L48 1NB
Nearest main town: West Kirby

Secretary:	Mr T. D. M. Bacon	Tel: 0151 625 5660
		Fax: 0151 625 7394
Professional:	Mr K. Jones	Tel: 0151 625 1818

Playing: Midweek: round £35.00; day £40.00. Weekend: round n/a; day n/a. Handicap certificate required.

Facilities: Bar: 11am–11pm. Food: Lunch and dinner from 11am–5pm. Bar snacks.

Comments: A marvellous parkland test ... Very long and not without difficulty ... Always worth a game ... Never seen it in bad condition ... Surprises you when you least expect it ... Very tidy.

Formby Golf Club ★★★★★

Golf Road, Formby, L37 1LQ
Nearest main town: Liverpool

Secretary:	Mr K. Wilcox	Tel: 01704 872164
		Fax: 01704 833028
Professional:	Mr C. Harrison	Tel: 01704 873090

Playing: Midweek: round £60.00; day £60.00. Weekend: round £60.00; day £60.00.

Facilities: Bar: 11am–11pm. Food: Lunch from 12pm–2.30pm.

Comments: Played the second round of my life here and never looked back ... Such a hard course ... Tough course ... Made welcome ... Well-drained course open all year ... Classic links, so much history between these sand dunes.

Grange Park Golf Club ★★★

Prescot Road, St Helens, WA10 3AD
Nearest main town: St Helens

Secretary: Mr C. V. Hadley   Tel: 01744 26318
                                   Fax: 01744 26318
Professional: Mr P. Roberts   Tel: 01744 28785

Playing: Midweek: round £24.00; day £36.00. Weekend: round £36.00; day n/a. Handicap certificate required.

Facilities: Bar: 11am–11pm. Food: Breakfast and lunch from 10.30am–6pm. Bar snacks.

Comments: Excellent greens ... Great course in bleak surroundings ... Class course with long par-3s – clue is they're all in the same direction.

Haydock Park Golf Club ★★

Golborne Park, Newton-le-Willows, WA12 0HX
Nearest main town: Liverpool

Secretary: Mr J. V. Smith   Tel: 01925 228525
                                  Fax: 01925 228525
Professional: Mr P. E. Kenwright   Tel: 01925 226944

Playing: Midweek: round £25.00; day £25.00. Weekend: round n/a; day n/a. Handicap certificate required.

Facilities: Bar: 11am–11pm. Food: Bar snacks.

Comments: Made welcome by members ... Close to racecourse ... Undulating parkland ... Cheap, value course with interesting members ... Generally in good condition.

Hesketh Golf Club ★★★★

Cockle Dick's Lane, Southport, PR9 9QQ
Nearest main town: Merseyside

Secretary: Mr M. G. Senior   Tel: 01704 530226
    Fax: 01704 538250
Professional: Mr J. Donoghue   Tel: 01704 530050

Playing: Midweek: round £35.00; day £40.00. Weekend: round n/a; day £50.00. Handicap certificate required.

Facilities: Bar: 11am–11pm. Food: Lunch and dinner from 11am–9pm, except Mondays.

Comments: Only let down by the welcome ... Pretty, links-type course ... Behind Hillside and Birkdale in Southport ... Superb clubhouse ... Historic club.

Heswall Golf Club ★★★★

Cottage Lane, Gayton, Chester, Wirral, L60 8PB
Nearest main town: Chester

Secretary: Mr R. J. Butler   Tel: 0151 342 1237
    Fax: 0151 342 1237
Professional: Mr A. E. Thompson   Tel: 0151 342 7431
    Fax: 0151 342 7431

Playing: Midweek: round £35.00; day £35.00. Weekend: round £40.00; day £40.00. Handicap certificate required.

Facilities: Bar: 11am–11pm. Food: Lunch and dinner from 11am–6pm.

Comments: 'Mary, call the cattle home across the sands of Dee' ... Idyllic setting on salt marshes and site of first RAF parachute jump ... Overlooks the River Dee with views into Wales ... Spectacular setting for a course where you need plenty of guile.

Hillside Golf Club ★★★★★

Hastings Road, Hillside, Southport, PR8 2LU
Nearest main town: Southport

Secretary: Mr J. G. Graham   Tel: 01704 567169
    Fax: 01704 563192

Professional: Mr B. Seddon   Tel: 01704 568360

Playing: Midweek: round £40.00; day £50.00. Weekend: round £50.00; day n/a. Handicap certificate required.

Facilities: Bar: 11am–11pm. Food: Breakfast, lunch and dinner from 7am–9pm.

Comments: Absolutely gorgeous ... Very memorable ... Best back nine in England ... The best course that I have played anywhere in the world ... Nice variety of holes ... Not to be underrated alongside its illustrious neighbour (Birkdale) ... Beautifully manicured fairways and greens – a test of any player ... Lovely clubhouse and pro shop ... Wonderful greens ... A natural beauty ... Greens like silk.

Hoylake Municipal Golf Club   ★★

Carr Lane, Hoylake, L47 4BQ
Nearest main town: Birkenhead

Secretary: Mr A. Peacock   Tel: 0151 632 2956
Professional: Mr S. Hooton

Playing: Midweek: round £6.50; day n/a. Weekend: round £6.50; day n/a.

Facilities: Bar: Club meetings only. Food: Breakfast and lunch from 9am–4pm.

Comments: Great course for a muni ... Windy links-type course ... Good value, knocks spots off municipals in the South ... Cheap, fun, value golf.

Royal Liverpool Golf Club   ★★★★

Meols Drive, Hoylake, L47 4AL
Nearest main town: Liverpool

Secretary: Gp Capt C. T. Moore CBE   Tel: 0151 632 3101
Fax: 0151 632 6737
Professional: Mr J. Heggarty   Tel: 0151 632 5868

Playing: Midweek: round £55.00; day £80.00. Weekend: round £70.00; day n/a. Handicap certificate required.

Facilities: Bar: 11am–9pm. Food: Lunch from 12pm–2.30pm.

Comments: Flat, uninteresting with no definition ... Didn't like the internal out of bounds ... Well presented and they let us use the medal tees – nice touch ... Quite simply the best greens I have ever seen ... Links legend.

Southport & Ainsdale Golf Club ★★★★

Bradshaws Lane, Ainsdale, Southport, PR8 3LG
Nearest main town: Southport

Secretary: Mr N. A. Wilson   Tel: 01704 578000
                                         Fax: 01704 570896
Professional: Mr M. Houghton   Tel: 01704 577316

Playing: Midweek: round £35.00; day £45.00. Weekend: round £45.00; day n/a. Handicap certificate required.

Facilities: Bar: 11am–11pm. Food: Lunch by arrangement.

Comments: Very good test with tricky greens ... Unusual par-3 start ... Historic course ... Where golf should be played.

Southport Old Links Golf Club ★★★

Moss Lane, Southport, PR9 7QS
Nearest main town: Churchtown

Secretary: Mr B. E. Kenyon   Tel: 01704 228207
Professional: None.

Playing: Midweek: round £18.50; day £25.50. Weekend: round £25.50; day n/a. Handicap certificate required.

Facilities: Bar: 11am–11pm. Food: Lunch from 11am–4pm, except Mondays.

Comments: Nine holes, two sets of tees – really nice course ... As tough as they come for a nine-hole ... One of the most respected clubs in Southport ... A brilliant, brilliant experience.

The Childwall Golf Club ★★★

Naylor's Road, Gateacre, Liverpool, L27 2YB
Nearest main town: Liverpool

Secretary: Mr K. G. Jennions   Tel: 0151 487 0654
                                         Fax: 0151 487 0882

Professional: Mr N. Parr   Tel: 0151 487 9871

Playing: Midweek: round £26.00; day £26.00. Weekend: round £35.00; day £35.00. Handicap certificate required.

Facilities: Bar: 11am–11pm. Food: Lunch from 12pm–2pm. Dinner from 6pm–9pm. Bar snacks.

Comments: Very good course with tree-lined fairways ... James Braid design ... Parkland pearl ... Accuracy the watchword ... For the price, it does not get much better.

Wallasey Golf Club ★★★

Bayswater Road, Wallasey, L45 8LA
Nearest main town: New Brighton

Secretary: Mrs L. M. Dolman   Tel: 0151 639 3630
Fax: 0151 638 8988
Professional: Mr M. Adams   Tel: 0151 638 3888

Playing: Midweek: round £35.00; day £40.00. Weekend: round £40.00; day n/a. Handicap certificate required.

Facilities: Bar: 11am–11pm. Food: Bar snacks from 10am–6pm.

Comments: Condition of course top class ... Pro shop high standard ... Gorgeous ... Very native course yet beautiful ... Quite exceptional ... So much trouble off the tee ... Fairly unknown ... Next to Hoylake so combine the two.

West Derby Golf Club ★★★★

Yew Tree Lane, Liverpool, L12 9HQ
Nearest main town: Liverpool

Secretary: Mr A. P. Milne   Tel: 0151 254 1034
Fax: 0151 259 0505
Professional: Mr A. Witherup   Tel: 0151 220 5478

Playing: Midweek: round £25.50; day £27.50. Weekend: round £30.50; day £35.50. Handicap certificate required.

Facilities: Bar: 11am–11pm. Food: Lunch from 11.30am–2.30pm. Dinner by arrangement.

Comments: Tempting mixture of parkland and woodland ... Condition top notch ... Very underrated ... Great clubhouse ... Nothing but praise for this course ... Shortish but enjoyable ... Front nine widely regarded as better.

West Lancashire Golf Club ★★★★★

Blundellsands, Crosby, L23 8SZ
Nearest main town: Liverpool

Secretary:	Mr D. D. Wilson	Tel: 0151 924 1076
		Fax: 0151 931 4448
Professional:	Mr T. Hastings	Tel: 0151 924 5662

Playing: Midweek: round £35.00; day £50.00. Weekend: round £60.00; day n/a. Handicap certificate required.

Facilities: Bar: 11am–11pm. Food: Lunch from 11am–4pm. Dinner by arrangement.

Comments: Good welcome, good food ... Fair golf course, well maintained ... A cracker, and open most of the year ... For all your golfing delights.

Middlesex

Fulwell Golf Club ★★★

Wellington Road, Hampton Hill, TW12 1JY
Nearest main town: Fulwell

Secretary:	Mr P. F. Butcher	Tel: 0181 977 2733
		Fax: 0181 977 7732
Professional:	Mr N. Turner	Tel: 0181 977 3844

Playing: Midweek: round n/a; day £30.00. Weekend: round n/a; day n/a.

Facilities: Bar: Members only. Food: Members only.

Comments: Nicely kept course ... Long but not too taxing ... Stylish and a fair price ... Too long for some at over 6,500 yards ... Worth paying a visit.

North Middlesex Golf Club ★★

The Manor House, Friern Barnet Lane, Barnet, N20 0NL
Nearest main town: London

Secretary:	Mr R. Tapsell	Tel: 0181 445 1604
Professional:	Mr A. Roberts	Tel: 0181 445 3060

Playing: Midweek: round £22.00; day £27.50. Weekend: round n/a; day n/a.

Facilities: Bar: 11am–11pm. Food: Bar snacks.

Comments: Neat and tidy parkland ... Great par-3 finish towards clubhouse ... Good condition ... Great greens.

Northwood Golf Club ★

Rickmansworth Road, Northwood, HA6 2QW
Nearest main town: Rickmansworth

Secretary:	Mr D. Thompson	Tel: 01923 821384
		Fax: 01923 840150
Professional:	Mr C. J. Holdsworth	Tel: 01923 820112

Playing: Midweek: round £27.00; day £35.00. Weekend: round n/a; day n/a.

Facilities: Bar: 11am–11pm. Food: Lunch from 10am–6pm. Bar snacks.

Comments: Traditional club ... Fairly flat ... Course in good order ... A little unfriendly ... Better to be had near London.

Stockley Park Golf Club   ★★★

The Clubhouse, Stockley Park, Uxbridge, UB11 1AQ
Nearest main town: Uxbridge

Secretary: Mr N. Munro   Tel: 0181 813 5700
                                         Fax: 0181 813 5655
Professional: Mr A. Knox   Tel: 0181 813 5700

Playing: Midweek: round £23.00; day n/a. Weekend: round £33.00; day n/a.

Facilities: Bar: 11am–11pm. Food: Breakfast, lunch and dinner from 7.30am– 9pm.

Comments: Planes rather distracting ... Set right by Heathrow ... A new course with much character ... A little hilly for my liking.

Trent Park Golf Club   ★★

Bramley Road, London, N14
Nearest main town: London

Secretary: None.
Professional: Mr R. Stocker   Tel: 0181 367 4653

Playing: Midweek: round £11.75; day £11.75. Weekend: round £14.75; day £14.75. Handicap certificate required.

Facilities: Bar: 11am–11pm. Food: Bar snacks.

Comments: Cheap inner city course ... Apart from some of the greens, it's a reasonable standard ... Short, popular course that is still good value ... For a municipal course it is faultless ... Easy to reach from the M25.

West Midlands

Little Aston Golf Club ★★★★

Streetly, Sutton Coldfield, B74 3AN
Nearest main town: Birmingham

Secretary: Mr M. Dibble (Manager) Tel: 0121 353 2942
Professional: Mr J. Anderson

Playing: Midweek: round £50.00; day n/a. Weekend: round n/a; day n/a.

Facilities: Bar: 11am–11pm. Food: Lunch and dinner from 11am–8pm. Bar snacks.

Comments: Exceptional parkland course ... Vardon masterpiece ... Bunkering is lethal ... Sand everywhere ... A special place for golfers ... Blasted sand traps ... The best in Birmingham ... Some fine short par-4s ... Held some memorable Dunlop Masters here ... Exemplary condition and course ... Play it as soon as you can.

Pype Hayes Golf Club ★★

Eachelhurst Road, Walmley, Sutton Coldfield, B76 8EP
Nearest main town: Sutton Coldfield

Secretary: Mr L. Brogan Tel: 0121 351 1014
  Fax: 0121 313 0206
Professional: Mr J. Bayliss Tel: 0121 351 1014

Playing: Midweek: round £9.00; day n/a. Weekend: round £10.00; day n/a.

Facilities: Bar: 11am–8pm. Food: Breakfast, lunch and dinner from 10am–7pm. Bar snacks.

Comments: Cracking pay-and-play ... Best value in the country ... How can they do it so cheap? ... Municipal course in better-than-average condition ... Very accessible.

Swindon Golf Club ★★★

Bridgnorth Road, Swindon, Dudley, DY3 4PH
Nearest main town: Dudley

Secretary:	Mrs R. Pope	Tel: 01902 897031
		Fax: 01902 326219
Professional:	Mr P. Tester	Tel: 01902 896191

Playing: Midweek: round £18.00; day £28.00. Weekend: round £27.00; day £40.00.

Facilities: Bar: 11am–10.30pm. Food: Breakfast and lunch from 8am–3pm. Dinner by arrangement.

Comments: Very fine layout on moorland ... Views make up for course deficiencies ... Right in the middle of the Black Country ... Not much room for error ... A very severe test ... One for the notebook.

Norfolk

Hunstanton Golf Club

Golf Course Road, Old Hunstanton, PE36 6JQ
Nearest main town: Hunstanton

For years, Hunstanton was known primarily for the quality of its greens. It was as if the smoothness and hard-to-read borrows of its putting surfaces overshadowed everything that went before them. The wild grasses, the camber fairways, the scratchy bushes speckling the course and, most importantly, the timeless course design were eclipsed by the fact that balls on Hunstanton greens held their line better than any other in the country.

This traditional club still prides itself on its greens, but there is so much more to discover. Hunstanton is located just a short drive from the holiday town at the western end of a magnificent stretch of golf courses including Royal West Norfolk, Sheringham and Royal Cromer. There are those that prefer the incredibly natural setting of Royal West Norfolk, but the majority of golfers in the area plump for Hunstanton, a traditional out-and-back links with no end of difficulties for the average player.

Once you've got over a 1st tee shot in front of the clubhouse over dunes, for the first three holes there is nothing to suggest this is a special golf course. But from the 4th onwards, every hole presents an individual challenge. It is not from the dunes, which in the context of links golf are merely dressing, or the rough, which barely rises above your ankle, but rather deep bunkers, pin-stripe fairways and an extremely penal design. There are angled greens, blind par-3s and drives to angled fairways, contriving to create a very knotty problem. You also need to watch the holidaymakers crossing the fairway at the 10th on their way to the beach.

In the pecking order of golf courses in Britain and Ireland, Hunstanton is not ranked in the top league. This is on account of the weak finishing holes, but do not let that put you off. This is an exhilarating adventure and one you won't forget.

Secretary:	Mr M. T. Whybrow	Tel: 01485 532811
		Fax: 01485 532319
Professional:	Mr J. Carter	Tel: 01485 532751
Playing:	Midweek: round n/a; day £50.00. Weekend: round n/a; day £60.00. Handicap certificate required.	

Facilities: Bar: 11am–11pm. Food: Lunch from 11.30am–2.30pm. Bar snacks. Dinner by arrangement.

Comments: Magnificent greens – large and receptive ... Very underrated, so do go ... Absolutely top-class links with superb greens and beautiful scenery.

Barnham Broom Hotel Golf Club   ★

Barnham Broom, Norwich, NR9 4DD
Nearest main town: Norwich

Secretary: Mr P. Ballingall   Tel: 01603 759393
                                              Fax: 01603 758224
Professional: Mr P. Ballingall   Tel: 01603 759552

Playing: Midweek: round £25.00; day £30.00. Weekend: round £35.00; day £40.00.

Facilities: Bar: 11am–11pm. Food: Breakfast, lunch and dinner from 7am–9pm.

Comments: Overrated, featureless slug over average terrain ... Unfriendly pro shop and hotel ... Nothing better for a winter break ... Two quality courses and comfortable hotel.

Bawburgh Golf Club   ★

Glen Lodge, Marlingford Road, Bawburgh, NR9 3LU
Nearest main town: Norwich

Secretary: Mr J. Barnard   Tel: 01603 740404
                                              Fax: 01603 740403
Professional: Mr C. Potter   Tel: 01603 742323
                                              Fax: 01603 742323

Playing: Midweek: round £18.00; day £26.00. Weekend: round £20.00; day £30.00.

Facilities: Bar: 11am–11pm. Food: Lunch from 12pm–4pm.

Comments: Interesting course that will mature into a fine one ... Parkland/heathland mix ... Cheap at the price ... Not one to go out of your way for, but still good.

Eaton Golf Club ★★★

Newmarket Road, Norwich, NR4 6SF
Nearest main town: Norwich

Secretary:	Mrs L. A. Bovill	Tel: 01603 451686
		Fax: 01603 451686
Professional:	Mr M. Allen	Tel: 01603 452478

Playing: Midweek: round £30.00; day £30.00. Weekend: round £40.00; day £40.00. Handicap certificate required.

Facilities: Bar: 11am–11pm. Food: Lunch from 12pm–2.30pm. Dinner by arrangement.

Comments: Hidden gem, superb greens and interesting holes ... Small greens and heavy rough make this a toughie ... Affordable golf in nice surroundings.

Gorleston Golf Club ★★

Warren Road, Gorleston, NR31 6JT
Nearest main town: Great Yarmouth

Secretary:	Mr N. P. Longbottom	Tel: 01493 661911
		Fax: 01493 661911
Professional:	Mr N. Brown	Tel: 01493 662103
		Fax: 01493 662103

Playing: Midweek: round £21.00; day £21.00. Weekend: round £25.00; day £25.00. Handicap certificate required.

Facilities: Bar: 11am–11pm. Food: Lunch and dinner from 11am–7pm. Bar snacks.

Comments: Presentation not up to scratch ... Holiday course ... Standard seaside course ... Better examples of seaside golf around.

Great Yarmouth & Caister Golf Club ★★★

Beach House, Caister-on-Sea, Great Yarmouth, NR30 5TD
Nearest main town: Great Yarmouth

Secretary:	Mr H. J. Harvey	Tel: 01493 728699
		Fax: 01493 728699
Professional:	Mr J. Hill	Tel: 01493 720421

Playing: Midweek: round n/a; day £27.00. Weekend: round n/a; day £30.00. Handicap certificate required.

Facilities: Bar: 11am–11pm. Food: Lunch from 12pm–2.30pm. Dinner from 6pm–9.30pm in summer (winter by arrangement).

Comments: Old club with colourful history ... Condition not what it once was ... Fine links ... A links to really get your teeth into ... Links with attitude.

Kings Lynn Golf Club   ★★★

Castle Rising, Kings Lynn, PE31 6BD
Nearest main town: Kings Lynn

Secretary: Mr B. S. Oldfield   Tel: 01553 631654
                                       Fax: 01553 631036
Professional: Mr J. Reynolds   Tel: 01553 631655

Playing: Midweek: round n/a; day £35.00. Weekend: round n/a; day n/a. Handicap certificate required.

Facilities: Bar: 11am–11pm. Food: Lunch from 11.30am–2.30pm. Bar snacks. Dinner from 6pm–9pm Thursday, Friday and Saturday.

Comments: An absolute joy to play and a clubhouse to match ... If you go to Norfolk this is a must visit ... Surprisingly good ... A real pleasure ... In top condition on visit ... Set up in a US Open style with narrow fairways and heavy rough ... Has the feel of a top-class club.

Royal Cromer Golf Club   ★★★

Overstrand Road, Cromer, NR27 OJH
Nearest main town: Cromer

Secretary: Mr B. A. Howson   Tel: 01263 512884
                                       Fax: 01263 512884
Professional: Mr R. J. Page   Tel: 01263 512267

Playing: Midweek: round n/a; day £30.00. Weekend: round n/a; day £36.00. Handicap certificate required.

Facilities: Bar: 11am–11pm. Food: Lunch and dinner from 11am–7pm. Bar snacks.

Comments: Always a pleasure to play ... Very tough in the wind ... Can get very windy ... Set on a cliff edge, Cromer is an experience not to be missed ... Awaken your senses at Cromer.

Royal Norwich Golf Club ★★★

Drayton High Road, Hellesdon, Norwich, NR6 5AH
Nearest main town: Norwich

Secretary: Mr J. Meggy   Tel: 01603 429928
                                  Fax: 01603 417945
Professional: Mr D. Futter   Tel: 01603 408459

Playing: Midweek: round n/a; day £30.00. Weekend: round n/a; day £36.00. Handicap certificate required.

Facilities: Bar: 11am–10.30pm. Food: Lunch from 10am–6pm.

Comments: One of the weakest Royal courses around ... Mixed selection of holes ... Parkland course ... Get tangled in the gorse ... Blasted gorse can make things tough here.

Royal West Norfolk Golf Club ★★★★

Hunstanton, Brancaster, PE31 8AX
Nearest main town: Hunstanton

Secretary: Maj N. A. Carrington-Smith   Tel: 01485 210087
                                            Fax: 01485 210087
Professional: Mr R. E. Kimber   Tel: 01485 210616

Playing: Midweek: round n/a; day £43.00. Weekend: round n/a; day £53.00. Handicap certificate required.

Facilities: Bar: 11am–11pm. Food: Lunch and dinner from 11am–7pm.

Comments: Great course and history, but not keen on visitors ... Old-fashioned links where the sea has an influence ... Stepping back in time 100 years to this traditional, rugged links ... Epitome of traditional links golf ... Nothing to match it.

Sheringham Golf Club   ★★★

Sheringham, Sheringham, NR26 8HG
Nearest main town: Sheringham

Secretary:	Mr M. J. Garrett	Tel: 01263 823488
		Fax: 01263 825189
Professional:	Mr M. W. Judd	Tel: 01263 822980

Playing: Midweek: round n/a; day £35.00. Weekend: round n/a; day £40.00. Handicap certificate required.

Facilities: Bar: 9am–11pm. Food: Bar snacks.

Comments: Go there for the views ... Watch out for the walkers, especially if you slice ... Don't forget this course when you are in Norfolk ... Pretty course, but don't be lulled into thinking it's easy.

The Norfolk Golf & Country Club   ★

Hingham Road, Reymerston, Norwich, NR9 4QQ
Nearest main town: Norwich

Secretary:	Mr M. Aho	Tel: 01362 850297
		Fax: 01362 850614
Professional:	Mr T. Varne	

Playing: Midweek: round £18.00; day £25.00. Weekend: round £22.00; day £30.00.

Facilities: Bar: 11am–11pm. Food: Breakfast, lunch and dinner from 9am–9pm. Bar snacks.

Comments: Soulless course created from farmland ... Flat and not very interesting ... Fairly good value ... Very open ... Nice condition – open all year.

Thetford Golf Club   ★★★

Brandon Road, Thetford, IP24 3NE
Nearest main town: Thetford

Secretary:	Mrs S. A. Redpath	Tel: 01842 752169
		Fax: 01842 766212
Professional:	Mr G. Kitley	Tel: 01842 752662
		Fax: 01842 752662

Playing: Midweek: round £32.00; day £32.00. Weekend: round n/a; day n/a. Handicap certificate required.

Facilities: Bar: 11am–8pm. Food: Lunch from 12pm–2.30pm.

Comments: Superb setting and condition throughout ... Not the best practice facilities ... Touched by many hands of greatness ... Unusual course with intimidating reputation.

Wensum Valley Golf Club   ★★

Beech Avenue, Taverham, NR8 6HP
Nearest main town: Norwich

Secretary: Miss B. Todd   Tel: 01603 261012
                                          Fax: 01603 261664
Professional: Mr P. Whittle   Tel: 01603 261012

Playing: Midweek: round £18.00; day £18.00. Weekend: round £18.00; day £18.00.

Facilities: Bar: 11am–11pm. Food: Lunch and dinner from 11am–9pm. Bar snacks.

Comments: Good scoring ... Golf centre for all abilities ... Nice condition ... Course not up to much ... Built on the side of a valley ... Friendly club ... Course can get boggy in winter.

Northamptonshire

Northamptonshire County Golf Club   ★★★★

Golf Lane, Church Brampton, Northampton, NN6 8AZ
Nearest main town: Northampton

Northamptonshire County has hosted county events for many years and such is its quality that it is now an Open Championship regional qualifying course. The condition of the course is always top class and, with the addition of a special fairway watering system in recent years, it is even better.

Located just four miles outside Northampton itself, tucked away in the quiet village of Church Brampton, the course is heathland, sculpted by the hand of Harry Colt. The master designer had fine raw materials with which to fashion the course, an advantageous mixture of peat/sand base for the fairways and natural, undulating positions on which to place the greens.

The members will tell you it is very easy to run up a big score on some of the holes here. But, in truth, it is not a particularly difficult heathland course, the gorse that lines the fairways not as tough as some of the Surrey courses and the sturdy fir trees rarely blocking your sight of the fairways and greens. All the hazards here are laid out clearly before you and are completely natural – a stream comes into play for some on the 9th and 15th.

Rather than easing the golfer into the round, Northamptonshire County starts fiercely with a 450-yard par-4, followed by a par-5 of 520 yards. For many amateurs, it is a disillusioning start. But if you crack it, things get easier – that is, until the 10th, 11th and 12th. The 10th looks an innocuous medium-length par-4 but is anything but that, while the 11th is another par-4 with out-of-bounds over the back and to the right of the green. It may look a tiddler, but the 12th has a habit of catching out the unwary, a short par-3 of 136 yards protected by a very deep bunker at the front and a small bunker to the right.

No one would ever claim that Northamptonshire County is an exceptional course, but for the average player it is very fair and probably the finest all-round test for the player in the county.

Secretary: Mrs M. E. Wadley   Tel: 01604 842951
                                      Fax: 01604 843025
Professional: Mr T. Rouse   Tel: 01604 842226

Playing: Midweek: round n/a; day £37.50. Weekend: round n/a; day n/a. Handicap certificate required.

Facilities: Bar: 11am–9.30pm. Food: Bar snacks.

Comments: Very good Open regional qualifying course ... Excellent greens and course presentation ... Carpet fairways and slippery greens ... Good test, particularly the bunkers ... Loved this one.

Cold Ashby Golf Club ★★

Stanford Road, Cold Ashby, NN6 6EP
Nearest main town: Northampton

Secretary: Mr D. A. Croxton   Tel: 01604 740548
                                    Fax: 01604 740548
Professional: Mr S. Rose   Tel: 01604 740099

Playing: Midweek: round £16.00; day £25.00. Weekend: round £19.00; day n/a.

Facilities: Bar: 11am–11pm. Food: Lunch and dinner from 11am–9pm. Bar snacks.

Comments: Nicely matured course with plenty of character ... Three loops of nine ... Nice individual holes, but as a whole average.

Collingtree Park Golf Club ★★★★

Windingbrook Lane, Northampton, NN4 0XN
Nearest main town: Northampton

Secretary: Miss J. Byrne   Tel: 01604 700000
                                Fax: 01604 702600
Professional: Mr G. Pook   Tel: 01604 700000

Playing: Midweek: round n/a; day £30.00. Weekend: round n/a; day £40.00. Handicap certificate required.

Facilities: Bar: 11am–11pm. Food: Bar snacks.

Comments: It is as hard as you make it ... Exciting layout with lots of water holes ... Everything a championship course should be ... 10th is a cracking hole.

Farthingstone Hotel Golf Club   ★

Farthingstone, Towcester, NN12 8HA
Nearest main town: Towcester

Secretary:	Mr D. C. Donaldson	Tel: 01327 361291
		Fax: 01327 361645
Professional:	Mr A. Curtis	Tel: 01327 361533

Playing: Midweek: round £16.00; day £18.50. Weekend: round £25.00; day £30.00.

Facilities: Bar: 11am–11pm. Food: Breakfast, lunch and dinner from 7am–10pm.

Comments: Very open, very bleak ... Variable condition and greens a little furry ... Nice panoramic views ... Shame course doesn't match the view.

Hellidon Lakes Hotel Golf & Country Club   ★★★

Daventry, Hellidon, NN11 6LN
Nearest main town: Daventry

Secretary:	Mr J. Nicoll	Tel: 01327 262550
		Fax: 01327 262559
Professional:	Mr G. Wills	Tel: 01327 262551

Playing: Midweek: round £15.00; day n/a. Weekend: round £25.00; day n/a.

Facilities: Bar: 11am–11pm. Food: Breakfast, lunch and dinner from 7am–9pm.

Comments: I never knew that they could breed greens this fast ... Excellent value for money and enjoyed every hole ... Very stuffy atmosphere ... 27-hole course with plenty of variation.

Kingsthorpe Golf Club   ★

Kingsley Road, Northampton, NN2 7BU
Nearest main town: Northampton

Secretary:	Mr J. E. Harris	Tel: 01604 710610
		Fax: 01604 710610
Professional:	Mr P. Armstrong	Tel: 01604 719602
		Fax: 01604 719602

Playing: Midweek: round n/a; day £25.00. Weekend: round n/a; day £25.00. Handicap certificate required.

Facilities: Bar: 11am–11pm. Food: Bar snacks.

Comments: Friendly club ... Course usually in good upkeep ... Short but competitive ... Parkland ... Value day rate.

Oundle Golf Club

Benefield Road, Oundle, PE8 4EZ
Nearest main town: Oundle

Secretary: Mr G. Brooks   Tel: 01832 273267
                                    Fax: 01832 273267
Professional: Mr R. Keys   Tel: 01832 272273

Playing: Midweek: round £22.50; day £22.50. Weekend: round £30.50; day £30.50.

Facilities: Bar: 11am–11pm. Food: Breakfast, lunch and dinner from 11am–9pm.

Comments: Nothing to see here ... No problems off the tee ... Fair value in the week ... A parkland track with little definition.

Staverton Park Golf Club ★★★

Staverton, Daventry, NN11 6JT
Nearest main town: Daventry

Secretary: Mr D. Entwhistle   Tel: 01327 302000
                                    Fax: 01327 311428
Professional: Mr R. Mudge   Tel: 01327 705506

Playing: Midweek: round £25.00; day n/a. Weekend: round £27.50; day n/a. Handicap certificate required.

Facilities: Bar: 11am–11pm. Food: Breakfast from 7.30am–9am. Lunch from 12.30pm–1.45pm. Dinner from 7.30pm–9pm.

Comments: Fairly open and bleak ... Plenty of room for the driver ... Wayward shots go unpenalised ... Not great condition.

Wellingborough Golf Club ★★★★

Harroween Hall, Great Harroween, Wellingborough, NN9 5AD
Nearest main town: Wellingborough

Secretary:	Mr R. Tomlin	Tel: 01933 673022
		Fax: 01933 679379
Professional:	Mr D. Clifford	Tel: 01933 678752

Playing: Midweek: round £25.00; day £35.00. Weekend: round n/a; day n/a. Handicap certificate required.

Facilities: Bar: 11am–11pm. Food: Lunch and dinner from 11am–9pm.

Comments: Magnificent clubhouse ... Excellent club course ... Right up there with the best in the county ... Condition always first class ... Rarely gets unplayable ... Nice provincial course.

Whittlebury Park Golf & Country Club ★★★

Whittlebury, Towcester, NN12 8XW
Nearest main town: Towcester

Secretary:	Mr P. J. Tomalin	Tel: 01327 858092
		Fax: 01327 858009
Professional:	To be appointed.	

Playing: Midweek: round £20.00; day £35.00. Weekend: round £30.00; day £45.00. Handicap certificate required.

Facilities: Bar: 11am–11pm. Food: Breakfast, lunch and dinner from 9am–9pm.

Comments: 36 holes at this parkland course ... Right next to Silverstone racetrack ... Interesting setting but course average ... Fair value for straightforward course ... Bland parkland.

Northumberland

Slaley Hall Golf & Country Club ★★★★

Corbridge, Slaley, NE47 0BY
Nearest main town: Corbridge

Just 20 minutes from Newcastle, Slaley Hall is a very striking new course (opened in 1991) in an area not exactly famed for its courses. With a hotel on site, it has been designed with Tour events in mind and as such has hosted the European Masters.

While the players rate the course highly, the terrible weather that has afflicted these tournaments – wiping out one – has not exactly put Slaley Hall in the shop window. Many have labelled it a 'Woburn of the North', but in truth it has been like a 'Manchester of the North East' every time a tournament goes there, such has been the deluge. This may have long term benefits for the course, and players in the area are now certainly blessed with a course to be proud of, and one that is not overbusy.

Designer Dave Thomas wanted to make every hole individual as well as challenging and to some extent he succeeded. The start at Slaley is tough, as is the finish, although it is fair to say that the opening holes are generally tighter, with much emphasis placed on accuracy off the tee. The back nine is more open and the place to open your shoulders.

The course stretches over 7,000 yards off the back tees and is carved through an 1,000 acre estate of impressive pine forests. The trees define the opening loop and golfers who can manoeuvre the ball will be the greatest beneficiaries of its layout. For many, the signature hole is the 450-yard par-4 9th, known as the 'Sleeping Giant', which is uphill all the way to a green surrounded by rhododendrons, magnificent when in summer bloom. With a pond and a ditch to the left, and towering pines to the right, it is quite a combination.

Secretary:	Mr M. Stancer	Tel: 01434 673350
		Fax: 01434 673152
Professional:	Mr M. Stancer	Tel: 01434 673154
Playing:	Midweek: round £50.00; day £80.00. Weekend: round n/a; day n/a. Handicap certificate required.	
Facilities:	Bar: 11am–11pm. Food: Breakfast, lunch and dinner from 7am–10pm. Bar snacks.	

Comments: Costly but very good course ... Excellent – no other words to describe this one ... Excellent condition and a good challenge ... Great new course and an exquisite restaurant ... A course that asks you many questions ... Products are just way too pricey ... Unquestionably one of the best new courses around ... Very well-managed and enjoyable club ... Straight tee shots required on a course that sparkles in the summer ... Has everything at a price ... Do not let the poor weather at the recent tour event put you off.

Allendale Golf Club   ★

High Studdon, Allenheads Road, Allendale, NE47 9DH
Nearest main town: Allendale

Secretary: Mr P. Mason   Tel: 01434 683623
Professional: None.

Playing: Midweek: round n/a; day £12.00. Weekend: round n/a; day £12.00.

Facilities: Bar: 11am–11pm Friday, Saturday & Sunday only. Food: Bar snacks.

Comments: Hilly parkland course recently extended to 18 holes ... Not up to much even with extension ... 1000ft up – wasn't worth the climb ... Cheap golf all that can be said.

Alnmouth Golf Club   ★★

Foxton Hall, Alnmouth, NE66 3BE
Nearest main town: Alnmouth

Secretary: Mr C. Jobson   Tel: 01665 830231
                                        Fax: 01665 830922
Professional: To be appointed.   Tel: 01665 830043

Playing: Midweek: round n/a; day £27.00. Weekend: round n/a; day n/a. Handicap certificate required.

Facilities: Bar: 11am–11pm. Food: Lunch and dinner from 11am–9pm. Bar snacks.

Comments: Hugs the Northumberland coastline ... Good, honest test at a fair price ... Popular course kept in decent nick ... Worth seeking out for something a bit different.

Bamburgh Castle Golf Club   ★★★★

The Club House, 40 The Wynding, Bamburgh, NE69 7DE
Nearest main town: Bamburgh

Secretary: Mr T. C. Osborne   Tel: 01668 214378
Professional: None.

Playing: Midweek: round n/a; day £25.00. Weekend: round
                    £30.00; day £35.00. Handicap certificate required.

Facilities: Bar: 11am–11pm. Food: Bar snacks.

Comments: Views really make this course what it is ... Fabulous
                    views ... Don't miss it ... Be on your game early, two
                    par-3s to open ... Scenic wonder ... Short course but
                    stunningly beautiful ... Book early for this one ...
                    Unheralded masterpiece.

Bedlingtonshire Golf Club   ★

Acorn Bank, Bedlington, NE22 6AA
Nearest main town: Bedlington

Secretary: Mr E. Ramsey   Tel: 01670 822457
Professional: Mr M. Webb   Tel: 01670 822087
                                         Fax: 01670 822087

Playing: Midweek: round £15.00; day £20.00. Weekend: round
                    £20.00; day £25.00.

Facilities: Bar: 11am–11pm. Food: Lunch and dinner from
                    11am–9pm. Bar snacks.

Comments: Facilities poor ... Too long for mere amateurs ... Very
                    flat ... Nothing that makes it stand out.

Bellingham Golf Club

Boggle Hole, Bellingham, NE48 2DT
Nearest main town: Hexham

Secretary: Mr P. Cordiner   Tel: 01434 220182
                                         Fax: 01434 220160
Professional: None.

Playing: Midweek: round £20.00; day £20.00. Weekend: round
                    £25.00; day £25.00.

Facilities: Bar: 11am–11pm. Food: Lunch and dinner from 11am–9pm. Bar snacks.

Comments: A tiny club that tries really hard ... Great welcome, great value ... Situated between Hadrian's Wall and the Scottish border.

Berwick-upon-Tweed Golf Club   ★★★★

Goswick Beal, Berwick-upon-Tweed, TD15 2RW
Nearest main town: Berwick-upon-Tweed

Secretary: Mr A. E. French   Tel: 01289 387256
                                           Fax: 01289 387256
Professional: Mr P. Terras   Tel: 01289 387380

Playing: Midweek: round £20.00; day £25.00. Weekend: round £25.00; day £32.00. Handicap certificate required.

Facilities: Bar: 11am–10pm. Food: Lunch and dinner from 11am–9pm, except Mondays.

Comments: Ideal links for competitive holiday golf ... Good fair test for a links and excellent greens ... Natural links.

Dunstanburgh Castle Golf Club   ★★

Alnwick, Embleton, NE66 3XQ
Nearest main town: Alnwick

Secretary: Mr E. Williams   Tel: 01665 576562
                                           Fax: 01665 576562
Professional: None.

Playing: Midweek: round n/a; day £15.00. Weekend: round £20.00; day £25.00.

Facilities: Bar: 11am–11pm. Food: Lunch and dinner from 11am–9pm. Bar snacks.

Comments: A romantic course as you approach the castle ... Great value ... A charming place, especially in the wind ... Variable condition but that's the beauty of this track ... Vintage course ... Bet they don't get this down South ... Ruins, rabbit scrape, howling gales, dunes, tidal burns, outstanding flora and fauna ... A real treat.

Hexham Golf Club ★★

Spital Park, Hexham, NE46 3RZ
Nearest main town: Hexham

Secretary:	Mr A. N. Harris	Tel: 01434 603072
		Fax: 01434 601865
Professional:	Mr M. W. Forster	Tel: 01434 604904

Playing: Midweek: round £27.00; day £35.00. Weekend: round £35.00; day n/a.

Facilities: Bar: 11am–11pm. Food: Lunch and dinner from 11am–6pm. Bar snacks.

Comments: Excellent layout in good condition ... Harry Vardon layout ... Undulating parkland with a bit of fizz ... Wonderful views from this charmingly contoured gem.

Linden Hall ★★★

Linden Hall Hotel, Longhorsley, Morpeth, NE65 8XF
Nearest main town: Morpeth

Secretary:	Mr D. Curry	Tel: 01670 788050
		Fax: 01670 788544
Professional:	Mr D. Curry	Tel: 01670 788050

Playing: Midweek: round £25.00; day £40.00. Weekend: round £27.50; day £45.00.

Facilities: Bar: 11am–11pm. Food: Lunch and dinner from 11am–9pm. Dinner by arrangement.

Comments: Excellent short par-3s ... Nice balance of holes ... Very promising course with nice feel ... Good condition ... Signs are this is a course with a future ... Best I've felt on a course for years ... Cultured design that keeps the player on their toes.

Magdalene Fields Golf Club ★

Magdalene Fields, Berwick-upon-Tweed, TV15 1NE
Nearest main town: Berwick-upon-Tweed

Secretary:	Mr M. J. Lynch	Tel: 01289 306384
		Fax: 01289 306384
Professional:	None.	

Playing: Midweek: round £16.00; day £21.00. Weekend: round £18.00; day £22.50.

Facilities: Bar: 11am–11pm. Food: Lunch from 12pm–2pm. Dinner from 7pm–9pm. Bar snacks.

Comments: Very natural seaside course ... Exposed and some severe wind chill ... Poor condition ... Gone to seed a bit.

Newbiggin-by-the-Sea Golf Club   ★

Newbiggin, Newbiggin-by-the-Sea, NE64 6DW
Nearest main town: Newbiggin

Secretary: Mr G. W. Beattie   Tel: 01670 852959
                                    Fax: 01670 520236
Professional: Mr M. Webb   Tel: 01670 817833

Playing: Midweek: round n/a; day £14.00. Weekend: round n/a; day £19.00.

Facilities: Bar: 11am–11pm. Food: Bar snacks.

Comments: Average links ... Condition not what it was ... Not much fun in the wind and rain.

Seahouses Golf Club   ★★★

Beadnell Road, Seahouses, NE68 7XT
Nearest main town: Alnwick

Secretary: Mr J. A. Stevens   Tel: 01665 720794
Professional: None.

Playing: Midweek: round £18.00; day £18.00. Weekend: round £25.00; day £25.00.

Facilities: Bar: 11am–11pm. Food: Lunch and dinner from 12pm–9pm, except Mondays. Bar snacks.

Comments: Very nice surrounding area and great fun to play the holes next to the sea ... Epitome of golf in the North – a rugged course across marshland ... Eccentric design and a cracking par-3 at the 10th ... Natural, undiluted golf ... Across coves and down dale – superb.

Wooler Golf Club   ★

Dod Law, Doddington, Wooler, NE71 6EA
Nearest main town: Wooler

Secretary: Mr N. Frizzell   Tel: 01668 281791
Professional: None.

Playing: Midweek: round £10.00; day n/a. Weekend: round
                   £15.00; day n/a.

Facilities: Bar: 11am–3pm (weather permitting). Food: Snacks
                   (weather permitting).

Comments: A little gem ... Hilltop moorland course with nine holes
                   and 18 tees ... Can always get a game ... Eccentric
                   course for nine-holer with one par-5 of 580 yards.

Nottinghamshire

Notts Golf Club

Hollinwell, Kirby-in-Ashfield, NG17 7QR
Nearest main town: Mansfield

Notts, or Hollinwell as it is more commonly known, must rank as one of the finest inland courses in Britain. Set within the boundaries of Sherwood Forest, Notts is blessed with outstanding natural scenery and a colourful past – many golfers will be unaware that Notts held the Dunlop Masters and John Player Classic in 1970, when the first prize of £25,000 was a world record.

The course, which is predominantly heather and gorse, dates back to the turn of the century with the original Willie Park design revised by John Henry Taylor. His revisions were primarily cosmetic, barely scratching the surface of the established layout apart from to add some bunkers. The silver birch and oak forest that framed the land was left untouched, as were the well-drained carpet fairways, which twist and turn through a lush valley.

You are reminded of the impressive location as early as the 2nd, where the rock behind the green is known as Robin Hood's Chair. It's a gentle start to the round with the longest hole on the course coming at the 6th, where its length is rather mitigated by being downhill.

The name of the course is derived from the 8th, named 'Holy Well'. Off the back tees, your drive needs to carry the lake some 180 yards to a fairway bordered by trees. As with many of the holes at Hollinwell, place your tee shot well and you are rewarded with a simple approach shot. The 205-yard 13th is another good hole, played from an elevated tee into a valley to a heavily bunkered green.

You will soon realise Notts is not a long course, but it is still very demanding. The shaping of the fairways (the 12th is a good example) means that a wrongly positioned ball meanders its way to the very edge of the playing surface. And when you have finished, Hollinwell boasts one of the finest and most homely clubhouses in the country. It is well worth lunching here as the surroundings and food both match each other in quality.

Secretary: Mr S. F. C. Goldie   Tel: 01623 753225
                                     Fax: 01623 753655
Professional: Mr A. Thomas   Tel: 01623 753087

Playing: Midweek: round £40.00; day £55.00. Weekend: round n/a; day n/a. Handicap certificate required.

Facilities: Bar: 11am–11pm. Food: Lunch and dinner from 11am–8pm. Bar snacks.

Comments: Did not feel that welcome at what is ostensibly a members' club ... Golf as it should be ... Tough course in excellent condition ... Superb day out on a renowned course ... Don't leave this area without playing Notts – there is nothing else like it.

Cotgrave Place Golf & Country Club ★★

Nottingham, Stragglethorpe, NG12 3HB
Nearest main town: Nottingham

Secretary:	Mr W. Carr	Tel: 0115 933 3344
		Fax: 0115 933 4567
Professional:	Mr R. Smith	Tel: 0115 933 3344

Playing: Midweek: round £15.00; day n/a. Weekend: round £20.00; day n/a.

Facilities: Bar: 11am–11pm. Food: Breakfast, lunch and dinner from 7am–10pm.

Comments: Could develop into an excellent golf centre with some long, demanding holes ... Challenging par-3s ... A new course with ideas nicked from across the pond ... Still improving ... 36 different challenging holes.

Coxmoor Golf Club ★★★

Coxmoor Road, Sutton-in-Ashfield, NG17 5LF
Nearest main town: Sutton-in-Ashfield

Secretary:	Mr N. Cockbill	Tel: 01623 557359
		Fax: 01623 557359
Professional:	Mr D. Ridley	Tel: 01623 559906

Playing: Midweek: round £28.00; day £40.00. Weekend: round n/a; day n/a. Handicap certificate required.

Facilities: Bar: 11am–11pm. Food: Breakfast and bar snacks from 10am–9pm.

Comments: Splendid value on a sparkling course ... Good quality course ... Undulating moorland track, generally in fine condition.

Mapperley Golf Club ★★

Central Avenue, Plains Road, Mapperley, NG3 5RH
Nearest main town: Nottingham

Secretary: Mr A. Newton   Tel: 0115 955 6672
Professional: Mr M. Allen   Tel: 0115 955 6673

Playing: Midweek: round £15.00; day £20.00. Weekend: round £20.00; day £25.00.

Facilities: Bar: 11am–11pm. Food: Lunch and dinner from 11am–7pm. Bar snacks.

Comments: Mature, hilly course ... Meadowland course ... Not the best in Notts ... Don't bust a gut to get there.

Newark Golf Club ★★

Kelwick, Coddington, NG24 2QX
Nearest main town: Newark

Secretary: Mr A. W. Morgan   Tel: 01636 626282
                                    Fax: 01636 626497
Professional: Mr P. A. Lockley Tel: 01636 626492
                                    Fax: 01636 626492

Playing: Midweek: round £22.00; day £27.00. Weekend: round £27.00; day n/a. Handicap certificate required.

Facilities: Bar: 11am–11pm. Food: Lunch and dinner from 11am–7pm. Bar snacks.

Comments: Pleasant parkland course with excellent 19th ... Not bad and good for the area ... Secluded, parkland course with friendly members.

Oakmere Park Golf Club ★

Oaks Lane, Oxton, NG25 0RH
Nearest main town: Nottingham

Secretary: Mr S. St John-Jones   Tel: 0115 965 3545
                                     Fax: 0115 965 5628
Professional: Mr S. St John-Jones   Tel: 0115 965 3545

Playing: Midweek: round £18.00; day £30.00. Weekend: round £24.00; day £40.00.

Facilities: Bar: 11am–11pm. Food: Lunch and dinner from 11am–9pm. Bar snacks.

Comments: Nice course but a bit untidy ... Complete golf centre where practice facilities overshadow the course ... Average parkland fare.

Ramsdale Park Golf Centre ★★

Oxton Road, Calverton, NG14 6NU
Nearest main town: Nottingham

Secretary: Mr B. Jenkinson   Tel: 0115 965 5600
                                           Fax: 0115 965 4105
Professional: Mr R. Macey   Tel: 0115 965 5600

Playing: Midweek: round £14.00; day £23.00. Weekend: round £16.00; day £27.00.

Facilities: Bar: 11am–11pm. Food: Lunch and dinner from 11am–9pm. Bar snacks.

Comments: Nice course if a little tiring ... Hilly parkland course ... Extensive practice facilities ... Basic golf at value price ... Two courses in fair condition.

Ruddington Grange Golf Club ★★

Wilford Road, Ruddington, NG11 6NB
Nearest main town: Nottingham

Secretary: Mr D. Dessaur   Tel: 0115 984 6141
                                           Fax: 0115 940 5165
Professional: Mr R. Simpson   Tel: 0115 921 1951

Playing: Midweek: round £15.00; day £18.00. Weekend: round £22.50; day £27.00.

Facilities: Bar: 11am–11pm. Food: Lunch and dinner from 11am–9pm. Bar snacks.

Comments: Superb new greens since change of ownership ... Plenty of water hazards on this young, uninspiring course.

Rufford Park Golf Centre ★★

Rufford Lane, Newark, NG22 9DG
Nearest main town: Newark

Secretary:	Miss J. Strange	Tel: 01623 825253
		Fax: 01623 825254
Professional:	Mr J. Vaughan	

Playing: Midweek: round £14.00; day £20.00. Weekend: round £18.00; day n/a.

Facilities: Bar: 11am–11pm. Food: Breakfast, lunch and dinner from 9am–9pm. Bar snacks.

Comments: Good course to learn the game ... Off-course facilites are improving ... Nice variety at this basic course.

Sherwood Forest Golf Club ★★★

Eakring Road, Mansfield, NG18 3EW
Nearest main town: Mansfield

Secretary:	Mr K. Hall	Tel: 01623 626689
		Fax: 01623 420412
Professional:	Mr K. Hall	Tel: 01623 627403

Playing: Prices on application. Handicap certificate required.

Facilities: Bar: 11am–11pm. Food: Lunch and dinner from 11am–9pm. Bar snacks.

Comments: Green fees on application ... Good course and club ... One of the best in the county and in lovely setting ... Delightful silver birch and pine trees ... Back nine the highlight.

Wollaton Park Golf Club ★★★

Wollaton Park, Nottingham, NG8 1BT
Nearest main town: Nottingham

Secretary:	Mr M T. Harvey	Tel: 0115 978 7574
		Fax: 0115 978 7574
Professional:	Mr J. Lower	Tel: 0115 978 4834

Playing: Midweek: round £25.00; day £35.00. Weekend: round £30.00; day £40.00. Handicap certificate required.

Facilities: Bar: 11am–11pm. Food: Lunch and dinner from 11am–11pm. Bar snacks.

Comments: Interesting parkland with lively deer roaming the fairways
... Teasing course with teasing holes ... Very enticing
course in public park ... Pleasant oasis just three miles
from centre of Nottingham ... Top quality inner city
course.

Worksop Golf Club   ★★★★

Windmill Lane, Worksop, S80 2SQ
Nearest main town: Worksop

Secretary: Mr G. L. Lord   Tel: 01909 477731
                                         Fax: 01909 477731
Professional: Mr C. Weatherhead   Tel: 01909 477732

Playing: Midweek: round £24.00; day £32.00. Weekend: round
£32.00; day n/a. Handicap certificate required.

Facilities: Bar: 11am–11pm. Food: Lunch and dinner from
11am–8pm. Bar snacks.

Comments: A wonderfully British course – immaculate ... Dem-
anding course, I can see why Lee Westwood is so good
... Lee Westwood plays here – enough said ...
Delightful parkland course with fast greens ... Fast
greens – just like Lee likes them ... Top-notch course ...
Right attitude at this friendly club.

Oxfordshire

Tadmarton Heath Golf Club ★★★★

Wigginton, Banbury, OX15 5HL
Nearest main town: Banbury

Before the construction of a golf course at Tadmarton Heath, Harry
Vardon was consulted about the viability of a course on the top of
Wigginton Hill. Without reservation he commented that 'God made it to
be a golf course'. Seventy-six years on, Tadmarton Heath is a joy to
play, a course that has stood the test of time and gets better with age.

Ironically for a heathland course, there is no heather, just gorse and
broom which defines all the fairways. There are plenty of other natural
features, including the ravine at the 7th (originally a holy well where the
water was reputed to have healing powers) and the natural plateaus
which form the fairways for the 11th and 12th. There are very few trees,
agronomy experts having recommended that they were of little use on
a heathland course.

As you would expect of a course that measures just under 6,000
yards, the fairways are very tight and much thought goes into each hole.
The course is generally flat but visually it is very exciting, a genuine test
despite its short length. The best holes are probably the 6th, where a
7-ft-deep bunker with railway sleepers guards the green, and the short
7th, played to a small green set in an embankment. It also finishes with
a flourish, the 18th a dogleg, but the bend in the fairway only starting
at around 240 yards.

Like many heathland courses, Tadmarton Heath is blessed with
excellent drainage, the sandy soil sitting above ironstone which means
all-year-round play. The members of this club are generally welcoming
and are happy to share their clubhouse, a delightful converted farm-
house, with visitors. There's a lovely lounge bar to sit in during the
evening.

Secretary:	Mr R. E. Wackrill	Tel: 01608 737278
		Fax: 01608 730548
Professional:	Mr T. Jones	Tel: 01608 730047
Playing:	Midweek: round n/a; day £26.00. Weekend: round n/a; day n/a. Handicap certificate required.	
Facilities:	Bar: 11am–2pm & 4pm–10pm. Food: Lunch from 8am–2pm. Dinner from 4pm–9.30pm. Bar snacks.	

Comments: Excellent condition ... Tight, short course ... One mistake can be very costly ... Favourite hole is the 7th ... Course with colourful history ... Heathland track with excellent drainage for year-round play.

Badgemore Park Golf Club ★★★

Henley on Thames, RG9 4NR
Nearest main town: Henley-on-Thames

Secretary: Mr J. Connell   Tel: 01491 572206
          (Manager)   Fax: 01491 576899
Professional: Mr J. Dunn   Tel: 01491 574175

Playing: Midweek: round £15.00; day £25.00. Weekend: round n/a; day n/a.

Facilities: Bar: 11am–11pm. Food: Lunch and dinner from 11am–10pm. Bar snacks.

Comments: Tricky ... Played it all my life and love it ... Trees in play on each hole.

Brailes Golf Club ★

Sutton Lane, Lower Brailes, Banbury, OX15 5BB
Nearest main town: Shipston-on-Stour

Secretary: Mr R. A. S. Malir   Tel: 01608 685336
          Fax: 01608 685205
Professional: Mr M. Bendall   Tel: 01608 685633

Playing: Midweek: round £18.00; day £27.00. Weekend: round £26.00; day £36.00.

Facilities: Bar: 11am–11pm. Food: Lunch and dinner from 11am–9pm. Bar snacks.

Comments: Magnificent links setting ... A little overplayed and has been know to be in poor condition ... Views of three counties from the 17th tee ... In fair condition but don't go out of your way.

Chesterton Country Golf Club ★

Bicester, Chesterton, OX6 8TE
Nearest main town: Bicester

Secretary: Mr B. T. Carter   Tel: 01869 241204
Professional: Mr J. W. Wilkshire   Tel: 01869 242023

Playing: Midweek: round £12.00; day £15.00. Weekend: round £15.00; day £20.00.

Facilities: Bar: 11am–11pm. Food: Lunch from 11am–3pm.

Comments: Flat course on old farmland ... Standard new course ... Flat terrain, not very interesting.

Chipping Norton Golf Club ★

Southcombe, Chipping Norton, OX7 5QH
Nearest main town: Chipping Norton

Secretary: Mr S. Chislett   Tel: 01608 642383
    Fax: 01608 645422
Professional: Mr D. Craik Jr   Tel: 01608 643356

Playing: Midweek: round £20.00; day £20.00. Weekend: round n/a; day n/a.

Facilities: Bar: 11am–11pm. Food: Lunch and dinner from 11am–9pm. Bar snacks.

Comments: Exposed downland course ... Not much to see ... Friendly club course ... Straightforward ... Well thought of in the area.

Drayton Park Golf Club ★★

Steventon Road, Drayton, OX14 2RR
Nearest main town: Abingdon

Secretary: None.   Tel: 01235 528989
    Fax: 01235 525731
Professional: Mrs D. Masey   Tel: 01235 550607

Playing: Midweek: round £13.00; day £20.00. Weekend: round £16.00; day n/a.

Facilities: Bar: 11am–11pm. Food: Lunch and dinner from 11am–9pm.

Comments: Challenging but forgiving ... Hawtree design with interesting use of water hazards ... Facile parkland course.

Frilford Heath Golf Club (Red)   ★★★★

Frilford Heath, Abingdon, OX13 5NW
Nearest main town: Abingdon

Secretary: Mr J. W. Kleynhans   Tel: 01865 390864
    Fax: 01865 390823
Professional: Mr D. C. Craik   Tel: 01865 390887

Playing: Midweek: round £35.00; day £60.00. Weekend: round £35.00; day £60.00. Handicap certificate required.

Facilities: Bar: 8am–11pm. Food: Breakfast, lunch and dinner from 8am–9pm. Bar snacks.

Comments: Clubhouse grand and welcoming ... Building of Blue Course means some holes out of style with the rest ... The best at Frilford Heath ... 8th the best hole, a long tight par-4 ... Nice par-3 through a spinney ... Good food in lovely clubhouse.

Frilford Heath Golf Club (Green)   ★★★

Frilford Heath, Abingdon, OX13 5NW
Nearest main town: Abingdon

Secretary: Mr J. W. Kleynhans   Tel: 01865 390864
    Fax: 01865 390823
Professional: Mr D. C. Craik   Tel: 01865 390887

Playing: Midweek: round £35.00; day £60.00. Weekend: round £35.00; day £60.00. Handicap certificate required.

Facilities: Bar: 8am–11pm. Food: Breakfast, lunch and dinner from 8am–9pm. Bar snacks.

Comments: Prettiest and shortest of three courses ... Some great long par-4s ... 7th and 16th very special ... Nice collection of par-3s.

Frilford Heath Golf Club (Blue)   ★★★

Frilford Heath, Abingdon, OX13 5NW
Nearest main town: Abingdon

Secretary: Mr J. W. Kleynhans   Tel: 01865 390864
    Fax: 01865 390823
Professional: Mr D. C. Craik   Tel: 01865 390887

Playing: Midweek: round £35.00; day £60.00. Weekend: round £35.00; day £60.00. Handicap certificate required.

Facilities: Bar: 8am–11pm. Food: Breakfast, lunch and dinner from 8am–9pm. Bar snacks.

Comments: Very open ... Modern design with large bunkers and water ... Thick rough and bunkers the hazards ... Tough start ... Par-3 3rd a cracker.

Henley Golf Club   ★★★

Harpsden, Henley-on-Thames, RG9 4HG
Nearest main town: Henley

Secretary: Mr A. M. Chaundy   Tel: 01491 575742
                                         Fax: 01491 412179
Professional: Mr M. Howell   Tel: 01491 575710
                                         Fax: 01491 575710

Playing: Midweek: round n/a; day £30.00. Weekend: round n/a; day n/a. Handicap certificate required.

Facilities: Bar: 11am–11pm. Food: Lunch and dinner from 11am–9pm. Bar snacks.

Comments: Short parkland course ... Basic facilities but quaint little course ... Charming course in pretty area ... Good golfing ... Never a problem to get a game.

Huntercombe Golf Club   ★★★

Nuffield, Henley-on-Thames, RG9 5SL
Nearest main town: Henley-on-Thames

Secretary: Lt Col T. J. Hutchison Tel: 01491 641207
                                         Fax: 01491 642060
Professional: Mr J. B. Draycott   Tel: 01491 641241

Playing: Midweek: round £27.00; day £35.00. Weekend: round n/a; day n/a. Handicap certificate required.

Facilities: Bar: 8am–11pm. Food: Breakfast, lunch and dinner from 8am–8pm. Bar snacks.

Comments: Quaintly, quintessentially English ... A jewel in the Chilterns – keep it quiet ... Superb condition and can be tricky ... Medium difficulty and greens in superb condition.

Lyneham Golf Club ★★★

Chipping Norton, Lyneham, OX7 6QQ
Nearest main town: Chipping Norton

Secretary:	Mr C. J. T. Howkins Tel: 01993 831841
	Fax: 01993 831775
Professional:	Mr R. Jefferies
Playing:	Midweek: round £15.00; day £22.00. Weekend: round £18.00; day £27.00.
Facilities:	Bar: 11am–11pm. Food: Lunch and dinner from 11am–9pm. Bar snacks.
Comments:	Tremendous value for money, good food and warm welcome ... Water in play on eight holes ... New course which looks natural for its age.

Southfield Golf Club ★★★

Hill Top Road, Oxford, OX4 1PF
Nearest main town: Oxford

Secretary:	Mrs S. Mathews Tel: 01865 242158
	Fax: 01865 242158
Professional:	Mr A. Rees Tel: 01865 244258
Playing:	Midweek: round £18.00; day £24.00. Weekend: round n/a; day n/a. Handicap certificate required.
Facilities:	Bar: 11am–11pm. Food: Lunch from 12pm–2pm. Dinner from 4pm–8pm. Bar snacks.
Comments:	Not too taxing ... Peaceful ... Course used by Oxford University ... Interesting course but there's better in the county.

The Oxfordshire Golf Club ★★★

Rycote Lane, Milton Common, Thame, OX9 2PU
Nearest main town: Thame

Secretary:	Mr M. O'Bata Tel: 01844 278300
	Fax: 01844 278003
Professional:	Mr I. Mosey Tel: 01844 278505
Playing:	Prices on application.

Facilities: Bar: Members only. Food: Members only.

Comments: Expensive, over-priced for an unnatural course ... Excellent new design with superb practice facilities ... Did the earth move for you? It certainly did for the designers ... Exciting, if unnatural course ... Links lovers steer a wide berth round this one.

Waterstock Golf Club   ★★

Thame Road, Waterstock, OX33 1HT
Nearest main town: Oxford

Secretary: Mr A. Wyatt   Tel: 01844 338093
                                       Fax: 01844 338036
Professional: Mr J. Goodman

Playing: Midweek: round £14.00; day £22.00. Weekend: round £17.00; day £30.00.

Facilities: Bar: 11am–11pm. Food: Lunch and dinner served from 11am–9pm. Bar snacks.

Comments: Very modern and interesting ... Donald Steel design ... Outstanding facilites for the visitor ... New course with character ... Clever design ... All the shots required.

Shropshire

Llanymynech Golf Club ★★★★

Pant, Oswestry, SY10 8LB
Nearest main town: Oswestry

Llanymynech, six miles north of Oswestry, is famed for its association with Ian Woosnam, who fashioned his skills here as a youngster. It is a spectacular layout, riding high on limestone outcrops and offering views extending 50 miles. Famously, on the 4th you tee off in Wales, but putt-out in England, and it is not until the 9th that you return.

The course is something of a throwback to the days when courses were built on high land so that the farmers could use the pasture land at lower levels. For years, the condition of the course was monitored by the sheep that roamed the site, but they left in 1973 and since then more traditional methods of greenkeeping have been used.

No one would ever claim that Llanymynech is in outstanding condition, and some would argue that there are better courses in the area, but the diversity of the holes creates much excitement for the player. The front nine is cut through a forest and requires clever placement of tee-shots to maximise the scoring opportunities. On the back nine, the course is at its most scenic with views overlooking Shropshire and out to the Welsh Hills. It is also a more open and satisfying part of the course, where you really feel the uniqueness of the golf experience.

As you would expect from a course located in a fairly barren golfing region, green fees are very good value. You can pay more for, say, Hawkstone Park Hotel, a very popular stop-off for golfers, but Llanymynech offers a more varied experience.

Secretary:	Mr D. R. Thomas	Tel: 01691 830983
Professional:	Mr A. Griffiths	Tel: 01691 830879

Playing: Midweek: round £15.00; day £23.00. Weekend: round £20.00; day £25.00. Handicap certificate required.

Facilities: Bar: 11am–11pm. Food: Lunch and dinner from 11am–11pm. Bar snacks.

Comments: Idiosyncratic mountain golf with fabulous views – a must for a clear spring or autumn day ... Most unusual course ... Scenic and invigorating ... A pilgrimage to this weird and wonderful course is highly recommended.

Arscott Golf Club ★

Arscott, Pomtesbury, SY5 OXP
Nearest main town: Shrewsbury

Secretary: Mr A. Petersen   Tel: 01743 860114
                                       Fax: 01743 860114
Professional: Mr I. Doran   Tel: 01743 860881

Playing: Midweek: round £16.00; day £18.00. Weekend: round
                   £20.00; day £22.00. Handicap certificate required.

Facilities: Bar: 11am–11pm. Food: Lunch from 12pm–3pm.
                   Dinner from 6pm–9pm at weekends only. Bar snacks.

Comments: Modern course with fine views over Wales ... Fairly hilly
                   ... Can only get better ... Plenty of water hazards ...
                   You can learn the game here.

Bridgnorth Golf Club ★

Stanley Lane, Bridgnorth, WV16 4SF
Nearest main town: Bridgnorth

Secretary: Mr K. D. Cole   Tel: 01746 763315
                                       Fax: 01746 761381
Professional: Mr P. Hinton   Tel: 01746 762045

Playing: Midweek: round £22.00; day £28.00. Weekend: round
                   £25.00; day £30.00. Handicap certificate required.

Facilities: Bar: 11am–11pm. Food: Lunch and dinner from
                   11am–9pm. Bar snacks.

Comments: Good value ... Friendly club ... Fine if you're in the
                   area, but otherwise no ... Friendly atmosphere ... Pro
                   very helpful.

Church Stretton Golf Club ★★★

Trevor Hill, Church Stretton, SY6 6JH
Nearest main town: Church Stretton

Secretary: Mr R. Broughton   Tel: 01694 722281
Professional: Mr P. Seal   Tel: 01743 873751

Playing: Midweek: round £19.00; day £24.00. Weekend: round
                   n/a; day £23.00. Handicap certificate required.

Facilities: Bar: 12pm–3pm & 5pm–9.30pm. Food: Lunch from 12pm–3pm. Dinner from 5pm–8pm. Bar snacks.

Comments: Good test for an inland course ... James Braid design ... Hilly course where wild things roam ... Unusual course but nice club attitude.

Hawkstone Park Hotel & Golf Club   ★★★★

Weston-under-Redcastle, SY4 5UY
Nearest main town: Shrewsbury

Secretary: Mr K. L. Brazier   Tel: 01939 200611
                                            Fax: 01939 200311
Professional: Mr P. Wesselingh   Tel: 01939 200611

Playing: Midweek: round £28.00; day £42.00. Weekend: round £36.00; day £50.00. Handicap certificate required.

Facilities: Bar: 11am–11pm. Food: Lunch and dinner from 11am–10pm. Bar snacks.

Comments: Very mature course in a lovely area ... Delightful golf experience with dramatic views ... A long weekend visit offered at a great value course ... Hotel and food both excellent ... Resort course that does the little things well ... Course looked in need of rest on last visit.

Hill Valley Golf and Country Club   ★★★

Terrick Road, Whitchurch, SY13 4JZ
Nearest main town: Whitchurch

Secretary: Mr A. J. Minshell   Tel: 01948 663584
                                            Fax: 01948 665927
Professional: Mr C. Burgess   Tel: 01948 663032

Playing: Midweek: round £20.00; day n/a. Weekend: round £25.00; day n/a.

Facilities: Bar: 11am–11pm. Food: Lunch from 11am–6pm. Dinner by arrangement.

Comments: US-style golf ... Very comfortable club ... Liked the numerous water hazards ... Really blends in with the landscape ... Nice course for a nice price.

Hill Valley Golf & Country Club   ★★★

Terrick Road, Whitchurch, SY13 4JZ
Nearest main town: Whitchurch

Secretary:	Mr P. Condliffe	Tel: 01948 663584
		Fax: 01948 665927
Professional:	Mr A. R. Minshall	Tel: 01948 663032

Playing: Midweek: round £20.00; day £26.00. Weekend: round £25.00; day £32.00. Handicap certificate required.

Facilities: Bar: 11am–11pm. Food: Lunch and dinner from 10am–10pm. Bar snacks.

Comments: Could not fault the way our society day was handled ... Two courses, one designed by Alliss/Thomas ... US-style layout – very unnatural ... Even the lakes and streams can't disguise a bland course.

Mile End Golf Club   ★

Mile End, Oswestry, SY11 4JE
Nearest main town: Oswestry

Secretary:	Mr R. Thompson	Tel: 01691 670580
		Fax: 01691 670580
Professional:	Mr S. Carpenter	Tel: 01691 671246

Playing: Midweek: round £14.00; day £20.00. Weekend: round £18.00; day £25.00.

Facilities: Bar: 11am–11pm. Food: Lunch from 11.30am–3pm. Dinner by arrangement.

Comments: Suitable for all standards ... Good facility for beginners ... Not the best in the area.

Shifnal Golf Club   ★★★

Decker Hill, Shifnal, TF11 8QL
Nearest main town: Telford

Secretary:	Mr P. W. Holden	Tel: 01952 460330
		Fax: 01952 460330
Professional:	Mr J. Flanaghan	Tel: 01952 460457

Playing: Midweek: round £25.00; day £30.00. Weekend: round n/a; day n/a.

Facilities: Bar: 11am–11pm. Food: Lunch and dinner from 11am–8pm. Bar snacks.

Comments: Clubhouse the best thing about this course ... Woodland/parkland course of variable standard ... Condition not the best ... Enjoyed it.

Telford Golf & Country Club   ★★★

Great Hay, Sutton Heights, Telford, TF7 4DT
Nearest main town: Telford

Secretary: Mr I. Lucas   Tel: 01952 429977
                                      Fax: 01952 586602
Professional: Mr D. Thorpe   Tel: 01952 586052

Playing: Midweek: round £25.00; day n/a. Weekend: round £30.00; day n/a. Handicap certificate required.

Facilities: Bar: 11am–11pm. Food: Breakfast, lunch and dinner from 7am–10pm.

Comments: Enormous lakes and bunkers ... Not much thought in the design ... Fine facilities ... Try and keep out of the water!

The Shropshire   ★★★

Muxton Grange, Muxton, TF2 8PQ
Nearest main town: Telford

Secretary: Miss L. Davies   Tel: 01952 677866
                                      Fax: 01952 677844
Professional: Mr D. Bateman   Tel: 01952 677800

Playing: Midweek: round £15.00; day £24.00. Weekend: round £20.00; day n/a. Handicap certificate required.

Facilities: Bar: 11am–11pm. Food: Lunch and dinner from 12pm–7pm. Bar snacks.

Comments: Ideal golf society venue with three loops of nine ... Gold/Silver course is the best combination ... A fine golfing day out ... New golf centre providing affordable golf for everyone ... Not a top course but it does the job well.

Worfield Golf Club ★

Worfield, Bridgnorth, WV15 5HE
Nearest main town: Wolverhampton

Secretary:	Mr W. Weaver	Tel: 01746 716372
		Fax: 01746 716302
Professional:	Mr S. Russell	Tel: 01746 716541

Playing: Midweek: round £16.00; day £22.00. Weekend: round £25.00; day n/a.

Facilities: Bar: 11am–11pm. Food: Bar snacks. Dinner from 6pm–9pm. Bar snacks.

Comments: Good standard new course ... All you would expect from new course ... Undulating greens ... Looks easy but is anything but.

Wrekin Golf Club ★★

Wellington, Telford, TF6 5BX
Nearest main town: Telford

Secretary:	Mr D. Briscoe	Tel: 01952 244032
		Fax: 01952 252906
Professional:	Mr K. Housden	Tel: 01952 223101

Playing: Midweek: round £20.00; day £25.00. Weekend: round £28.00; day n/a.

Facilities: Bar: 11am–11pm. Food: Lunch and dinner from 11am–11pm. Bar snacks.

Comments: Very hilly but worth the effort ... Condition not always what you would expect.

Somerset

Burnham & Berrow Golf Club ★★★★★

St Christopher's Way, Burnham-on-Sea, TA8 2PE
Nearest main town: Burnhan-on-Sea

Some golfers find the out-and-back links rather an outdated layout, so they should be well warned off Burnham and Berrow, a very traditional course set on the North Somerset coast, with views of the Bristol Channel and the distant Glamorgan shore. Players who balk at playing the course on this basis are, however, missing out, because Burnham and Berrow delights in so many ways that the rigidness of the layout becomes a secondary consideration.

The out-and-back links was immortalised by St Andrews, a course that, when golf was first played, was essentially a fairway which stretched out for nine holes, then a fairway that stretched back for nine holes. Burnham and Berrow is just like this. A strip of coastal land that was left when the seas receded after the last Ice Age, it is sparsely vegetated with fine-bladed grass for fairways and wild, rough grasses forming the course's primary protection against good scoring.

The course has been altered many times in the twentieth century to cut out a lot of blind shots that existed and in particular to avoid hitting church-goers who walked across the fairways to reach the church in the middle of the course. They have also taken steps to preserve the plant-life which is abundant in the wild grasses, particularly the orchids.

As befits a grand course, it is the finishing holes at Burnham and Berrow that prove the highlight of any round. The 15th is a long par-4, followed by the short par-4 16th which requires a short pitch to a small, elevated green (a feature of Burnham and Berrow are the small greens, which slope in all directions). A long par-3 at the 17th that can require a driver at times, precedes the finishing hole, a par-4 sculpted through small sandhills. The course will test all your shots, and offers you some spectacular positions from which to play. If you're to score well, you'd better have your short game in good nick, as the chances are you will fail to hold many of the greens at your first attempt.

Secretary: Mrs E. L. Sloman — Tel: 01278 785760
Fax: 01278 795440
Professional: Mr M. Crowther-Smith — Tel: 01278 784545

Playing: Midweek: round £36.00; day £36.00. Weekend: round £50.00; day £50.00. Handicap certificate required.

Facilities: Bar: 11am–11pm. Food: Lunch and dinner from 11am–9pm. Bar snacks.

Comments: Classic links with plenty of variety ... Lovely links ... Hard course when the wind is blowing ... Vicious rough ... Excellent, knowledgable staff ... Magnificent links with some of the best greens anywhere ... Not quite a traditional links but seaside golf at its best ... Tough links with the character of an old smooth malt whisky ... Best course in the UK for the price ... Twilight fee is unbeatable value.

Bath Golf Club   ★★★

Sham Castle, North Road, Bath, BA2 6JG
Nearest main town: Bath

Secretary: Mr P. E. Ware   Tel: 01225 463834
                                        Fax: 01225 331027
Professional: Mr P. Hancock   Tel: 01225 466953

Playing: Midweek: round £25.00; day £30.00. Weekend: round £30.00; day £35.00. Handicap certificate required.

Facilities: Bar: 11am–11pm. Food: Lunch and dinner from 11am–7pm. Bar snacks.

Comments: A lot of thought required here ... Accuracy rather than brute strength rewarded ... Best in Bath ... Ranks alongside some of Bristol's best ... Views over the city and countryside.

Clevedon Golf Club   ★★★

Castle Road, Clevedon, BS21 7AA
Nearest main town: Clevedon

Secretary: Mr M. Heggie   Tel: 01275 874057
                                        Fax: 01275 341228
Professional: Mr M. Heggie   Tel: 01275 874704

Playing: Midweek: round £20.00; day £25.00. Weekend: round £30.00; day £30.00. Handicap certificate required.

Facilities: Bar: 11am–11pm. Food: Lunch and dinner from 11am–7pm. Bar snacks.

Comments: Long walks ... Variety and challenge in abundance ... Views over the Severn Estuary ... Exhilarating golf with a perfect backdrop.

Farrington Golf Club ★★★

Marsh Lane, Farrington Gurney, BS39 6TS
Nearest main town: Bath

Secretary: Mrs P. M. Thompson Tel: 01761 453440
                                    Fax: 01761 241274
Professional: Mr P. Thompson   Tel: 01761 241787

Playing: Midweek: round £20.00; day £25.00. Weekend: round £30.00; day £36.00.

Facilities: Bar: 11am–11pm. Food: Lunch and dinner from 11am–9pm. Bar snacks.

Comments: Not very pretty but excellent value ... New course catering to every standard of golfer ... 27 holes of undiluted US-style golf ... Unimaginative design on unremarkable piece of land ... Valuable addition for area's golfers.

Isle of Wedmore Golf Club ★★

Lineage, Lascotts Hill, Wedmore, BS28 4QT
Nearest main town: Wedmore

Secretary: Mr A. C. Edwards   Tel: 01934 713649
                                  Fax: 01934 713696
Professional: Mr G. Coombe   Tel: 01934 712452

Playing: Midweek: round £18.00; day £22.00. Weekend: round £22.00; day £25.00.

Facilities: Bar: 11am–11pm. Food: Lunch and dinner from 11am–9pm. Bar snacks.

Comments: Greens were pretty poor on visit ... Natural course ... Views of Cheddar Valley make up for otherwise plain track ... Odd course, the 12th green cut at a 50-degree slope.

Mendip Golf Club ★

Gurney Slade, Bath, BA3 4UT
Nearest main town: Bath

Secretary: Mrs J. P. Howe   Tel: 01749 840570
Fax: 01749 841439
Professional: Mr R. F. Lee   Tel: 01749 841439

Playing: Midweek: round n/a; day £20.00. Weekend: round n/a; day £30.00. Handicap certificate required.

Facilities: Bar: 11am–11pm. Food: Lunch and dinner from 10am–10pm. Bar snacks.

Comments: Lovely springy turf ... Compact course ... Ordinary clubhouse ... Nice course, a little overrated in the area ... Above average condition ... Recommended at a fair price.

Mendip Spring Golf Club ★★★

Honeyhall Lane, Congresbury, BS49 5JT
Nearest main town: Congresbury

Secretary: Mrs L. Lovell   Tel: 01934 852322
Fax: 01934 853021
Professional: Mr J. Blackburn   Tel: 01934 853337

Playing: Midweek: round £22.00; day £29.00. Weekend: round £25.00; day £32.00. Handicap certificate required.

Facilities: Bar: 11am–11pm. Food: Lunch and dinner from 11am–9pm. Bar snacks.

Comments: Pleasant, friendly, well-laid-out course ... Best hole named Kin-el ... Good facilities, food and welcome ... Island green at the 12th ... Imaginative new course kept in good order ... High-class golf facility.

Minehead & West Somerset Golf Club ★★

The Warren, Warren Road, Minehead, TA24 5SJ
Nearest main town: Minehead

Secretary: Mr L. S. Harper   Tel: 01643 702057
Fax: 01643 705095
Professional: Mr I. Read   Tel: 01643 704378

Playing: Midweek: round n/a; day £22.00. Weekend: round n/a; day £25.00. Handicap certificate required.

Facilities: Bar: 11am–11pm. Food: Lunch and dinner from 10am–10pm. Bar snacks.

Comments: Links course set on a shingle spit ... Par-3 finish ... Can get windy ... Average condition ... Very flat and exposed.

Oake Manor Golf Club   ★★★

Taunton, Oake, TA4 1BA
Nearest main town: Taunton

Secretary: Mr R. Gardner   Tel: 01823 461993
                                       Fax: 01823 461995
Professional: Mr R. Gardner   Tel: 01823 461993

Playing: Midweek: round £16.50; day £20.00. Weekend: round £20.00; day £25.00.

Facilities: Bar: 11am–11pm. Food: Lunch and dinner from 11am–10pm. Bar snacks.

Comments: Perfect parkland course at a bargain price ... Great condition for fairly new course ... Plenty of water hazards ... Flat course but difficult ... Great fun ... One of some high quality new courses in Somerset ... Surrounding countryside makes this course.

Orchardleigh Golf Club   ★★★

Frome, Somerset, BA11 2PH
Nearest main town: Frome

Secretary: Mr J. Willder   Tel: 01373 454200
                                       Fax: 01373 454202
Professional: Mr P. Green   Tel: 01373 454200

Playing: Midweek: round £30.00; day £35.00. Weekend: round £40.00; day n/a. Handicap certificate required.

Facilities: Bar: 11am–11pm. Food: Lunch and dinner from 11am–9pm. Bar snacks.

Comments: Been there every season and course always in good condition ... Superb new course in established parkland ... Feels as if it has been around for a long time ... Hats off to Brian Huggett for a fine design ... Another quality course in the West Country.

Weston-super-Mare Golf Club   ★★

Uphill Road North, Weston-super-Mare, BS23 4NQ
Nearest main town: Weston-super-Mare

Secretary: Mr J. Keight   Tel: 01934 626968
Fax: 01934 626968
Professional: Mr M. La Band   Tel: 01934 633360

Playing: Midweek: round n/a; day £24.00. Weekend: round n/a; day £35.00. Handicap certificate required.

Facilities: Bar: 11am–11pm. Food: Lunch and dinner from 11am–10pm. Bar snacks.

Comments: Great opening hole right next to the beach ... Historic course that's part of the town ... Great condition ... Fine test ... So hard on the first try ... Never stop loving it.

Windwhistle Golf Club   ★

Chard, Cricket St Thomas, TA20 4DG
Nearest main town: Chard

Secretary: Mr I. N. Dodd   Tel: 01460 30231
Fax: 01460 30055
Professional: Mr D. Driver

Playing: Midweek: round £14.00; day £16.00. Weekend: round £18.00; day £20.00.

Facilities: Bar: 11am–11pm. Food: Lunch and dinner from 10am–9pm. Bar snacks.

Comments: Relatively new course still establishing itself ... Great views at this course in the clouds ... Respected country club with eccentric course.

Yeovil Golf Club   ★★★

Sherborne Road, Yeovil, BA21 5BW
Nearest main town: Yeovil

Secretary:	Mr R. Wilmott	Tel: 01935 422965
		Fax: 01935 411283
Professional:	Mr G. Kite	Tel: 01935 473763

Playing: Midweek: round £25.00; day £30.00. Weekend: round £30.00; day n/a. Handicap certificate required.

Facilities: Bar: 11am–11pm. Food: Lunch from 11am–4pm. Dinner by arrangement.

Comments: Mature, interesting course ... Attractive layout ... Not too punishing ... Best holes on the back nine ... Good value for condition of course ... Variable catering.

Staffordshire

Beau Desert Golf Club ★★★★

Hazel Slade, Cannock, WS12 5PJ
Nearest main town: Cannock

There were no trees at Beau Desert until the 1950s. The Forestry Commission, who planted them, did such a good job that now this heathland course is overrun with them. It makes for a wonderful forest setting, where you will enjoy a memorable golfing day out.

The course was initially the property of the Marquess of Anglesey but just after the First World War he sold it to a group of members and 1921 is now considered the birth date of the club. It was a favourite course for the affluent of the day, including Edward VIII, who played regularly there, as the numerous pictures in the clubhouse testify.

Beau Desert is very tight off the tee with heather and gorse framing the fairways. Approach shots are played to large, undulating greens, indeed the 18th green, when it is cut to its fullest extent, is reputed to be the largest in the country. It's very tough, and when the Open qualifying rounds have been held here only a handful will break the standard scratch score of 71.

You can be in trouble almost before you have started at Beau Desert as the opening tee shot is played over a pit 100 yards wide – if you don't clear it you are staring at a double bogey. Even the second shot is tough, a difficult-to-judge short iron played uphill to a blind green. Another hole to watch for is the 7th, a par-3 played across a valley to a smallish green.

There is a superb variety of holes at Beau Desert and, unusually, there is no water on the course. It feels very isolated at times in the tunnel of trees, but it allows you to concentrate on your game and learn the nuances of this course.

Secretary:	Mr A. J. R. Fairfield	Tel: 01543 422626
		Fax: 01543 451137
Professional:	Mr B. Stevens	Tel: 01543 422492
Playing:	Midweek: round n/a; day £35.00. Weekend: round n/a; day £45.00. Handicap certificate required.	
Facilities:	Bar: 8am–11pm. Food: Breakfast, lunch and dinner from 8am–9pm.	

Comments: A hidden gem for the average player ... Heathland cut into pine forest ... Little gem in the Midlands ... Real test of golf ... Long carries off many tees and punishing rough ... A Herbert Fowler gem, always making you think ... Wicked heather, fascinating greens and lovely situation ... Every hole a pleasure ... What a charming course with great conditions throughout.

Branston Golf & Country Club ★★★

Burton Road, Branston, Burton-on-Trent, DE14 2DP
Nearest main town: Burton

Secretary:	Mr G. Pyle	Tel: 01283 512211
		Fax: 01283 566984
Professional:	Mr S. Stiff	Tel: 01283 512211

Playing: Midweek: round £27.00; day £37.00. Weekend: round £37.00; day n/a. Handicap certificate required.

Facilities: Bar: 11am–11pm. Food: Breakfast, lunch and dinner from 7am–10pm.

Comments: Testing course that requires accurate irons ... A lot of golf clubs could learn from this one ... Flat course with natural water hazards ... Water torture ... Next to the River Trent.

Brocton Hall Golf Club ★★★

Brocton, Stafford, ST17 0TH
Nearest main town: Stafford

Secretary:	Mr W. Lanyon	Tel: 01785 661901
		Fax: 01785 661591
Professional:	Mr R. Johnson	Tel: 01785 661485

Playing: Midweek: round n/a; day £30.00. Weekend: round n/a; day £35.00.

Facilities: Bar: 11am–11pm. Food: Lunch and dinner from 11am–11pm. Bar snacks.

Comments: Parkland course, kept in fine condition ... Greens consistently good for this type of course ... Will go back ... Not well known but excellent value.

Druids Heath Golf Club   ★★

Stonnall Road, Aldridge, WS9 8JZ
Nearest main town: Sutton Coldfield

Secretary:	Mr D. Woodhall	Tel: 01922 455595
Professional:	Mr G. Williams	Tel: 01922 459523

Playing: Midweek: round £25.00; day £25.00. Weekend: round £32.00; day £32.00. Handicap certificate required.

Facilities: Bar: 11am–11pm. Food: Lunch and dinner from 11am–3pm. Bar snacks.

Comments: Nice course but very pretentious clubhouse ... A bit unwelcoming and too many rules ... Wonderful example of how a new course can be transformed ... Heathland course.

Enville Golf Club (Highgate)   ★★★

Highgate Common, Enville, Stourbridge, DY7 5BN
Nearest main town: Stourbridge

Secretary:	Mr R. J. Bannister	Tel: 01384 872074
		Fax: 01384 873396
Professional:	Mr S. Power	Tel: 01384 872585

Playing: Midweek: round £28.00; day £38.00. Weekend: round n/a; day n/a. Handicap certificate required.

Facilities: Bar: 11am–7.30pm. Food: Lunch and dinner from 11am–7.30pm. Bar snacks.

Comments: Excellent greens and fairways surrounded by heather and trees ... Flat moorland course ... Far superior to the Lodge ... Overpriced.

Enville Golf Club (Lodge)   ★★★

Highgate Common, Enville, Stourbridge, DY7 5BN
Nearest main town: Stourbridge

Secretary:	Mr R. J. Bannister	Tel: 01384 872074
		Fax: 01384 873396
Professional:	Mr S. Power	Tel: 01384 872585

Playing: Midweek: round £28.00; day £38.00. Weekend: round n/a; day n/a. Handicap certificate required.

Facilities: Bar: 11am–7.30pm. Food: Lunch and dinner from 11am–7.30pm. Bar snacks.

Comments: Not far behind the Highgate course ... Similar style to the main course ... Emphasis on accuracy ... Nicely balanced.

Leek Golf Club ★★

Big Birchall, Leek, ST13 5RE
Nearest main town: Leek

Secretary: Mr F. Cutts   Tel: 01538 384779
                              Fax: 01538 384535
Professional: Mr P. Stubbs   Tel: 01538 384767

Playing: Midweek: round £24.00; day £24.00. Weekend: round £30.00; day £30.00. Handicap certificate required.

Facilities: Bar: 11am–11pm. Food: Bar snacks. Dinner by arrangement.

Comments: Excellent condition ... Very challenging ... Always enjoy it here ... One for the notebook if you're around.

Patshull Park Hotel Golf & Country Club ★★

Pattingham, Wolverhampton, WV6 7HR
Nearest main town: Wolverhampton

Secretary: Mr K. Roberts   Tel: 01902 700100
                              Fax: 01902 700874
Professional: Mr R. Bissell   Tel: 01902 700342
                              Fax: 01902 700874

Playing: Midweek: round £22.50; day £40.00. Weekend: round £27.50; day £45.00. Handicap certificate required.

Facilities: Bar: 11am–11pm. Food: Breakfast, lunch and dinner from 7am–10pm. Bar snacks.

Comments: A natural course in tune with the landscape ... Very expensive for what you get ... Not in the same league as other Jacobs designs ... Good facilities.

Sandwell Park Golf Club ★★

Birmingham Road, West Bromwich, B71 4JJ
Nearest main town: West Bromwich

Secretary:	Mr D. A. Paterson	Tel: 0121 553 4637
		Fax: 0121 525 1651
Professional:	Mr N. Wylie	Tel: 0121 553 4384

Playing: Midweek: round £30.00; day £35.00. Weekend: round n/a; day n/a. Handicap certificate required.

Facilities: Bar: 11am–11pm. Food: Lunch from 11am–9pm. Bar snacks.

Comments: Tight tree-lined course with fast greens the norm ... Heathland course in the Sandwell Valley ... Excellent value course – an oasis in a concrete jungle.

Seedy Mill Golf Club ★★

Elmhurst, Lichfield, WS13 3HE
Nearest main town: Lichfield

Secretary:	Mr J. Martin	Tel: 01543 417333
		Fax: 01543 418098
Professional:	Mr R. O'Hanlon	Tel: 01543 417333

Playing: Midweek: round £19.00; day £28.00. Weekend: round £24.00; day £28.00.

Facilities: Bar: 11am–11pm. Food: Bar snacks.

Comments: Simple course protected by heavy rough ... Greens not always in best shape ... New course with lakes, sculpted bunkers and excessive contouring ... Rolling parkland.

Trentham Park Golf Club ★

Trentham Park, Stoke-on-Trent, ST4 8AE
Nearest main town: Newcastle-under-Lyme

Secretary:	Mr T. Beresford	Tel: 01782 658800
		Fax: 01782 658800
Professional:	Mr B. Rimmer	Tel: 01782 642125

Playing: Midweek: round £22.50; day £25.00. Weekend: round n/a; day £30.00. Handicap certificate required.

Facilities: Bar: 11am–11pm. Food: Lunch and dinner from 11am–9pm, except Mondays.

Comments: Woodland course that constantly surprises ... Condition not all it should be ... Very helpful pro and staff.

Westwood Golf Club (Leek)   ★★

Newcastle Road, Wallbridge, ST13 7AA
Nearest main town: Leek

Secretary: Mr C. Plant   Tel: 01538 398385
                                             Fax: 01538 382485
Professional: Mr N. Hyde   Tel: 01538 398897

Playing: Midweek: round £18.00; day £25.00. Weekend: round £20.00; day n/a.

Facilities: Bar: 11am–11pm. Food: Lunch and dinner from 11am–9pm. Bar snacks.

Comments: A great welcome and interesting course ... Moorland course, nice and natural ... Value price for above average course.

Whittington Heath Golf Club   ★★★

Tamworth Road, Lichfield, WS14 9PW
Nearest main town: Lichfield

Secretary: Mrs J. A. Burton   Tel: 01543 432317
                                             Fax: 01543 432317
Professional: Mr A. R. Sadler   Tel: 01543 432261

Playing: Midweek: round £24.00; day £32.00. Weekend: round n/a; day n/a. Handicap certificate required.

Facilities: Bar: 11am–9pm. Food: Breakfast, lunch and dinner from 8am–9pm. Bar snacks.

Comments: Heathland in woods ... Difficult well-guarded greens make up for lack of length ... Course in good nick and company excellent ... Peaceful, calm course ... Great doglegs ... Views of Lichfield Cathedral.

Suffolk

Royal Worlington & Newmarket Golf Club ★★★★

Golf Links Road, Worlington, Bury St Edmunds, IP28 8SD
Nearest main town: Newmarket

Nine-hole courses are traditionally regarded with a certain amount of suspicion by golfers, who rather blithely dismiss them as 'fun' courses, lacking sufficient variety and length to prove a discernible challenge. Players who visit Royal Worlington generally have these illusions shattered by what is a very challenging and picturesque course, and almost certainly one of the best nine-hole courses in the world.

Suffolk is blessed with an excellent variety of courses, including the fiendishly difficult Aldeburgh, Purdis Heath, Woodbridge and Thorpeness, which prove excellent for holiday golfers to this quiet corner of England. Royal Worlington is situated some way away in the racing town of Newmarket, but is well worth the trip, particularly if you take in Gog Magog, a course that is situated on the southern side of the university town of Cambridge.

Royal Worlington, inaugurated in 1890, has a very linksy feel for an inland course, an impression which can in someway be put down to the rather haphazard arrangement of holes, with a couple of par-3s crossing fairways, and drives almost being played straight over greens. This calls for a certain amount of courtesy to fellow players and a great deal of concentration to cope with the unusual layout. The links feel is also on account of the sandy soil which provides excellent drainage.

The best holes come from halfway with the 5th a stunning, bunkerless short hole, where an overlong shot is punished by the trees behind the green. The 7th is another fine par-3, with a classic saucer green leaving only the top of the pin visible from the tee.

It is hard not to come away from here being impressed, and the plaudits heaped upon the course, particularly by journalists who have been known to get it wrong, in this case are completely justified.

Secretary: Maj G. W. M. Hipkin Tel: 01638 717787
Fax: 01638 717787
Professional: Mr M. Hawkins Tel: 01638 715224

Playing: Midweek: round n/a; day £35.00. Weekend: round n/a; day n/a. Handicap certificate required.

Facilities: Bar: 11am–11pm. Food: Lunch from 12pm–2.30pm. Bar snacks.

Comments: How did they design such a great nine holes in a large field? ... A real treat and will return soon ... The best nine hole course in the world? ... Wonderfully traditional ... Who needs 18 when you've got nine of this quality? ... Will be back ... Stunning short course.

Aldeburgh Golf Club   ★★★★

Aldeburgh, IP15 5PE
Nearest main town: Aldeburgh

Secretary: Mr I. M. Simpson   Tel: 01728 452890
Fax: 01728 452937
Professional: Mr K. Preston   Tel: 01728 453309

Playing: Midweek: round n/a; day £35.00. Weekend: round n/a; day £42.00. Handicap certificate required.

Facilities: Bar: 11am–11pm. Food: Lunch from 11am–4pm.

Comments: A hard course to play to your handicap ... Terrific collection of par-4s, bunkers and gorse ... Tight and difficult ... Hard-running at times ... Real tough cookie ... Standard scratch says it all.

Brett Vale Golf Club

Noakes Road, Raydon, Ipswich, IP7 5LR
Nearest main town: Ipswich

Secretary: Mr D. Reid   Tel: 01473 310718
Fax: 01473 824482
Professional: Mr R. Taylor   Tel: 01473 310718

Playing: Midweek: round £15.00; day £25.00. Weekend: round £20.00; day £30.00.

Facilities: Bar: 11am–11pm. Food: Bar snacks.

Comments: Well-fashioned course that runs through a nature reserve ... A course completely in tune with the surroundings ... Condition generally good ... Will always have affection for this place.

Bury St Edmunds Golf Club ★★★

Tut Hill, Bury St Edmunds, IP28 6LG
Nearest main town: Bury St Edmunds

Secretary:	Mr J. C. Sayer	Tel: 01284 755979
		Fax: 01284 763288
Professional:	Mr M. Jillings	Tel: 01284 755978

Playing: Midweek: round £24.00; day £26.00. Weekend: round n/a; day n/a.

Facilities: Bar: 11am–11pm. Food: Bar snacks. Dinner by arrangement.

Comments: Welcoming members' course ... Parkland with a few twists along the way ... Heartily recommended ... Another quality Suffolk course.

Felixstowe Ferry Golf Club ★★★

Ferry Road, Felixstowe, IP4 9RY
Nearest main town: Felixstowe

Secretary:	Mr R. H. Owens	Tel: 01394 286834
Professional:	Mr I. Macpherson	Tel: 01394 283975

Playing: Midweek: round n/a; day £22.00. Weekend: round n/a; day n/a. Handicap certificate required.

Facilities: Bar: 11am–11pm. Food: Bar snacks.

Comments: Links for the purist ... Bleak but warming landscape ... Feels very fresh and exciting here ... Very unusual course for Suffolk ... Plays like a dream.

Hintlesham Hall Golf Club ★

Hintlesham, Suffolk, IP8 3NS
Nearest main town: Ipswich

Secretary:	Mr I. Procter	Tel: 01473 652761
		Fax: 01473 652700
Professional:	Mr A. Spink	Tel: 01473 652761

Playing: Midweek: round £27.00; day £47.00. Weekend: round £27.00; day £47.00. Handicap certificate required.

Facilities: Bar: 11am–11pm. Food: Lunch and dinner from 11am–9pm. Bar snacks.

Comments: Mature parkland course in grounds of sumptuous hotel ... Very regal atmosphere ... Quality through and through ... Very established and inviting.

Ipswich Golf Club (Purdis Heath)   ★★★

Purdis Heath, Bucklesham Road, Ipswich, IP3 8UQ
Nearest main town: Ipswich

Secretary: Mr R. A. J. Rayner   Tel: 01473 728941
                                       Fax: 01473 715236
Professional: Mr S. J. Whymark   Tel: 01473 724017

Playing: Midweek: round £25.00; day £35.00. Weekend: round £28.00; day £38.00. Handicap certificate required.

Facilities: Bar: 11am–11pm. Food: Breakfast, lunch and dinner from 8am–7pm. Bar snacks.

Comments: A hidden gem in Suffolk ... Heathland beauty, well worth the visit ... Nothing else like it in Suffolk ... As good as it gets.

Rushmere Golf Club   ★★★

Rushmere Heath, Ipswich, IP4 5QQ
Nearest main town: Ipswich

Secretary: Mr P. L. Coles   Tel: 01473 725648
                                       Fax: 01473 725648
Professional: Mr N. T. J. McNeill Tel: 01473 728076

Playing: Midweek: round £20.00; day £20.00. Weekend: round £20.00; day £20.00. Handicap certificate required.

Facilities: Bar: 11am–11pm. Food: Lunch from 12pm–2.30pm. Bar snacks. Dinner by arrangment.

Comments: Rather ragged heathland course ... At the mercy of the wind ... Watch out you don't get blown away.

Seckford Golf Club   ★★★

Seckford Hall Road, Great Bealings, Woodbridge, IP13 6NT
Nearest main town: Woodbridge

Secretary:	Mr J. Skinner	Tel: 01394 388000
		Fax: 01394 382818
Professional:	Mr J. Skinner	Tel: 01394 388000

Playing: Midweek: round £15.00; day £18.00. Weekend: round £17.50; day £20.00.

Facilities: Bar: 11am–11pm. Food: Lunch and dinner from 11am–8pm. Bar snacks.

Comments: Short course but not without charm ... Keeps getting better ... Riveting stretch of finishing holes ... A little open ... Too easy.

The Suffolk Golf & Country Club   ★★★

St John's Plantation, The Street, Bury St Edmunds, IP28 6JS
Nearest main town: Bury St Edmunds

Secretary:	Mr I. Dalyrimple	Tel: 01284 706777
		Fax: 01284 706721
Professional:	Mr S. Hall	Tel: 01284 706777

Playing: Midweek: round £20.00; day n/a. Weekend: round £25.00; day n/a.

Facilities: Bar: 11am–11pm. Food: Breakfast, lunch and dinner from 7am–9pm. Bar snacks.

Comments: A country club course that's very boring ... Flat and rather dull ... Condition good ... Smattering of water hazards ... Tough for beginners.

Thorpeness Golf Club & Hotel   ★★★★

Thorpeness, Leiston, IP16 4NH
Nearest main town: Aldeburgh

Secretary:	Mr N. W. Griffin	Tel: 01728 452176
		Fax: 01728 453868
Professional:	Mr F. Hill	Tel: 01728 454926

Playing: Midweek: round n/a; day £25.00. Weekend: round n/a; day £30.00. Handicap certificate required.

Facilities: Bar: 11am–11pm. Food: Breakfast, lunch and dinner from 7am–10pm. Bar snacks.

Comments: This course has it all – especially gorse ... Takes golf to the next level ... Excellent society venue and good value for money ... Tough, interesting track with super practice facilities and catering ... James Braid design of classic brilliance.

Ufford Park Hotel Golf Club ★★

Yarmouth Road, Ufford, IP12 1QW
Nearest main town: Woodbridge

Secretary:	Mr B. Tidy	Tel: 01394 382836
		Fax: 01394 383582
Professional:	Mr S. Robertson	Tel: 01394 382836

Playing: Midweek: round £16.00; day £24.00. Weekend: round £20.00; day £30.00.

Facilities: Bar: 11am–11pm. Food: Breakfast, lunch and dinner from 7am–10pm. Bar snacks.

Comments: Recent irrigation improved greens no end ... Natural parkland track making good use of unremarkable land ... Leisure complex more than a golf club ... Facility for beginners.

Woodbridge Golf Club ★★★

Bromeswell Heath, Woodbridge, IP12 2PF
Nearest main town: Woodbridge

Secretary:	Capt. L. A. Harpum RN	Tel: 01394 382038
		Fax: 01394 382392
Professional:	Mr A. Hubbert	Tel: 01394 383213

Playing: Midweek: round £20.00; day £30.00. Weekend: round n/a; day n/a. Handicap certificate required.

Facilities: Bar: 11am–11pm. Food: Breakfast, lunch and dinner from 9am–9pm. Bar snacks.

Comments: Old fashioned atmosphere ... One of the best courses in East Anglia ... Heavenly place on high ground ... At its best in the autumn ... A magical place – the best in Suffolk.

Surrey

St George's Hill Golf Club

Golf Club Road, St George's Hill, Weybridge, KT13 ONL
Nearest main town: Weybridge

Shots rang out through the trees on St George's Hill long before any golfers were set loose on the land. The sounds would emanate from the pond that is now flanked by the 9th fairway. Dead man's pond to be exact, for it was here that the last duel to be fought on British soil is believed to have taken place.

Today the only shots to be heard echoing through the trees are those from golfers as they plot their way round one of the most scenically beautiful courses that the heathlands of Surrey have to offer. St George's Hill, near Weybridge, has long been regarded in high esteem and is, frankly, a gem.

The estate of St George's Hill exudes exclusivity. The fairways roll past properties that sit amid meticulously mown lawns, but that was the way it was always meant to be when a local builder, a Mr Tarrant, acquired the land, in the 1900s. He engaged Harry Colt to design the course, but due to a shortage of funds, he sold the site to concentrate on another course sited at Virginia Water, which came to be known as Wentworth.

While many of Surrey's heath and heather courses appear to be clones of each other, St George's Hill stands apart. There is the profusion of heather and gorse that you would expect from a course in this part of the country, but unlike its neighbours, St George's Hill is played over very undulating, spectacular terrain, making for exhilarating golf with deep drops and blind drives. There are no weak holes here. From the 1st, where you drive over a valley, it's one classic after another.

The beauty of St George's Hill goes unchallenged. As Bernard Darwin once wrote: 'The prettiest courses are also the best and certainly one of the best is St George's Hill.'

Secretary:	Mr J. Robinson	Tel: 01932 847758
		Fax: 01932 821564
Professional:	Mr A. C. Rattue	Tel: 01932 843523
Playing:	Midweek: round £60.00; day £70.00. Weekend: round n/a; day n/a. Handicap certificate required.	

Facilities:	Bar: 11am–11pm. Food: Lunch from 11am–3pm. Bar snacks. Dinner by arrangement.
Comments:	Wonderful tall pines ... Tee shots very intimidating ... A match for any course in the country ... Better than Wentworth and without the attitude ... Grandeur nested in beauty ... Very old, very traditional, but welcoming ... Wooded course with spilling heather.

Burhill Golf Club   ★★★

Burwood Road, Walton-on-Thames, KT12 4BL
Nearest main town: Walton-on-Thames

Secretary:	Mr G. Hogg	Tel: 01932 227345
		Fax: 01932 267159
Professional:	Mr L. Johnson	Tel: 01932 221729
Playing:	Midweek: round £32.00; day £45.00. Weekend: round n/a; day n/a. Handicap certificate required.	
Facilities:	Bar: 11am–11pm. Food: Lunch from 11.30am–2.30pm. Bar snacks.	
Comments:	Lots of long par-4s and a great clubhouse ... Never known it in anything but immaculate condition ... True greens ... Welcoming clubhouse ... One of the friendlier clubs in Surrey ... Short and difficult ... Give me the keys to this place!	

Camberley Heath Golf Club   ★★★

Golf Drive, Camberley, GU15 1JG
Nearest main town: Camberley

Secretary:	Mr J. Greenwood	Tel: 01276 23258
		Fax: 01276 692505
Professional:	Mr G. Ralph	Tel: 01276 27905
Playing:	Midweek: round £36.00; day £56.00. Weekend: round n/a; day n/a. Handicap certificate required.	
Facilities:	Bar: 11am–9pm. Food: Bar snacks.	
Comments:	Good quality of service ... Odd course with tight fairways and a lot of heather ... Heath and heather – what a treat ... One of Harry Colt's best ... A delight ... Typical Surrey course – heather and gorse spilling everywhere.	

Coombe Hill Golf Club ★★★

Golf Club Drive, Coome Lane West, Kingston, KT2 7DF
Nearest main town: New Maldon

Secretary: Mrs C. De Foy   Tel: 0181 942 2284
                                    Fax: 0181 336 7601
Professional: Mr C. De Foy   Tel: 0181 949 3713

Playing: Midweek: round £65.00; day £65.00. Weekend: round n/a; day n/a. Handicap certificate required.

Facilities: Bar: 11am–11pm. Food: Lunch from 11am–6pm. Bar snacks.

Comments: Conditioning always top class ... Far too pricey ... Charming course but not at that price ... At best during spring and early summer.

Drift Golf Club ★★★

The Drift, East Horsley, KT24 5HD
Nearest main town: East Horsley

Secretary: Mr D. Rutter   Tel: 01483 284641
                                    Fax: 01483 284642
Professional: Mr P. Fuller   Tel: 01483 284772

Playing: Midweek: round £25.00; day £45.00. Weekend: round n/a; day n/a.

Facilities: Bar: 11am–11pm. Food: Lunch from 11.30am–2.30pm. Bar snacks.

Comments: Tight, tree-lined course with very fast greens ... Long woodland course ... Par-73 and feels it ... Get away from it all here ... A great place to contemplate.

Duke's Dene Golf Club ★★

Slines New Road, Woldingham, CR3 7HA
Nearest main town: Woldingham

Secretary: Mr T. Del Sol   Tel: 01883 653501
                                     Fax: 01883 653502
Professional: Mr P. Thornley   Tel: 01883 653541

Playing: Midweek: round £25.00; day £45.00. Weekend: round £30.00; day n/a.

Facilities: Bar: 11am–11pm. Food: Bar snacks. Sunday lunch only.

Comments: Great layout with some difficult holes ... Excellent clubhouse and food ... Valley course ... A little bit different to normal Surrey fare ... Food excellent ... A pleasure to play.

Effingham Golf Club ★★★

Effingham Crossroads, Effingham, KT24 5PZ
Nearest main town: Guildford

Secretary:	Mr R. W. Lamb	Tel: 01372 452203
		Fax: 01372 459959
Professional:	Mr S. Hoatson	Tel: 01372 452606

Playing: Midweek: round £28.50; day £35.00. Weekend: round n/a; day n/a. Handicap certificate required.

Facilities: Bar: 11am–11pm. Food: Lunch from 11.30am–2.30pm. Bar snacks.

Comments: A treat to play ... Well presented all year round ... Exhausting long course ... Downland track ... A warm reception at this mature club.

Epsom Golf Club ★★

Longdown Lane South, Epsom, KT17 4JR
Nearest main town: Epsom

Secretary:	Mr J. H. Carter	Tel: 01372 721666
		Fax: 01372 817183
Professional:	Mr R. Goudie	Tel: 01372 741867

Playing: Midweek: round £20.00; day £30.00. Weekend: round £20.00; day n/a.

Facilities: Bar: 11am–11pm. Food: Bar snacks.

Comments: A short course with quality holes on the back nine ... Right next to the racecourse ... Consistently good greens throughout the year ... Undulating turf ... Something about the grandstands that makes this course special.

Farnham Golf Club ★★

The Sands, Farnham, GU10 1PX
Nearest main town: Farnham

Secretary: Mrs J. Brazill   Tel: 01252 782109
                                       Fax: 01252 781185
Professional: Mr G. Cowlishaw   Tel: 01252 782198

Playing: Midweek: round £30.00; day £37.50. Weekend: round
n/a; day n/a. Handicap certificate required.

Facilities: Bar: 11am–11pm. Food: Bar snacks.

Comments: Good front nine, full of character ... Worth a look ...
Opening nine far superior ... Longish course worth
playing once or twice ... Enjoyed every minute.

Foxhills Golf Club ★★★★

Stonehill Road, Ottershaw, KT16 OEL
Nearest main town: Chertsey

Secretary: Mr A. Laking   Tel: 01932 872050
                                       Fax: 01932 874762
Professional: Mr A. Good   Tel: 01932 873961
                                       Fax: 01932 872913

Playing: Midweek: round £50.00; day £70.00. Weekend: round
£65.00; day n/a.

Facilities: Bar: 11am–11pm. Food: Lunch from 11am–3pm.
Dinner from 7pm–9.30pm. Bar snacks.

Comments: Tree-lined treasure ... Excellent golf club ... Courses
both have distinctive character ... Chertsey almost
unanimously preferred to the Longcross.

Gatton Manor Hotel Golf & Country Club ★★

Standon Lane, Ockley, RH5 5PQ
Nearest main town: Dorking

Secretary: Mrs L. C. Heath   Tel: 01306 627555
                                       Fax: 01306 627713
Professional: Mr R. Sargent   Tel: 01306 627557
                                       Fax: 01306 627752

Playing: Midweek: round £21.00; day £38.00. Weekend: round £28.00; day n/a.

Facilities: Bar: 11am–11pm. Food: Lunch and dinner from 11am–10pm. Bar snacks.

Comments: Sprawling country-club course ... Standard country-club fare ... A little soulless ... Water hazards will test your nerves.

Guildford Golf Club   ★★★

High Path Road, Merrow, Guildford, GU1 2HL
Nearest main town: Guildford

Secretary: Mr B. J. Green   Tel: 01483 563941
                                          Fax: 01483 453228
Professional: Mr P. G. Hollington   Tel: 01483 566765

Playing: Midweek: round £25.00; day £35.00. Weekend: round n/a; day n/a.

Facilities: Bar: 11am–11pm. Food: Lunch and dinner from 11am–9pm. Bar snacks.

Comments: Unusual course but pleasant ... Excellent greens ... Setting ensures all-year-round play ... Clear away the cobwebs on this invigorating course ... One for the notebook ... Easily missed but you will regret it.

Hankley Common Golf Club   ★★★★★

Tiford, Farnham, GU10 2DD
Nearest main town: Farnham

Secretary: Mr F. Scott   Tel: 01252 792493
                                          Fax: 01252 795699
Professional: Mr P. Stow   Tel: 01252 793761

Playing: Midweek: round £42.00; day £55.00. Weekend: round £55.00; day n/a. Handicap certificate required.

Facilities: Bar: 11am–11pm. Food: Lunch from 11.20am–3pm. Bar snacks. Dinner by arrangement.

Comments: Excellent course – better than Sunningdale ... Superb greens ... Unexpected links character in places ... Greens first class ... Many memorable holes on this heathland masterpiece ... Give me this anyday ... Highly rated course that matches its billing ... Oh, to live in Surrey.

Hindhead Golf Club   ★★★★

Churt Road, Hindhead, GU26 6HX
Nearest main town: Hindhead

Secretary:	Mr P. Owen	Tel: 01428 604614
		Fax: 01428 608508
Professional:	Mr N. Ogilvy	Tel: 01428 604458

Playing: Midweek: round £32.00; day £43.00. Weekend: round £42.00; day £53.00. Handicap certificate required.

Facilities: Bar: 11am–11pm. Food: Bar snacks.

Comments: Elevated tees looking down on heather – magnificent ... Made very welcome ... Visually preferred the first nine in the valley ... Great view from the bar onto the 18th ... Two different nines but heath and heather all the way ... Take this any day over links golf ... One of the best in Surrey.

Merrist Wood Golf Club   ★★★

Coombe Lane, Worplesdon, Guildford, GU3 3PE
Nearest main town: Worplesdon

Secretary:	Mr R. Penley-Martin	Tel: 01483 884045
		Fax: 01483 884045
Professional:	Mr A. Kirk	Tel: 01483 884050

Playing: Midweek: round £35.00; day n/a. Weekend: round £50.00; day n/a.

Facilities: Bar: 11am–11pm. Food: Breakfast, lunch and dinner from 10am–10pm.

Comments: Course, pro shop, welcome and food all very good ...
Good day's golf ... Unusual Surrey course with little
heather ... Relaxed atmosphere at this private members'
club ... Good fun, if a little open ... Rather play nearby
Worplesdon and Woking ... As if Surrey needed another
course.

New Zealand Golf Club ★★★

Woodham Lane, Addlestone, KT15 3QD
Nearest main town: Woking

Secretary:	Mr R. Merrett	Tel: 01932 342891
		Fax: 01932 342891
Professional:	Mr V. Elvidge	Tel: 01932 349619

Playing: Midweek: round £45.00; day £48.00. Weekend: round
n/a; day n/a.

Facilities: Bar: 11am–7pm. Food: Lunch from 12pm–2.30pm. Bar
snacks.

Comments: Never have a bad time here ... Riveting course ...
Heathland with bags of style ... Up there with the best.

Pyrford Golf Club ★★★

Warren Lane, Pyrford, GU22 8XR
Nearest main town: Ripley

Secretary:	Mr N. Sharratt	Tel: 01483 723555
		Fax: 01483 729777
Professional:	Mr J. Bennett	Tel: 01483 751070

Playing: Midweek: round £38.00; day £50.00. Weekend: round
£52.00; day n/a.

Facilities: Bar: 11am–11pm. Food: Bar snacks.

Comments: Don't count your chickens until you've played the final
two holes – tough ... Nice attempt to recreate links feel
in middle of Surrey ... 25 acres of water ... Try the
Pyrford experience ... Water fun that you will remember.

Reigate Heath Golf Club ★★

The Club House, Reigate Heath, RH2 8QR
Nearest main town: Reigate

Secretary:	Mr R. J. Perkins	Tel: 01737 226793
		Fax: 01737 226793
Professional:	Mr B. Davies	Tel: 01737 226793

Playing: Midweek: round n/a; day £20.00. Weekend: round n/a; day n/a. Handicap certificate required.

Facilities: Bar: 11am–11pm. Food: Lunch from 11.30am–2.30pm. Bar snacks.

Comments: The best nine hole course in Surrey ... Real heath and heather course of charm ... Not the best condition but good fun ... Members very proud of their course ... Pine and birch trees the backdrop for shots.

Reigate Hill Golf Club ★

Gatton Bottom, Reigate, RH2 0TU
Nearest main town: Reigate

Secretary:	Mr A. P. Barclay	Tel: 01737 645577
		Fax: 01737 642650
Professional:	Mr M. Platt	Tel: 01737 646070

Playing: Midweek: round £25.00; day £35.00. Weekend: round £35.00; day n/a.

Facilities: Bar: 11am–11pm. Food: Lunch from 11am–6pm. Bar snacks.

Comments: A golf centre devoid of character ... Opened four years ago but not fully mature ... Some exciting holes ... A little tedious on the back nine ... A cheap alternative to the overpriced courses in Surrey.

Richmond Golf Club ★

Sudbrook Park, Richmond, London, SW15 5JR
Nearest main town: Richmond

Secretary:	Mr R. L. Wilkins	Tel: 0181 940 4351
		Fax: 0181 332 7914
Professional:	Mr N. Job	Tel: 0181 940 7792

Playing: Midweek: round £27.00; day £45.00. Weekend: round n/a; day n/a. Handicap certificate required.

Facilities: Bar: 11am–11pm. Food: Lunch from 12pm–2.30pm. Bar snacks.

Comments: Lovely Georgian clubhouse ... Great collection of six par-3s ... One to treasure ... You need a strategy ... Par-3s are course's trademark.

Richmond Park Golf Club   ★

Roehampton Gate, London, SW15 5JR
Nearest main town: London

Secretary: Mr A. J. Gourvish   Tel: 0181 876 3205
                                      Fax: 0181 878 1354
Professional: Mr D. Brown   Tel: 0181 876 3205

Playing: Midweek: round £13.50; day n/a. Weekend: round £16.80; day n/a.

Facilities: Bar: None. Food: None.

Comments: Decent value ... Presentation could be improved ... Well-worn course ... Better than average for the price.

Royal Mid-Surrey Golf Club   ★★★

Old Deer Park, Richmond, TW9 2SB
Nearest main town: Richmond

Secretary: Mr A. J. Perkins   Tel: 0181 940 1894
                                      Fax: 0181 332 2957
Professional: Mr D. Talbot   Tel: 0181 940 0459

Playing: Midweek: round £60.00; day n/a. Weekend: round n/a; day n/a. Handicap certificate required.

Facilities: Bar: 11am–11pm. Food: Lunch from 12pm–2.30pm. Dinner on Thursdays only.

Comments: Was looking forward to it and wasn't disappointed ... One of the best in London ... Bunkers cunningly placed ... Flat course protected by bunkers.

Royal Wimbledon Golf Club   ★★

29 Camp Road, Wimbledon, London, SW19 4UW
Nearest main town: London

Secretary:	Mr N. Smith	Tel: 0181 946 2125
		Fax: 0181 944 8652
Professional:	Mr H. Boyle	Tel: 0181 946 4606

Playing: Prices on application.

Facilities: Bar: Members only. Food: Members only.

Comments: Classic Surrey course with sandy loam soil and heather ... Always in good condition ... How does Surrey have so many great courses? ... Tradition through and through ... Very traditional, a litte staid ... Course that has aged wonderfully.

Selsdon Park Hotel Golf Club   ★★★

Addington Road, Sanderstead, South Croydon, CR2 8YA
Nearest main town: Croydon

Secretary:	Mrs C. Screene	Tel: 0181 657 8811
		Fax: 0181 651 3401
Professional:	Mr M. Churchill	Tel: 0181 6574129

Playing: Midweek: round £22.50; day £40.00. Weekend: round £27.50; day £50.00.

Facilities: Bar: 11am–11pm. Food: Lunch from 12pm–2pm. Dinner from 7pm–10pm.

Comments: A visually attractive course ... Always a pleasure to play ... Parkland with unbelievable facilities ... One of the best welcomes anywhere ... Great welcome to a beginner with no handicap.

Shirley Park Golf Club   ★★

194 Addiscombe Road, Croydon, CR0 7LB
Nearest main town: Croydon

Secretary:	Mr A. Baird	Tel: 0181 654 1143
		Fax: 0181 654 6733
Professional:	Mr P. Webb	Tel: 0181 654 8767

Playing: Midweek: round £25.00; day n/a. Weekend: round n/a; day n/a.

Facilities: Bar: 11am–11pm. Food: Lunch and dinner from 10am–7pm. Bar snacks.

Comments: Very good society course ... Good value ... Felt very welcome ... 7th a cracking par-3 ... Short holes make this ... Can't think of a better day out.

Sunningdale Golf Club (Old)   ★★★★★

Ridgemount Road, Sunningdale, SL5 9RW
Nearest main town: Sunningdale

Secretary:	Mr S. Zuill	Tel: 01344 621681
		Fax: 01344 624154
Professional:	Mr K. Maxwell	Tel: 01344 620128
		Fax: 01344 874903

Playing: Midweek: round £100.00; day £125.00. Weekend: round n/a; day n/a. Handicap certificate required.

Facilities: Bar: 11am–8pm. Food: Lunch and dinner from 10am–6pm.

Comments: Magical heathland course ... What golf is all about ... Requires real thought ... Wonderful course and club ... Lovely course, requiring straight-hitting ... Expensive but just has to be played ... As good as you can get – at a price ... Traditional course – always enjoyable but too expensive ... My choice for the final round of my life ... The blueprint for all courses ... Not bad, but overpriced and surely an easy course ... No better place to play an inland course than at Sunningdale ... Stand on the 10th tee and just take a deep breath – magic.

Sunningdale Golf Club (New)   ★★★★

Ridgemount Road, Sunningdale, SL5 9RW
Nearest main town: Sunningdale

Secretary:	Mr S. Zuill	Tel: 01344 621681
		Fax: 01344 624154
Professional:	Mr K. Maxwell	Tel: 01344 620128
		Fax: 01344 874903

Playing: Midweek: round £75.00; day £125.00. Weekend: round n/a; day n/a. Handicap certificate required.

Facilities: Bar: 11am–8pm. Food: Lunch and dinner from 10am–6pm.

Comments: Simply perfect condition for a traditional golf club ... Has a real championship feel to it now ... Old Course? Give me the New anyday ... Cheaper than the Old in the week and worth the saving.

Tandridge Golf Club   ★★★★

Oxted, Surrey, RH8 9NQ
Nearest main town: Redhill

Secretary: Lt Cdr S. E. Kennard   Tel: 01883 712274
                                        Fax: 01883 730537
Professional: Mr A. Farquhar   Tel: 01883 713701

Playing: Midweek: round £35.00; day £45.00. Weekend: round n/a; day n/a. Handicap certificate required.

Facilities: Bar: 11am–11pm. Food: Snack bar from 11am–3pm. Dinner by arrangement.

Comments: Two distinct halves – very tidy course ... Mature, tight and enjoyable course ... Well established layout ... Harry Colt design ... Underrated course.

The Addington Golf Club   ★★★★

205 Shirley Church Road, Croydon, CRO 5AB
Nearest main town: Croydon

Secretary: Mr J. W. Beale   Tel: 0181 777 1055
Professional: None.

Playing: Midweek: round £35.00; day £35.00. Weekend: round n/a; day n/a. Handicap certificate required.

Facilities: Bar: 11am–11pm. Food: Lunch from 12pm–2.30pm.

Comments: Very good course tucked away in suburbia ... A forgotten gem in London – beautiful ... Some stunning holes, but course lacked condition ... A wonderful course, forgotten by golfers everywhere ... Just the best experience in 10 years of golf – will be back.

The Wentworth Golf Club (West) ★★★★

Wentworth Drive, Virginia Water, GU25 4LS
Nearest main town: Guildford

Secretary:	Mr S. Christie	Tel: 01344 842201
		Fax: 01344 842804
Professional:	Mr D. Rennie	Tel: 01344 846306

Playing: Prices on application. Handicap certificate required.

Facilities: Bar: 11am–11pm. Food: Lunch from 12pm–2.30pm. Dinner from 6pm–9.30pm. Bar snacks.

Comments: Green fees on application ... Course always in excellent condition ... Any serious golfers must play this course ... Exceptional course, well laid out ... Truly a championship course ... Corporate membership has proved exceptional value for money ... Wonderful, peaceful setting ... Front tees can mess up this course and take driver out of your hands ... Not as hard as it looks but still good quality ... For the money, is it really worth it? ... Good condition but what should you expect for the price?

The Wentworth Golf Club (East) ★★★★

Wentworth Drive, Virginia Water, GU25 4LS
Nearest main town: Guildford

Secretary:	Mr S. Christie	Tel: 01344 842201
		Fax: 01344 842804
Professional:	Mr D. Rennie	Tel: 01344 846306

Playing: Prices on application. Handicap certificate required.

Facilities: Bar: 11am–11pm. Food: Lunch from 12pm–2.30pm. Dinner from 6pm–9.30pm. Bar snacks.

Comments: Green fees on application ... Some good, challenging par-4s and par-3s, notably the 2nd, 6th and 7th ... Tough, condition not as good as it should be ... Always in A1 condition ... Good test of golf ... Prefer it to the West – and I'm not alone ... More fun than the West ... A cracking day out ... Was thinking about the West all the time I was playing here.

The Wisley Golf Club   ★★★

Ripley, Surrey, GU23 6QU
Nearest main town: Woking

Secretary:	Mr J. R. Arthur OBE	Tel: 01483 211022
		Fax: 01483 211662
Professional:	Mr W. Reid	Tel: 01483 211213

Playing: Prices on application.

Facilities: Bar: Members only. Food: Members only

Comments: Very impressive – trusting and sophisticated ... Robert Trent Jones Jr design to a high calibre ... Undeniably good course, but who wants to be in the club? ... No-one is missing much here.

Walton Heath Golf Club (Old)   ★★★★★

Deans Lane, Walton-on-the-Thames, Tadworth, KT20 7TP
Nearest main town: Tadworth

Secretary:	Mr N. C. Lomas	Tel: 01737 812380
		Fax: 01737 814225
Professional:	Mr K. Macpherson	Tel: 01737 812152

Playing: Midweek: round £68.00; day n/a. Weekend: round n/a; day n/a. Handicap certificate required.

Facilities: Bar: 11am–9pm. Food: Lunch from 11.30am–2.30pm. Afternoon tea.

Comments: Make use of the caddies – most helpful ... Suffers from ludicrously high heather ... Best course near London ... Fantastic course in very good condition ... Hard but fair ... Bloody heather ... Superb food after damn difficult game ... Will be back again and again.

Walton Heath Golf Club (New)   ★★★

Deans Lane, Walton-on-the-Thames, Tadworth, KT20 7TP
Nearest main town: Tadworth

Secretary:	Mr N. C. Lomas	Tel: 01737 812380
		Fax: 01737 814225
Professional:	Mr K. Macpherson	Tel: 01737 812152

Playing: Midweek: round £68.00; day n/a. Weekend: round n/a; day n/a. Handicap certificate required.

Facilities: Bar: 11am–9pm. Food: Lunch from 11.30am–2.30pm. Afternoon tea.

Comments: Easy start (1st and 2nd), but great par-4s later on, notably the 9th, 12th, 14th and 18th ... Not far behind the Old Course ... A treat to play.

West Byfleet Golf Club   ★★★

Sheerwater Road, West Byfleet, KT14 6AA
Nearest main town: West Byfleet

Secretary: Mr D. G. Lee   Tel: 01932 343433
                                     Fax: 01932 340667
Professional: Mr D. Regan   Tel: 01932 346584

Playing: Midweek: round £29.50; day n/a. Weekend: round n/a; day n/a. Handicap certificate required.

Facilities: Bar: 11am–variable. Food: Bar snacks.

Comments: Traditional club, pretty and challenging ... A difficult par-70 with atttractive woodland ... Nice club and fair value in area of high green fees ... Not as celebrated as many of Surrey's greats, but worth a visit.

West Hill Golf Club   ★★★★

Bagshot Road, Brookwood, GU24 OBH
Nearest main town: Woking

Secretary: Mr M. C. Swatton   Tel: 01483 474365
                                      Fax: 01483 474252
Professional: Mr J. A. Clements   Tel: 01483 473172
                                      Fax: 01483 473172

Playing: Midweek: round £40.00; day £55.00. Weekend: round n/a; day n/a.

Facilities: Bar: 11am–9pm. Food: Lunch and dinner by arrangement.

Comments: A great course to test your outer limits ... Charming course ... Better than Woking and Worplesdon ... Narrow, twisty course with smallish greens ... Long carries to the fairways ... Champion course ... Right next door to Worplesdon ... Heath and heather monster.

West Surrey Golf Club   ★★★★

Enton Green, Godalming, GU8 5AF
Nearest main town: Milford

Secretary: Mr R. T. Crabb   Tel: 01483 421275
                                            Fax: 01483 415419
Professional: Mr A. Tawse   Tel: 01483 417278

Playing: Midweek: round £27.00; day £39.00. Weekend: round
                   £48.00; day £48.00. Handicap certificate required.

Facilities: Bar: 11am–11pm. Food: Bar snacks.

Comments: Real struggle in the summer with running fairways ...
                   Best time to play is in autumn ... Good facilities for
                   traditional club ... Short course with birdie opportunities
                   ... Rather underrated in Surrey.

Wildwood Country Club   ★★★

Horsham Road, Alford, GU6 8JE
Nearest main town: Guildford

Secretary: Mr B. McMillon   Tel: 01403 753255
                                            Fax: 01403 752005
Professional: Mr N. Parfrement   Tel: 01403 753255

Playing: Midweek: round £19.00; day £30.00. Weekend: round
                   £29.00; day £40.00.

Facilities: Bar: 11am–11pm. Food: Lunch from 10am–5pm. Bar
                   snacks.

Comments: Serious golf ... Difficult course and excellent greens ...
                   Facilities for the visitor are first class ... Old oak trees
                   dominate this homely club ... True, fast greens.

Wimbledon Common Golf Club   ★

19 Camp Road, London, SW19 4UW
Nearest main town: London

Secretary: Mr J. Vincent   Tel: 0181 946 1250
                                            Fax: 0181 668 2788
Professional: Mr J. S. Jukes

Playing: Midweek: round £15.00; day £22.00. Weekend: round
                   n/a; day n/a.

Facilities:	Bar: 11am–11pm. Food: Lunch and dinner from 11am–8.30pm. Bar snacks.
Comments:	Another with the red clothing rule ... Nice woodland in parts ... Special aura about this short, challenging course ... Good value.

Windlesham Golf Club   ★★

Grove End, Bagshot, GU19 5HY
Nearest main town: Bagshot

Secretary:	Mr C. J. Lumley	Tel: 01276 452220
		Fax: 01276 452290
Professional:	Mr L. Mucklow	Tel: 01276 472323
Playing:	Midweek: round £40.00; day n/a. Weekend: round £50.00; day n/a. Handicap certificate required.	
Facilities:	Bar: 11am–11pm. Food: Lunch from 11.30am–3pm. Bar snacks. Dinner by arrangement.	
Comments:	Very long course by Tommy Horton ... Charming course but not without difficulty ... Some rather long, boring par-4s ... Fine facilities ... Uninteresting parkland track.	

Woking Golf Club   ★★★★

Pond Road, Hook Heath, Woking, GU22 0JZ
Nearest main town: Woking

Secretary:	Lt Col I. J. Holmes	Tel: 01483 760053
		Fax: 01483 772441
Professional:	Mr J. Thorne	Tel: 01483 769582
Playing:	Midweek: round £40.00; day £50.00. Weekend: round n/a; day n/a. Handicap certificate required.	
Facilities:	Bar: 11am–7.30pm. Food: Lunch from 11.30am–3pm. Bar snacks. Dinner by arrangement.	
Comments:	The spilling heather can be a real struggle ... You can forget about balls landing in the heather ... Touch of class here ... Very traditional place ... Choice course ... On a par with the best in Surrey ... What heathland golf is all about ... Rather stuffy atmosphere ... Super ... Value golf.	

Worplesdon Golf Club   ★★★★

Heath House Road, Woking, GU22 0RA
Nearest main town: Woking

Secretary:	Mr J. T. Christine	Tel: 01483 472277
		Fax: 01483 473303
Professional:	Mr J. T. Christine	Tel: 01483 473287

Playing: Midweek: round £44.00; day £57.00. Weekend: round n/a; day n/a. Handicap certificate required.

Facilities: Bar: 11am–3pm & 5pm–10pm. Food: Lunch from 11.30am–3pm. Bar snacks.

Comments: Just like playing Augusta ... A course of privilege ... Quick greens ... Very tight course, perhaps the toughest in Surrey ... Short 10th the highlight ... Narrow, twisty course.

East Sussex

East Sussex National Golf Club (East) ★★★★★

Little Horsted, Uckfield, TN22 5ES
Nearest main town: Uckfield

Originally the concept of Canadian Brian Turner, East Sussex National was intended as a golf complex the likes of which the British Isles had never seen before. It was to be a facility that oozed class and quality, its fairways would be sculpted through the hills and vales of the South Downs, and its range of tees would be designed to suit players of every ability.

Although Turner had to sell out, the dream lives on. East Sussex National stands as one of the most welcoming clubs in the country, with a vast clubhouse and impressive driving range, where average players can enjoy the trappings of stardom – as many will testify, you feel like a professional turning up for a tournament here.

There are two courses, but the West is primarily reserved for the members – no matter, the East is far superior. The East, to use the American terminology, is a 'stadium course'. It offers superb viewing facilities. Many greens are cut into hillsides and large mounds flank most of the fairways. It perhaps does not have the aesthetic appeal of the West, although both courses are appealing to the eye. With few trees to offer protection on the East, you are at the mercy of the elements on the front nine that is immediately reminiscent of the target-golf game found predominantly on the other side of the Atlantic. The opening hole is not all that long and the fairway generous. The green, however, is small and is generally missed at one's cost. It lies above the level of the fairway, and a large water-filled gully lies between fairway and green.

And so it goes on – one fine, testing hole after another. Water plays a leading role on the back nine, too, especially over the closing holes. The 16th, a par-3, is played across a lake, and the 17th, a par-4 of 450 yards, has a stretch of water that bisects the fairway in the driving zone and then threatens again down the right side of the fairway.

There are holes at East Sussex where it's possible to run the ball onto the green, but they are few and far between. By and large it is an imaginative course for a modern design. You're missing out if you don't try East Sussex at least once.

Secretary:	Mr P. Lewin	Tel: 01825 880088
		Fax: 01825 880066
Professional:	Mr I. Naylor	Tel: 01825 880256

Playing: Midweek: round £35.00; day £55.00. Weekend: round £45.00; day £80.00. Handicap certificate required.

Facilities: Bar: 11am–11pm. Food: Lunch from 12pm–3pm. Bar snacks.

Comments: Service and course presentation excellent ... An inspiring course ... A superb facility every club player should enjoy ... Superb course design, lovely tees and greens, great off-course facilities ... Sussex Hills put to excellent use ... A Tour course ... They make you feel like a pro here – everything you could hope from a golf club ... Great condition ... Service and facilities are the best ever ... Members' course is the better ... Shame about US-type grasses ... East Sussex – the top dog ... Excellent course condition and practice facilities ... A little expensive ... They treat you as though you have won the lottery here ... Need one say more, the best so far ... Course is just superb ... US-style courses but in many cases you can play bump-and-run shots ... West course for members is more intimate.

Ashdown Forest Golf Hotel (Old)   ★★★

Chapel Lane, Forest Row, RH18 5BB
Nearest main town: East Grinstead

Secretary:	Mr D. J. Scrivens	Tel: 01342 824866
		Fax: 01342 824869
Professional:	Mr M. Landsborough	Tel: 01342 822247

Playing: Midweek: round £16.00; day £21.00. Weekend: round £21.00; day £26.00. Handicap certificate required.

Facilities: Bar: 11am–8pm. Food: Bar snacks.

Comments: Typical Sussex course with heather and undulating, quick-drying ground ... No bunkers ... Nice layout but nothing special ... Testing dunes.

Ashdown Forest Golf Hotel (Hotel)   ★★★

Chapel Lane, Forest Row, RH18 5LR
Nearest main town: East Grinstead

Secretary:	Mr D. J. Scrivens	Tel: 01342 824866
		Fax: 01342 824869
Professional:	Mr M. A. Landsborough	Tel: 01342 822247

Playing: Midweek: round £30.00; day £40.00. Weekend: round £40.00; day £45.00. Handicap certificate required.

Facilities: Bar: 11am–8pm. Food: Bar snacks.

Comments: Not a single bunker on this course ... Carries over heather ... One of East Sussex's best ... Keep coming back time and time again ... Very natural ... Imaginative and intriguing ... A complete delight.

Cooden Beach Golf Club ★★★

Cooden Beach, Bexhill-on-Sea, TN39 4TR
Nearest main town: Bexhill

Secretary:	Mr T. E. Hawes	Tel: 01424 842040
		Fax: 01424 842040
Professional:	Mr J. Sim	Tel: 01424 843938

Playing: Midweek: round £29.00; day £29.00. Weekend: round £35.00; day £35.00. Handicap certificate required.

Facilities: Bar: 11am–11pm. Food: Lunch from 12pm–3pm.

Comments: Always welcoming at this great club ... Must keep on the fairways ... Pro shop is consistently helpful ... Playable throughout the year.

Crowborough Beacon Golf Club ★★★

Beacon Road, Crowborough, TN6 1UJ
Nearest main town: Tunbridge Wells

Secretary:	Mrs V. Harwood	Tel: 01892 661511
		Fax: 01892 667339
Professional:	Mr D. Newnham	Tel: 01892 653877

Playing: Midweek: round £25.00; day £40.00. Weekend: round £30.00; day n/a. Handicap certificate required.

Facilities: Bar: 11am–11pm. Food: Breakfast, lunch and dinner from 8am–9pm. Bar snacks.

Comments: Beautiful course with great views ... A gem in God's country – please keep it that way ... Heathland masterpiece.

Eastbourne Downs Golf Club   ★★

East Dean Road, Eastbourne, BN20 8ES
Nearest main town: Eastbourne

Secretary:	Mr A. J. Reeves	Tel: 01323 720827
		Fax: 01323 412506
Professional:	Mr T. Marshall	Tel: 01323 732264

Playing: Midweek: round £16.00; day £20.00. Weekend: round £20.00; day £23.00. Handicap certificate required.

Facilities: Bar: 11am–11pm. Food: Lunch and dinner from 11am–9pm. Bar snacks.

Comments: Could be my least favourite course despite the views ... Interesting course on South Downs, not many flat lies ... Excellent food here ... Open gorseland on top of Beachy Head, rough to get lost in, greens that hold, horizontal trees – simple! ... A cracker.

Hastings Golf Club   ★

Beauport Park, Battle Road, St Leonards-on-Sea, TN38 0TA
Nearest main town: Hastings

Secretary:	Mrs H. Hovenden	Tel: 01424 852977
Professional:	Mr C. Giddins	Tel: 01424 852981
		Fax: 01424 852981

Playing: Midweek: round £10.30; day £10.30. Weekend: round £13.00; day n/a.

Facilities: Bar: 11am–11pm. Food: Lunch from 11am–6pm. Bar snacks.

Comments: Evocative course with fine views ... Very undulating ... Typical public course ... Cheap and charming ... Not great condition.

Mid Sussex Golf Club

Spatham Lane, Ditchling, BN6 8XJ
Nearest main town: Eastbourne

Secretary:	Mr J. Tippett-Iles	Tel: 01273 846567
		Fax: 01273 845767
Professional:	Mr C. Connell	

Playing: Midweek: round £22.50; day n/a. Weekend: round £25.00; day n/a.

Facilities: Bar: 11am–11pm. Food: Lunch and dinner from 11am–9pm. Bar snacks.

Comments: A little parkland jewel ... Tight driving holes to small, well-guarded greens ... Wanted to play the 14th again and again ... Mature course ... Driving key to making a good score.

Nevill Golf Club   ★★★

Benhall Mill Road, Tunbridge Wells, TN2 5JW
Nearest main town: Tunbridge Wells

Secretary: Miss K. N. R. Pudner Tel: 01892 525818
                                      Fax: 01892 517861
Professional: Mr P. Huggett   Tel: 01892 532941

Playing: Midweek: round £23.00; day £33.00. Weekend: round £46.00; day £46.00. Handicap certificate required.

Facilities: Bar: 11am–11pm. Food: Bar snacks. Sunday lunch.

Comments: Interesting front nine, tails off a bit ... Course always well maintained ... Excellent clubhouse ... Nice mixture of heathland and woodland ... Open in places, not too claustrophobic.

Piltdown Golf Club   ★★★★

Piltdown, Uckfield, TN22 3XB
Nearest main town: Uckfield

Secretary: Mr J. C. Duncan Tel: 01825 722033
                                 Fax: 01825 724192
Professional: Mr J. Amos   Tel: 01825 722389

Playing: Midweek: round £27.50; day £32.00. Weekend: round n/a; day n/a. Handicap certificate required.

Facilities: Bar: 11am–11pm. Food: Bar snacks. Dinner by arrangement.

Comments: Well designed with excellent greens ... Charming clubhouse and good value day's golf ... Natural heathland ... Charming course but brutal.

Royal Ashdown Forest Golf Club (Old)   ★★★★

Chapel Lane, Forest Row, RH18 5LR
Nearest main town: East Grinstead

Secretary: Mr D. J. Scrivens   Tel: 01342 822018
                                              Fax: 01342 825211
Professional: Mr M. A. Landsborough Tel: 01342 822247

Playing: Midweek: round £30.00; day £40.00. Weekend: round
                  £40.00; day £45.00. Handicap certificate required.

Facilities: Bar: 11am–8pm. Food: Bar snacks.

Comments: What about all that heather and gorse – just brilliant ...
                  A challenging, heathery, rugged course requiring great
                  accuracy ... Pines and birches ... Quick greens in the
                  summer ... As natural a course as you will find ... Well
                  worth the visit.

Royal Eastbourne Golf Club   ★★★

Paradise Drive, Eastbourne, BN20 8BP
Nearest main town: Eastbourne

Secretary: Mr P. G. White   Tel: 01323 729738
                                           Fax: 01323 729738
Professional: Mr R. Wooler   Tel: 01323 736986
                                           Fax: 01323 736986

Playing: Midweek: round £20.00; day £20.00. Weekend: round
                  £25.00; day £25.00. Handicap certificate required.

Facilities: Bar: 11am–11pm. Food: Lunch from 10am–5.30pm.
                  Bar snacks.

Comments: Two different nines, first fairly flat, second in the dunes
                  ... Four classic par-3s make this a fine course ... Short,
                  easy course ... Par-3s the highlight.

Rye Golf Club   ★★★

Camber, Rye, TN31 7QS
Nearest main town: Rye

Secretary: Mr C. J. W. Gilbert   Tel: 01797 225241
                                           Fax: 01797 225460
Professional: Mr M. P. Lee   Tel: 01797 225218

Playing: Prices on application.

Facilities: Bar: Members only. Food: Members only.

Comments: One of the most difficult courses around – and it wasn't even windy ... Classic links golf ... Lots of character and tradition ... Dream to eventually play it.

Seaford Golf Club ★★★★

East Blatchington, Seaford, BN25 2JD
Nearest main town: Seaford

Secretary: Mr R. N. Vandenbergh Tel: 01323 892442
Fax: 01323 894113
Professional: Mr D. Mills Tel: 01323 894160

Playing: Midweek: round £25.00; day n/a. Weekend: round n/a; day n/a. Handicap certificate required.

Facilities: Bar: 11am–11pm. Food: Lunch and dinner from 10am–9pm. Bar snacks.

Comments: Very good value for the money, warm welcome ... Massively underrated ... Brilliant links with excellent views – simply great value ... Tricky in the wind ... Welcoming dormy house ... Finest inland course in the south.

Seaford Head Golf Club ★★

Southdown Road, Seaford, BN25 4JS
Nearest main town: Eastbourne

Secretary: Mr J. T. Wass Tel: 01323 890139
Professional: Mr A. J. Lowies Tel: 01323 890139

Playing: Midweek: round £13.00; day £19.00. Weekend: round £15.50; day £21.00.

Facilities: Bar: 11am–11pm. Food: Lunch from 11.30am–5pm. Bar snacks.

Comments: Great views ... Like Seaford, good quality ... Highlight is the 'Hell Hole' ... Quality layout with interesting and diverse challenges ... Cliff-top links of the highest order.

Sedlescombe Golf Club   ★★

Kent Street, Sedlescombe, TN33 0SD
Nearest main town: Hastings

Secretary: Mr J. Feezy   Tel: 01424 870898
Professional: Mr J. Andrews   Tel: 01424 870898

Playing: Midweek: round £15.00; day £20.00. Weekend: round
                  £18.00; day £24.00.

Facilities: Bar: 11am–11pm. Food: Lunch from 10am–2pm. Bar
                  snacks.

Comments: Simple but fun ... Needs to mature ... Recently estab-
                  lished parkland but going the right way ... Fairly
                  exposed.

The Dyke Golf Club   ★

Devil's Dyke, Dyke Road, Brighton, BN1 8YJ
Nearest main town: Brighton

Secretary: Mr T. R. White   Tel: 01273 857296
                                        Fax: 01273 857078
Professional: Mr R. Arnold   Tel: 01273 857260
                                        Fax: 01273 857564

Playing: Midweek: round £28.00; day £38.00. Weekend: round
                  £40.00; day n/a. Handicap certificate required.

Facilities: Bar: 11am–11pm. Food: Lunch from 11.30am–3pm.
                  Bar snacks. Dinner by arrangement.

Comments: Greens are always good and so is scoring ... Too many
                  poor holes – badly defined, blind with average greens
                  ... Great views but didn't enjoy the course ... You either
                  love it or hate it – I loved it.

West Hove Golf Club   ★★

Church Farm, Hangleton, Hove, BN3 8AN
Nearest main town: Hove

Secretary: Mr K. Haste   Tel: 01273 419738
                                        Fax: 01273 439988
Professional: Mr D. Cook   Tel: 01273 413494

Playing: Midweek: round £14.00; day n/a. Weekend: round
                  £18.00; day n/a.

Facilities: Bar: 11am–11pm. Food: Lunch and dinner from 10am–9pm. Bar snacks.

Comments: Hawtree-designed downland course with nice variety of holes ... Built on chalk so in play most of the year.

West Sussex

West Sussex Golf Club ★★★★

Golf Club Lane, Wiggonholt, Pulborough, RH20 2EN
Nearest main town: Pulborough

It comes as quite a relief to visit West Sussex. As modern course design gets to grip with the improvements in golf club technology, so courses are getting longer and longer, pushing the 7,000-yard barrier and over. West Sussex, situated in a luxuriant basin of pines, heather and sandy turf just below the Chanctonbury Ring, stands as an example of classic design, its total length of 6,156 yards no reflection of the perils that lurk on every hole.

That said, long, accurate driving is the game you want here, setting up mid to short iron approaches to fairly defenceless greens. Sounds easy, but standing on the tee, the fairways are not what catches your eye. Rather, it's the heather, vast expanses of deep purple, hugging the fairways and edging to the bases of the indigenous pines and silver birches. Not only will you struggle to find your ball in there, but you'll be forced to play out sideways, the roots of the heather twisting the club face as you muster all your strength to escape.

Although this challenge exists on almost every hole, West Sussex is also marked for greatness by the variety and excitement of its par-3s. There are five in total, three coming in the space of four holes. The 6th plays over 200 yards from an elevated tee, over a lake to a thin green, while the 12th is a long iron over a heather-filled gully with out-of-bounds all the way down the left. The course's most attractive hole is the 15th, a par-3 played through a funnel of mature trees over a lake to a back-to-front sloping green. All three are memorable.

You'll be hypnotised by the lush beauty of West Sussex, and if you get the chance, visit in the autumn when the heather blooms and the leaves take on their tawny colours. Also, make sure to have a meal here after the round – the food is consistently good.

Secretary: Mr C. P. Simpson   Tel: 01798 872563
Fax: 01798 872033
Professional: Mr T. Packham   Tel: 01798 872426

Playing: Midweek: round £40.00; day £50.00. Weekend: round n/a; day n/a. Handicap certificate required.

Facilities: Bar: 11am–11pm. Food: Lunch from 11am–3pm. Bar snacks.

Comments: Kept in superb condition ... Clubhouse outstanding ... Members a little overprotective of their beautiful course ... Charming and an excellent test, although members were a little stuffy ... Nearest to a classic links inland ... Tougher than it looks.

Bognor Regis Golf Club   ★★

Downview Road, Felpham, Bognor Regis, PO22 8JD
Nearest main town: Bognor Regis

Secretary: Mr B. D. Poston   Tel: 01243 821929
                                          Fax: 01243 860719
Professional: Mr S. Bassil   Tel: 01243 865209

Playing: Midweek: round £25.00; day £25.00. Weekend: round n/a; day n/a. Handicap certificate required.

Facilities: Bar: 11am–11pm. Food: Bar snacks.

Comments: A fine day out ... Holidaying golfers give this course a special atmosphere ... They don't take the game too seriously here ... Flat but certainly not dull.

Chichester Golf Club (Cathedral)   ★★

Hunston Village, Chichester, PO20 6AX
Nearest main town: Chichester

Secretary: Mr M. Palmer   Tel: 01243 536666
                                          Fax: 01243 539922
Professional: Mr J. Slinger   Tel: 01243 528999

Playing: Midweek: round £15.00; day £20.00. Weekend: round £19.50; day £27.00.

Facilities: Bar: 11am–11pm. Food: Lunch from 11am–3pm.

Comments: New course protected by too many water hazards ... Tried to recreate Florida in West Sussex – doesn't work.

Chichester Golf Club (Tower)   ★★

Hunston Village, Chichester, PO20 6AX
Nearest main town: Chichester

Secretary:	Mr M. Palmer	Tel: 01243 536666
		Fax: 01243 539922
Professional:	Mr J. Slinger	Tel: 01243 528999

Playing: Midweek: round £20.00; day £30.00. Weekend: round £28.00; day £38.00. Handicap certificate required.

Facilities: Bar: 11am–11pm. Food: Lunch from 11am–3pm.

Comments: More established than the Cathedral but not much better ... Condition not up to much ... Cheap golf for the family.

Copthorne Golf Club   ★★★

Borers Arm Road, Copthorne, RH10 3LL
Nearest main town: Copthorne

Secretary:	Mr J. P. Pyne	Tel: 01342 712033
		Fax: 01342 717682
Professional:	Mr J. Burrell	Tel: 01342 712405

Playing: Midweek: round £30.00; day £38.00. Weekend: round £32.00; day n/a. Handicap certificate required.

Facilities: Bar: 11am–11pm. Food: Lunch from 11am–5pm. Dinner by arrangement.

Comments: Excellent wooded heathland course ... A good test of golf ... Very attractive course unknown outside Sussex ... Mystery why this course is so underrated.

Cottesmore Golf & Country Club   ★

Buchan Hill, Pease Pottage, Crawley, RH11 9AT
Nearest main town: Crawley

Secretary:	Mr M. Topper	Tel: 01293 528256
		Fax: 01293 522819
Professional:	Mr A. Prior	Tel: 01293 535399

Playing: Midweek: round £25.00; day £32.00. Weekend: round £31.00; day £42.00.

Facilities: Bar: 11am–11pm. Food: Breakfast and lunch from 8am–3pm. Dinner from 6pm–9.30pm.

Comments: Newish course, a little overpriced ... Fairly pretty but triumph of style over substance ... Nice to look at ... Appealing simple course ... Too expensive for what you get.

Goodwood Golf Club   ★★

Goodwood, West Sussex, PO18 0PN
Nearest main town: Chichester

Secretary: Mr J. Stevens   Tel: 01243 774968
                                 Fax: 01243 781741
Professional: Mr K. MacDonald   Tel: 01243 774994

Playing: Midweek: round £32.00; day £32.00. Weekend: round £42.00; day £42.00. Handicap certificate required.

Facilities: Bar: 11am–11pm. Food: Lunch from 11am–6pm.

Comments: Tough downland course ... Very entertaining ... Braid design ... Marvellous beech trees frame each hole at this pleasant course ... Views across the Downs.

Ham Manor Golf Club   ★★

West Drive, Angmering, Littlehampton, BN16 4JE
Nearest main town: Littlehampton

Secretary: Mr V. J. Chaszczewski Tel: 01903 783288
                                     Fax: 01903 850886
Professional: Mr S. Buckley   Tel: 01903 783732

Playing: Midweek: round £26.00; day £26.00. Weekend: round £40.00; day £40.00. Handicap certificate required.

Facilities: Bar: 11am–2.30pm & 5pm–10pm (all day Saturday). Food: Lunch from 11.30am–3pm. Dinner from 6pm–9pm. No food on Mondays.

Comments: Look out for Des Lynam, this is his course ... Fairly uninteresting design but nice feel to the club ... Nice course with soft turf, but better around.

Littlehampton Golf Club   ★★★

170 Rope Walk, Littlehampton, BN17 5DL
Nearest main town: Littlehampton

Secretary: Mr K. R. Palmer   Tel: 01903 717170
                                          Fax: 01903 726629
Professional: Mr G. McQuitty   Tel: 01903 716369

Playing: Midweek: round £24.00; day £24.00. Weekend: round
                   £24.00; day £24.00. Handicap certificate required.

Facilities: Bar: 11am–9pm. Food: Breakfast and lunch from
                   8am–5.30pm. Bar snacks.

Comments: Part links, part parkland ... Excellent club ... Links is
                   very hard in the wind ... Links with great par-3s ... Nice,
                   fast greens ... One to treasure.

Mannings Heath Golf Club (Waterfall)   ★★★★

Fullers, Hammerpond Road, Horsham, RH13 6PG
Nearest main town: Horsham

Secretary: Mr J. Curtis   Tel: 01403 210228
                                          Fax: 01403 270974
Professional: Mr C. Tucker   Tel: 01403 210228

Playing: Midweek: round £32.00; day £40.00. Weekend: round
                   £40.00; day £55.00. Handicap certificate required.

Facilities: Bar: 11am–11pm. Food: Breakfast, lunch and dinner
                   from 7am–8pm. Bar snacks.

Comments: Value for money ... Pleasure to play ... Outstanding
                   facilities ... Best in the South – value and quality in
                   spades ... Improvement to two holes and this would be
                   unbeatable ... Tiring course ... 10th and 11th fabulous
                   back-to-back holes ... Lovely clubhouse.

Mannings Heath Golf Club (Kingfisher)   ★★★

Fullers, Hammerpond Road, Horsham, RH13 6PG
Nearest main town: Horsham

Secretary: Mr J. Curtis   Tel: 01403 210228
                                          Fax: 01403 270974
Professional: Mr C. Tucker   Tel: 01403 210228

Playing:	Midweek: round £32.00; day £40.00. Weekend: round £40.00; day £55.00. Handicap certificate required.
Facilities:	Bar: 11am–11pm. Food: Breakfast, lunch and dinner from 7am–8pm. Bar snacks.
Comments:	Tradition makes this course appear timeless ... Pleasant but not as testing as the Waterfall course ... Not a good value course.

Pyecombe Golf Club   ★

Pyecombe, West Sussex, BN45 7FF
Nearest main town: Brighton

Secretary:	Mr I. Bradbury	Tel: 01273 845372
		Fax: 01273 843338
Professional:	Mr C. R. White	Tel: 01273 845398

Playing:	Midweek: round £15.00; day £20.00. Weekend: round £20.00; day n/a. Handicap certificate required.
Facilities:	Bar: 11am–11pm. Food: Lunch and dinner from 11am–6pm.
Comments:	Views were the highlight of this round ... Course lacks a little pizzazz ... Course doesn't match the views ... In the heart of the South Downs ... Natural setting for this typical downland course.

Singing Hills Golf Club   ★

Albourne, West Sussex, BN6 9EB
Nearest main town: Brighton

Secretary:	Mr V. Street	Tel: 01273 835353
		Fax: 01273 835444
Professional:	Mr W. Street	

Playing:	Midweek: round £18.00; day £28.00. Weekend: round £18.00; day £36.00.
Facilities:	Bar: 11am–10pm. Food: Lunch from 12pm–9pm. Bar snacks.
Comments:	No special feeling here ... Island green a little different ... Lots of water, very unnatural ... Seen it all before and done better.

Slinford Park Golf Club ★

Stane Street, Slinford, RH13 7RE
Nearest main town: Horsham

Secretary:	To be appointed.	Tel: 01403 791154
		Fax: 01403 791465
Professional:	Mr G. McKay	Tel: 01403 791555

Playing: Midweek: round £25.00; day n/a. Weekend: round n/a; day n/a.

Facilities: Bar: 11am–11pm. Food: Lunch from 11.30am–3pm. Dinner from 6pm–9pm. Bar snacks.

Comments: Quite dramatic for a new course ... Maturing well ... Will be better in ten years ... Condition variable ... Can get a little wet ... Two large lakes form focus of many holes.

Tilgate Forest Golf Club ★★★★

Titmus Drive, Tilgate, Crawley, RH10 5EU
Nearest main town: Crawley

Secretary:	Mr S. Priest	Tel: 01293 530103
		Fax: 01293 523478
Professional:	Mr S. Trussell	Tel: 01293 530103

Playing: Midweek: round £12.30; day £21.30. Weekend: round £17.00; day n/a.

Facilities: Bar: 11am–11pm. Food: Lunch from 12pm–3pm. Dinner from 6pm–9pm. Bar snacks.

Comments: One drawback to this lovely course was a five-hour round ... Left me feeling completely at one with the world – smashing course ... Magical splendour guarantees a dream golf day fulfilled ... Absolutely sublime golfing pleasure.

Worthing Golf Club ★★★

Links Road, Worthing, BN14 9QZ
Nearest main town: Worthing

Secretary:	Mr I. J. Evans	Tel: 01903 260801
		Fax: 01903 694664
Professional:	Mr S. Rolley	Tel: 01903 260718

Playing: Midweek: round £25.00; day £30.00. Weekend: round £30.00; day £40.00. Handicap certificate required.

Facilities: Bar: 11am–9pm. Food: Lunch from 11am–3pm. Bar snacks. Dinner from 6pm–9pm from Wednesday–Friday.

Comments: Very enjoyable downland course ... Entertaining ... Would go back ... Better to be had in West Sussex ... Easy walking.

Tyne & Wear

Boldon Golf Club ★★

Dipe Lane, East Boldon, NE36 0PQ
Nearest main town: Newcastle

Secretary: Mr R. W. Benton   Tel: 0191 536 5360
                                 Fax: 0191 536 5835
Professional: Mr R. Phipps   Tel: 0191 536 5835

Playing: Midweek: round £18.00; day £18.00. Weekend: round £22.00; day n/a. Handicap certificate required.

Facilities: Bar: 11am–11pm. Food: Lunch from 11am–2pm.

Comments: Pleasant course with some difficult holes ... Excellent pro shop ... Pro-shop staff very knowledgable ... Rugged course with interesting features ... A tough course and horrific in a gale ... Exposed but exciting value course.

Garesfield Golf Club ★★

Chopwell, NE17 7AP
Nearest main town: Newcastle

Secretary: Mr E. M. Thirlwell   Tel: 01207 561278
                                    Fax: 01207 561309
Professional: Mr D. Race   Tel: 01207 563082

Playing: Midweek: round £15.00; day £17.00. Weekend: round £17.00; day £21.00.

Facilities: Bar: 11am–11pm. Food: Lunch and dinner from 11am–9pm. Bar snacks.

Comments: Stonking value for money ... Really good for the price ... Woodland surroundings ... Won't make a point of going back ... Price neglects the course's shortcomings.

George Washington Hotel Golf Club ★★

Stone Cellar Road, Usworth, Washington, NE37 1PH
Nearest main town: Newcastle

Secretary: Mr D. V. Duffy   Tel: 0191 402 9988
                                    Fax: 0191 415 1166
Professional: Mr W. Marshall   Tel: 0191 417 8346

Playing: Midweek: round £20.00; day n/a. Weekend: round £30.00; day n/a. Handicap certificate required.

Facilities: Bar: 11am–11pm. Food: Breakfast, lunch and dinner from 8am–10pm. Bar snacks.

Comments: Facilities good ... Course and facilities fairly middle of the road ... Rather overplayed ... Not known for its condition.

Northumberland Golf Club ★

High Gosforth Park, Newcastle-upon-Tyne, NE3 5HT
Nearest main town: Newcastle

Secretary: Mr J. M. Forteath   Tel: 0191 236 2498
                                    Fax: 0191 236 2498
Professional: None.

Playing: Midweek: round £35.00; day £45.00. Weekend: round n/a; day n/a. Handicap certificate required.

Facilities: Bar: 11am–11pm. Food: Lunch from 12pm–2pm. Dinner from 6pm–9pm. Bar snacks.

Comments: Shortish course with plenty of heather ... Narrow fairways ... Situated in the middle of a racecourse ... Course affects play on eight holes ... Some drives over racecourse rails ... Unique course.

Parklands Golf Club ★

High Gosforth Park, Newcastle-upon-Tyne, NE3 5HQ
Nearest main town: Newcastle

Secretary: Mr B. Woof   Tel: 0191 236 4480
                                    Fax: 0191 236 3322
Professional: Mr B. Rumney Tel: 0191 236 4480

Playing: Midweek: round £15.00; day n/a. Weekend: round £18.00; day n/a.

Facilities: Bar: 11am–11pm. Food: Bar snacks.

Comments: Fairly mundane ... Couldn't get my enthusiasm up for this one ... Easily missable.

South Shields Golf Club   ★

Cleadon Hills, South Shields, NE34 8EG
Nearest main town: Newcastle

Secretary: Mr W. H. Loades   Tel: 0191 456 8942
Professional: Mr G. Parsons   Tel: 0191 456 0110

Playing: Midweek: round £20.00; day £20.00. Weekend: round £25.00; day £25.00. Handicap certificate required.

Facilities: Bar: 11am–11pm. Food: Lunch and dinner from 11am–9pm.

Comments: Opens with a par-3 ... True greens and marvellous views ... Rough can transform this course ... Blasted boundary wall affects many of the holes ... Good fun ... Nice matchplay course.

Wearside Golf Club

Coxgreen, Sunderland, SR4 9JT
Nearest main town: Sunderland

Secretary: Mr N. Hildrew   Tel: 0191 534 2518
                                          Fax: 0191 534 2518
Professional: Mr D. Brolls   Tel: 0191 534 4269

Playing: Midweek: round £25.00; day £25.00. Weekend: round £32.00; day £32.00. Handicap certificate required.

Facilities: Bar: 11am–11pm. Food: Lunch and dinner from 11am–9pm, except Mondays.

Comments: Lovely layout ... Opens with a par-3 ... Watch out for Penshaw Monument ... Fair condition ... Interesting, historic course.

Whitley Bay Golf Club ★

Claremont Road, Whitley Bay, NE26 3UF
Nearest main town: Newcastle

Secretary:	Mr B. Dockar	Tel: 0191 252 0180
		Fax: 0191 297 0030
Professional:	Mr G. Shipley	Tel: 0191 252 5688

Playing: Midweek: round £22.00; day £30.00. Weekend: round n/a; day n/a.

Facilities: Bar: 11am–11pm. Food: Lunch and dinner from 11am–9pm. Bar snacks.

Comments: Not up to much ... Bracing ... Not really a visitor's course ... Basic facilities ... One to avoid for visitors.

Warwickshire

Marriott Forest of Arden Golf Club   ★★★★

Maxstoke Lane, Meriden, Coventry, CV7 7HR
Nearest main town: Coventry

Set in the heart of the Midlands, the Forest of Arden is a golf complex of exceptional quality. Its glamourisation on account of hosting the English Open and British Masters in recent years in no way overshadows the quality of the course, which combines very modern design methods with a traditional feel.

The man responsible was Donald Steel. Demanding but fair would be an accurate description of the course he conceived, and it is one that is constantly evolving. Despite being a very young course, already it has undergone major changes, particularly at the 4th and 14th, where the greens have been rebuilt and re-contoured.

You get the impression that the Forest of Arden is a very modern course from the opening holes. It starts gently with a short par-4, but soon toughens up, on the front nine seemingly using all the clubs in the bag. The 9th is widely acknowledged as the most difficult on the course, particularly when it plays into the prevailing wind – it's been known for top Tour pros to have to use a driver and wood off the fairway to reach this 470-yarder.

Traditionally the back nine has always played a little bit harder, but there are compensations for the weary and disillusioned golfer who has cracked by this point. Deer roam freely on this part of the Packington Estate, seemingly unperturbed by the golfing fraternity. And in the summer, the heather in bloom is also a welcome sight.

As you would expect for a modern course, water comes into play on five holes – the 4th, 8th, 12th, 17th and most notably the 18th, which demands a 220-yard-plus carry over a lake to one of the best finishing holes of any modern course in England.

Secretary:	Mr D. MacLaren	Tel: 01676 522335
		Fax: 01676 523711
Professional:	Mr K. Thomas	Tel: 0958 632170
Playing:	Midweek: round £45.00; day £90.00. Weekend: round £55.00; day £110.00. Handicap certificate required.	
Facilities:	Bar: 11am–11pm. Food: Breakfast, lunch and dinner from 8am–9.30pm. Bar snacks.	

Comments: Quiet atmosphere – loved it ... Disappointing for club of supposed standing ... Interesting course on the right day ... Technically interesting ... Thick rough ... Can get wet ... Extremely tricky for amateurs and pros.

The Belfry

Lichfield Road, Wishaw, B76 9PR
Nearest main town: Wishaw

Golfers everywhere breathed a collective sigh of despair when it was announced that the 2001 Ryder Cup was to be held at The Belfry. Once a favourite among golfers, its stock has fallen with its increasing familiarity and now invites the sort of criticism reserved for few other courses. The recent redesign, where a number of holes have been re-routed and had challenges added, may reverse the tide and propel it back upwards to its former position of pre-eminence.

However, much of the fun of playing The Belfry comes from its familiarity. Holes that you have watched on the TV come to life standing on the tee, and you track your progress down each one comparing your own shots to those of the professionals. The 10th and the 18th are the most famous examples, the former a short par-4 where it is possible to drive the green depending on the position of the tee and wind conditions and the latter a dogleg par-4 where you cross the water twice.

What's for certain is you won't find the course set up in the same way as it was for the Ryder Cup. The thick rough will certainly be shorter and the course will not play as long. That's good news for amateurs, because The Belfry is no pushover despite the professional scores that have been shot here in the past. Neither will the fairways and greens be in the same excellent condition. The Belfry has at times over the last few years resembled a field that has been put out to fallow – rather disappointing if you've made the visit to play this famed course.

The Belfry is fairly exposed to the wind and you will need to take it into account on most days. Otherwise, everything is laid out in front of you and any difficulties you get into will be entirely of your own making. A very fair test.

Secretary: Mr R. Maxfield   Tel: 01675 470301
                              Fax: 01675 470178
Professional: Mr P. McGovern   Tel: 01675 470301

Playing: Prices on application.

Facilities: Bar: 11am–11pm. Food: Breakfast, lunch and dinner from 10am–10pm.

Comments: Green fees on application ... Everyone knows it but playing experience is top class ... Disappointing ... Redesign should improve course ... Been looking a little tired lately ... 18th is still one of the memorable holes in British golf ... Its light may be fading but for average punter still a magic experience ... One of the top courses and hospitality to match ... Not as challenging as the TV suggests.

Bidford Grange Golf Club   ★

Stratford Road, Bidford-on-Avon, B50 4LY
Nearest main town: Stratford-upon-Avon

Secretary: Mr E. Cash   Tel: 01789 490319
                                     Fax: 01789 778184

Professional: None.

Playing: Midweek: round £12.00; day £20.00. Weekend: round £15.00; day £25.00.

Facilities: Bar: 11am–11pm. Food: Lunch by arrangement.

Comments: A water sports venue ... Very testing and sometimes too long ... Meant to feel like a links ... Too long at almost 7,300 yards ... Good value society location ... Not for those afraid of water.

Copt Heath Golf Club   ★★

1220 Warwick Road, Knowle, Solihull, B93 9LN
Nearest main town: Solihull

Secretary: Mr W. Lenton   Tel: 01564 772650
                                     Fax: 01564 771022
Professional: Mr B. J. Barton   Tel: 01564 776155

Playing: Midweek: round £35.00; day £40.00. Weekend: round n/a; day n/a. Handicap certificate required.

Facilities: Bar: 11am–11pm. Food: Lunch from 11.30pm–2.30pm.

Comments: Easy walking course with hundreds of bunkers – great fun! ... Designed by Harry Vardon ... Parkland beauty ... Homely club.

Coventry Golf Club ★★★

Finham Park, Coventry, CV3 6PJ
Nearest main town: Coventry

Secretary: Mr B. Fox Tel: 01203 414152
Fax: 01203 690131
Professional: Mr P. Weaver Tel: 01203 411298

Playing: Midweek: round £30.00; day £30.00. Weekend: round n/a; day n/a. Handicap certificate required.

Facilities: Bar: 11am–11pm. Food: Lunch and dinner from 11am–9pm. Bar snacks.

Comments: Hard course in fine fettle ... Why the segregation of sexes – come on! ... Extremely tough course, well worth seeking out ... Go for the course, not the club.

Edgbaston Golf Club ★★★

Church Road, Edgbaston, B15 3TB
Nearest main town: Birmingham

Secretary: Mr P. Heath Tel: 0121 454 1736
Fax: 0121 454 2395
Professional: Mr J. Cundy Tel: 0121 454 3226

Playing: Midweek: round £35.00; day £50.00. Weekend: round £50.00; day n/a. Handicap certificate required.

Facilities: Bar: 11am–2pm & 6pm–10pm. Food: Lunch from 12pm–2pm. Dinner from 6pm–9pm.

Comments: Honest track ... Sublime woodland/parkland setting ... Gorgeous parkland with Georgian clubhouse ... Overpriced but such a perfect setting ... Deserves more recognition ... Not a hit-and-hope course, you need a brain ... Just what a golfing day out should be ... .Only three miles out of the city but you feel very at one with nature ... Kept in exceptional condition ... If someone offers, go ... Play it every year and it just gets better.

Leamington & County Golf Club ★

Golf Lane, Whitnash, Leamington Spa, CV31 2QA
Nearest main town: Leamington Spa

Secretary:	Mrs S. M. Cooknell	Tel: 01926 425961
		Fax: 01926 425961
Professional:	Mr I. Grant	Tel: 01926 428014

Playing: Midweek: round £25.00; day £28.00. Weekend: round £40.00; day n/a. Handicap certificate required.

Facilities: Bar: 11am–11pm. Food: Lunch and dinner from 11am–6pm. Bar snacks.

Comments: A course with a good pedigree ... Many dull holes ... Rather barren and windswept ... Bleak clubhouse.

Oakridge Golf Club ★★

Arley Lane, Ansley Village, Nuneaton, CV10 9PH
Nearest main town: Nuneaton

Secretary:	Mrs S. Lovric	Tel: 01676 541389
		Fax: 01676 542709
Professional:	Mr I. Sadler	Tel: 01676 540542

Playing: Midweek: round £15.00; day n/a. Weekend: round n/a; day n/a.

Facilities: Bar: 11am–11pm. Food: Lunch and dinner from 12pm–9pm. Bar snacks.

Comments: A bit of a walkover ... Water hazards, but nothing too frightening ... Little protection for this open course ... Facilities don't cater to beginner.

Robin Hood Golf Club ★★

St Bernards Road, Solihull, B92 7DJ
Nearest main town: Birmingham

Secretary:	Mrs T. A. Rennie	Tel: 0121 706 0061
		Fax: 0121 706 0806
Professional:	Mr A. Harvey	Tel: 0121 706 0806

Playing: Midweek: round £29.00; day £35.00. Weekend: round £29.00; day £35.00. Handicap certificate required.

Facilities: Bar: 11am–11pm. Food: Bar snacks.

Comments: Riveting course with much variety ... Difficulty factor very high ... A little long for the novice ... You need to give it a belt here ... Not a chance of matching your handicap ... Really stiff finish.

Stratford-upon-Avon Golf Club ★★★

Tiddington Road, Stratford-upon-Avon, CV37 7BA
Nearest main town: Stratford-upon-Avon

Secretary: Mr M. Wilson Tel: 01789 297296
Professional: Mr D. Sutherland Tel: 01789 205677
Fax: 01789 292608

Playing: Midweek: round £28.00; day £32.00. Weekend: round £35.00; day n/a. Handicap certificate required.

Facilities: Bar: 11am–11pm. Food: Breakfast, lunch and dinner from 8am–9pm. Bar snacks.

Comments: Presentation can't be faulted ... Best finishing holes in the county ... Highly rated in the area ... Always ruin my card at the finish.

Sutton Coldfield Golf Club ★★★

110 Thornhill Road, Sutton Coldfield, B74 3ER
Nearest main town: Birmingham

Secretary: Mr R. F. Fletcher Tel: 0121 353 9633
Fax: 0121 353 5503
Professional: Mr J K. Hayes Tel: 0121 353 9633

Playing: Midweek: round £25.00; day £35.00. Weekend: round £35.00; day £35.00. Handicap certificate required.

Facilities: Bar: 11am–11pm. Food: Bar snacks.

Comments: Gorse everywhere ... Enjoyable course with good facilities ... Made very welcome on this tricky layout.

The Belfry (PGA National) ★★★

Lichfield Road, Wishaw, B76 9PR
Nearest main town: Wishaw

Secretary: Mr R. Maxfield Tel: 01675 470301
Fax: 01675 470301
Professional: Mr P. McGovern Tel: 01675 470301

Playing: Midweek: round £50.00; day n/a. Weekend: round £50.00; day n/a.

Facilities: Bar: 11am–11pm. Food: Breakfast, lunch and dinner from 10am–10pm.

Comments: Completely artificial course ... Unimpressive site with mounds everywhere ... Exciting golf on a course for the pros ... Designed purely for tournament golf ... Could not get excited about it ... Very unnatural but will appeal to lovers of modern design ... Walked off a happy man.

The Warwickshire (SE)   ★★★

Leek Wootton, Warwick, CV35 7QT
Nearest main town: Warwick

Secretary: Mr G. Ivory   Tel: 01926 409409
                                           Fax: 01926 408409
Professional: Mr J. Cook   Tel: 01926 409409

Playing: Midweek: round £45.00; day £75.00. Weekend: round £45.00; day £75.00. Handicap certificate required.

Facilities: Bar: 11am–11pm. Food: Bar snacks.

Comments: Play a pro's course ... A joy to play ... Tight holes making for accurate drives ... No soul at this new US-style course ... Get me back to a links.

The Warwickshire (NW)   ★★

Leek Wootton, Warwick, CV35 7QT
Nearest main town: Warwick

Secretary: Mr G. Ivory   Tel: 01926 409409
                                           Fax: 01926 408409
Professional: Mr J. Cook   Tel: 01926 409409

Playing: Midweek: round £45.00; day £75.00. Weekend: round £45.00; day £75.00. Handicap certificate required.

Facilities: Bar: 11am–11pm. Food: Bar snacks.

Comments: Corporate golf at its best ... Good course and food ... Great challenge and how golf should be played ... Great facilities but golf could be better.

Welcombe Hotel & Golf Club   ★★★★

Warwick Road, Stratford-upon-Avon, CV37 0NR
Nearest main town: Stratford-upon-Avon

Secretary:	Mr J. Moore	Tel: 01789 295252
		Fax: 01789 414666
Professional:	Mr K. Hayler	Tel: 01789 299012

Playing: Midweek: round £35.00; day £55.00. Weekend: round £35.00; day £55.00. Handicap certificate required.

Facilities: Bar: 11am–11pm. Food: Breakfast, lunch and dinner from 8am–9.30pm. Bar snacks.

Comments: Can't fault its presentation ... Overpriced but money should go to greenkeepers ... Visually very attractive ... Woodland course in terrific nick.

Whitefields Hotel Golf Club ★

Coventry Road, Thurlaston, Rugby, CV23 9JR
Nearest main town: Rugby

Secretary:	Mr B. Coleman	Tel: 01788 521800
		Fax: 01788 521695
Professional:	Mr M. Chamberlain	Tel: 01788 817777
		Fax: 01788 817777

Playing: Midweek: round £18.00; day £25.00. Weekend: round £22.00; day £30.00. Handicap certificate required.

Facilities: Bar: 11am–11pm. Food: Breakfast, lunch and dinner from 7am–10pm. Bar snacks.

Comments: Fairly unimaginative ... Practice facilities deserve a better course ... Always enjoy society days here ... A course for the higher handicappers ... Caters for the learner.

Windmill Village Golf Club ★

Birmingham Road, Allesley, CV5 9AL
Nearest main town: Coventry

Secretary:	Mr M. Harrhy	Tel: 01203 404041
	(Manager)	Fax: 01203 407016
Professional:	Mr R. Hunter	Tel: 01203 404041

Playing: Midweek: round £9.95; day £16.00. Weekend: round £13.95; day £20.00.

Facilities: Bar: 11am–11pm. Food: Breakfast, lunch and dinner from 10am–10pm. Bar snacks.

Comments: Recently redesigned and improving in all aspects ...
Very short course ... Fun for beginners with water
hazards ... Better places to play in the West Midlands.

Wiltshire

Bowood Golf & Country Club ★★★★

Derry Hill, Calne, SN11 9PQ
Nearest main town: Chippenham

The early 1990s saw a trend towards a new breed of 'luxury' golf resorts as developers attempted to match the standards set by the likes of Turnberry and Gleneagles, far-flung but long-established favourites in Britain. Many of these big-dollar, high-maintenance country clubs failed, but some, like Bowood, flourished, and even today remains a popular West Country retreat.

On what is essentially a flat site, although majestic in its own way with mature woodland encasing the Bowood estate, the course is a fair test of golf, blending 18 holes with the property's 2,000-acre Great Park, originally the creation of Capability Brown in the late 1700s. The cavernous moulded bunkers, skilfully planned hillocks that skirt and define the fairways, vast greens, and the occasional lake or stream are in complete harmony with the surroundings – a refreshing discovery in these times of New Age golf craziness.

From the very back tees, Bowood weighs in at 7,317 yards, which includes a 600-yard par-5. Anyone with any sanity will settle for the more user-friendly, although still long, 6,890 yards from the whites. Given its length, you could be forgiven for thinking this is some US Open-style course with pencil-thin fairways and punishing rough. In fact, the rough is loose knit and relatively benign, but, by and large, like so many quintessentially English designs, it begs you to think on every hole.

Pick of the holes are the 13th (Wyatt's Spire) the green framed by dense woodland and an old towering church spire, and the 15th (The Moors), a scenic dogleg with a couple of huge oak trees dominating parts of the fairway. The 18th (Home Farm) with water all the way down the right and another small lake sitting just short and left of the green, is a bit of a cliché, but these designers like to finish with a flourish.

Secretary:	Mr E. Scholfield	Tel: 01249 822228
		Fax: 01249 822218
Professional:	Mr N. Blenkarne	Tel: 01249 822228
Playing:	Midweek: round £32.00; day £37.00. Weekend: round £39.00; day £42.00. Handicap certificate required.	

Facilities: Bar: 11am–11pm. Food: Breakfast, lunch and dinner from 8am–10pm. Bar snacks.

Comments: Long and demanding ... Well-thought-out course ... Hazard warning ... Gets wet in winter ... Excellent course but poor drainage so avoid in winter.

Cumberwell Park Golf Club   ★★★★

Bradford-on-Avon, BA15 2PQ
Nearest main town: Bath

Secretary: Mr J. Jacobs   Tel: 01225 863322
                 (Golf Director)   Fax: 01225 868160
Professional: Mr J. Jacobs   Tel: 01255 863322

Playing: Midweek: round £20.00; day £35.00. Weekend: round £25.00; day £40.00.

Facilities: Bar: 11am–11pm. Food: Sunday lunch and bar snacks.

Comments: One of the best new courses around ... No excessive contouring, just natural golf ... What golf clubs should be all about – friendly and accessible ... Best in Wiltshire ... Very long from the tiger tees.

High Post Golf Club   ★★★

Great Durnford, Salisbury, SP4 6AT
Nearest main town: Salisbury

Secretary: Mr N. I. Symington   Tel: 01722 782231
                                      Fax: 01722 782356
Professional: Mr I. Welding   Tel: 01722 782219

Playing: Midweek: round £23.00; day £35.00. Weekend: round £28.00; day £35.00. Handicap certificate required.

Facilities: Bar: 11am–10pm. Food: Lunch and dinner from 11am–9pm.

Comments: Very open course on Salisbury Plain ... Watch out for jet fighters overhead ... A treat ... Very English and tradi- tional ... One of the best in Wiltshire ... Great value ... Tremendous ... Facilities a little basic.

Manor House Golf Club ★★★★

Castle Coombe, SN14 7PL
Nearest main town: Chippenham

Secretary:	Mrs S. Auld	Tel: 01249 782982
		Fax: 01249 782992
Professional:	Mr C. Smith	Tel: 01249 783101
		Fax: 01249 783103

Playing: Midweek: round £37.50; day £60.00. Weekend: round £50.00; day £80.00. Handicap certificate required.

Facilities: Bar: 11am–11pm. Food: Lunch and dinner from 11am–9pm. Bar snacks.

Comments: The best Alliss/Clark layout ... You have to plot your way round here ... Rather hilly and exhausting ... A cracker ... Expensive ... Get a strategy ready ... Modern club with excellent facilities ... Complete course with pot bunkers, loads of water and rollercoaster greens.

Marlborough Golf Club ★★

The Common, Marlborough, SN8 1DU
Nearest main town: Marlborough

Secretary:	Mr J. A. D. Sullivan	Tel: 01672 512147
		Fax: 01672 513164
Professional:	Mr S. Amor	Tel: 01672 512493

Playing: Midweek: round £22.00; day £32.00. Weekend: round £30.00; day £40.00. Handicap certificate required.

Facilities: Bar: 11am–11pm. Food: Lunch from 11am–4pm. Dinner by arrangement.

Comments: Good reputation ... Decent value ... Smart club ... Tranquil and attractive ... Could come here more often ... Have a day out at the course and town.

North Wilts Golf Club ★★

Bishop's Cannings, Devizes, SN10 2LP
Nearest main town: Devizes

Secretary:	Mrs P. Stephenson	Tel: 01380 860627
		Fax: 01380 860877
Professional:	Mr G J. Laing	Tel: 01380 860330

Playing: Midweek: round £19.00; day £28.00. Weekend: round £25.00; day £40.00. Handicap certificate required.

Facilities: Bar: 11am–11pm. Food: Lunch and dinner from 11am–10pm. Bar snacks.

Comments: Well-presented course and a very friendly welcome ... Downland course with fine views.

Ogbourne Downs Golf Club ★

Ogbourne St George, Marlborough, SN8 1TB
Nearest main town: Marlborough

Secretary: Mr D. J. Knight   Tel: 01672 841327
                                         Fax: 01672 841327
Professional: Mr C. Harraway   Tel: 01672 841287

Playing: Midweek: round £20.00; day £20.00. Weekend: round £30.00; day £30.00. Handicap certificate required.

Facilities: Bar: 11am–11pm. Food: Lunch and dinner from 11am–6pm.

Comments: Nice welcome ... Course a little down the pecking order ... Better examples of downland golf elsewhere ... Missable ... A little tiresome.

Salisbury & South Wilts Golf Club ★★★

Netherhampton, Salisbury, SP2 8PR
Nearest main town: Salisbury

Secretary: Mr G. Pearce   Tel: 01722 742645
                                         Fax: 01722 742645
Professional: Mr J. Cave   Tel: 01722 742929

Playing: Midweek: round £25.00; day £30.00. Weekend: round £40.00; day £55.00.

Facilities: Bar: 11am–11pm. Food: Lunch and dinner from 11am–9pm.

Comments: Excellent presentation ... Kept in mint condition ... Really had fun ... Not too busy like a lot of courses in the area ... Large and welcoming membership ... Have grown to love it over the years.

The Wiltshire Golf Club ★★

Vastern, Swindon, SN4 7PB
Nearest main town: Wootton Bassett

Secretary: Mr D. Martin   Tel: 01793 849999
                               Fax: 01793 849988
Professional: Mr A. Gray   Tel: 01793 851360

Playing: Midweek: round n/a; day £30.00. Weekend: round n/a; day £30.00. Handicap certificate required.

Facilities: Bar: 11am–11pm. Food: Lunch and dinner from 11am–6pm.

Comments: Tight fairways with many lakes and ponds ... Nothing special ... Water hazards the primary defence to this average course.

Tidworth Garrison Golf Club ★★★

Bulford Road, Tidworth, SP9 7AF
Nearest main town: Tidworth

Secretary: Mr T. Harris   Tel: 01980 842301
                               Fax: 01980 842301
Professional: Mr T. Gosden   Tel: 01980 842393

Playing: Midweek: round £22.00; day £22.00. Weekend: round £22.00; day £22.00. Handicap certificate required.

Facilities: Bar: 11am–11pm. Food: Lunch from 11am–4pm.

Comments: Views of Salisbury Plain ... Perhaps overrated ... Always in neat order ... Very dry in the summer ... Bouncy course when dry ... Downland – best in the spring or autumn ... Exciting par-5s.

Upavon Golf Club ★★

Douglas Avenue, Upavon, SN9 6BQ
Nearest main town: Upavon

Secretary: Mr L. Mitchell   Tel: 01980 630787
                                 Fax: 01980 630787
Professional: Mr R. Blake   Tel: 01980 630281
                                 Fax: 01980 635103

Playing: Midweek: round £16.00; day £22.00. Weekend: round £16.00; day £22.00.

Facilities: Bar: 11am–11pm. Food: Lunch from 11am–4pm.

Comments: Nice example of downland course ... Can always get a game ... Never busy ... Straightforward ... Plenty of birdie chances ... Great welcome at this uncrowded course.

West Wilts Golf Club   ★★

Elm Hill, Warminster, BA12 0AU
Nearest main town: Westbury

Secretary: Mr D. J. Spratt   Tel: 01985 213133
                                          Fax: 01985 219809
Professional: Mr A. J. Lamb   Tel: 01985 212110

Playing: Midweek: round £18.00; day £28.00. Weekend: round £36.00; day £36.00. Handicap certificate required.

Facilities: Bar: 11am–9pm. Food: Lunch from 11am–3pm.

Comments: Short course with tight fairways ... Well thought out ... Good all-round club ... Downland course with excellent drainage ... Condition tip-top.

East Yorkshire

Beverley & East Riding Golf Club ★★

The Westwood, Beverley, HU17 8RG
Nearest main town: Beverley

Secretary:	Mr B. Gregory	Tel: 01482 868757
		Fax: 01482 868757
Professional:	Mr I. Mackie	Tel: 01482 869519

Playing: Midweek: round £12.00; day £16.00. Weekend: round £16.00; day £21.00.

Facilities: Bar: 11am–11pm. Food: Lunch from 12pm–3pm. Dinner by arrangement.

Comments: Outstanding greens for a commonland course ... Watch out for the sheep ... Natural layout – not everyone's choice ... Rugged ... Gorse the main defence.

Bridlington Golf Club ★

Belvedere Road, Bridlington, YO15 3NA
Nearest main town: Bridlington

Secretary:	Mr C. Greenwood	Tel: 01262 606367
		Fax: 01262 606367
Professional:	Mr A. R. A. Howarth	Tel: 01262 674721
		Fax: 01262 674721

Playing: Midweek: round £14.00; day £22.00. Weekend: round £25.00; day £30.00.

Facilities: Bar: 11am–11pm. Food: Lunch and dinner from 11am–9pm. Bar snacks.

Comments: Excellent and unusual club – beautiful waitresses ... Seaside course ... Unmanicured, wild course on top of cliffs ... On a cold day can be brutal ... Enjoyable, natural course.

Cave Castle Golf Hotel ★

South Cave, Hull, HU15 2EU
Nearest main town: Hull

Secretary:	Mrs C. Welton	Tel: 01430 421286
		Fax: 01430 421118
Professional:	Mr S. Mackinder	Tel: 01430 421286

Playing: Midweek: round £12.50; day £18.00. Weekend: round £18.00; day £25.00.

Facilities: Bar: 11am–11pm. Food: Breakfast, lunch and dinner from 7am–10pm. Bar snacks.

Comments: Young course with improving standards ... Great value course where beginners are welcome ... Enjoyed every minute of it ... Some way to go, but good future.

Flamborough Head Golf Club ★

Lighthouse Road, Flamborough, YO15 1AR
Nearest main town: Bridlington

Secretary:	Mr G. S. Thornton	Tel: 850333
		Fax: 01262 850279
Professional:	None.	

Playing: Midweek: round n/a; day £20.00. Weekend: round n/a; day n/a.

Facilities: Bar: 11am–9pm. Food: Lunch and dinner by arrangement. Bar snacks.

Comments: Unusual links ... Could be better ... Old-style club with remarkable course ... Very English.

Hornsea Golf Club

Rolston Road, Hornsea, HU18 1XG
Nearest main town: Hornsea

Secretary:	Mr B. W. Kirton	Tel: 01964 532020
		Fax: 01964 532020
Professional:	Mr B. Thompson	Tel: 01964 534989

Playing: Midweek: round £19.00; day £26.00. Weekend: round £30.00; day n/a.

Facilities: Bar: 11am–11pm. Food: Lunch from 11am–5pm. Bar snacks.

Comments: Members only before 3pm at weekends ... Parkland course ... Greens exceptional on visit ... Nothing special ... Homely club.

North Yorkshire

Ganton Golf Club ★★★★★

Station Road, Ganton, YO12 4PA
Nearest main town: Scarborough

All that is missing from Ganton is the sea. The course feels as if it should have been moulded by the crushing of waves against cliffs, but despite the freshness of the air and the sea shells that can be found in some of the bunkers, it remains indelibly moorland with gorse and heather carpeting the edges of the fairways. Links lovers might snobbishly label it inadequate on this count, but any honest golfer would agree that Ganton is a magnificent course.

It has been likened to some of the great courses in Surrey in its character, but the similarity is very tenuous, with trees only affecting play on four holes. There are no great avenues of trees and only occasionally, where great banks of gorse can threaten, is there not an awareness of space. In truth, it bears a similarity to Woodhall Spa, another heathland course which is located in Lincolnshire.

Situated in the Vale of Pickering not far from Scarborough, Ganton is a terrific challenge on a windy day and a good one on a calm day. The gorse and heather dictate the style and pace of play, but so do the bunkers, which are expansive (none more so than the huge bunker on the 16th, in which you could get two coaches and still have room for a car) on the fairways and deeply potted around the greens.

Ganton is unique for a course of such standing in that it has only two par-3s and two par-5s to make a par of 72. The monotony of the par-4s is thankfully broken with some excellent examples of the short par-4, and few walk off the 18th green bored or non-plussed with the examination that they have just sat.

Memorable holes include the 4th, a 397-yard par-4 which is played over a gully to a plateau green with a water hazard guarding the left-hand side of the green, and the 17th with a carry over a road and cross bunker to a far green, closely trapped and exposed to all the winds. In some ways the best is saved until last, a dogleg where if you drive too far to the left, you will find your second shot, requiring a long-iron, screened by a copse of pines.

Secretary: Maj R. G. Woolsey   Tel: 01944 710329
                                        Fax: 01944 710922
Professional: Mr G. Brown   Tel: 01944 710260

Playing: Midweek: round £50.00; day £50.00. Weekend: round £56.00; day £56.00. Handicap certificate required.

Facilities: Bar: 11am–11pm. Food: Lunch and dinner by arrangement.

Comments: Secretary and members could not have been more friendly ... A real thinking man's course ... Very tough track in the wind ... Terrific course, and what bunkers! ... Get the European Tour to play here in the wind ... Interesting and varied ... Genuine course ... Shame it can't hold tour events any more ... Many links characteristics but essentially moorland.

Catterick Golf Club   ★

Leyburn Road, Catterick Garrison, DL9 3QE
Nearest main town: Scotch Corner

Secretary: Mrs D. Hopkins   Tel: 01748 833268
                                      Fax: 01748 833268
Professional: Mr A. Marshall   Tel: 01748 833671

Playing: Midweek: round £15.00; day £20.00. Weekend: round £25.00; day n/a. Handicap certificate required.

Facilities: Bar: 11am–11pm. Food: Lunch and dinner from 11am–9pm. Bar snacks.

Comments: Played here many times and always a new set of problems ... Watch out for Heartbreak Hill ... Opens as it means to go on – tough ... Fairly unkempt course but interesting ... Plenty of out of bounds.

Cleveland Golf Club

Queen Street, Redcar, TS10 1BT
Nearest main town: Redcar

Secretary: Mr P. Fletcher   Tel: 01642 471798
                                      Fax: 01642 471798
Professional: Mr S. Wynn   Tel: 01642 483462

Playing: Midweek: round £20.00; day £22.00. Weekend: round £22.00; day £26.00.

Facilities: Bar: 11am–11pm. Food: Lunch and dinner from 11am–7pm. Bar snacks.

Comments: A potentially fine links ... Spoiled by its dreadfully industrial surroundings ... A spirited club ... Only links in Yorkshire ... Polluted air spoils otherwise fine course ... Steelworks a blot on the landscape ... A monster on a windy day ... Very long for the amateur.

Cocksford Golf Club ★★

Stutton, Tadcaster, LS24 9NG
Nearest main town: Tadcaster

Secretary:	Mrs G. Coxon	Tel: 01937 834253
		Fax: 01937 834253
Professional:	Mr G. Thompson	Tel: 01937 834253

Playing: Midweek: round £17.00; day £21.00. Weekend: round £23.00; day £26.00.

Facilities: Bar: 11am–11pm. Food: Lunch from 12pm–2pm. Dinner from 6pm–9pm. Bar snacks.

Comments: Caters for all standards ... Slightly poor condition ... Historic setting on scene of battle ... Main hazard a beck that affects half the 27 holes ... Won't be going again ... Cheap, fun golf.

Forest Park Golf Club ★★

Stockton-on-Forest, York, YO3 9UW
Nearest main town: York

Secretary:	Miss N. Crossley	Tel: 01904 400425
Professional:	None.	

Playing: Midweek: round £16.00; day £22.00. Weekend: round £21.00; day £28.00.

Facilities: Bar: 11am–11pm. Food: Bar snacks.

Comments: Improving all the time ... Parkland setting with mature trees and strategic design ... Very average ... 27 holes ... Improving ... Some way to go.

Fulford Golf Club

Heslington Lane, York, YO1 5DY
Nearest main town: York

Secretary:	Mr R. Bramley	Tel: 01904 413579
		Fax: 01904 416918
Professional:	Mr B. Hessay	Tel: 01904 412882

Playing: Midweek: round £35.00; day £45.00. Weekend: round £45.00; day £45.00. Handicap certificate required.

Facilities: Bar: 11am–11pm. Food: Lunch and dinner from 11am–9pm.

Comments: Excellent all round and good value ... Nice memories of Bernhard Langer and Peter Baker ... Traditional and superb ... Excellent facilities ... Nice, peaceful with good greens, fairways and beer ... It may have been easy for the pros, but great for 15-handicapper ... Condition always superb, too easy for the pros but just about perfect for us ... Par-4s make this course super all round ... Welcomed with open arms ... Surely could be used for a tour event ... Oozes nostalgia.

Harrogate Golf Club ★★★★

Forest Lane Head, Harrogate, HG2 7TF
Nearest main town: Harrogate

Secretary:	Mr G. Merryweather	Tel: 01423 862999
		Fax: 01423 860073
Professional:	Mr P. Johnson	Tel: 01423 862547

Playing: Midweek: round £28.00; day £32.00. Weekend: round £40.00; day £40.00. Handicap certificate required.

Facilities: Bar: 11am–11pm. Food: Lunch and dinner from 11am–9pm. Bar snacks.

Comments: Very mature ... Delightful in every way ... One of the finest in Yorkshire ... 14th overlooked by Knaresborough Castle ... Straightforward and honest ... Quality in spades.

Kirkbymoorside Golf Club ★★★

Manor Vale, Kirkbymoorside, York, YO6 6EG
Nearest main town: Pickering

Secretary:	Mr A. R. Holmes	Tel: 01751 431525
		Fax: 01751 433190
Professional:	None.	

Playing: Midweek: round £18.00; day £18.00. Weekend: round £25.00; day £25.00.

Facilities: Bar: 11am–11pm. Food: Lunch from 12pm–3pm. Dinner by arrangement.

Comments: A wonderful welcome ... Every hole a potential card-killer ... A nice test with imagination in the design ... Well-kept greens.

Malton & Norton Golf Club   ★★

Welham Park, Welham Road, York, Malton, YO17 9QE
Nearest main town: York

Secretary: Mr E. Harrison   Tel: 01653 697912
                                        Fax: 01653 697912
Professional: Mr S. I. Robinson   Tel: 01653 693882

Playing: Midweek: round £22.00; day £22.00. Weekend: round £28.00; day £28.00. Handicap certificate required.

Facilities: Bar: 11am–11pm. Food: Lunch from 12pm–3pm. Dinner by arrangement.

Comments: Average course with 27 holes ... Holes work in all directions ... Mixed quality ... A mixture of flat and sloping parkland ... Nothing out of the ordinary ... Pretty decent value.

Oakdale Golf Club   ★★

Oakdale, Harrogate, HG1 2LN
Nearest main town: Harrogate

Secretary: Mr D. Rodgers   Tel: 01423 567162
                                        Fax: 01423 536030
Professional: Mr C. Dell   Tel: 01423 560510

Playing: Midweek: round £27.00; day £32.00. Weekend: round £32.00; day £40.00. Handicap certificate required.

Facilities: Bar: 11am–11pm. Food: Lunch from 12pm–3pm. Dinner from 7pm–9.30pm. No food on Mondays.

Comments: High quality ... Another touch of Mackenzie in Yorkshire ... Subtle ... Makes you think ... Not a great, but bubbling under ... You never have the course licked.

Pannal Golf Club   ★★★

Follifoot Road, Pannal, HG3 1ES
Nearest main town: Harrogate

Secretary:	Mr R. Braddon	Tel: 01423 872628
		Fax: 01423 870043
Professional:	Mr M. Burgess	Tel: 01423 872620

Playing: Midweek: round £37.00; day £45.00. Weekend: round £45.00; day n/a. Handicap certificate required.

Facilities: Bar: 11am–11pm. Food: Lunch and dinner from 12pm–9pm.

Comments: Very exposed ... Fascinating moorland course ... Rather barren and bleak ... Overpriced ... A driver's course ... Natural course where you have to feel the layout ... Greens of the highest order ... Presentation an absolute dream.

Romanby Golf Club   ★★★

Yafforth Road, Northallerton, DL7 0PE
Nearest main town: Northallerton

Secretary:	Mr G. McDonnell	Tel: 01609 778855
		Fax: 01609 779084
Professional:	Mr T. Jenkins	

Playing: Midweek: round £15.00; day £21.50. Weekend: round £20.00; day £30.00.

Facilities: Bar: 11am–11pm. Food: Lunch and dinner from 10am–9pm. Bar snacks.

Comments: Still a young course but the best is yet to come ... Excellent course and catering ... Outstanding pay-as-you-play ... Water in play on seven holes ... Considerate design ... Makes full use of natural terrain ... Everything a new course should be ... First-class facilities.

Rudding Park Golf Club   ★★★

Ruddong Park, Harrogate, HG3 1DJ
Nearest main town: Harrogate

Secretary:	Mr M. Mackaness	Tel: 01423 872100
		Fax: 01423 873011
Professional:	Mr S. Hotham	Tel: 01423 873400

Playing: Midweek: round £18.50; day £30.00. Weekend: round £20.00; day £32.50. Handicap certificate required.

Facilities: Bar: 11am–11pm. Food: Lunch and dinner from 11am–8pm. Bar snacks.

Comments: Skill needed on these slick greens ... No problems off the tee ... Nice new complex with hotel on site ... Much imagination needed to interpret these sloping greens ... Course has an 'old' feel for a modern layout ... Excellent covered driving range ... A place to learn the game.

Scarborough North Cliff Golf Club ★★★

North Cliff Avenue, Burniston Road, Scarborough, YO12 6PP
Nearest main town: Scarborough

Secretary:	Mr J. R. Freeman	Tel: 01723 360786
		Fax: 01723 362134
Professional:	Mr S. N. Deller	Tel: 01723 365920

Playing: Midweek: round £18.00; day £25.00. Weekend: round £22.00; day £28.00. Handicap certificate required.

Facilities: Bar: 11am–11pm. Food: Lunch from 12pm–2pm.

Comments: A stunning location ... Views over the North Sea ... A very natural course with spectacular views ... Views over choice countryside ... Superior to South Cliff.

Scarborough South Cliff Golf Club ★★★

Deepdale Avenue, Scarborough, YO11 2UE
Nearest main town: Scarborough

Secretary:	Mr C. Weir	Tel: 01723 374737
		Fax: 01723 376969
Professional:	Mr A. R. Skingle	Tel: 01723 365150

Playing: Midweek: round £18.00; day £25.00. Weekend: round £25.00; day £30.00. Handicap certificate required.

Facilities: Bar: 11am–11pm. Food: Lunch and dinner from 12pm–8pm.

Comments: Very different feel to the North Cliff ... Course has its own 'Amen Corner' at the 15th, 16th and 17th ... Ian Woosnam has won here ... Problems start on the green ... Multi-tiered greens ... Tricky, hard-to-read greens.

York Golf Club

Lords Moor Lane, Strensall, York, YO3 5XF
Nearest main town: York

Secretary: Mr S. G. Watson   Tel: 01904 491840
                                       Fax: 01904 491852
Professional: Mr A. Mason   Tel: 01904 490304

Playing: Midweek: round £25.00; day £32.00. Weekend: round n/a; day n/a.

Facilities: Bar: 11am–11pm. Food: Lunch from 12pm–2pm. Dinner from 7pm–9pm. Bar snacks.

Comments: Overshadowed by Ganton and Fulford but a great day's golf nonetheless ... Friendly, enjoyable place to play ... Heathland gem ... Felt like a member for the day ... Not too tiring ... Bar meals out of this world.

South Yorkshire

Rotherham Golf Club

Thrybergh Park, Rotherham, S65 4NU
Nearest main town: Rotherham

Rotherham Golf Club could not be more removed from the typical picture people might have of the area of industrial bleakness. Indeed, only standing on the 17th tee can you see any evidence that this is the industrial heartland of England, such is the protection that the mature deciduous trees give the course.

Only three miles out of the city centre, you approach the course on a road that gives you the impression that Rotherham could be a mini-Sunningdale or Wentworth in the heart of Yorkshire. Indeed, the impression is confirmed when you reach the clubhouse, a country mansion that was once owned by the Rearsby family. In front of the club-house is a massive beech tree, and standing by the first tee an intimidating oak that you feel you will see more of once you are out on the course.

But, some might say disappointingly, that is not the case, as you will find that Rotherham is an open and undulating course, the trees not really interfering with play but simply forming the boundaries of the course.

A par-70 with two par-5s and four par-3s, Rotherham is not particularly difficult in terms of losing balls, but rather in scoring. For sheer difficulty, Hallamshire or nearby Lindrick (Derbyshire) come out tops, but Rotherham makes you think, particularly when you are playing approach shots to small undulating greens, protected by deep bunkers. The par-3s are excellent examples of this where, with the exception of the 9th, all are played to raised and elevated greens on banks.

Rotherham is a friendly and compact course that is very popular with societies. There's a lively atmosphere in the impressive clubhouse and the course weathers well in the winter.

Secretary: Mr G. Smalley   Tel: 01709 850812
                                         Fax: 01709 855288
Professional: Mr S. Thornhill   Tel: 01709 850480

Playing: Midweek: round £28.00; day £28.00. Weekend: round
                    £35.00; day £35.00.

Facilities: Bar: 11am–11pm. Food: Lunch and dinner from 11am–9pm.

Comments: Tests your skills to the limit ... Great value for money on this mature course ... Fairly straightforward established course ... Enjoyed it ... Will be back.

Doncaster Golf Club ★★

Bawtry Road, Besscarr, Doncaster, DN4 5HU
Nearest main town: Doncaster

Secretary:	Mr R. Perkins	Tel: 01302 865632
		Fax: 01302 865994
Professional:	Mr G. Bailey	Tel: 01302 868404

Playing: Midweek: round £20.00; day £25.00. Weekend: round £25.00; day n/a. Handicap certificate required.

Facilities: Bar: 11am–11pm. Food: Bar snacks. Sunday lunch by arrangement.

Comments: Parkland/heathland with nice feel ... Wouldn't return in a hurry ... A few too many parallel fairways ... Well bunkered ... One for the long hitters with plenty of room ... Undulating with well-placed bunkers.

Hallamshire Golf Club ★★★

Sandygate, Sheffield, S10 4LA
Nearest main town: Sheffield

Secretary:	Mrs K. E. Redshaw	Tel: 0114 230 2153
		Fax: 0114 230 2153
Professional:	Mr G. Tickell	Tel: 0114 230 5222

Playing: Midweek: round £36.00; day n/a. Weekend: round £41.00; day n/a. Handicap certificate required.

Facilities: Bar: 11am–10pm. Food: Lunch from 11.30am–3pm.

Comments: Very difficult front nine due to the wind ... Greens hard and fast on visit ... Superbly natural course at 800ft ... Excellent condition ... Can always get a game here ... A cracker of a moorland course.

Hallowes Golf Club   ★★

Dronfield, Sheffield, S18 6UR
Nearest main town: Sheffield

Secretary: Mr R. Wariss   Tel: 01246 413734
                                         Fax: 01246 411196
Professional: Mr P. Dunn   Tel: 01246 411196

Playing: Midweek: round £25.00; day £34.00. Weekend: round
                    n/a; day n/a.

Facilities: Bar: 11am–11pm. Food: Breakfast, lunch and dinner
                    from 7am–9pm. Closed on Mondays.

Comments: A favourite course in the area ... Good layout and
                    always friendly ... Moorland course with good atmos-
                    phere ... Unlikely to be on a must-play list.

Hillsborough Golf Club   ★★★

Worrall Road, Sheffield, S6 4BE
Nearest main town: Sheffield

Secretary: Mr K. A. Dungey   Tel: 0114 234 9151
                                         Fax: 0114 234 9151
Professional: Mr G. Walker   Tel: 0114 233 2666

Playing: Midweek: round £28.00; day £28.00. Weekend: round
                    £35.00; day £35.00. Handicap certificate required.

Facilities: Bar: 11am–11pm. Food: Lunch from 11.30am–3pm.

Comments: Not a bunker to be seen ... Mature parkland of some
                    reputation ... Hard to beat in Yorkshire ... Opening
                    hole an absolute cracker ... Very stiff test ... Pick of the
                    bunch the par-3 3rd.

Lindrick Golf Club   ★★★★

Lindrick Common, Worksop, S81 8BH
Nearest main town: Worksop

Secretary: Lt Sdr R. J. M. Jack RN   Tel: 01909 475282
                                              Fax: 01909 488685
Professional: Mr J. King   Tel: 01909 475820

Playing: Midweek: round n/a; day £45.00. Weekend: round
                    £30.00; day n/a. Handicap certificate required.

Facilities: Bar: 11am–11pm. Food: Lunch and dinner from 11am–9pm. Bar snacks.

Comments: Excellent course but could be friendlier ... Just pop off the M1 to find this great course ... Course not as good as I was led to believe ... Overrated – only three or four good holes and not very friendly ... Expected more from this heathland course.

Silkstone Golf Club   ★

Field Head, Elmhirst Lane, Silkstone, S75 4LD
Nearest main town: Barnsley

Secretary: Mr J. Goulding   Tel: 01226 790328
Professional: Mr K. Guy   Tel: 01226 790128

Playing: Midweek: round £26.00; day £26.00. Weekend: round n/a; day n/a. Handicap certificate required.

Facilities: Bar: 11am–11pm. Food: Bar snacks.

Comments: A little too hilly for my liking ... Extremely tough walking ... Can be a struggle ... Heavily sloping fairways approaching small greens ... Very stiff test with terrible par-3 finish.

Tankersley Park Golf Club   ★

High Green, Sheffield, S30 4LG
Nearest main town: Sheffield

Secretary: Mr A. Brownhill   Tel: 0114 246 8247
                                           Fax: 0114 245 5583
Professional: Mr I. Kirk   Tel: 0114 245 5583

Playing: Midweek: round £24.00; day £28.00. Weekend: round £28.00; day n/a.

Facilities: Bar: 11am–11pm. Food: Lunch and dinner from 11am–9.30pm.

Comments: Good condition with some tough holes, especially the 18th ... Nice course to play ... Nice welcome ... Views over the Pennines.

West Yorkshire

Alwoodley Golf Club ★★★★★

Wigton Lane, Alwoodley, LS17 8SA
Nearest main town: Leeds

With Moor Allerton, Sand Moor, Ilkley and Moortown in close proximity, The Alwoodley is the centrepiece of an outstanding selection of courses just north of Leeds. For golf lovers, it is just sheer heaven, and it's never too busy – the area is not exactly known for its tourism, with holidaying golfers few and far between.

Perhaps it is not surprising that The Alwoodley should be such a superb golf course given the quality of the men who have fashioned it through the years. Harry Colt and Alister Mackenzie supervised its birth and formative years and Mackenzie liked the product so much that he became the first club secretary. Minor alterations have been implemented down the years, and the greens and tees have recently been upgraded, while keeping the spirit of the original layout.

The layout of the course is The Alwoodley's best feature, with each hole being very individual. The danger comes not from the mature stands of trees, but from the heather, which must be avoided at all costs. The course's bunkering is fairly sparse, but what there is is cleverly placed and designed.

An indication of The Alwoodley's challenge comes as early as the 2nd, where the tee shot must carry 150 yards over gorse and heather to an unseen fairway, before twisting left to an angled green which is completely unprotected. The run from the 5th to the 8th is a particularly strong stretch of holes, while there are a number of devious doglegs, particularly the 15th and 16th which form half of a wonderful finishing stretch running back to the clubhouse with each hole over 400 yards.

With only two par-5s and three of the four par-3s requiring long irons, The Alwoodley has a reputation for being one of the hardest courses in the country. Once you've experienced it, you'll find it hard to disagree. This really is a challenge.

Secretary: Mr R. C. W. Banks   Tel: 0113 268 1680
                                          Fax: 0113 293 9458
Professional: Mr J. R. Green   Tel: 0113 268 9603

Playing: Midweek: round £50.00; day £50.00. Weekend: round £60.00; day £60.00.

Facilities:	Bar: 11am–11pm. Food: Lunch and dinner from 11am–9pm. Bar snacks.
Comments:	Quality course in excellent condition ... Lovely new clubhouse ... Just five minutes outside Leeds – unbelievable ... Mackenzie masterpiece ... Play the designer who worked on Augusta ... Wonderful ... Exclusive club but possible to play ... Best in Yorkshire by far.

Bingley St Ives Golf Club ★★★★

St Ives Estate, Bingley, BD16 1AT
Nearest main town: Bradford

Secretary:	Mrs M. Welch (Manager)	Tel: 01274 562436 Fax: 01274 511788
Professional:	Mr R. Firth	Tel: 01274 562506

Playing:	Midweek: round £24.00; day £29.00. Weekend: round n/a; day n/a. Handicap certificate required.
Facilities:	Bar: 11am–11pm. Food: Lunch from 11am–5.30pm. Dinner by arrangement. Bar snacks.
Comments:	Used to be municipal, now private ... Three courses in one with moorland, woodland and parkland ... Touched by the great Bobby Jones and Alistair Mackenzie ... Hallowed fairways ... Much improved ... Sleeping giant reawakened ... Cracking finish ... Deserves more recognition ... Quality new clubhouse.

Garforth Golf Club ★★★

Long Lane, Garforth, Leeds, LS25 2DS
Nearest main town: Leeds

Secretary:	Mr N. C. Brown	Tel: 0113 286 3308 Fax: 0113 286 3308
Professional:	Mr K. Findlater	Tel: 0113 286 2063 Fax: 0113 286 2063

Playing:	Midweek: round £26.00; day £30.00. Weekend: round n/a; day n/a.
Facilities:	Bar: 11am–11pm. Food: Bar snacks.

Comments: Wouldn't mind being a member here ... Practice ground one of the best around ... Course really sets the pulse racing ... So natural, so enjoyable ... Great location with Cock Beck providing natural water hazards ... Beck comes into play on 10 holes.

Halifax Bradley Hall Golf Club   ★

Holywell Green, Halifax, HX4 9AN
Nearest main town: Halifax

Secretary: Mr J. R. Burton   Tel: 01422 374108
Professional: Mr P. Wood   Tel: 01422 370231

Playing: Midweek: round £18.00; day £23.00. Weekend: round £28.00; day £35.00. Handicap certificate required.

Facilities: Bar: 11am–11pm. Food: Lunch from 11am–2pm. Dinner from 6pm–9pm.

Comments: Super closing holes ... Not particularly memorable ... Far superior front nine ... Moorland with plenty of heather ... Lovely setting but course doesn't match it.

Halifax Golf Club   ★★★

Union Lane, Ogden, Halifax, HX2 8XR
Nearest main town: Halifax

Secretary: Mr G. Horrocks-Taylor   Tel: 01422 244171
    Fax: 01422 241459
Professional: Mr M. Allison   Tel: 01422 240047

Playing: Midweek: round £15.00; day £20.00. Weekend: round £20.00; day £30.00.

Facilities: Bar: 11am–11pm. Food: Lunch and dinner from 11am–9pm. Bar snacks.

Comments: Fascinating course with holes spilling in all directions ... Great design with wind a huge factor ... Design that has stood the test of time ... Excellent short par-4s ... Sprawling moorland ... Clever course ... Not one you can overpower ... Excellent variation.

Headingley Golf Club   ★★

Back Church Lane, Adel, Leeds, LS16 8DW
Nearest main town: Leeds

Secretary:	Mr J. R. Burns	Tel: 0113 267 9573
		Fax: 0113 281 7334
Professional:	Mr S. A. Foster	Tel: 0113 267 5100

Playing: Midweek: round £30.00; day £35.00. Weekend: round £40.00; day £40.00. Handicap certificate required.

Facilities: Bar: 11am–11pm. Food: Lunch and dinner from 11am–9pm. Bar snacks.

Comments: Another Mackenzie special ... One of the best in Leeds ... Trademark Mackenzie layout ... Fantastic blend of heathland and woodland ... Enjoyed every minute of it ... Loved it ... Some nice Augusta touches ... A real tribute to the members.

Huddersfield Golf Club   ★★★

Fixby Hall, Lightridge Road, Huddersfield, HD2 2EP
Nearest main town: Huddersfield

Secretary:	Mr J. M. Seatter	Tel: 01484 420110
		Fax: 01484 424623
Professional:	Mr P. Carman	Tel: 01484 426463

Playing: Midweek: round £33.00; day £45.00. Weekend: round £45.00; day £60.00. Handicap certificate required.

Facilities: Bar: 11am–11pm. Food: Bar snacks. Dinner by arrangement (jackets required).

Comments: One of Yorkshire's finest and most respected clubs ... Very imaginative layout ... Fine golf in exulted setting ... Makes full use of natural contours of the land ... Hilly in parts ... Condition top class ... A very fair and rewarding course.

Ilkley Golf Club   ★★★★

Myddleton, Ilkley, LS29 0BE
Nearest main town: Ilkley

Secretary:	Mr A. K. Hatfield	Tel: 01943 600214
		Fax: 01943 816130

Professional: Mr J. L. Hammond   Tel: 01943 607463
                                      Fax: 01943 607463

Playing: Midweek: round £37.00; day £37.00. Weekend: round £42.00; day £42.00.

Facilities: Bar: 11am–11pm. Food: Bar snacks or lunch by arrangement.

Comments: Maintained to perfection ... Pork pies at lunch were the best ever ... Immaculate fairways ... Nice greens and great scenery ... Unusual and consistently rewarding course ... Front nine gets my vote ... Had a great time.

Keighley Golf Club   ★★

Howden Park, Utley, Keighley, BD20 6DH
Nearest main town: Keighley

Secretary: Mr J. P. Cole   Tel: 01535 604778
                 (Manager)   Fax: 01535 604778
Professional: Mr M. Bradley   Tel: 01535 665370

Playing: Midweek: round £24.00; day £28.00. Weekend: round £28.00; day £34.00. Handicap certificate required.

Facilities: Bar: 11am–11pm. Food: Lunch and dinner from 10am–9pm. Bar snacks.

Comments: Nightmare finish ... Nothing special ... Nestling in the Aire Valley ... Fairly tight with good finish.

Leeds Golf Club   ★★

Elmete Road, Roundhay, Leeds, LS8 2LJ
Nearest main town: Leeds

Secretary: Mr S. J. Clarkson   Tel: 0113 265 9203
                                      Fax: 0113 232 3369
Professional: Mr S. Longster   Tel: 0113 265 8786

Playing: Midweek: round £25.00; day n/a. Weekend: round n/a; day n/a. Handicap certificate required.

Facilities: Bar: 11am–11pm. Food: Lunch and dinner from 10am–10pm. Bar snacks.

Comments: Unusual finish with a par-3 ... Very rural feel to this parkland course ... The oldest club in Leeds ... Very picturesque ... 11th a terror ... Traditional ... Well worth the money.

Mid Yorkshire Golf Club ★

Havercroft Lane, Darrington, Pontefract, WF8 3BP
Nearest main town: Pontefract

Secretary: Mr I. M. Collins   Tel: 01977 704522
                                         Fax: 01977 600823
Professional: Mr A. Corbett   Tel: 01977 600844
                                         Fax: 01977 600844

Playing: Midweek: round £18.00; day £27.00. Weekend: round £25.00; day n/a. Handicap certificate required.

Facilities: Bar: 11am–11pm. Food: Lunch from 11am–5pm. Dinner by arrangement.

Comments: Brand new development ... Ideal society venue ... Extensive facilities for the beginner ... What you would expect from a new venue ... Course doesn't quite match the facilities ... Sweeping well-maintained fairways.

Moor Allerton Golf Club

Coal Road, Wike, Leeds, LS17 9NH
Nearest main town: Leeds

Secretary: Mr J. Denton   Tel: 0113 266 1154
                                         Fax: 0113 237 1124
Professional: Mr R. Lane   Tel: 0113 266 5209

Playing: Midweek: round £41.00; day £45.00. Weekend: round n/a; day n/a. Handicap certificate required.

Facilities: Bar: 11am–11pm. Food: Lunch and dinner from 10am–9pm.

Comments: Quiet, beautifully presented ... A serious challenge ... Relaxed atmosphere ... First Robert Trent Jones design in the UK ... Views across Vale of York ... Clever course with good, imaginative use of water hazards ... Thoroughly enjoyed it.

Moortown Golf Club   ★★★★

Harrogate Road, Leeds, LS17 7DB
Nearest main town: Leeds

Secretary: Mr C. A. Moore   Tel: 0113 268 6521
                                        Fax: 0113 268 0986
Professional: Mr B. Hutchinson   Tel: 0113 268 3636

Playing: Midweek: round £42.00; day £50.00. Weekend: round
                  £47.00; day £55.00. Handicap certificate required.

Facilities: Bar: 11am–11pm. Food: Lunch from 11am–3pm.

Comments: Mackenzie masterpiece – top class ... Wonderful old
                  clubhouse dominates a very tough course ... Springy
                  turf ... Written into Ryder Cup legend ... Gorse,
                  heather, streams, hollows – has it all.

Northcliffe Golf Club   ★★★

High Bank Lane, Shipley, BD18 4LJ
Nearest main town: Bradford

Secretary: Mr H. R. Archer   Tel: 01274 596731
                                          Fax: 01274 596731
Professional: Mr M. Hillas   Tel: 01274 587193

Playing: Midweek: round £20.00; day £20.00. Weekend: round
                  £25.00; day £25.00. Handicap certificate required.

Facilities: Bar: 11am–11pm. Food: Lunch and dinner from
                  11am–10pm. Bar snacks.

Comments: A homely club, stamina is a prerequisite ... Great 1st
                  and 18th ... Very welcoming ... 18th green is 110ft
                  below tee ... Go for the views.

Otley Golf Club   ★

West Busk Lane, Otley, LS21 3NG
Nearest main town: Leeds

Secretary: Mrs P. Bates   Tel: 01943 465329
                                         Fax: 01943 850387
Professional: Mr S. Tomkinson   Tel: 01943 463403

Playing: Midweek: round £26.00; day £33.00. Weekend: round
                  £33.00; day £39.00.

Facilities: Bar: 11am–11pm. Food: Bar snacks.

Comments: Attractive club course with views to match ... Traditional woodland course ... Rather basic facilities ... Definitely worth the money ... A woodland special ... Really felt away from it all here ... My kind of golf course.

Sand Moor Golf Club ★★★★

Alwoodley Lane, Leeds, LS17 7DJ
Nearest main town: Leeds

Secretary: Mr B. F. Precious   Tel: 0113 268 5180
Fax: 0113 268 5180
Professional: Mr P. Tupling   Tel: 0113 268 3925
Fax: 0113 268 3925

Playing: Midweek: round £30.00; day £38.00. Weekend: round £40.00; day £40.00. Handicap certificate required.

Facilities: Bar: 11am–11pm. Food: Lunch and dinner from 11am–9pm.

Comments: A bit on the short side ... Classic Mackenzie course with natural hazards used ingeniously ... Excellent pro shop ... Facilities first class for visitors – it wasn't always that way here ... Very hilly ... A fine second-string course ... Spacious course with notable par-3s.

Scarcroft Golf Club ★★★★

Syke Lane, Leeds, LS14 3BQ
Nearest main town: Leeds

Secretary: Mr T. B. Davey   Tel: 0113 289 2311
Professional: Mr D. Tear   Tel: 0113 289 2780

Playing: Midweek: round £28.00; day £35.00. Weekend: round £40.00; day n/a. Handicap certificate required.

Facilities: Bar: 11am–11pm. Food: Lunch and dinner from 10am–9pm. Bar snacks.

Comments: Friendly atmosphere ... Well-cut fairways and greens ... Lovely course – peaceful, modern and good fun ... Popular course for visitors ... Well worth the visit.

Shipley Golf Club ★★★

Beckfoot Lane, Cottingley Bridge, Bingley, BD16 1LX
Nearest main town: Bradford

Secretary:	Mr G. M. Shaw	Tel: 01274 568652
		Fax: 01274 568652
Professional:	Mr J. R. Parry	Tel: 01274 563674

Playing: Midweek: round £27.00; day £27.00. Weekend: round £32.00; day £32.00. Handicap certificate required.

Facilities: Bar: 11am–11pm. Food: Breakfast, lunch and dinner from 9am–9pm. Bar snacks.

Comments: Superb examples of the Mackenzie green ... Situated in a verdant valley bottom ... Good condition ... Trees just keep getting in the way.

Wakefield Golf Club ★★★

28 Woodthorpe Lane, Sandal, Wakefield, WF2 6JH
Nearest main town: Wakefield

Secretary:	Mr J. W. Wood	Tel: 01924 258778
		Fax: 01924 242752
Professional:	Mr I. M. Wright	Tel: 01924 255380

Playing: Midweek: round £22.00; day £27.50. Weekend: round £30.00; day £30.00. Handicap certificate required.

Facilities: Bar: 11am–11pm. Food: Lunch and dinner from 12pm–9pm. Bar snacks.

Comments: Fairly straightforward with the exception of the left-hand dogleg at the 13th ... A few too many parallel holes ... Good par-3s ... Condition not consistent ... Plenty of bunkers.

West Bowling Golf Club ★

Newall Hall, Rooley Lane, Bradford, BD5 8LB
Nearest main town: Bradford

Secretary:	Mr M. E. L. Lynn	Tel: 01274 393207
		Fax: 01274 393207
Professional:	Mr I. A. Marshall	Tel: 01274 728036

Playing: Midweek: round £20.00; day £24.00. Weekend: round n/a; day n/a.

Facilities: Bar: 11am–11pm. Food: Lunch from 10am–5pm. Bar snacks. Dinner by arrangement.

Comments: Beautiful small course in urban surroundings ... Unheralded course ... Short but very good fun ... Recommended.

Woodsome Hall Golf Club   ★★

Woodsome Hall, Fenay Bridge, Huddersfield, HD8 0LQ
Nearest main town: Huddersfield

Secretary: Mr A. S. Guest   Tel: 01484 602739
                                       Fax: 01484 608260
Professional: Mr M. Higginbottom   Tel: 01484 602034

Playing: Midweek: round £27.50; day £35.00. Weekend: round £35.00; day £40.00. Handicap certificate required.

Facilities: Bar: 11am–11pm. Food: Breakfast, lunch and dinner from 9am–10pm.

Comments: Tradition, style, one of the best in Yorkshire ... Quality ... Clubhouse makes the course ... Good, old-fashioned values at this club ... Real treat.

SCOTLAND

Strathclyde

Royal Troon Golf Club ★★★★★

Craigend Road, Troon, KA10 6EP
Nearest main town: Troon

Royal Troon is the centrepiece of a magnificent stretch of courses on the coast of the Firth of Clyde that includes Prestwick and Western Gailes. Unlike, say, Open venues like Muirfield or Turnberry, which are showered with praise by almost all who play there, Troon is a links that suffers from the imbalance of its two halves. They are not that different in length, but the prevailing wind from the south-west makes the back nine very harrowing. On the first day of the 1997 Open Championship, only two players could match the par of 36 on the back nine.

This impression is not helped by the fact that Troon is essentially an out-and-back links, so by the time you step into the teeth of the gale on the 13th, the batteries are already running low. By the time you have reached the 18th, you can feel thoroughly disillusioned with the game and swear never to return to Troon.

Whether you label this a design fault, or merely package it as the slings-and-arrows of playing a championship course, you can't fail to be impressed with some of the holes at Troon. The best holes are at the farthest extreme of the course, starting with the 7th, a sharp dogleg protected by a conical sandhill on the right. They say the next, the Postage Stamp 8th, a par-3 of just 126 yards, is the most difficult stamp in the world to lick, played from an elevated tee into the prevailing wind to a green just 25 feet across at its widest point. The green is protected by a gully, a sandhill and crater bunkers. The 9th runs round the back of the Postage Stamp, a par-4 of 419 yards where the bunkers on the left protect the best line in – if you're too far right there's no sight of the green, which, unusually, is completely unprotected.

The 10th and 11th are Troon's best two holes. On both occasions, you drive over sandhills to unreceptive, bumpy fairways, from where it's uphill into the wind with a long iron. The 11th, with the railway running just over the stone wall, plays as a par-5 for the members but is one of the most difficult par-4s in the world for the pros.

Troon does not have the dramatic landscapes of other links courses, its definition confined to long wispy grasses and watchtower sandhills. The compensation comes in the form of dramatic views over the Firth of Clyde to the Isle of Arran and the Mull of Kintyre.

Secretary: Mr J. W. Chandler   Tel: 01292 311555
                                     Fax: 01292 318204
Professional: Mr R. B. Anderson   Tel: 01292 313281
                                       Fax: 01292 315977

Playing: Midweek: round £110.00; day n/a. Weekend: round n/a; day n/a. Handicap certificate required.

Facilities: Bar: 11am–11pm. Food: Lunch for visitors on Monday, Tuesday and Thursday only. Includes buffet lunch.

Comments: Visitors Monday, Tuesday & Thursday only. Price includes Old Course round as well ... Have not played it but walked it and reckon the Postage Stamp is one of the best holes in the world ... Overpriced ... Back nine is too tough ... Into the wind on the back nine is toughest experience I've had on any course ... A long, hard slog back ... Best holes are at far end of course ... Best holes from the 9th to the 13th ... Hard to fault ... Still one of the best around ... For the money, not worth it ... Loved it and will be back.

Turnberry Hotel Golf Club (Ailsa)   ★★★★★

Turnberry, KA26 9LT
Nearest main town: Girvan

Turnberry is arguably the most scenically stunning course on the Open Championship rota. The views across to the Isle of Arran and Mull of Kintyre are wondrous, and on a clear day you can sometimes see all the way to Ireland. And looming out of the mid-Atlantic swell is the sinister and primeval Ailsa Craig, a 1208ft bulging hunk of rock which lends its name to Turnberry's famous links.

The course, unusually for a links, is run entirely as a commercial operation. There are none of the Rottweiler secretaries you associate with the top private courses, so you should be able to play, although the waiting list is growing. Guests of the first-class hotel, which looms over the course, get preference, so if you really want to treat yourself, book in. If not, you'll just have to wait, but it's worth it.

Turnberry is maintained in absolutely stunning condition. The warts-and-all nature of links golf doesn't seem to apply here, where the fairways rarely get dry and the greens are always holding. It is hard to imagine there would be a first-class links here in 1945 when the course was used as an airstrip in the war, a transformation that destroyed many of its natural features. But, under the guidance of

Mackenzie Ross, it was revived and stands as a monument to that architect's brilliance.

Turnberry is also blessed with a pleasant micro-climate, the warm air on the Gulf Stream making for pleasant golfing conditions. There are all the perils you associate with Open courses, such as wiry rough, protected greens and sandhills, but it is not particularly wild and many of the tee shots are attractive from elevated tees to valley fairways. It truly is a very fair test of golf.

For many, the experience of playing Turnberry is purely to stand on the 9th tee, with the waves bludgeoning the rocky outcrop tee, with a drive across cliffs to a camber fairway marked by a stone cairn. But you wouldn't label it Turnberry's best hole. The 16th, a short par-4 called Wee Burn, could lay claim to that; so could any of the eight holes along the coast. The course truly will appeal to all and is the most accessible links for those who prefer the inland game.

Secretary:	Mr E. Bowman	Tel: 01655 331000
		Fax: 01655 331706
Professional:	Mr B. Gunson	Tel: 01655 331000
	(Golf Dir)	Fax: 01655 331069

Playing: Midweek: round £120.00; day n/a. Weekend: round £150.00; day n/a.

Facilities: Bar: 11am–11pm. Food: Breakfast, lunch and dinner from 7am–10pm. Bar snacks.

Comments: An experience that will live in the memory forever ... Just a wonderful place to play and forget about the world ... Forget the cost, you must play it at least once ... Not to be missed ... Playing the final hole towards the hotel is just a bit special ... Very beautiful ... History, tradition and a superb hotel ... Worth every penny.

Western Gailes Golf Club

Gailes, Irvine, KA11 5AE
Nearest main town: Troon

Western Gailes will never win any awards for equal opportunities (there are no ladies' tees here), but as a test of golf it is first class. It is not the type of links where the scenery distracts you from your game, neither is there a great deal of variety. The attraction of Western Gailes lies in staying mentally strong enough to combat the ferocious winds that can pick up here. In fact, the second name of the club could not be more appropriate.

The course is completely exposed to the winds that race in from the south-west, much like neighbouring Royal Troon. The winds that make the incoming holes at Troon such a contest are the same ones that will send your ball ballooning in the air from the 6th to the 13th at Western Gailes. It is here that you must protect your score before the comparatively easy finishing holes.

The unusual layout of the course, with the clubhouse set in the middle of a narrow piece of tortured, bumpy land, and the holes spreading out in both directions, is intriguing. With the toughest part of the course in the middle, you can completely lose your appetite for the game if things are going badly, and the sorry golfers trudging off the 18th are testament to that. The impression is further confirmed by looking at the faces of the members in the bar, carved completely by the strong winds, and more akin to North Sea shrimp fishermen than golfers.

One of the club's most distinguished members, Lord Brabazon, once said: 'If you have the time, play just three courses – Western Gailes, Prestwick and Turnberry.' Advice taken with a pinch of salt, although you should play Western Gailes.

Secretary: Mr A. M. McBean   Tel: 01294 311649
                                        Fax: 01294 312312

Professional: None.

Playing: Midweek: round £60.00; day £90.00. Weekend: round
                  n/a; day n/a.

Facilities: Bar: 11am–11pm. Food: Lunch and dinner from
                  11am–10pm.

Comments: Beautifully maintained and managed course ...
                  Excellent facilitites ... What a wonderful traditional
                  course with a warm Scottish welcome ... Warm and
                  friendly clubhouse.

Ballochmyle Golf Club   ★★

Ballochmyle, Mauchline, KA5 6LE
Nearest main town: Mauchline

Secretary: Mr A. Williams   Tel: 01290 550469
                                      Fax: 01290 550469

Professional: None.

Playing: Midweek: round £18.00; day £25.00. Weekend: round
                  n/a; day £30.00.

Facilities: Bar: 11am–11pm. Food: Bar snacks.

Comments: Small greens, plenty of trees ... Greens give this course protection against good scoring ... Friendly attitude ... Will go back for the welcome ... Unpretentious club ... Course honest, if somewhat unspectacular.

Belleisle Golf Club ★★★★

Belleisle Park, Doonfoot Road, Ayr, KA7 4DU
Nearest main town: Ayr

Secretary:	Mr T. Culter (Manager)	Tel: 01292 441258 Fax: 01292 442632
Professional:	Mr D. Gemmell	Tel: 01292 441314 Fax: 01292 441314

Playing: Midweek: round £19.00; day £27.00. Weekend: round £21.00; day £31.00.

Facilities: Bar: 11am–11pm. Food: Breakfast, lunch and dinner from 7am–10pm. Bar snacks.

Comments: One of the best kept and presented public courses ... Always in excellent condition – summer or winter ... True and fast greens on visit ... Tough and pretty.

Brunston Castle Golf Club

Daily, Girvan, KA26 9RH
Nearest main town: Girvan

Secretary:	Mr P. McCloy (Gen Manager)	Tel: 01465 811471 Fax: 01465 811545
Professional:	Mr S. Forbes	Tel: 01465 811474

Playing: Midweek: round £26.00; day £40.00. Weekend: round £30.00; day £45.00.

Facilities: Bar: 11am–11pm. Food: Lunch and dinner from 10am–10pm. Bar snacks.

Comments: Nice new course ... Tends to get boggy in wet conditions ... New Donald Steel course ... Praiseworthy design but course can get wet ... Perfect golf facility for novice.

Buchanan Castle Golf Club   ★★★

Drymen, G63 0HY
Nearest main town: Glasgow

Secretary: Mr R. Kinsella   Tel: 01360 660307
Professional: Mr K. Baxter   Tel: 01360 660330
                                  Fax: 01360 660330

Playing: Midweek: round £30.00; day £40.00. Weekend: round £30.00; day £40.00. Handicap certificate required.

Facilities: Bar: 11am–11pm. Food: Lunch and dinner from 10am–9pm. Bar snacks.

Comments: Very welcoming ... Loch Lomond is nearby ... Plenty of water in play ... Nice mix of natural hazards ... Conditioning out of the top drawer ... Shamefully underrated.

Carradale Golf Club   ★

Carradale, PA28 6SA
Nearest main town: Campbeltown

Secretary: Mr E. Graham   Tel: 01583 431335 (Home)
Professional: None.

Playing: Midweek: round n/a; day £8.00. Weekend: round n/a; day £8.00.

Facilities: Bar/Food: Hotels next to the course open for catering.

Comments: Nine-holer overlooking the Isle of Arran ... Good reviews ... So difficult ... Rough terrain and Lilliputian greens – very uncomfortable ... Pay it a visit.

Cathcart Castle Golf Club

Mearns Road, Clarkston, G76 7YL
Nearest main town: Clarkston

Secretary: Mr I. G. Sutherland   Tel: 0141 638 9449
Professional: Mr S. Duncan   Tel: 0141 638 3436

Playing: Midweek: round £25.00; day £35.00. Weekend: round n/a; day n/a.

Facilities: Bar: 11am–11pm. Food: Lunch and dinner from 10am–9pm. Bar snacks.

Comments: Straightforward course with few tricks ... Mature tree-lined course ... Excellent value for money ... Rather short and unmemorable.

Cathkin Braes Golf Club ★★★

Cathkin Road, Rutherglen, G73 4SE
Nearest main town: Glasgow

Secretary:	Mr H. Millar	Tel: 0141 634 6605
		Fax: 0141 634 6605
Professional:	Mr S. Bree	Tel: 0141 634 0650
		Fax: 0141 634 0650

Playing: Midweek: round £25.00; day £35.00. Weekend: round n/a; day n/a. Handicap certificate required.

Facilities: Bar: 11am–11pm. Food: Lunch and dinner from 10am–9pm.

Comments: Magnificent course prone to waterlogging and midgies ... Wonderful layout but exclusivity should give it a minus rating ... Demanding but expensive ... Absolute luxury ... Fantastic service ... Wonderful course with fantastic scenery ... A dream whether wet or dry ... Moorland treat.

Cowglen Golf Club ★

301 Barrhead Road, Glasgow, G43
Nearest main town: Glasgow

Secretary:	Mr R. J. G. Jamieson	Tel: 0141 632 0556
Professional:	Mr J. McTear	Tel: 0141 649 9401

Playing: Midweek: round £20.00; day n/a. Weekend: round £20.00; day n/a.

Facilities: Bar: 11am–11pm. Food: Lunch and dinner from 10am–10pm.

Comments: There's better around Glasgow ... A club course, not really worth it for visitors ... Views of the Campsie Hills ... You're not missing much if you swerve it.

Dullatur Golf Club ★

Dullatur, Glasgow, G68 0AR
Nearest main town: Cumbernauld

Secretary:	Mrs C. Miller	Tel: 01236 723230
		Fax: 01236 727271
Professional:	Mr D. Sinclair	

Playing: Midweek: round £20.00; day £30.00. Weekend: round £25.00; day £35.00.

Facilities: Bar: 11am–11pm. Food: Lunch and dinner from 10am–9pm.

Comments: Poor holes to get up and down from on lower part of course but otherwise pretty good ... New course designed by Dave Thomas ... Depressing name, depressing course ... Two courses and fair facilities for novice ... Fairly natural new course.

East Renfrewshire Golf Club ★★★

Loganswell, Pilmuir, Newton Mearns, G77 6RT
Nearest main town: Newton Mearns

Secretary:	Mr A. L. Gillespie	Tel: 0141 333 9989
		Fax: 0141 333 9979
Professional:	Mr G. D. Clarke	Tel: 01355 500206

Playing: Midweek: round £30.00; day £40.00. Weekend: round n/a; day n/a. Handicap certificate required.

Facilities: Bar: 11am–11pm. Food: Lunch and dinner from 10am–9pm. Bar snacks.

Comments: Superbly laid out and challenging course ... Very busy ... Holiday course that can get crowded ... Flattish course with plenty of intrigue.

Elderslie Golf Club

63 Main Road, Elderslie, G77 6RX
Nearest main town: Glasgow

Secretary:	Mrs A. Anderson	Tel: 01505 323956
Professional:	Mr R. Bowman	Tel: 01505 320032
		Fax: 01505 320032

Playing: Midweek: round £20.00; day £30.00. Weekend: round n/a; day n/a. Handicap certificate required.

Facilities: Bar: 11am–11pm. Food: Lunch and dinner from 10am–8pm. Bar snacks.

Comments: Fairly easy ... Drop in if you are near Glasgow ... Simple parkland course with little trouble ... Not great value ... Large and welcoming membership.

Glasgow Gailes Golf Club ★★★★★

Gailes, Irvine, KA11 5AE
Nearest main town: Irvine

Secretary: Mr D. W. Deas   Tel: 01294 311258
                                      Fax: 01294 279366
Professional: Mr J. Steven   Tel: 01294 311561

Playing: Midweek: round £42.00; day £52.00. Weekend: round £47.00; day £47.00. Handicap certificate required.

Facilities: Bar: 11am–11pm. Food: Lunch from 11am–4pm. Bar snacks all day.

Comments: Beguiling course, just heavenly when the sun shines ... Heather-lined course of infinite character ... Ninth-oldest course in the world ... Qualifying course for the Open ... Championship standard links with interesting and varied holes ... A real beauty tucked away on some precious turf ... Always in good order ... Make sure you play it.

Glasgow Golf Club ★★★

Killermont, Glasgow, G61 2TW
Nearest main town: Glasgow

Secretary: Mr D. W. Deas   Tel: 0141 942 2011
                                      Fax: 0141 942 0770
Professional: Mr J. Steven   Tel: 0141 942 8507

Playing: Prices on application.

Facilities: Bar: Members only. Food: Members only

Comments: One of the oldest clubs in the world ... Course a little outdated ... Absolutely superb clubhouse ... Wonderful club which also owns Glasgow Gailes ... Very fine parkland course ... Get your driver out here.

Glencruitten Golf Club   ★

Glencruitten Road, Oban, PA34 4PU
Nearest main town: Oban

Secretary: Mr A. G. Brown   Tel: 01631 562868
Professional: Mr G. Clark   Tel: 01631 564115

Playing: Midweek: round £16.00; day £16.00. Weekend: round £19.00; day £19.00.

Facilities: Bar: 11am–11pm. Food: Lunch and dinner from 10am–9pm.

Comments: Very short and isolated ... Fun to play ... Don't take it too seriously ... A picture ... Hard walking ... Loads of blind shots.

Gourock Golf Club   ★★

Cowal View, Gourock, PA19 1HD
Nearest main town: Greenock

Secretary: Mr A. D. Taylor   Tel: 01475 631001
                                           Fax: 01475 631001
Professional: Mr G. Coyle   Tel: 01475 636834

Playing: Midweek: round £18.00; day £25.00. Weekend: round £22.00; day £27.00. Handicap certificate required.

Facilities: Bar: 11am–11pm. Food: Lunch from 12pm–2pm. Dinner from 5pm–7pm.

Comments: Rather hilly moorland track ... Nice facilities at this friendly club ... Views over the Firth of Clyde ... Nothing special for the area.

Haggs Castle Golf Club   ★★★

70 Dumbreck Road, Dumbreck, G41 4SN
Nearest main town: Glasgow

Secretary:	Mr I. Harvey	Tel: 0141 427 1157
		Fax: 0141 427 1157
Professional:	Mr J. McAlister	Tel: 0141 427 3355
		Fax: 0141 427 3355

Playing: Midweek: round £27.00; day £38.00. Weekend: round n/a; day n/a. Handicap certificate required.

Facilities: Bar: 11am–11pm. Food: Lunch from 11am–4pm. Dinner by arrangement.

Comments: Mature course which has hosted the Scottish Open ... High, lofted shots needed to elevated greens ... Welcoming private club ... Thoroughly enjoyed it ... Will be back one day ... Well maintained.

Hayston Golf Club ★

Campsie Road, Glasgow, G66 1RN
Nearest main town: Glasgow

Secretary:	Mr J. V. Carmichael	Tel: 0141 775 0723
		Fax: 0141 775 0723
Professional:	Mr S. Barnett	Tel: 0141 775 0882

Playing: Midweek: round £20.00; day £30.00. Weekend: round n/a; day n/a.

Facilities: Bar: 11am–11pm. Food: Lunch and dinner from 10am–9pm.

Comments: Very undulating parkland course ... Fair test with good facilities ... By no means a classic but fair to the average player ... Not in great condition.

Hilton Park Golf Club ★★★

Auldmarroch Estate, Milngavie, G62 7HB
Nearest main town: Glasgow

Secretary:	Mrs J. A. Warnock	Tel: 0141 956 4657
		Fax: 0141 956 4657
Professional:	Mr W. McCondichie	Tel: 0141 956 5125
		Fax: 0141 956 5125

Playing: Midweek: round £20.00; day £28.00. Weekend: round n/a; day n/a. Handicap certificate required.

Facilities: Bar: 11am–11pm. Food: Members & guests only.

Comments: Very scenic ... Interesting moorland course with trouble at every turn ... The Hilton far superior to the Allander course ... Good quality course.

Irvine Golf Club   ★★★★

Bogside, Irvine, KA12 8SR
Nearest main town: Irvine

Secretary:	Mr M. McMann	Tel: 01294 275979
Professional:	Mr K. Erskine	Tel: 01294 275626
		Fax: 01294 275626

Playing: Midweek: round £38.00; day £55.00. Weekend: round £55.00; day n/a.

Facilities: Bar: 11am–11pm. Food: Lunch and dinner from 10am–9pm. Bar snacks.

Comments: Very tricky course with good variety of holes ... Excellent variation ... Good welcome ... Interesting parkland course ... Will go again ... Just the ticket for holiday golf.

Kilmacolm Golf Club   ★★★

Porterfield Road, Kilmacolm, PA13 4PD
Nearest main town: Paisley

Secretary:	Mr D. W. Tinton	Tel: 01505 872139
		Fax: 01505 874007
Professional:	Mr D. Stewart	Tel: 01505 872695

Playing: Midweek: round £20.50; day £30.50. Weekend: round £20.50; day £30.50. Handicap certificate required.

Facilities: Bar: 11am–11pm. Food: Lunch and dinner from 12pm–9pm. Bar snacks.

Comments: One of the best value smaller courses ... 7th is a bit special ... Moorland course of character.

Kilmarnock Golf Club   ★★★★

29 Hillhouse Road, Barassie, Troon, KA10 6SY
Nearest main town: Troon

Secretary:	Mr R. L. Bryce	Tel: 01292 313920
		Fax: 01292 313920

Professional: Mr G. Howie   Tel: 01292 311322
                                     Fax: 01292 311322

Playing: Midweek: round £38.00; day £58.00. Weekend: round
                  n/a; day n/a. Handicap certificate required.

Facilities: Bar: 11am–11pm. Food: Lunch and dinner from
                  11am–9pm. Bar snacks.

Comments: Beautifully presented ... Hard test ... Open qualifying
                  course ... Some blind shots ... A must play in the area
                  ... Better than Troon ... New nine holes a little out of
                  character with the rest ... Sensational seaside links ...
                  Heather-lined fairways and small greens – it's awesome.

Kirkhill Golf Club   ★

Greenlees Road, Glasgow, G72 8YN
Nearest main town: Glasgow

Secretary: Mr J. Sweeney   Tel: 0141 641 3083
                                        Fax: 0141 641 3083
Professional: Mr D. Williamson   Tel: 0141 641 7972
                                        Fax: 0141 641 7972

Playing: Midweek: round £20.00; day £25.00. Weekend: round
                   n/a; day n/a.

Facilities: Bar: 11am–11pm. Food: Lunch and dinner from
                   10am–9pm. Bar snacks.

Comments: Designed by the master craftsman, James Braid ... Hard
                   walking ... Need to be fit ... Blasted 1st hole a good
                   indication of what's to come.

Lanark Golf Club   ★★

The Moor, Lanark, ML11 7RX
Nearest main town: Glasgow

Secretary: Mr G. H. Cuthill   Tel: 01555 663219
                                         Fax: 01555 663219
Professional: Mr A. White   Tel: 01555 661456

Playing: Midweek: round £24.00; day £36.00. Weekend: round
                   n/a; day n/a. Handicap certificate required.

Facilities: Bar: 11am–11pm. Food: Lunch and dinner from
                   10am–9pm. Bar snacks.

Comments: Difficult-to-read greens made this a struggle ... Superb condition ... Always in good nick and a varied challenge ... A few blind shots ... Short and hilly ... Something different from the norm ... Heathland golf at its best.

Largs Golf Club   ★★

Irvine Road, Largs, KA30 8EU
Nearest main town: Largs

Secretary: Mr D. H. MacGillivray Tel: 01475 673594
                                      Fax: 01475 673594
Professional: Mr R. Collinson   Tel: 01475 686192

Playing: Midweek: round £25.00; day £35.00. Weekend: round £35.00; day £35.00. Handicap certificate required.

Facilities: Bar: 11am–11pm. Food: Lunch and dinner from 11am–9pm. Bar snacks.

Comments: Very good club with lovely welcome ... Parkland course of some stature ... Great parkland course with streams affecting several holes ... Good hospitality ... Scotland not known for its parkland golf, but this is an exception ... Homely club ... Made very welcome.

Loch Lomond Golf Club   ★★★★

Rossdhu House, Alexandria, G83 8NT
Nearest main town: Glasgow

Secretary: Mr D. MacDonald   Tel: 01436 655555
                                      Fax: 01436 655550
Professional: Mr C. Campbell   Tel: 01436 655535

Playing: Midweek: round £150.00; day n/a. Weekend: round £150.00; day n/a. Handicap certificate required.

Facilities: Bar: 11am–11pm. Food: Breakfast, lunch and dinner from 7am–10pm. Bar snacks.

Comments: Wonderful layout but very expensive ... Too wet and fragile for extensive playing ... Great practice facilities ... Worth the cost if you get the chance.

Lochranza Golf Club ★

Lochranza, Isle of Arran, KA27 8HL
Nearest main town: Brodick

Secretary: Mr I. M. Robertson   Tel: 01770 830273
                                     Fax: 01770 830600

Professional: None.

Playing: Midweek: round £12.00; day £16.00. Weekend: round
£12.00; day £16.00.

Facilities: Ring for information.

Comments: Closed for half the year ... Worth playing if you're going
to Machrie ... Very tough and windy nine-holer on the
Isle of Arran ... Great fun.

Lochwinnoch Golf Club ★

Burnfoot Road, Lochwinnoch, PA12 4AN
Nearest main town: Paisley

Secretary: Mrs E. Wilson   Tel: 01505 842153
                               Fax: 01505 843668

Professional: Mr G. Reilly   Tel: 01505 843029

Playing: Midweek: round £15.00; day £20.00. Weekend: round
£15.00; day £20.00. Handicap certificate required.

Facilities: Bar: 11am–11pm. Food: Lunch and dinner from
10am–9pm.

Comments: Well kept but not a difficult course ... Useful practice for
the high-handicapper ... Rather hilly parkland course.

Loudoun Gowf Golf Club ★★

Galston, KA4 8PA
Nearest main town: Kilmarnock

Secretary: Mr T. R. Richmond   Tel: 01563 820551
                                   Fax: 01563 822229

Professional: None.

Playing: Midweek: round £18.00; day £30.00. Weekend: round
n/a; day n/a.

Facilities: Bar: 11am–11pm. Food: Lunch and dinner from 11am–10pm. Bar snacks.

Comments: Very difficult parkland course ... Short but designed to high order ... Nothing you won't find elsewhere ... Worthy of note ... Delightfully named, charming short course.

Machrie Hotel Golf Club ★★★★

Port Ellen, Isle of Islay, PA42 7AN
Nearest main town: Port Ellen

Secretary: Mr T. Dunn   Tel: 01496 302310
Fax: 01496 302404

Professional: None.

Playing: Midweek: round £20.00; day £30.00. Weekend: round £20.00; day £30.00.

Facilities: Bar: 11am–11pm. Food: Breakfast, lunch and dinner from 7am–10pm. Bar snacks.

Comments: Unique atmosphere and incredibly challenging ... Almost unplayable in really bad weather ... New holes a bit of a let down ... Enjoy the whisky and peat fire in the clubhouse ... Surprising course design but very interesting ... Condition excellent ... Incredibly natural course ... Thrilling from start to finish.

Machrihanish Golf Club ★★★★

Machrihanish, PA28 6PT
Nearest main town: Campbeltown

Secretary: Mrs M. Anderson   Tel: 01586 810213
Fax: 01586 810221
Professional: Mr K. Campbell   Tel: 01586 810277
Fax: 01586 810277

Playing: Midweek: round £25.00; day £40.00. Weekend: round £30.00; day £50.00.

Facilities: Bar: 11am–11pm. Food: Breakfast, lunch and dinner from 9am–9pm. Bar snacks.

Comments: Natural setting offering stiff test of golf ... Great links course that is open to the elements ... A wild, windswept course ... Great malt and fantastic people ... Brilliant and what a nice welcome and people ... A mini Turnberry despite its modest facilities ... Tremendous opening hole to a fantastic links course ... Undulating, wonderful greens ... Cracking opening par-4 over the sea.

Millport Golf Club ★★★

Millport, Isle of Cumbrae, KA28 0HB
Nearest main town: Millport

Secretary:	Mr D. Donnelly	Tel: 01475 530306
		Fax: 01475 530306
Professional:	Mr K. Docherty	Tel: 01475 530305

Playing: Midweek: round £14.50; day £18.50. Weekend: round £18.50; day £24.50.

Facilities: Bar: 11am–11pm. Food: Lunch and dinner from 10am–9pm. Bar snacks.

Comments: Superb views to Bute, Arran and Kintyre ... Moorland course that can get windy ... Felt very alive here.

Milngavie Golf Club ★★

Laighpark, Glasgow, G62 8EP
Nearest main town: Glasgow

Secretary:	Ms S. McGuinness	Tel: 0141 956 1619
		Fax: 0141 956 4252
Professional:	None.	

Playing: Midweek: round £20.00; day £30.00. Weekend: round n/a; day n/a. Handicap certificate required.

Facilities: Bar: 11am–11pm. Food: Bar snacks. Dinner by arrangement.

Comments: You need to hit the fairways running here ... 1st is a bit special ... Drive over the burn at the 1st is a great way to start ... Scenic course with elements of moorland golf ... Less than 6,000 yards.

Paisley Golf Club ★★

Braehead, Paisley, PA2 8TZ
Nearest main town: Paisley

Secretary: Mr M. MacPherson   Tel: 0141 884 3903
                                    Fax: 0141 884 3903
Professional: Mr G. Stewart   Tel: 0141 884 4114

Playing: Midweek: round £20.00; day £28.00. Weekend: round
£20.00; day £28.00. Handicap certificate required.

Facilities: Bar: 11am–11pm. Food: Lunch and dinner from
10am–9pm. Bar snacks.

Comments: Terrific views and some fine hilly holes ... Good course
and interesting greens ... Very windy at times ... Wind
the main challenge.

Port Glasgow Golf Club ★

Devol Farm, Port Glasgow, PA14 5XE
Nearest main town: Port Glasgow

Secretary: Mr N. L. Mitchell   Tel: 01475 700334
Professional: None.

Playing: Midweek: round £15.00; day £20.00. Weekend: round
n/a; day n/a.

Facilities: Bar: 11am–11pm. Food: Lunch and dinner from
12pm–9pm. Bar snacks.

Comments: Views of the Clyde ... Cheap course primarily for beginners ... Short course with basic facilities ... Moorland
track open most of the year.

Prestwick Golf Club ★★★★

2 Links Road, Prestwick, KA9 1QG
Nearest main town: Prestwick

Secretary: Mr I. T. Bunch   Tel: 01292 477404
                                  Fax: 01292 477255
Professional: Mr F. C. Rennie   Tel: 01292 479483

Playing: Midweek: round £65.00; day £90.00. Weekend: round
n/a; day n/a. Handicap certificate required.

Facilities: Bar: 11am–11pm. Food: Lunch from 11am–3pm.

Comments: 1st is just so tough, you feel disillusioned before you've got going ... Good fun ... Plenty of blind holes ... History and tradition with terrific holes next to the Firth ... Great value ... So difficult ... Walking in the footsteps of the greats ... An intoxicating experience.

Prestwick St Cuthbert Golf Club   ★★★

East Road, Prestwick, KA9 2SX
Nearest main town: Prestwick

Secretary: Mr J. C. Rutherford   Tel: 01292 477101
                                        Fax: 01292 671730

Professional: None.

Playing: Midweek: round £22.00; day £30.00. Weekend: round n/a; day n/a.

Facilities: Bar: 11am–11pm. Food: Lunch and dinner from 11am–9pm.

Comments: Good test ... Only minus point is flatness of course ... Flat and exposed ... Little attractive to the eye ... Fun on an historic course.

Prestwick St Nicholas Golf Club   ★★

Grangemuir Road, Prestwick, KA9 1SN
Nearest main town: Prestwick

Secretary: Mr G. B. S. Thomson Tel: 01292 477608
                                        Fax: 01292 473900

Professional: None.

Playing: Midweek: round £30.00; day £50.00. Weekend: round £35.00; day n/a.

Facilities: Bar: 11am–11pm. Food: Lunch from 12pm–4pm. Dinner by arrangement.

Comments: Weekend play Sunday only ... Laid out between the sea and the railway line ... A very honest links ... One to savour ... Enormous greens ... Don't leave Prestwick without playing here ... Won't forget it in a hurry.

Ranfurly Castle Golf Club ★

Golf Road, Bridge of Weir, PA11 3HN
Nearest main town: Paisley

Secretary:	Mr J. Walker	Tel: 01505 612609
		Fax: 01505 612609
Professional:	Mr T. Eckford	Tel: 01505 614795

Playing: Midweek: round £30.00; day £40.00. Weekend: round n/a; day n/a. Handicap certificate required.

Facilities: Bar: 11am–11pm. Food: Lunch and dinner from 10am–9pm. Bar snacks.

Comments: Good Scottish inland golf ... Very challenging and visually attractive ... Not out the top drawer but good value ... Hard walking ... Tough.

Shiskine Golf Club ★★★

Shiskine, Isle of Arran, KA27 8HA
Nearest main town: Brodick

Secretary:	Mr I. Robertson	Tel: 01770 860226
		Fax: 01770 860205
Professional:	None.	

Playing: Midweek: round £12.00; day £18.00. Weekend: round £15.00; day £20.00.

Facilities: Bar: None. Food: Tea room and snacks all day.

Comments: Wonderful views but course did not match them ... Plenty of blind shots ... Could be best value in Britain ... Good greens, great setting and great fun although can get congested ... More boys and girls have learned golf here than at all the private Glasgow and Edinburgh clubs combined ... A gem ... 12 holes only ... Great value ... Great views to Mull of Kintyre ... A pilgrimage to repeat again and again ... You will either love it or hate it.

Stirling Golf Club ★

Queen's Road, Stirling, FK8 3AA
Nearest main town: Stirling

Secretary:	Mr W. C. McArthur	Tel: 01786 464098
		Fax: 01786 450748

Professional: Mr I. Collins   Tel: 01786 471490

Playing: Midweek: round £20.00; day £30.00. Weekend: round n/a; day n/a.

Facilities: Bar: 11am–11pm. Food: Breakfast, lunch and dinner from 10am–9pm. Bar snacks.

Comments: Nondescript rolling parkland course ... Usually in good condition ... Stirling Castle broods over the course ... Surprisingly difficult.

Strathaven Golf Club   ★★★

Glasgow Road, Strathaven, ML10 6NL
Nearest main town: Glasgow

Secretary: Mr A. W. Wallace   Tel: 01357 520421
                                        Fax: 01357 520539
Professional: Mr M. McCrorie   Tel: 01357 521812

Playing: Midweek: round £22.00; day £32.00. Weekend: round n/a; day n/a. Handicap certificate required.

Facilities: Bar: 11am–11pm. Food: Lunch and dinner from 10am–9pm.

Comments: Tree-lined course with oodles of character ... One to note ... A respite from the surfeit of links golf in Scotland ... Tight driving and tricky greens ... Always in good condition.

Troon Portland Golf Club   ★★★

Troon, KA10 6EP
Nearest main town: Troon

Secretary: Mr J. W. Chandler   Tel: 01292 311555
                                        Fax: 01292 318204
Professional: Mr R. Anderson

Playing: Midweek: round n/a; day £35.00. Weekend: round n/a; day £45.00.

Facilities: Bar: 11am–11pm. Food: Lunch and dinner by arrangement. Bar snacks.

Comments: You don't go to Troon to play here ... Enjoyed it but only a warm up to the main challenge ... Good fun.

Turnberry Hotel Golf Club (Arran)   ★★★

Turnberry, KA26 9LT
Nearest main town: Girvan

Secretary:	Mr E. Bowman	Tel: 01655 331000
		Fax: 01655 331706
Professional:	Mr B. Gunson	Tel: 01655 331000
	(Golf Dir)	Fax: 01655 331069

Playing: Midweek: round £55.00; day n/a. Weekend: round £55.00; day n/a.

Facilities: Bar: 11am–11pm. Food: Breakfast, lunch and dinner from 7am–10pm. Bar snacks.

Comments: Wonderful foil to the Ailsa ... Not easy and sometimes in better condition than the Ailsa ... Top-class second-string course at this luxurious hotel ... Very technical course, very rewarding.

Vale of Leven Golf Club   ★

Northfield Road, Alexandria, G83 9ET
Nearest main town: Dumbarton

Secretary:	Mr J. Stewart	Tel: 01389 752351
Professional:	None.	

Playing: Midweek: round £18.00; day n/a. Weekend: round £22.00; day n/a.

Facilities: Bar: 12am–11pm. Food: Breakfast, lunch and dinner from 8am–9pm.

Comments: Holes overlook Loch Lomond ... Not in the same league as nearby Loch Lomond ... Very short but unbelievably tricky ... Can get very wet.

West Kilbride Golf Club   ★★

Fullerton Drive, Seamill, West Kilbride, KA23 9HT
Nearest main town: West Kilbride

Secretary:	Mr H. Armour	Tel: 01294 823911
		Fax: 01294 823911
Professional:	Mr G. Ross	Tel: 01294 823042

Playing: Midweek: round n/a; day £37.00. Weekend: round n/a; day n/a. Handicap certificate required.

Facilities: Bar: 11am–11pm. Food: Lunch and dinner from 11am–10pm.

Comments: A really strong test off blue tees ... Invariably in great condition ... Warm welcome at a beautiful setting ... Views of the Isle of Arran ... Unheralded but excellent ... Good value compared to a lot of Scottish courses.

Westerwood Hotel Golf & Country Club ★★

St Andrews Drive, Cumbernauld, G68 1RN
Nearest main town: Glasgow

Secretary: Mr S. Killin   Tel: 01236 452772
                              Fax: 01236 738478
Professional: Mr S. Killin   Tel: 01236 725281

Playing: Midweek: round £22.50; day £35.00. Weekend: round £27.50; day £45.00.

Facilities: Bar: 11am–11pm. Food: Breakfast, lunch and dinner from 7am–10pm. Bar snacks.

Comments: Need to be long and straight, unlike its designer, Mr Ballesteros ... Will get better ... Imaginative course, what you would expect from Seve ... Beautiful location which course does not live up to ... Ambitious course ... Maybe Seve should stick to his day job.

Windyhill Golf Club ★★★

Windyhill, Bearsden, G61 4QQ
Nearest main town: Glasgow

Secretary: Mr B. Davidson   Tel: 0141 942 2349
                                Fax: 0141 942 5874
Professional: Mr G. Collinson   Tel: 0141 942 7157

Playing: Midweek: round n/a; day £20.00. Weekend: round n/a; day n/a. Handicap certificate required.

Facilities: Bar: 11am–11pm. Food: Lunch and dinner from 10am–9pm.

Comments: Not the best near Glasgow but worth a shout ... Nice feel to this open parkland course ... Some good technical holes on the back nine ... Front nine much harder.

Borders and
Dumfries & Galloway

Southerness Golf Club ★★★★★

Southerness, Southerness, DG2 8AZ
Nearest main town: Dumfries

When you mention the Solway Firth as an area of natural outstanding golf, Silloth-on-Solway springs immediately to mind. But located almost directly opposite Silloth, across the pond-like calm of the Firth, in Scotland, is a course few have heard of. Mention its name, Southerness, and you might still be corrected and told Southerndown, the fine Welsh course. On the map of Britain's golf courses, someone's left a crumb of cake on Southerness.

The course's low profile is possibly because it is something of a rarity, a links course that was opened only in 1947, a second generation course without the traditional feel and established nature of many of Scotland's great links; it may be because it is not blessed with the same outstanding natural scenery that one expects from a links; or it may be because it was designed by Mackenzie Ross, almost as an afterthought while he was working on the exceptional Ailsa course at Turnberry. Whatever it is, Southerness does not get the credit it deserves.

In design terms it is first class. There are no blind holes, where you hit your ball and scamper over a dune or hill to see which trap your ball has fallen into. Neither do balls bounce off the fairways after a good drive. Situated on flat piece of land by the Solway Firth, and covered in gorse, heather and bracken, Southerness is very fair, the scores on each day governed by the wind that rushes in off the sea.

With the character of each hole at the mercy of the wind, Southerness is in a constant flux. One thing that never changes is the quality of the par-4s, particular the 12th, played to a green nestling precariously on the edge of the beach. Neither does the welcome, which is warm and hearty on arrival and in the clubhouse afterwards.

Secretary: Mr W. D. Ramage Tel: 01387 880677
Fax: 01387 880644

Professional: Mr G. Gray

Playing: Midweek: round £30.00; day £30.00. Weekend: round £40.00; day £40.00. Handicap certificate required.

Facilities: Bar: 11am–11pm. Food: Lunch and dinner from 11am–9pm. Bar snacks.

Comments: Not a well-known course so invariably in good condition ... Long and windy ... A gem of a course, well worth the visit ... Greens very good ... People just superb.

Dumfries & County Golf Club   ★★★

Nunfield, Edinburgh Road, Dumfries, DG1 1JX
Nearest main town: Dumfries

Secretary: Mr E. C. Pringle   Tel: 01387 253585
Professional: Mr S. Syme   Tel: 01387 268918
    Fax: 01387 268918

Playing: Midweek: round £23.00; day £23.00. Weekend: round £26.00; day £26.00.

Facilities: Bar: 11am–11pm. Food: Lunch and dinner from 11am–9pm. Bar snacks.

Comments: Runs alongside River Nith ... A long journey to find it but worth the effort ... Parkland beauty sculpted by Willie Fernie ... One of the best examples of Scottish parkland golf ... An unforgettable par-3 14th ... Informative pro shop ... Off the beaten track but good for visitors.

Duns Golf Club   ★

Hardens Road, Duns, TD11 3NR
Nearest main town: Duns

Secretary: Mr A. Campbell   Tel: 01361 882194
Professional: None.

Playing: Midweek: round £12.00; day £15.00. Weekend: round £15.00; day £20.00.

Facilities: Bar: 11am–11pm. Food: Bar snacks.

Comments: Need to be fit here ... Odd course for an oddly named club ... Burn runs through middle of the course ... Burn dominates the 15th ... A warm welcome guaranteed ... A real Braveheart of a course.

Moffat Golf Club   ★★★

Coatshill, Moffat, DG10 9SB
Nearest main town: Beattock

Secretary: Mr T. A. Rankin   Tel: 01683 220020
Professional: None.

Playing: Midweek: round £18.50; day £20.00. Weekend: round
                  £28.00; day £30.00.

Facilities: Bar: 11am–11pm. Food: Bar snacks.

Comments: Take your oxygen tank with you ... Up in the gods – you
                  certainly need a head for heights ... Warm welcome but
                  freezing cold course ... Scenic course overlooking the
                  town.

Portpatrick Golf Club   ★★★★

Golf Course Road, Portpatrick, DG9 8TB
Nearest main town: Stranraer

Secretary: Mr J. A. Horberry   Tel: 01776 810273
                                         Fax: 01776 810811

Professional: None.

Playing: Midweek: round £18.00; day £27.00. Weekend: round
                  £21.00; day £32.00. Handicap certificate required.

Facilities: Bar: 11am–11pm. Food: Lunch and dinner from
                  11am–9pm. Bar snacks.

Comments: Remote links with bundles of character ... Course
                  defence entirely dictated by the wind ... Wonderfully
                  old-fashioned links ... Will linger in the memory for a
                  long time ... Village simply breathes golf ... Very
                  exposed.

Powfoot Golf Club   ★★★★

Cummertrees, Annan, DG12 5QE
Nearest main town: Annan

Secretary: Mr B. W. Sutherland   Tel: 01461 700276
                  (Manager)   Fax: 01461 700276
Professional: Mr G. Dick   Tel: 01461 700327
                                         Fax: 01461 700327

Playing: Midweek: round £23.00; day £30.00. Weekend: round £23.00; day £30.00.

Facilities: Bar: 11am–11pm. Food: Lunch and dinner from 11am–9pm. Bar snacks.

Comments: Superb condition and nice surroundings ... A classic links ... Good layout, difficult in the wind.

The Roxburgh Golf Course   ★★★★

Sunlaws House Hotel, Kelso, TD5 8JZ
Nearest main town: Kelso

Secretary: Mr D. MacIntyre   Tel: 01573 450331
Professional: Mr G. Niven   Tel: 01573 450333
                                        Fax: 01573 450611

Playing: Midweek: round £35.00; day n/a. Weekend: round £60.00; day n/a. Handicap certificate required.

Facilities: Bar: 11am–11pm. Food: Breakfast, lunch and dinner from 9am–9pm. Bar snacks.

Comments: Excellent new course ... The 5th and 6th are exceptional holes ... Shop and food a little pricey ... When fully mature this will be a bit special ... Was allowed to use championship tees so a great welcome ... Anyone know a better new course? ... Best new course in Scotland since Loch Lomond.

Fife and Clackmanan

Ladybank Golf Club ★★★★★

Annsmuir, Ladybank, KY15 7RA
Nearest main town: Cupar

Ladybank is, unquestionably, one of the great inland courses of Scotland. While Gleneagles is often rated the premier inland course on account of the combined grace and splendour of its clubhouse and course, Ladybank is sold purely on the strength of its heathland charm. Situated in the heart of Fife, it is a picturesque course with a profusion of heather, wiry broom and pine trees. It's a course you'll want to play at least once.

The course was originally laid out by Tom Morris in 1879 and has gradually been extended. But the new holes that were added are in keeping with the original design, and there's an agreed game-plan for the player to adhere to – namely, accuracy. Ladybank is not a course where you blithely whip the driver out of the bag on the tee, but rather one where the view from the tee consistently argues with you to take an iron. This makes it a very long course at over 6,600 yards, but with usually only one safe way in to the green it is a prudent policy.

Of course, the technical aspects of the game are not what everyone comes to Ladybank for, rather they come to marvel at the pines, heather and gorse, which give the course a sublime feel and smell. In many respects it resembles the famed Surrey heath and heather courses, but unlike them there's also thick swathes of wild grasses and secondary rough of an almost brush-wire character, which clings to the hosel of your club.

The best hole on the course is probably the 16th, a sharp dogleg to the left where there is only one real line – down the middle – followed by an approach shot to a left-to-right sloping green with trees on the left. It's indicative of many holes at Ladybank, a visual and technical puzzle that you leave feeling as though you've only scratched the surface.

Secretary: Mr I. F. Sproule   Tel: 01337 830814
                                          Fax: 01337 831505
Professional: Mr M. J. Gray   Tel: 01337 830725

Playing: Midweek: round £28.00; day £40.00. Weekend: round £35.00; day n/a. Handicap certificate required.

Facilities: Bar: 11am–11pm. Food: Lunch and dinner from 10am–9pm. Bar snacks.

Comments: Excellent test of golf in beautiful surroundings ... Well prepared ... Good all-round test ... Gorse is the main hazard here ... Excellent practice facilities ... Best time to play is in the autumn ... Very nice experience – warm clubhouse and course in top nick ... Forget about St Andrews, this is the best in Fife ... A golfer's golf course ... Tough but rewarding ... Set in exquisite mature woodland ... Pine trees, heather and gorse – perfect ... Really is the business ... Preferred it to all the Open courses ... Very easy on the eye.

St Andrews Old Golf Course   ★★★★★

St Andrews Links Trust, St Andrews, KY16 9SF
Nearest main town: St Andrews

No more than a flat, vast open playing field. Made redundant by the improvements in golf club technology. These are just two of the criticisms levelled at the Old Course at St Andrews, the home of the Royal and Ancient Golf Club and the most famous golf course in the world. It has almost become fashionable to have a pop at the Old Course, once, they say, a venerable work of art, but now its colours fading and its brush strokes criticised for their broadness and depth.

It wasn't always like this. The bunkers were once praised for their depth and singularity, the double greens for their design and surreal appearance, the double fairways for their uniqueness. But opinions change, and as the game of golf grows and players seek out virgin territory, so the memories of the Old Course fade. Why the stark, barrenness of the Old Course when you can have the deep colours and exhilaration of a County Down or a Turnberry?

What the Old Course will do is make you think. If the design is such a joke, why is it so difficult? Huge greens and wide fairways are normally associated with good scoring, and yet, with the exception of the pros, who can make a mockery of the front nine at times, you'll struggle to better your handicap. The answer lies in the illusions the landscape offers. From the tee you are presented with huge fairways, but you see only rutted, unreceptive ones. For your approaches, you are presented with huge greens, but they are often blind and so contoured that your ball runs off in all directions. Then there's the fickle wind, which can grab your ball in mid-flight and deposit it in a scrape or burn.

The Old Course will also make you nervous. First-tee nerves for golfers are as normal as the common cold, but you'll never have experienced anything like this – and the irony is the fairway you'll be aiming at is the biggest anywhere in the world. Then there's the 17th, a hole so difficult you'll treat it like walking on egg shells and leave with an eight. That's the difficulty at St Andrews. Much like meeting your favourite celebrity, you'll clam up and the right words won't come out.

Secretary: Mr A. J. R. McGregor Tel: 01334 466666
(General Manager)   Fax: 01334 477036
Professional: None.

Playing: Midweek: round £75.00; day n/a. Weekend: round £75.00; day n/a. Handicap certificate required.

Facilities: Bar: 11am–11pm. Food: Breakfast, lunch and dinner from 7am–9pm.

Comments: Sheer magic ... Anyone who's ever professed to be a golfer must play ... Take a caddie ... So subtle ... Feel the nerves on the 1st tee ... The course and the people, the best anywhere ... Tee shot at the 1st is so special ... Take away the 1st, 17th and 18th and this is a very ordinary links ... Course not up to much but the special feeling makes up for it ... It can be both cruel and kind ... A wonderful and mystical venue – not to be missed ... Treasure the experience.

Aberdour Golf Club   ★★★

Seaside Place, Aberdour, Aberdour, KT3 OTX
Nearest main town: Dunfermline

Secretary: Mr T. H. McIntyre   Tel: 01383 860080
Fax: 01383 860050
Professional: Mr G. McCallum   Tel: 01383 860256
Fax: 01383 860256

Playing: Midweek: round £17.00; day £28.00. Weekend: round £17.00; day £28.00. Handicap certificate required.

Facilities: Bar: 11am–11pm. Food: Lunch and dinner from 11am–9pm. Bar snacks.

Comments: Short course on nice piece of coastline ... Good views ... Great wee seaside course with lovely views.

Alloa Golf Club ★★★

Schawpark, Sauchie, Alloa, FK10 3AX
Nearest main town: Alloa

Secretary: Mr T. Crampton   Tel: 01259 722745
Professional: Mr W. Bennett   Tel: 01259 724476
                                    Fax: 01259 724476

Playing: Midweek: round £20.00; day £30.00. Weekend: round £25.00; day £35.00.

Facilities: Bar: 11am–11pm. Food: Lunch and dinner from 11am–9pm. Bar snacks.

Comments: Hilly course with plenty of blind shots ... Strategic bunkering with sunken greens ... Nice stop-over in otherwise barren golfing region ... Worth seeking out ... Reasonable green fees.

Balbirnie Park Golf Club ★★★★

Balbirnie Park, Markinch, Glenrothes, KY7 6NR
Nearest main town: Glenrothes

Secretary: Mr S. Oliver   Tel: 01592 612095
                                Fax: 01592 612383
Professional: Mr D. F. G. Scott   Tel: 01592 752006
                                        Fax: 01592 752006

Playing: Midweek: round £25.00; day £33.00. Weekend: round £30.00; day £40.00.

Facilities: Bar: 11am–11pm. Food: Lunch and dinner from 12pm–9pm. Bar snacks.

Comments: One of the best parkland courses around with a high degree of difficulty ... Still quite young but great fairways, and greens will improve ... Excellent and unusual club ... Compact links with views of Isle of Man on a clear day.

Braehead Golf Club ★★

Cambus, Alloa, FK10 2NT
Nearest main town: Alloa

Secretary: Mr P. MacMichael   Tel: 01259 725766
                                    Fax: 01259 725766

Professional: Mr P. Brookes   Tel: 01259 722078
                                          Fax: 01259 720731

Playing: Midweek: round £18.50; day £24.50. Weekend: round
                  £24.50; day £32.50.

Facilities: Bar: 11am–11pm. Food: Lunch and dinner from
                  10am–9pm. Bar snacks.

Comments: Some testing par-3s, particularly the 14th ... Not much
                  to look at ... Nice design, fair to all standards.

Crail Golfing Society   ★★★★

Balcomie Clubhouse, Fifeness, Crail, KY10 3XN
Nearest main town: St Andrews

Secretary: Mr J. F. Horsfield   Tel: 01333 450686
                                           Fax: 01333 450416
Professional: Mr G. Lennie   Tel: 01333 450960
                                           Fax: 01333 450960

Playing: Midweek: round £22.00; day £35.00. Weekend: round
                  £27.00; day £45.00.

Facilities: Bar: 11am–11pm. Food: Breakfast, lunch and dinner
                  from 7am–10pm. Bar snacks.

Comments: Beautiful part of the world ... Course in excellent nick
                  ... Best holes by the sea ... Very friendly ... One of
                  the oldest clubs in the world ... Superb little links ...
                  Very hospitable ... Friendly Scottish links of the
                  highest quality ... Greens true and fast ... Good
                  holiday golf.

Dunfermline Golf Club   ★★

Pitfirrane, Crossford, Dunfermline, KY12 8QW
Nearest main town: Dunfermline

Secretary: Mr R. De Rose   Tel: 01383 723534
Professional: Mr S. Craig   Tel: 01383 729061

Playing: Midweek: round £20.00; day £30.00. Weekend: round
                  £25.00; day £35.00.

Facilities: Bar: 11am–11pm. Food: Lunch and dinner from
                  11am–9pm. Bar snacks.

Comments: Weekend play on Sundays only ... Nice parkland course ... Have fun ... Course has stood the test of time ... Rough and semi-rough too punishing on visitors ... Internal out of bounds very frustrating.

Golf House Club ★★★

Elie, Leven, KY9 1AS
Nearest main town: St Andrews

Secretary:	Mr A. Sneddon	Tel: 01333 330301
		Fax: 01333 330895
Professional:	Mr R. Wilson	Tel: 01333 330955
		Fax: 01333 330955

Playing: Midweek: round £32.00; day £45.00. Weekend: round £40.00; day £55.00. Handicap certificate required.

Facilities: Bar: 11am–11pm. Food: Breakfast, lunch and dinner from 9am–9pm. Bar snacks.

Comments: With 16 par-4s and two par-3s this course is full of quirks ... Excellent holiday golf here ... James Braid grew up here ... Located virtually in the middle of the village ... Bump-and-run is a shot you need ... Eccentric course with numerous semi-blind shots.

Kirkcaldy Golf Club ★★★

Balwearie Road, Kirkcaldy, KY2 5LT
Nearest main town: Kirkcaldy

Secretary:	Mr A. C. Thomson	Tel: 01592 205240
		Fax: 01592 205240
Professional:	Mr A. Caira (Director of Golf)	Tel: 01592 203258

Playing: Midweek: round £16.00; day £22.00. Weekend: round £22.00; day £32.00.

Facilities: Bar: 11am–11pm. Food: Lunch and dinner from 12pm–9pm. Bar snacks.

Comments: Challenging parkland course ... Nicely kept, simple course that is surprisingly challenging ... In play most of the year.

Leven Links ★★★★

The Promenade, Leven, KY8 4HS
Nearest main town: Leven

Secretary:	Mr S. Herd	Tel: 01333 421390
		Fax: 01333 428859

Professional: None.

Playing: Midweek: round £25.00; day £35.00. Weekend: round £30.00; day £40.00. Handicap certificate required.

Facilities: Bar: 11am–11pm. Food: Breakfast, lunch and dinner from 8am–9pm. Bar snacks.

Comments: Short course but wind stiffens things up ... Right next to Lundin ... Pure links ... Finishes with a flourish ... Real appreciation of the game at this club ... Has stood the test of time ... Always beautifully prepared.

Lundin Golf Club ★★★★

Golf Road, Lundin Links, KY8 6BA
Nearest main town: Leven

Secretary:	Mr D. R. Thomson	Tel: 01333 320202
		Fax: 01333 329743
Professional:	Mr D. K. Webster	Tel: 01333 320051

Playing: Midweek: round £28.00; day £36.00. Weekend: round £36.00; day n/a.

Facilities: Bar: 11am–11pm. Food: Lunch and dinner from 10am–9pm. Bar snacks.

Comments: Weekend play on Saturday afternoons only ... Very hard and interesting course ... Greens are exceptional, while fairways can be scrappy ... Superb welcome ... Unusual course with challenging tee shots ... A parkland/links hybrid that's fun to play ... Old railway runs through the middle ... Let creativity be your watchword.

Scotscraig Golf Club ★★★★

Golf Road, Tayport, DD6 9DZ
Nearest main town: St Andrews

Secretary: Mr K. Gourlay   Tel: 01382 552515
                                        Fax: 01382 553130
Professional: Mr S. J. Campbell   Tel: 01382 552855

Playing: Midweek: round £27.00; day £36.00. Weekend: round £32.00; day £44.00.

Facilities: Bar: 11am–11pm. Food: Lunch and dinner from 10am–9pm. Bar snacks.

Comments: Almost as hard as Carnoustie but without the hype ... Deep bunkers on this links/heathland track ... Enjoyed it immensely ... Lives up to its brutal reputation ... Greens hard to read.

St Andrews Eden Golf Course   ★★★★

St Andrews Links Trust, St Andrews, KY16 9SF
Nearest main town: St Andrews

Secretary: Mr A. J. R. McGregor Tel: 01334 466666
                                        Fax: 01334 477036
Professional: None.

Playing: Midweek: round £23.00; day n/a. Weekend: round £23.00; day n/a.

Facilities: Bar: 11am–11pm. Food: Breakfast, lunch and dinner from 7am–9pm.

Comments: Excellent condition of greens ... The flair of St Andrews also very nice ... A great course for winter golf ... Play it every year ... Much more fun than other St Andrews courses ... Outstanding group of par-3s ... Played it in a sea mist – excellent!

St Andrews Golf Course (Dukes)   ★★★★

Old Course Hotel Golf Resort & Spa, St Andrews, KY16 9NSP
Nearest main town: St Andrews

Secretary: Mr S. Toon   Tel: 01334 479947
                                        Fax: 01334 479456
Professional: Mr J. Kelly

Playing: Midweek: round £50.00; day n/a. Weekend: round £55.00; day n/a.

Facilities: Bar: 11am–11pm. Food: Breakfast, lunch and dinner from 7am–10pm. Bar snacks.

Comments: Quality course ... Panoramic views over the old town ... Can be extremely difficult when the wind blows ... Can tear your game apart ... If you like to be humbled, go here ... Harder than the Old Course ... Who said St Andrews was just about the Old Course?

St Andrews Jubilee Golf Course   ★★★★

St Andrews Links Trust, St Andrews, KY16 9SF
Nearest main town: St Andrews

Secretary: Mr A. J. R. McGregor Tel: 01334 466666
            (General Manager)   Fax: 01334 477036
Professional: None.

Playing: Midweek: round £35.00; day n/a. Weekend: round £35.00; day n/a.

Facilities: Bar: 11am–11pm. Food: Breakfast, lunch and dinner from 7am–9pm.

Comments: Tough cookie when the wind blows ... From the back tees this can be a real challenge ... Longest course at St Andrews ... Requires deep reserves of concentration ... The toughest of all the St Andrews courses ... Found it so tough in the wind ... Lacks a bit of atmosphere ... Hard in the wind.

St Andrews New Golf Course   ★★★★

St Andrews Links Trust, St Andrews, KY16 9SF
Nearest main town: St Andrews

Secretary: Mr A. J. R. McGregor Tel: 01334 466666
            (General Manager)   Fax: 01334 477036
Professional: None.

Playing: Midweek: round £35.00; day n/a. Weekend: round £35.00; day n/a.

Facilities: Bar: 11am–11pm. Food: Breakfast, lunch and dinner from 7am–9pm.

Comments: Better than the Old Course with some very strong holes
... Similar demands to the Old Course ... Preferred it to
the Old ... Great experience but too expensive ...
Surprisingly undulating – soak up the atmosphere and
prepare for the Old Course.

Lothian

Muirfield Golf Club

Gullane, Gullane, EH31 2EG
Nearest main town: Edinburgh

If you have managed to arrange a game at Muirfield, what you score on the course is largely of secondary importance. This, after all, is the course that not even the reigning US Open champion, Payne Stewart, could get on after being told it was a members' day. Stewart played instead at Gullane, from where the views of Muirfield suggested it was almost empty.

Protocol has become more relaxed since those days. The club, the Honourable Company of Edinburgh Golfers, is more open to approaches from players wishing to play the course, for years considered the best course in Britain and Ireland.

Muirfield is an astonishing links. It consists of nine holes arranged in a circular shape around the boundaries of the club, with the back nine forming the inner circle. There are no dunes as such, just yawning bunkers, thick rough and 18 subtly contoured greens. One of Muirfield's outstanding features is its turf, which is very fine and tends to dry out quickly as it lies on top of pure sand. This can give the course a different character day in, day out; on the Saturday, an American-style target-golf course and on the Sunday, a typical links.

You get an early indication of what is to come at the 1st, a 449-yard par-4, where the pitfalls of missing the fairway will become immediately apparent. By the time you come off the par-3 4th, you will be doing better than average if you've yet to land in one of the bunkers, which seem to be depositaries for balls which land short of the green.

An unusual split-level fairway, situated on a dogleg, defines the 6th, before the final three holes on the front nine that will make or break your score. The 8th is probably the toughest of the trio, where 12 bunkers guard the right-hand side of the fairway, forcing you to the left and giving you a longer approach shot.

The back nine is not as tough as say a Troon or a Carnoustie, with birdie chances at the 14th, 15th and 17th, but it finishes with a bang, a devilish par-4 18th that is a fitting climax. Jack Nicklaus once described Muirfield as the fairest Open course he knew, and there is no greater praise than that.

Secretary: Mr J. A. Prideaux   Tel: 01620 842123
Fax: 01620 842977

Professional: None.

Playing: Midweek: round £70.00; day £95.00. Weekend: round n/a; day n/a. Handicap certificate required.

Facilities: Bar: 11am–11pm. Food: Lunch from 12pm–2pm.

Comments: Visitors on Tuesday & Thursday only ... The best course I have ever played which is what it is all about ... A bit of a mystery why it is voted No. 1 in the rankings ... Sadly, strange rules if you want to play ... Died and gone to heaven ... Just heaven ... True sense of history ... Thick rough, deep bunkering.

Braid Hills Golf Club ★

Braid Hills Road, Edinburgh, EH10 6JY
Nearest main town: Edinburgh

Secretary: None.   Tel: 0131 447 6666

Professional: None.

Playing: Midweek: round £8.50; day n/a. Weekend: round £8.50; day n/a.

Facilities: Food: Bar snacks.

Comments: One of the best public courses in the UK ... Tough, challenging with tight fairways and gorse ... Fun to play.

Bruntsfield Links Golfing Society ★★★

The Clubhouse, 32 Barnton Avenue, Edinburgh, EH4 6JH
Nearest main town: Edinburgh

Secretary: Cdr D. M. Sandford   Tel: 0131 336 2006
Fax: 0131 336 5538

Professional: Mr B. Mackenzie   Tel: 0131 336 4050

Playing: Midweek: round £36.00; day £50.00. Weekend: round £42.00; day £55.00. Handicap certificate required.

Facilities: Bar: 11am–11pm. Food: Lunch from 12.30pm–2.30pm.

Comments: Magnificent parkland ... Heavenly scenery ... Good course and best lunch to be had in Edinburgh ... Excellent restaurant ... Food better than the course.

Duddingston Golf Club ★★★

Duddington Road West, Edinburgh, EH15 3QD
Nearest main town: Edinburgh

Secretary:	Mr M. Corsa	Tel: 0131 661 7688
	(Manager)	Fax: 0131 661 4301
Professional:	Mr A. Mclean	Tel: 0131 661 4301

Playing: Midweek: round £27.00; day £36.00. Weekend: round £27.00; day £36.00.

Facilities: Bar: 11am–11pm. Food: Lunch from 12pm–2pm. Dinner by arrangement.

Comments: The most welcoming and challenging of the parkland courses around Edinburgh – underrated ... Braid's Burn the main hazard ... A course designed for the average player ... Sporting track very near centre of Edinburgh.

Dunbar Golf Club ★★★★

East Links, Dunbar, EH42 1LT
Nearest main town: Dunbar

Secretary:	Mrs L. Thom	Tel: 01368 862317
		Fax: 01368 865202
Professional:	Mr D. Small	Tel: 01368 862086
		Fax: 01368 862086

Playing: Midweek: round £25.00; day £35.00. Weekend: round £35.00; day £45.00.

Facilities: Bar: 11am–11pm. Food: Lunch and dinner from 10am–9pm.

Comments: Singular links character ... A cracking links and a great test in the wind ... Great hospitality and value ... Excellent links with tight fairways and slap-you-on-the-back welcome ... Classic East Lothian links ... Bracing ... On a rocky outcrop, this is marvellous ... Wind races around this links ... A lonely experience on a cold day ... Best holes around the turn.

Gullane Golf Club (No. 1) ★★★★★

Gullane, Lothian, EH31 2BB
Nearest main town: Edinburgh

Secretary:	Mr S. C. Owram	Tel: 01620 842255
		Fax: 01620 842327
Professional:	Mr J. Hume	Tel: 01620 843111

Playing: Midweek: round £54.00; day £80.00. Weekend: round £67.00; day n/a. Handicap certificate required.

Facilities: Bar: 11am–11pm. Food: Lunch from 12pm–2.30pm except Monday–Wednesday.

Comments: Beautiful links course ... .Excellent greens ... Bunkers are almost unfair ... Vastly underrated ... Greens as fast as anything played ... Great greens and view ... Wonderful greens and a windy course ... Austere-looking course ... Basic course but golf as it should be played ... Don't bother with No. 2 or No. 3, this is the one ... You can see Muirfield from the highest point here.

Gullane Golf Club (No. 2)   ★★★

Gullane, Lothian, EH31 2BB
Nearest main town: Edinburgh

Secretary:	Mr S. C. Owram	Tel: 01620 842255
		Fax: 01620 842327
Professional:	Mr J. Hume	Tel: 01620 843111

Playing: Midweek: round £23.00; day £35.00. Weekend: round £29.00; day £44.00.

Facilities: Bar: 11am–11pm. Food: Lunch from 12pm–2.30pm except Monday–Wednesday.

Comments: Clearly the second best links at Gullane ... Fairly open ... Not far behind No. 1 ... Lives in the shadow of No. 1.

Gullane Golf Club (No. 3)   ★★★

Gullane, Lothian, EH31 2BB
Nearest main town: Edinburgh

Secretary:	Mr S. C. Owram	Tel: 01620 842255
		Fax: 01620 842327
Professional:	Mr J. Hume	Tel: 01620 843111

Playing: Midweek: round £14.00; day £21.00. Weekend: round £18.00; day £26.00.

Facilities: Bar: 11am–11pm. Food: Lunch from 12pm–2.30pm except Monday–Wednesday.

Comments: Very well presented and managed – businesslike approach ... Fair welcome from helpful staff ... Comfortable, modern clubhouse ... Excellent short links to play with friends.

Kilspindie Golf Club ★★★

Aberlady, Longniddry, EH32 0QD
Nearest main town: Aberlady

Secretary: Mr R. M. McInnes   Tel: 01875 870358
Fax: 01875 870358

Professional: Mr G. J. Sked   Tel: 01875 870695

Playing: Midweek: round £20.00; day £30.00. Weekend: round £25.00; day £35.00.

Facilities: Bar: 11am–11pm. Food: Lunch from 10am–3pm.

Comments: Old course which has been overtaken by technology ... Short and tight ... Old links with superb bunkering ... Natural test of any golfer ... 8th is a stunner ... Everything links golf should be ... A little short ... Step back in time.

Liberton Golf Club ★

297 Gilmerton Road, Edinburgh, EH16 5UJ
Nearest main town: Edinburgh

Secretary: Mrs B. Giefer   Tel: 0131 664 3009
Fax: 0131 664 0853

Professional: Mr I. Seath   Tel: 0131 664 1056
Fax: 0131 658 1988

Playing: Midweek: round £17.00; day £30.00. Weekend: round £30.00; day n/a.

Facilities: Bar: 11am–11pm. Food: Lunch and dinner from 11am–10pm. Bar snacks.

Comments: A bit of everything at this short parkland course ... A little easy ... Nice routeing ... Wooded in places.

Longniddry Golf Club   ★★★

Links Road, Longniddry, EH32 0NL
Nearest main town: Edinburgh

Secretary:	Mr N. Robertson	Tel: 01875 852141
		Fax: 01875 853371
Professional:	Mr W. J. Gray	Tel: 01875 852228

Playing: Midweek: round £27.50; day £38.50. Weekend: round £35.50; day n/a. Handicap certificate required.

Facilities: Bar: 11am–11pm. Food: Lunch from 10am–8pm. Bar snacks.

Comments: Pleasant mixture of parkland and links golf with better-than-average greens ... Well-presented course with many feature holes ... Fair value for parkland course.

Lothianburn Golf Club   ★

106a Biggar Road, Edinburgh, EH10 7DU
Nearest main town: Edinburgh

Secretary:	Mr W. F. A. Jardine	Tel: 0131 445 5067
Professional:	Mr K. Mungall	Tel: 0131 445 2288
		Fax: 0131 445 2288

Playing: Midweek: round £15.00; day £22.00. Weekend: round £21.00; day n/a. Handicap certificate required.

Facilities: Bar: 11am–11pm. Food: Lunch from 11am–3pm. Dinner by arrangement.

Comments: Very traditional club ... Too hilly by far ... Sloping lies make scoring difficult ... Course to learn the vagaries of the game ... All those sloping lies can mess up your game ... Just as well this exhausting course is fairly short.

Luffness Golf Club   ★★★★

Aberlady, Lothian, EH32 0QA
Nearest main town: Gullane

Secretary:	Lt Col J. G. Tedford	Tel: 01620 843336
		Fax: 01620 842933
Professional:	None.	

Playing: Midweek: round £35.00; day £50.00. Weekend: round n/a; day n/a. Handicap certificate required.

Facilities: Bar: 11am–11pm. Food: Lunch from 12pm–2pm.

Comments: Stop off on the way to Muirfield ... Holes go in all directions ... Wind plays havoc ... Combine with Gullane, Muirfield and North Berwick ... One of the toughest courses in Scotland.

Marriott Dalmahoy Hotel & Country Club ★★★★

Dalmayhoy, Kirk Newton, EH27 8BD
Nearest main town: Edinburgh

Secretary: Mr B. Anderson (Golf Dir)   Tel: 0131 333 4105
Fax: 0131 335 3203
Professional: Mr N. Graham

Playing: Midweek: round £55.00; day n/a. Weekend: round £75.00; day n/a. Handicap certificate required.

Facilities: Bar: 11am–11pm. Food: Breakfast, lunch and dinner from 7am–10pm. Bar snacks.

Comments: Corporate venue ... Expensive pay-and-play ... Choice of two good courses with excellent country club attached ... Narrow fairways are difficult to play but lots of fun ... Requires concentration ... Two courses, the East was used for the Solheim Cup.

Mortonhall Golf Club ★★

231 Braid Road, Edinburgh, EH10 6PB
Nearest main town: Edinburgh

Secretary: Mrs C. D. Morrison   Tel: 0131 447 6974
Fax: 0131 447 8712
Professional: Mr D. B. Horn   Tel: 0131 447 5185

Playing: Midweek: round £30.00; day £40.00. Weekend: round £30.00; day £40.00. Handicap certificate required.

Facilities: Bar: 11am–11pm. Food: Lunch from 12pm–2.30pm.

Comments: Views of Edinburgh ... Best part of course are the views ... Welcoming club with simple course ... Very long but worth the walk.

Musselburgh Golf Club   ★★★

Monktonhall, Musselburgh, EH21 6SA
Nearest main town: Musselburgh

Secretary: Mr E. Stoddart   Tel: 0131 665 2005
Professional: Mr F. Mann   Tel: 0131 665 7055
                                         Fax: 0131 665 7055

Playing: Midweek: round £18.00; day £25.00. Weekend: round
                   £21.00; day £30.00.

Facilities: Bar: 11am–11pm. Food: Lunch and dinner from
                   10am–8pm. Bar snacks.

Comments: Really interesting course ... Not overly challenging until
                   the 18th ... Course right next to an oil production plant
                   ... The view has to be seen to be believed.

North Berwick Golf Club   ★★★★

West Links, Beach Road, North Berwick, EH39 4BB
Nearest main town: North Berwick

Secretary: Mr A. G. Flood   Tel: 01620 895040
                                         Fax: 01620 893274
Professional: Mr D. Huish   Tel: 01620 893233

Playing: Midweek: round £36.00; day £54.00. Weekend: round
                   £54.00; day £70.00. Handicap certificate required.

Facilities: Bar: 11am–11pm. Food: Lunch and dinner from
                   10am–10pm. Bar snacks.

Comments: Attractive, welcoming course ... Real links golf with
                   roads, walls, burns, humps and hollows ... Knee-length
                   rough a bit of a bind ... A course with everything ...
                   Really fun course – what the game is all about ... The
                   ideal place to be, not as busy as Gullane and twice as
                   welcoming ... Great location and best course in the
                   area ... Designed by the sands of time ... Watch out for
                   the famous Redan ... Prepare to be humbled by the
                   North Berwick experience ... We would die for some-
                   thing like this in the States.

Royal Burgess Golfing Society of Edinburgh   ★★★

181 Whitehouse Road, Barnton, Edinburgh, EH4 6BY
Nearest main town: Edinburgh

Secretary:	Mr J. P. Audis	Tel: 0131 339 2075
		Fax: 0131 339 3712
Professional:	Mr G. Yuille	Tel: 0131 339 6474
		Fax: 0131 339 6474

Playing: Midweek: round £37.00; day £47.00. Weekend: round n/a; day n/a. Handicap certificate required.

Facilities: Bar: 11am–11pm. Food: Bar snacks.

Comments: Highly conditioned ... Fairways like greens at some clubs ... Magnificent ... Accuracy more important than distance ... Historic course with many nice features ... Greens superb.

Royal Musselburgh Golf Club   ★★★★

Prestongrange House, Prestonpans, EH32 9RP
Nearest main town: Edinburgh

Secretary:	Mr T. H. Hardie	Tel: 01875 810276
		Fax: 01875 810276
Professional:	Mr J. Henderson	Tel: 01875 810139
		Fax: 01875 810139

Playing: Midweek: round £20.00; day £35.00. Weekend: round £35.00; day n/a. Handicap certificate required.

Facilities: Bar: 11am–11pm. Food: Lunch from 10am–4pm. Dinner by arrangement.

Comments: Rather unbalanced with just one par-5 ... Special feel to this venerable parkland layout ... Spirit in which golf should be played ... Very strategic bunkering ... Usually can be found in fine condition.

The Glen Golf Club   ★★★★

East Links, North Berwick, EH39 4LE
Nearest main town: North Berwick

Secretary:	Mr D. R. Montgomery	Tel: 01620 895288
		Fax: 01620 895447
Professional:	None.	

Playing: Midweek: round £17.00; day £26.00. Weekend: round £22.00; day £30.00.

Facilities: Bar: 11am–11pm. Food: Lunch and dinner from 10am–8pm.

Comments: Good old-fashioned golf club with no over-the-top features ... The East links of North Berwick ... Views over the Firth of Forth ... Blind shots all over the place ... Highlight was the 18th, left me with great impression of the course.

Whitekirk Golf Course   ★★★

Whitekirk, EH39 5PR
Nearest main town: North Berwick

Secretary: Mr G. Tuer   Tel: 01620 870300
                                          Fax: 01620 870330
Professional: None.

Playing: Midweek: round £18.00; day £30.00. Weekend: round £25.00; day £35.00.

Facilities: Bar: 11am–11pm. Food: Lunch and dinner from 10am–9pm. Bar snacks.

Comments: Relatively new course with wonderful views from the hill-tops ... First class catering ... Excellent value for money ... Practice facilities first class ... Outstanding golf.

Highland and Moray

Royal Dornoch Golf Club ★★★★★

Golf Road, Dornoch, IV25 3LW
Nearest main town: Dornoch

If you're travelling north towards the Highlands to play Royal Dornoch, chances are you're also going to take in a great quartet of courses, including Tain, Golspie and Brora. A word of advice – make sure to leave Dornoch until last and leave on a high note.

This is one of the finest golfing outposts in Britain. Unburdened by the weight of holding an Open Championship (although it surely could) and handed an air of mystique by its isolation, Royal Dornoch is an exceptional course for visitors. The whole place is shrouded in peace and tranquillity, and only serious golfers with an appreciation of the history and elegance of the game head out this way, so you can be sure of a respectful and warm welcome.

The course itself is a something of a conundrum. It's a straightforward, fair links, with few blind shots and all the trouble laid out clearly before you. But the classic links shot, the bump-and-run, can feel slightly redundant, the greens too well protected to allow you a straight line in, and they are often set on small plateaus. This is not a criticism, just the character of the course. You'll also find dramatic tee shots from elevated tees falling into basin fairways, gorse-covered dunes and hills and greens nestled in the shadow of hills.

It is a timeless design, touched by the hands of Donald Ross and Tom Morris. (Ross emigrated to North America in 1898 and went on to become one of the greatest course designers of all time – trademark Dornoch traits can be found on most of Ross's courses throughout the world). Highlights include the 5th, an exciting driving hole, and the 14th, called 'Foxy', appropriately so, including, as it does, an inventive double dogleg.

Secretary:	Mr J. S. Duncan	Tel: 01862 811220
		Fax: 01862 810792
Professional:	Mr A. Skinner	Tel: 01862 810902
		Fax: 01862 811095
Playing:	Midweek: round £45.00; day n/a. Weekend: round £55.00; day n/a. Handicap certificate required.	

Facilities: Bar: 11am–11pm. Food: Breakfast, lunch and dinner from 7am–10pm. Bar snacks.

Comments: So many cherished memories ... Finest links anywhere ... Golf as it should be ... Magical Northern gem ... Course and facilities excellent ... Good test of golf and good facilities ... Only drawback is remoteness, but still worth the journey ... It's not a frightening course but it can put egg on your face quite easily ... Very hard but fair course ... Just about worth the price of the trip ... A magical, classical links of charm and beauty ... A natural beauty ... Donald Ross country ... Miles from anywhere, a haven of tranquillity ... The best experience in 40 years of golf ... A real tear jerker.

Boat of Garten Golf Club   ★★★★★

Boat of Garten, PH24 3BQ
Nearest main town: Inverness

Secretary: Mr P. Smyth   Tel: 01479 831282
                                      Fax: 01479 831523
Professional: Mr J R. Ingram   Tel: 01479 831282

Playing: Midweek: round £21.00; day £26.00. Weekend: round £26.00; day £31.00. Handicap certificate required.

Facilities: Bar: 11am–11pm. Food: Breakfast, lunch and dinner from 9.30am–8pm. Bar snacks.

Comments: Good food, not to be missed ... Magnificent surroundings ... How golf should be played ... Maybe overrated ... An unfair course in the summer when the ball bounces everywhere ... Great location – I want to die here ... They get everything right here ... Superb scenery, absolutely compelling golf ... A little too hilly in places to be considered a great ... Had a great day.

Brora Golf Club   ★★★

Golf Road, Brora, KW9 6QS
Nearest main town: Dornoch

Secretary: Mr J. Fraser   Tel: 01408 621417
                                       Fax: 01408 622157
Professional: None.

Playing: Midweek: round £20.00; day £25.00. Weekend: round £20.00; day £25.00.

Facilities: Bar: 11am–11pm. Food: Lunch and dinner from 12pm–9pm.

Comments: Excellent hospitality ... Nice links course with good holes ... Electric fences rather annoying ... Friendly sheep on the fairways ... Perfect hospitality ... Any weaknesses the course has are made up in the 19th ... An experience ... Elevated tees.

Elgin Golf Club   ★★★

Hardhillock, Birnie Road, Elgin, IV30 3SX
Nearest main town: Elgin

Secretary: Mr D. F. Black   Tel: 01343 542338
                                     Fax: 01343 542341
Professional: Mr I. Rodger   Tel: 01343 542884
                                     Fax: 01343 542884

Playing: Midweek: round £22.00; day £29.00. Weekend: round £28.00; day £35.00. Handicap certificate required.

Facilities: Bar: 11am–11pm. Food: Lunch and dinner from 10am–9pm. Bar snacks.

Comments: Good course, useful driving range ... Pro shop is consistently helpful to visitors ... Short but don't be fooled ... One of the best inland courses in Scotland ... In the top three parkland courses in Scotland ... A nice change from the surfeit of links.

Forres Golf Club   ★★★

Muiryshade, Forres, IV36 0RD
Nearest main town: Forres

Secretary: Mrs M. Greenaway   Tel: 01309 672949
Professional: Mr S. Aird   Tel: 01309 672250
                                     Fax: 01309 672250

Playing: Midweek: round £18.00; day £25.00. Weekend: round £20.00; day £27.00.

Facilities: Bar: 11am–11pm. Food: Lunch and dinner from 10am–9pm. Bar snacks.

Comments: People at club could not do enough for the visitors ... Very up and down but nicely run club with good reception ... Well drained ... Welcoming visitors course.

Fortrose & Rosemarkie Golf Club   ★★★

Ness Road East, Fortrose, IV10 8SE
Nearest main town: Inverness

Secretary: Mrs M. Collier   Tel: 01381 620529
                                       Fax: 01381 620529

Professional: None.

Playing: Midweek: round £17.00; day £25.00. Weekend: round £23.00; day £30.00.

Facilities: Bar: 11am–11pm. Food: Lunch from 12pm–2pm. Dinner by arrangement.

Comments: Tight and tricky, but excellent ... Good place to play and absorb the game ... Sited on Black Isle ... Brute force the main weapon here ... Value for money ... Sea often in play ... Tough nut to crack.

Golspie Golf Club   ★★★

Ferry Road, Golspie, KW10 6ST
Nearest main town: Dornoch

Secretary: Mrs M. MacLeod   Tel: 01408 633266
                                        Fax: 01408 633393

Professional: None.

Playing: Midweek: round £18.00; day £20.00. Weekend: round £18.00; day £25.00.

Facilities: Bar: 11am–11pm. Food: Lunch from 12pm–3pm. Dinner by arrangement.

Comments: Part links, part heathland ... Good variety of golf in pretty surroundings ... The only course with six seaside holes, six heathland holes and six inland holes ... Well kept and visitors made very welcome ... Far from the crowds ... A must in conjunction with Brora and Royal Dornoch.

Grantown-on-Spey Golf Club   ★★★

Golf Course Road, Grantown-on-Spey, PH26 3HY
Nearest main town: Aviemore

Secretary: Mr J. A. Matheson   Tel: 01479 872079
                                         Fax: 01479 873725
Professional: Mr B. Mitchell   Tel: 01479 872398

Playing: Midweek: round n/a; day £18.00. Weekend: round n/a;
                   day £23.00.

Facilities: Bar: 11am–11pm. Food: Lunch and dinner from
                   11am–9pm. Bar snacks.

Comments: Play it along with Boat of Garten ... Enjoy the air up
                   here ... Wonderfully fresh and exhilarating course ... A
                   little easy but the scenery is just perfect ... A treasured
                   location near the rambling centre of Aviemore ...
                   Completely unknown so excellent value ... Who said
                   short courses were boring? ... Very eccentric but had a
                   ball.

Hopeman Golf Club   ★★★

Hopeman, Moray, IV30 2YA
Nearest main town: Elgin

Secretary: Mr R. Johnston   Tel: 01343 830578
                                         Fax: 01343 830152
Professional: None.

Playing: Midweek: round £15.00; day £20.00. Weekend: round
                   £20.00; day £25.00.

Facilities: Bar: 11am–11pm. Food: Lunch and dinner from
                   10am–3pm. Dinner by arrangement.

Comments: Cracking course ... The 12th one of the best par-3s in
                   all of golf ... Links near the Moray Firth ... You hit and
                   hope at the 12th ... Par-3 is so memorable ...
                   Unbelievable value for classic links experience.

Inverness Golf Club   ★★★

Culcabock Road, Inverness, IV2 3XQ
Nearest main town: Inverness

Secretary: Mr G. Thomson   Tel: 01463 239882
                                 Fax: 01463 239882
Professional: Mr A. P. Thomson   Tel: 01463 231989

Playing: Midweek: round £25.00; day n/a. Weekend: round £30.00; day n/a. Handicap certificate required.

Facilities: Bar: 11am–11pm. Food: Lunch from 12pm–3pm. Dinner by arrangement.

Comments: Flattish with very little definition ... A little overpriced for what you get ... Enjoyed myself thoroughly at this perfect little venue ... Parkland track in prime golfing country.

Kingussie Golf Club   ★★★★

Gynack Road, Kingussie, PH21 1LR
Nearest main town: Kingussie

Secretary: Mr N. D. MacWilliam Tel: 01540 661600
                                    Fax: 01540 662066
Professional: None.

Playing: Midweek: round £15.00; day £18.00. Weekend: round £17.00; day £22.00.

Facilities: Bar: 11am–11pm. Food: Breakfast, lunch and dinner from 10am–8pm.

Comments: Short but has all the shots and wonderful greens ... Highlands course up in the sky ... Very soft fairways ... Course plays longer than length ... Epitome of golfing in Scotland – scenic and good welcome ... Good value but could do with a practice ground.

Moray Golf Club (Old)   ★★★★

Stotfield Road, Lossiemouth, IV31 6QS
Nearest main town: Elgin

Secretary: Mr B. Russell   Tel: 01343 812018
                                Fax: 01343 815102
Professional: Mr A. Thomson   Tel: 01343 813330
                                   Fax: 01343 813330

Playing: Midweek: round £30.00; day £40.00. Weekend: round £40.00; day £50.00. Handicap certificate required.

Facilities: Bar: 11am–11pm. Food: Breakfast, lunch and dinner from 9am–9pm. Bar snacks.

Comments: Finishing hole is a cracker ... Unknown links ... Starts and ends in the town ... Views over the Moray Firth.

Moray Golf Club (New) ★★★

Stotfield Road, Lossiemouth, IV31 6QS
Nearest main town: Elgin

Secretary: Mr B. Russell   Tel: 01343 812018
   Fax: 01343 815102
Professional: Mr A. Thomson   Tel: 01343 813330

Playing: Midweek: round £17.00; day £22.00. Weekend: round £25.00; day £30.00.

Facilities: Bar: 11am–11pm. Food: Breakfast, lunch and dinner from 9am–9pm. Bar snacks.

Comments: Designed by Henry Cotton ... Does not have the same special feel as the Old ... .Very favourable climate for good golf ... Not a patch on the Old.

Muir of Ord Golf Club ★

Great North Road, Muir of Ord, IV6 7SX
Nearest main town: Inverness

Secretary: Mr D. Noble   Tel: 01463 870825
   Fax: 01463 870825
Professional: Mr G. Legett   Tel: 01463 871311

Playing: Midweek: round £12.50; day £14.50. Weekend: round £16.50; day £18.50.

Facilities: Bar: 11am–11pm. Food: Bar snacks.

Comments: Very short, eccentric heathland course ... Will test your patience ... Fairways you can stick a cigarette paper between – very tight and suffocating.

Nairn Dunbar Golf Club ★★★

Lochloy Road, Nairn, IV12 5AE
Nearest main town: Nairn

Secretary:	Mr J. Scott-Falconer	Tel: 01667 452741
		Fax: 01667 456897
Professional:	Mr B. R. Mason	Tel: 01667 453964

Playing: Midweek: round £25.00; day £33.00. Weekend: round £30.00; day £40.00.

Facilities: Bar: 11am–11pm. Food: Breakfast, lunch and dinner from 7am–9pm.

Comments: Hard slog but technically good ... Three new holes are poor and badly out of character ... Good new clubhouse but the other Nairn has Scotland's best new clubhouse ... 10th hole the best ... Unattractive course devoid of a links feel.

Nairn Golf Club   ★★★★

Seabank Road, Nairn, IV12 4HB
Nearest main town: Nairn

Secretary:	Mr J. Somerville	Tel: 01667 453208
		Fax: 01667 456328
Professional:	Mr R. Fyfe	Tel: 01667 452787
		Fax: 01667 451315

Playing: Midweek: round £50.00; day n/a. Weekend: round £50.00; day n/a. Handicap certificate required.

Facilities: Bar: 11am–11pm. Food: Lunch and dinner from 10am–9pm. Bar snacks.

Comments: Course was a bit disappointing and not worth the trip ... Joy to play ... Long way north but well worth the trip ... Memorable challenge you want to repeat again and again ... Very reasonable course ... Wonderful course presentation and greens ... Outstanding new clubhouse ... A little expensive but well worth the treat ... One of the truly great Scottish links ... Greens quick ... Silky, fast greens ... Devoid of natural beauty but tough as old boots ... Don't forget to take your game with you ... Bunkering and greens exceptional.

Tain Golf Club   ★★★★

Tain, IV19 1PA
Nearest main town: Dornoch

Secretary: Mrs K. D. Ross Tel: 01862 892314
Fax: 01862 892099

Professional: None.

Playing: Midweek: round £21.00; day £27.00. Weekend: round £25.00; day £31.00.

Facilities: Bar: 11am–11pm. Food: Lunch from 10am–3pm. Dinner by arrangement.

Comments: Dornoch is the top course in the area but you must visit this one too ... Heather and links, a great combination ... Exceptional value ... Very unfashionable course ... Playing here is like a chess match ... Have a clear game plan.

The Carnegie Club ★★★★

Skibo Castle, Clashmore, Dornoch, IV25 3RQ
Nearest main town: Dornoch

Secretary: Mr C. Oak Tel: 01862 894600
Fax: 01862 894601

Professional: Mr G. Finleyson Tel: 01862 881260

Playing: Midweek: round £130.00; day n/a. Weekend: round n/a; day n/a. Handicap certificate required.

Facilities: Bar: 11am–11pm. Food: Lunch from 12.30pm–3pm.

Comments: Some tight holes near Dornoch Firth, but excellent for a new course ... Not worth the cost but undoubted brilliance ... Gulped at the price and course.

Traigh Golf Course ★★

Traigh, Arisaig, PH39 4NT
Nearest main town: Fort William

Secretary: Mr W. Henderson Tel: 01687 450645

Professional: None.

Playing: Midweek: round £12.00; day £12.00. Weekend: round £12.00; day £12.00.

Facilities: Call for information.

Comments: Marvellous evocative course with vistas to the islands of Rhum and Skye ... Only nine holes but don't let that put you off ... A couple of memorable holes ... Views make up for what course so noticeably lacks.

Wick Golf Club   ★★★

Reiss, Wick, KW1 4RW
Nearest main town: Wick

Secretary: Mr D. Shearer   Tel: 01955 602935
Professional: None.

Playing: Midweek: round n/a; day £15.00. Weekend: round n/a; day £15.00.

Facilities: Bar: 12pm–8pm. Food: Bar snacks. Lunch and dinner by arrangement.

Comments: Not worth the trek ... Northernmost course in the British Isles ... Very rugged and a little unfair in places ... Wonderful people here ... Course a little eccentric.

Angus and Perth & Kinross

Carnoustie Golf Club ★★★★★

Links Parade, Carnoustie, DD7 7JE
Nearest main town: Dundee

When the Open Championship returns to Carnoustie this year, the reputation of this sleeping giant will once again be on the line. For years, the passing of this course, and the condition of its fairways and greens, have been lamented. But now, back in first-class order and with a newly constructed hotel to replace the old 1960s abomination, the world's best players will take on this historic links and test whether it really is the toughest course in the British Isles.

Visually it could not be more intimidating. The land is very cheerless, furnished with scrubs, scrapes and ditches. There are none of the moon-scape dunes that you associate with the great Open courses, neither is it a traditional out-and-back links. Instead, the severity of the course is entirely governed by the strength of the wind and the height of the rough.

Players have to hit the ground running at Carnoustie, requiring a long iron to a hidden green at the 1st, and then having to avoid a bunker in the middle of the fairway at the long par-4 2nd. There is a brief respite until the 6th, a par-5 with out-of-bounds all the way up the left and, once again, strategic bunkers placed in the middle of the fairway. From there, you need to thread a line through the out-of-bounds and a burn to set up a pitch to the green.

But it's the closing holes for which Carnoustie is famed, starting with the 15th, a 460-yard par-4 swinging spectacularly around a rolling ridge. The 16th is, wait for it, a 248-yard par-3, followed by the 17th, where you face a drive to a fairway which is almost completely surrounded by a stream. Both the 17th and the 18th, which cross the stream twice, provide a very un-links-style finish but are excellent for matchplay and could provide some thrills and spills at the Open.

Carnoustie's regeneration gives the links a very fresh feel. Its stock is set to rise with the return of the Open, so play it before it's too late.

Secretary: Mr E. J. C. Smith   Tel: 01241 853789
                                            Fax: 01241 852720
Professional: Mr L. Vannet   Tel: 01241 853789

Playing: Midweek: round £52.00; day n/a. Weekend: round £52.00; day n/a. Handicap certificate required.

Facilities: Bar/Food: Full facilities from April 1999.

Comments: Best in the country ... Ultimate test of golf overrides lack
of facilities ... Course only lacks playability ... Need to
cut back rough for amateurs ... Don't play this beast in
any more than a breeze ... What a course, a must ... A
real education although expensive ... The No. 1 in
Scotland ... If the wind blows in the Open watch out ...
18th is a classic finishing hole ... New clubhouse will
improve this club no end ... Most difficult I've played ...
Great test – in the Portmarnock class ... No dunes, no
long rough – it's the design that is so punishing ...
Greens are the killer ... Finish is the toughest anywhere.

The Gleneagles Hotel (King's)   ★★★★★

Auchterarder, PH3 1NF
Nearest main town: Perth

If you think of Scottish golf courses as wild and unkempt, then think
again. Gleneagles will blow away any preconceptions you might have.
There are four courses at this exclusive golf and hotel bolt-hole, all
beautifully manicured with a very modern feel. The King's Course is the
best of them all and few come away from it without falling in love with
this very sensuous and natural course.

The King's lays claim to be the best inland course in Scotland, and
the claim is founded on very solid arguments. It is kept in consistently
superb condition, but not even the heather-clad Grampian Mountains
which form the backdrop to the course, or the silver birch and rowan,
can persuade you that this is a victory of style over content. There are
18 very individual holes here, providing a varied technical test. There
are drives from elevated tees to camber fairways, approach shots to
elevated greens, sweeping plateau doglegs, angled greens, downhill
approaches and more.

Many of the best holes come towards the end of the round. There's
the driveable short par-4 14th, where you can gamble on setting up an
eagle or birdie, the plunge approach to the par-4 15th and the par-3
16th played to an angled green protected by an enormous hill covered
in wild grasses. The 17th swings around the side of a hill to a sloping,
elevated green and, finally, the par-5 18th, the first half of which is a
very natural roller-coaster fairway.

What will strike you about the King's Course is the shaping and
artistry of the holes. The fairways and greens have very curvy lines, and
even the bunkers seem to draw your vision. With the bushes and grassy
hills teeming with wildlife, it's a riveting experience. And if you're staying

at the Gleneagles Hotel, a standard bearer for service and welcome in Scotland, you will truly be the envy of your golfing compatriots.

Secretary: Miss H. Edment Tel: 01764 663543
Fax: 01764 694383

Professional: Mr G. Schofield Tel: 01764 663543

Playing: Midweek: round £85.00; day £100.00. Weekend: round n/a; day n/a.

Facilities: Bar: 11am–11pm. Food: Breakfast, lunch and dinner from 7am–10pm. Bar snacks.

Comments: Famed Gleneagles quality ... Palatial course ... A haven for wildlife ... Sculpted masterpiece with elements of all the classics ... Can get windy ... A right royal experience ... On a fine spring morning, it is paradise ... Fantastic ... Nothing better, but at a price ... Outstanding in every way, only the cost is off-putting ... Beautiful, natural layout with fabulous practice facilities ... Perfect in every way ... Played like a rabbit, would like to go back and play well ... Heaven in the Glens ... Everything is excellent ... Layout and course condition second to none.

Alyth Golf Club ★★★

Pitcrocknie, Alyth, PH11 8HF
Nearest main town: Dundee

Secretary: Mr J. Docherty Tel: 01828 632268
Fax: 01828 633491

Professional: Mr T. Melville Tel: 01828 632411
Fax: 01828 632411

Playing: Midweek: round £20.00; day £30.00. Weekend: round £25.00; day £40.00. Handicap certificate required.

Facilities: Bar: 11am–11pm. Food: Bar snacks. Dinner by arrangement.

Comments: Beautifully looked after, hard-to-master course ... Well-protected greens ... Does not get recognition it deserves ... Variety in abundance ... Far from straightforward parkland course ... In the shadow of a nearby classic links.

Auchterarder Golf Club ★★★

Ochil Road, Auchterarder, PH3 1LS
Nearest main town: Auchterarder

Secretary:	Mr W. M. Campbell	Tel: 01764 662804
		Fax: 01764 662804
Professional:	Mr G. Baxter	Tel: 01764 663711
		Fax: 01764 663711

Playing: Midweek: round £18.00; day £26.00. Weekend: round £24.00; day £36.00.

Facilities: Bar: 11am–11pm. Food: Lunch and dinner from 11am–9pm. Bar snacks.

Comments: Great holiday golf ... Not too long or demanding ... Made to feel very welcome ... A mini Gleneagles ... No par-5s but still very enjoyable ... Good bar.

Blairgowrie Golf Club (Rosemount) ★★★★

Rosemount, Blairgowie, PH10 6LG
Nearest main town: Perth

Secretary:	Mr J. N. Simpson	Tel: 01250 872622
		Fax: 01250 875451
Professional:	Mr C. Dernie	Tel: 01250 873116
		Fax: 01250 873116

Playing: Midweek: round £50.00; day £60.00. Weekend: round £55.00; day £75.00.

Facilities: Bar: 11am–11pm. Food: Lunch and dinner from 10am–9pm. Bar snacks.

Comments: Setting and presentation could not be bettered ... Greatly overrated ... Unique in Scotland but not a patch on Sunningdale, Liphook, Swinley Forest, West Sussex ... Expensive with poor facilities for visitors ... If I lived in Scotland this is the club I would join ... Visitors are not made to feel welcome ... Unique in Scotland ... Each hole separated from the others ... Great flora and fauna.

Blairgowrie Golf Club (Lansdowne) ★★

Rosemount, Blairgowrie, PH10 6LG
Nearest main town: Perth

Secretary:	Mr J. N. Simpson	Tel: 01250 872622
		Fax: 01250 875451
Professional:	Mr C. Dernie	Tel: 01250 873116
		Fax: 01250 873116

Playing: Midweek: round £40.00; day £60.00. Weekend: round £45.00; day £75.00.

Facilities: Bar: 11am–11pm. Food: Lunch and dinner from 10am–9pm. Bar snacks.

Comments: Like Rosemount, greatly overrated but even less fun to play ... Trademark Alliss/Thomas design ... Very narrow driving areas ... Couldn't pick which course I prefered ... Somewhat monotonous layout ... Great clubhouse.

Callander Golf Club   ★★★

Aveland Road, Callander, FK17 8EN
Nearest main town: Callander

Secretary:	Mr D. Allan	Tel: 01877 330090
	(Manager)	Fax: 01877 330062
Professional:	To be appointed.	

Playing: Midweek: round £18.00; day £26.00. Weekend: round £31.00; day £36.00.

Facilities: Bar: 11am–11pm. Food: Lunch and dinner from 10am–9pm. Bar snacks.

Comments: Good course from back tees but visitors only play about 4,000 yards from front tees or bits of fairway ... Nice test in the Trossachs ... Design by Tom Morris Snr ... Members too protective of course ... Very poor value for visitors.

Crieff Golf Club   ★★★★★

Perth Road, Crieff, PH7 3LR
Nearest main town: Perth

Secretary:	Mr J. S. Miller	Tel: 01764 652397
		Fax: 01764 655093
Professional:	Mr D. J. W. Murchie	Tel: 01764 652909

Playing: Midweek: round £20.00; day £34.00. Weekend: round £28.00; day n/a. Handicap certificate required.

Facilities: Bar: 11am–10pm. Food: Lunch and dinner from 10am–9pm.

Comments: Parkland course where every shot needs careful thought ... Built on the side of a hill ... People are what make the club ... Sloping lies ad nauseam ... Only one blind hole and long par-4s ... Best golf experience in Scotland ... Nine in the morning, 18 in the afternoon – perfect.

Downfield Golf Club   ★★★★

Turnberry Avenue, Dundee, DD2 3QP
Nearest main town: Dundee

Secretary: Mr B. D. Liddle   Tel: 01382 825595
                                              Fax: 01382 813111
Professional: Mr K. S. Hutton   Tel: 01382 889246

Playing: Midweek: round £26.00; day £36.00. Weekend: round £31.00; day n/a. Handicap certificate required.

Facilities: Bar: 11am–11pm. Food: Lunch and dinner from 10am–9pm. Bar snacks.

Comments: Slightly disappointed at condition on last visit as it is normally top class ... Best inland course I have played ... A bit of everything here ... Bit pricey ... Good practice and pro facilities ... Not well known outside Scotland ... Heavily wooded inland course ... Not what you expect in Scotland ... Don't miss it.

Edzell Golf Club   ★★★★

High Street, Edzell, DD9 7TF
Nearest main town: Brechin

Secretary: Mr I. G. Farquhar   Tel: 01356 647283
                                              Fax: 01356 648094
Professional: Mr A. J. Webster   Tel: 01356 648462
                                              Fax: 01356 648884

Playing: Midweek: round £21.00; day £31.00. Weekend: round £27.00; day £41.00.

Facilities: Bar: 11am–11pm. Food: Lunch and dinner from 10am–9pm. Bar snacks.

Comments: Highly regarded but not all it's made out to be ... Would not rush back ... A course that combines challenge and chasm ... Friendliest club in Scotland ... One of Scotland's best kept secrets ... Gets wet in winter ... Outstanding finishing hole and great greens ... Picturesque, interesting and friendly ... Small, compact course with tiny greens and quaint holes ... A treat ... Hospitality first class.

Forfar Golf Club   ★★★

Cunninghill, Arbroath Road, Forfar, DD8 2RL
Nearest main town: Forfar

Secretary:	Mr W. Baird	Tel: 01307 463773
		Fax: 01307 468495
Professional:	Mr P. McNiven	Tel: 01307 465683
		Fax: 01307 465683

Playing: Midweek: round £17.00; day £17.00. Weekend: round £25.00; day £30.00.

Facilities: Bar: 11am–11pm. Food: Lunch and dinner from 12pm–8pm. Bar snacks.

Comments: Tree-lined course always in immaculate condition ... A joy to play ... First-class condition ... Layout suspect but condition superb ... A little short, but undeniably sweet.

Kirriemuir Golf Club   ★★

Northmuir, Kirriemuir, DD8 4PN
Nearest main town: Dundee

Secretary:	Mr C. Garry	Tel: 01575 573317
		Fax: 01575 574608
Professional:	Mrs K. Ellis	Tel: 01575 573317

Playing: Midweek: round £18.00; day £24.00. Weekend: round n/a; day n/a.

Facilities: Bar: 11am–11pm. Food: Bar snacks.

Comments: Interesting and enjoyable but not that difficult ... Views of the Angus glens ... Short but not that sweet ... Better to be found in the area.

Letham Grange Golf Club   ★★★

Letham Grange, Colliston, DD11 4RL
Nearest main town: Arbroath

Secretary:	Miss C. Grainger	Tel: 01241 890377
		Fax: 01241 890414
Professional:	Mr S. Moir	Tel: 01241 890377

Playing: Midweek: round £27.50; day £40.00. Weekend: round
£35.00; day £55.00.

Facilities: Bar: 11am–11pm. Food: Breakfast, lunch and dinner
from 9am–11pm. Bar snacks

Comments: Meant to be a Scottish Augusta but far from it ... Very
un-Scottish course but good fun ... Target golf with a
few blind shots thrown in ... New course complements
the superior Old well ... Nice change from links golf ...
Tranquil setting for this US-style course ... Excellent
facilities and a course to match ... Felt very peaceful
and golf was fun ... Had a great laugh ... One of
Donald Steel's best courses ... Water hazards a constant
peril ... Prefer it to all those links.

Monifieth Golf Links (Medal)   ★★★★

Medal Starter's Box, Princes Street, Monifieth, DD5 4AW
Nearest main town: Dundee

Secretary:	Mr H. R. Nicoll	Tel: 01382 532767
		Fax: 01382 535553
Professional:	Mr I. McLeod	Tel: 01382 532945

Playing: Midweek: round £26.00; day £36.00. Weekend: round
£30.00; day n/a.

Facilities: Bar: 11am–11pm. Food: Breakfast, lunch and dinner
from 7am–10pm. Bar snacks.

Comments: A links with a friendly membership, unfriendly wind and
lovely well-tended greens and fairways ... Straightforward links ... Near Carnoustie ... Very exposed.

Monifieth Golf Links (Ashludie)   ★★★

Medal Starter's Box, Princes Street, Monifieth, DD5 4AW
Nearest main town: Dundee

Secretary:	Mr H. R. Nicoll	Tel: 01382 532767
		Fax: 01382 535553
Professional:	Mr I. McLeod	Tel: 01382 532945

Playing: Midweek: round £15.00; day £21.00. Weekend: round £16.00; day £24.00.

Facilities: Bar: 11am–11pm. Food: Breakfast, lunch and dinner from 7am–10pm. Bar snacks.

Comments: Don't come to Monifieth for this one ... Short links of some character ... Ticket to play both is good value.

Montrose Links Trust   ★★★★★

Traill Drive, Montrose, DD10 8SW
Nearest main town: Montrose

Secretary:	Mrs M. Stewart	Tel: 01674 672932
		Fax: 01674 671800
Professional:	Mr K. Stables	Tel: 01674 672634

Playing: Midweek: round £22.00; day £33.00. Weekend: round £30.00; day £45.00. Handicap certificate required.

Facilities: Bar: 11am–11pm. Food: Lunch from 12pm–8pm.

Comments: Forgotten stern links that is part of the life of the town ... Superb course ... Tricky – just what you would expect from a links ... Good value and a joy to play ... Golf played here since the 16th century ... Historic master-piece ... A links legend ... Deep bunkers, springy turf, towering sand dunes.

Murrayshall Hotel Golf Club   ★★★

Murrayshall, New Scone, Perth, PH2 7PH
Nearest main town: Perth

Secretary:	Mr A. Bryan	Tel: 01738 551171
	(Manager)	Fax: 01738 552595
Professional:	Mr A. T. Reid	Tel: 01738 552784

Playing: Midweek: round £22.00; day £32.00. Weekend: round £27.00; day £40.00.

Facilities: Bar: 11am–11pm. Food: Breakfast, lunch and dinner from 7am–10pm.

Comments: Some uninteresting holes on a course in average condition ... Take three trees out of the middle of the fairways and this would be a great course ... Difficult to find any faults ... Greens well protected and pins difficult to attack.

Panmure Golf Club   ★★★

Barry, Carnoustie, DD7 7RT
Nearest main town: Carnoustie

Secretary: Maj G. W. Paton   Tel: 01241 855120
                                            Fax: 01241 859737
Professional: Mr N. Mackintosh   Tel: 01241 852460

Playing: Midweek: round £30.00; day £45.00. Weekend: round £30.00; day £45.00.

Facilities: Bar: 11am–11pm. Food: Lunch from 10am–9pm. Bar snacks.

Comments: Weekend play on Sundays only ... Members not keen on visitors playing their course or using their clubhouse – just like Elie ... Complements nearby Carnoustie and Monifieth ... Bump-and-run golf ... Awkward bounces, narrow fairways, rough devastating ... Short but feels like 7,000 yards in the wind.

Pitlochry Golf Club   ★★★

Golf Course Road, Pitlochry, PH16 5QY
Nearest main town: Perth

Secretary: Mr D. C. M. McKenzie   Tel: 01796 472114
                                            Fax: 01796 473599
Professional: Mr G. Hampton   Tel: 01796 472792

Playing: Midweek: round £14.00; day £21.00. Weekend: round £18.00; day £27.00. Handicap certificate required.

Facilities: Bar: 11am–11pm. Food: Lunch and dinner from 10am–9pm. Bar snacks.

Comments: Stunning setting and top value for money ... A delight to play ... First four holes go straight uphill and are exhausting ... Meanders back down and is worth a visit ... Hard opener and gets easier ... Up hill and down dale at this course on the side of a mountain ... Second shot to the 4th is a thriller ... Plunging approach shots and driveable par-4s, great fun.

The Gleneagles Hotel (Monarch)   ★★★★

Auchterarder, PH3 1NF
Nearest main town: Perth

Secretary:	Miss H. Edment	Tel: 01764 663543
		Fax: 01764 694383
Professional:	Mr G. Schofield	Tel: 01764 6635543

Playing: Midweek: round £85.00; day £100.00. Weekend: round n/a; day n/a.

Facilities: Bar: 11am–11pm. Food: Breakfast, lunch and dinner from 7am–10pm. Bar snacks.

Comments: A fantastic set-up with course presentation out of this world ... Only snag way too pricey ... Some good holes but overall a bit of a let-down ... Poor ground in places and rather ordinary greens ... Stunning US-style course not normally associated with Scotland ... Excellent presentation and condition.

The Gleneagles Hotel (Queens)   ★★★★

Auchterarder, PH3 1NF
Nearest main town: Perth

Secretary:	Miss H. Edment	Tel: 01764 663543
		Fax: 01764 694383
Professional:	Mr G. Schofield	Tel: 01764 663543

Playing: Midweek: round £85.00; day £100.00. Weekend: round n/a; day n/a.

Facilities: Bar: 11am–11pm. Food: Breakfast, lunch and dinner from 7am–10pm. Bar snacks.

Comments: A good course in its own right ... Inevitably overshadowed by neighbours ... Condition a match for anything around ... Easiest course here ... Facilities just out of this world ... Surprisingly good ... Enjoyed it immensely ... Not far behind the other two.

Aberdeen

Cruden Bay Golf Club ★★★★★

Cruden Bay, Peterhead, AB42 0NN
Nearest main town: Peterhead

It's often said of Cruden Bay that no present-day designer in the world would have the cheek to design such a quirky, eccentric course as this. For instance, the 14th has no view of the fairway from the tee, or the green from the fairway; the 15th is a blind par-3; and the 3rd and the 8th were seemingly thrown in without much thought, as par-4s of well less than 300 yards.

Whether you view Cruden Bay as a hoot, or the epitome of links golf, you can't fail to be impressed by the location. Such was its desirability, a luxurious hotel occupied the site from the turn of the century to 1947, to which the rich and famous came to be spoilt – or more likely to play Cruden Bay. The 'Palace in the Sandhills', as it was tagged, was knocked down, and so, having had its turn in the limelight, Cruden Bay was shuffled off stage.

At least this saved Cruden Bay from being lumbered with the cachet of, say, Ballybunion. It is not overcrowded with visitors and its condition is normally good. Indeed, it seems to get better with age, the sandhills standing prouder, the fairways gnarled and more resistant to the footprints of holiday golfers. Even Cruden Bay beach, where the sands are 'as smooth and firm as the floor of a cathedral' seem to act as a stronger barrier between the North Sea and the course itself.

You can see it all from the clubhouse, laid out below you. This view, where you can see the holes threading their way through the dunes, really sets the adrenalin flowing, and you can only excitedly rush to the 1st tee from there. You'll be terrified, amused, humbled and downright knackered when you finish, but, most importantly of all, you'll remember Cruden Bay fondly.

Secretary:	Mrs R. Pittendrigh	Tel: 01779 812285
		Fax: 01779 812945
Professional:	Mr R. G. Stewart	Tel: 01779 812414
		Fax: 01779 812414
Playing:		Midweek: round £35.00; day £50.00. Weekend: round £45.00; day n/a. Handicap certificate required.

Facilities: Bar: 11am–11pm. Food: Breakfast, lunch and dinner from 9am–10pm. Bar snacks.

Comments: Tough links between high sand dunes ... Lovely views over the bay ... Experience not to be forgotten ... Wonderful location ... A true rival to courses across the UK ... Full of surprises, every hole is memorable ... Wonderfully peaceful and natural place to play ... Any number of exciting and unusual shots ... Holes 4–8 are great ... A real links course apart from one silly hole – magnificent ... View from 10th tee is the best in golf ... The best ... Who needs Pebble Beach? ... Outstanding scenery ... It's got the lot ... The most difficult links course around ... Everything you would want from a golf course ... A tactician's course ... Gobsmacked ... Unbelievable.

Aboyne Golf Club ★★

Formaston Park, Aboyne, AB34 5GL
Nearest main town: Aberdeen

Secretary: Mrs M. MacLean   Tel: 013398 87078
                                         Fax: 013398 87078

Professional: Mr I. Wright   Tel: 013398 86328

Playing: Midweek: round £18.00; day £24.00. Weekend: round £22.00; day £28.00.

Facilities: Bar: 11am–11pm. Food: Lunch from 10am–3pm.

Comments: Good pro shop ... Was impressed with condition ... Very flat and little definition ... Not bad value for fair quality golf ... Shoot the lights out ... Accessible first-time course ... Very straightforward.

Braemar Golf Club ★★★

Cluniebank Road, Braemar, AB35 5XX
Nearest main town: Ballater

Secretary: Mr J. Pennet   Tel: 013397 41618
Professional: None.

Playing: Midweek: round £13.00; day £18.00. Weekend: round £16.00; day £21.00.

Facilities: Bar: 11am–11pm. Food: Bar snacks.

Comments: Enchanting for many reasons ... Must have some of the most difficult par-3s and easiest par-4s anywhere ... Wonderful setting for great golf ... Beautiful scenery ... Short course with good par-3s.

Cullen Golf Club   ★★

The Links, Cullen, AB56 2UU
Nearest main town: Buckie

Secretary: Mr L. I. G. Findlay   Tel: 01542 840685
Professional: None.

Playing: Midweek: round £10.00; day £15.00. Weekend: round £13.00; day £18.00.

Facilities: Bar: 11am–11pm. Food: Bar snacks.

Comments: Eccentric little links ... So natural, pity the course can't be extended ... Balls can bounce off the rocks ... Beach can come into play for wayward shots ... An unusual golfing day out.

Deeside Golf Club   ★★★

Bieldside, Aberdeen, AB15 9DL
Nearest main town: Aberdeen

Secretary: Mr A. G. Macdonald   Tel: 01224 869457
                                     Fax: 01224 869457
Professional: Mr F J. Courts   Tel: 01224 861041
                                     Fax: 01224 861041

Playing: Midweek: round £25.00; day n/a. Weekend: round £30.00; day n/a. Handicap certificate required.

Facilities: Bar: 11am–11pm. Food: Lunch and dinner from 10am–9pm. Bar snacks.

Comments: Quality club ... Riverside course with brooks and streams ... All sorts of dangers lurking here ... Not long but not short on interest.

Duff House Royal Golf Club   ★★★★

The Barnyards, Banff, AB45 3SX
Nearest main town: Buckie

Secretary:	Mrs J. Maison	Tel: 01261 812062
		Fax: 01261 812224
Professional:	Mr R. S. Strachan	Tel: 01261 812075
		Fax: 01261 812075

Playing: Midweek: round £18.00; day £24.00. Weekend: round £25.00; day £30.00.

Facilities: Bar: 11am–11pm. Food: Lunch and dinner from 10am–9pm. Bar snacks.

Comments: Cracking value for an interesting, challenging and subtle course of substance ... Could not fault the course ... Greens like silk and food that says 'more please' and it's in Scotland! ... Never too busy ... Great condition ... Course protected by tricky greens ... Exceptional greens.

Kemnay Golf Club ★★

Monymusk Road, Kemnay, AB51 5RA
Nearest main town: Aberdeen

Secretary:	Mr B. Robertson	Tel: 01467 643746
		Fax: 01467 643746
Professional:	Mr R. MacDonald	Tel: 01467 642225

Playing: Midweek: round £16.00; day £20.00. Weekend: round £18.00; day £22.00.

Facilities: Bar: 11am–11pm. Food: Bar snacks. Dinner by arrangement.

Comments: Undulating and exciting ... Always easy to get a round ... Excellent views ... Fairly ordinary parkland.

Kintore Golf Club ★★

Kintore, AB51 0UR
Nearest main town: Aberdeen

Secretary:	Mrs V. Graham	Tel: 01467 632631
Professional:	None.	

Playing: Midweek: round £11.00; day £15.00. Weekend: round £16.00; day £20.00. Handicap certificate required.

Facilities: Bar: 11am–11pm. Food: Lunch from 12pm–2pm. Dinner from 6pm–9pm.

Comments: Moorland/woodland course of character ... Excellent
round rate for this charming club ... Nothing special ...
Made welcome.

Murcar Golf Club   ★★★

Bridge of Don, Aberdeen, AB23 8BD
Nearest main town: Aberdeen

Secretary: Mr D. Corstorphine   Tel: 01224 704354
                                           Fax: 01224 704354
Professional: Mr G. Forbes   Tel: 01224 704370

Playing: Midweek: round £30.00; day £40.00. Weekend: round
                     £35.00; day £45.00. Handicap certificate required.

Facilities: Bar: 11am–11pm. Food: Lunch and dinner from
                     10am–10pm. Bar snacks.

Comments: The total package ... Fantastic setting ... Great fun
                     (avoid a windy day, though) ... .Great short par-4s ...
                     Improved condition.

Newburgh-on-Ythan   ★★★

Newburgh, Ellon, AB41 0FB
Nearest main town: Aberdeen

Secretary: Mr E. Leslie   Tel: 01358 789956
                                           Fax: 01358 789956
Professional: None.

Playing: Midweek: round n/a; day £18.00. Weekend: round n/a;
                     day £25.00.

Facilities: Bar: 11am–8pm. Food: Bar snacks.

Comments: Played every hole 100 times but still look forward to
                     seeing them ... Founded in the 19th century and reeks
                     of history ... Forgotten course ... Lovely club with
                     course to be proud of.

Newmacher Golf Club (Hawkshill)   ★★★

Swailend, Newmacher, AB21 7UU
Nearest main town: Aberdeen

Secretary:	Mr G. McIntosh	Tel: 01651 863002
		Fax: 01651 863055
Professional:	Mr P. Smith	Tel: 01651 862127

Playing: Midweek: round £25.00; day £35.00. Weekend: round £30.00; day £40.00. Handicap certificate required.

Facilities: Bar: 11am–11pm. Food: Lunch and dinner by arrangement. Bar snacks.

Comments: Excellent layout and good mix of holes ... Superb home stretch ... Dave Thomas design of considerable flair.

Newmacher Golf Club (Swailend)

Swailend, Newmacher, AB21 7UU
Nearest main town: Aberdeen

Secretary:	Mr G. McIntosh	Tel: 01651 863002
		Fax: 01651 863055
Professional:	Mr P. Smith	Tel: 01651 862127

Playing: Midweek: round £15.00; day £25.00. Weekend: round £30.00; day £30.00.

Facilities: Bar: 11am–11pm. Food: Lunch and dinner by arrangement. Bar snacks.

Comments: Top course for one so young ... Newer than the Hawkshill and it shows ... Nice variety but wouldn't go back ... Other fish to fry in Scotland, I'm afraid.

Peterculter Golf Club ★★

Oldtown, Burnside Road, Peterculter, AB14 0LN
Nearest main town: Aberdeen

Secretary:	Mr K. Anderson	Tel: 01224 735245
		Fax: 01224 735580
Professional:	Mr D. Vannet	Tel: 01224 734994

Playing: Midweek: round £14.00; day £20.00. Weekend: round £17.00; day £23.00.

Facilities: Bar: 11am–11pm. Food: Lunch and dinner from 10am–9pm, except Mondays.

Comments: Great greens – lots of birdies ... Lovely wildlife by the River Dee ... Narrow course and tough par ... Interesting holes, the pick is the 2nd.

Peterhead Golf Club ★

Craigewan Links, Peterhead, AB42 1LT
Nearest main town: Aberdeen

Secretary: Mr M. Sexton   Tel: 01779 472149
                                     Fax: 01779 480725

Professional: None.

Playing: Midweek: round £16.00; day £22.00. Weekend: round £20.00; day £27.00. Handicap certificate required.

Facilities: Bar: 11am–11pm. Food: Lunch from 10am–3pm. Dinner by arrangement.

Comments: Very basic facilities but course is good ... Natural delight ... Ditches, streams, bunkers and bushes ... A design that seems timeless ... Very intimidating in the wind ... Near to Cruden Bay, so combine the two.

Portlethen Golf Club ★★★

Badentoy Road, Portlethen, AB12 4YA
Nearest main town: Aberdeen

Secretary: None.   Tel: 01224 781090
                                     Fax: 01224 781090
Professional: Mrs M. Thomson   Tel: 01224 782571

Playing: Midweek: round £14.00; day £21.00. Weekend: round £21.00; day £30.00.

Facilities: Bar: 11am–11pm. Food: Lunch and dinner from 10am–10pm. Bar snacks.

Comments: Longish parkland course ... Worth popping in ... Good value ... Back nine a little tougher than front ... Four par-4s over 420 yards ... A long hitter's paradise.

Royal Aberdeen Golf Club ★★★★

Balgownie, Bridge of Don, Aberdeen, AB23 8AT
Nearest main town: Aberdeen

Secretary: Mr G. F. Webster   Tel: 01224 702571
                                     Fax: 01224 826591
Professional: Mr R. MacAskill   Tel: 01224 702221

Playing: Midweek: round £55.00; day £75.00. Weekend: round £65.00; day n/a. Handicap certificate required.

Facilities: Bar: 11am–11pm. Food: Lunch from 12pm–3pm. Dinner by arrangement.

Comments: A forgotten links that is a privilege to play ... Inaccessible course that is so natural ... Bodies lurk in the rough here ... A treat for overseas visitors ... There's nothing else like it ... A classic of its type ... So much history here ... Where the game was born.

Royal Tarlair Golf Club ★★

Buchan Street, Macduff, AB44 1TA
Nearest main town: Banff

Secretary: Mrs C. Davidson   Tel: 01261 832897
Professional: None.

Playing: Midweek: round £10.00; day £15.00. Weekend: round £13.00; day £20.00. Handicap certificate required.

Facilities: Bar: 11am–11pm. Food: Lunch and dinner from 10am–9pm.

Comments: Superb views over the Moray Firth ... Cliff-top course, very attractive ... One of the weakest Royal courses ... Views the highlight of otherwise humdrum course.

Stonehaven Golf Club ★★★

Cowie, Stonehaven, AB39 3RH
Nearest main town: Stonehaven

Secretary: Mr W. A. Donald   Tel: 01569 762124
                                    Fax: 01569 765973
Professional: None.

Playing: Midweek: round n/a; day £15.00. Weekend: round n/a; day £20.00. Handicap certificate required.

Facilities: Bar: 11am–11pm. Food: Breakfast, lunch and dinner from 9am–9pm. Bar snacks.

Comments: Very remote ... Short but a real battle ... Wish I'd never turned up – too tough ... If you like a challenge ... Seven par-3s ... At the mercy of the elements, as golf should be.

Strathlene Golf Club ★

Buckie, AB5 2DJ
Nearest main town: Buckie

Secretary: To be appointed.   Tel: 01542 831798
Professional: None.

Playing: Midweek: round £12.00; day £18.00. Weekend: round £16.00; day £20.00.

Facilities: Bar: 11am–11pm. Food: Bar snacks.

Comments: Excellent value seaside course ... Plenty of elevated greens ... Always felt part of the club, even as a visitor ... Didn't mind leaving ... Wind plays havoc here.

WALES

Mid Wales

Aberdovey Golf Club ★★★★

Aberdovey, Gwynedd, LL35 0RT
Nearest main town: Aberdovey

It took over 100 years for the Welsh to start boasting about their golf courses – so long, in fact, that not even the Welsh themselves were aware of the fairway treasures hidden around the country's rugged coastline and amid its mountains and valleys. At the north of the Dovey Estuary, you will find two such cracking courses. Borth and Ynyslas is excellent value for money, while Aberdovey is a fabulous course, which the esteemed Bernard Darwin famously eulogised as the course 'that my soul loves best in this world'.

This is an historic course, and the railway that runs alongside it harks back to an era where gentlemen would travel to play golf by train. The train would also deliver the caddies to the course to carry the bags of the affluent golfers, who would choose to play the favoured form of the game in that day, matchplay, on this lovely links.

Aberdovey, like the Victorian seafront terraces of the town, can seem utterly forlorn in the winter. But in the summer, when the crowds make the town come alive, so does the course, as holidaying golfers enjoy the delights of this very individual test.

Whilst the course runs straight out and straight back in the manner of a traditional links, there is a marvellous diversity to the two nines, and indeed the holes themselves. On the front nine, the drive between the dunes at the 2nd is particularly memorable, as is the blind drive at the 3rd.

After posing such stern questions early on, there is a brief rest until the marsh-ridden 10th, and the problems intensify on the 12th, where the second shot is played to a green set high amid the dunes.

Various designers have amended Aberdovey, like many famous courses, with Colt, Fowler and Braid adding their expertise to the original design. It remains a spiritually uplifting and varied experience.

Secretary:	Mr J. M. Griffiths	Tel: 01654 767493
		Fax: 01654 767027
Professional:	Mr J. Davies	Tel: 01654 767602
Playing:	Midweek: round £25.00; day £38.00. Weekend: round £30.00; day £44.00. Handicap certificate required.	

Facilities: Bar: 11am–11pm. Food: Lunch and dinner from 11am–9pm. Bar snacks.

Comments: A well-run links with new clubhouse of high standard ... Railway runs alongside the course ... Straight out, straight back ... The classic design ... Brilliant course in every way ... Company, course and welcome all in place ... Superb day out in scenic surroundings.

Aberystwyth Golf Club   ★★

Bryn-y-Mor, Aberstwyth, Cardiganshire, SY23 2HY
Nearest main town: Aberystwyth

Secretary: To be appointed.   Tel: 01970 615104
                                           Fax: 01970 626622
Professional: Mr M. Newson   Tel: 01970 625301

Playing: Midweek: round £18.00; day £22.00. Weekend: round £22.00; day £25.00.

Facilities: Bar: 11am–11pm. Food: Lunch and dinner from 11am–9pm. Bar snacks.

Comments: Cracking finish ... On a clear day the views over Cardigan Bay are fabulous ... Great drive along the coastal road to the course ... Course matches the quality of views.

Borth & Ynyslas Golf Club   ★★★★

Borth, Cardiganshire, SY24 5JS
Nearest main town: Aberystwyth

Secretary: Miss S. Wilson   Tel: 01970 871202
                                           Fax: 01970 871202
Professional: Mr J. G. Lewis   Tel: 01970 871557

Playing: Midweek: round £20.00; day £25.00. Weekend: round £26.00; day £31.00.

Facilities: Bar: 11am–11pm. Food: Lunch and dinner from 11am–9pm. Bar snacks.

Comments: Top value, condition and character ... An unknown course that should remain that way ... Friendly and fun ... Testing links course with basic facilities.

Cradoc Golf Club ★★★

Penoyre Park, Cradoc, Brecon, Powys, LD3 9LP
Nearest main town: Brecon

Secretary: Mrs E. G. Pryce   Tel: 01874 623658
                              Fax: 01874 611711
Professional: Mr R. Davies   Tel: 01874 625524

Playing: Midweek: round £20.00; day £20.00. Weekend: round £25.00; day £25.00. Handicap certificate required.

Facilities: Bar: 11am–11pm. Food: Lunch and dinner from 10am–9pm. Bar snacks.

Comments: You need a strategy for each hole ... Spectacular views of the Brecon Beacons ... Remote course worth finding.

Llandrindod Wells Golf Club ★★

Llandrindod Wells, Powys, LD1 5NY
Nearest main town: Llandrindod Wells

Secretary: Mr G. R. Harris   Tel: 01597 823873
                              Fax: 01597 823873
Professional: None.

Playing: Midweek: round £12.00; day £15.00. Weekend: round £18.00; day £22.00.

Facilities: Bar: 11am–11pm. Food: Lunch and dinner from 10am–9pm. Bar snacks.

Comments: Delightful club with stupendous views ... Views magnificent ... Quiet, lazy golf that's very enjoyable ... Nice feel about this club ... Relaxed atmosphere ... Stunning on a warm summer's day.

Penrhos Golf & Country Club ★★

Llanrhystud, Aberystwyth, Cardiganshire, SY23 5AY
Nearest main town: Aberystwyth

Secretary: Mr R. Rees-Evans   Tel: 01974 202999
                              Fax: 01974 202100
Professional: Mr P. Diamond

Playing: Midweek: round £17.00; day £25.00. Weekend: round £22.00; day £30.00.

Facilities: Bar: 11am–11pm. Food: Breakfast, lunch and dinner from 9am–9pm. Bar snacks.

Comments: Country club with fine facilities ... Basic golf with a few lakes and fine views ... Long course with high standard scratch ... Deceptively difficult.

North Wales

Nefyn & District Golf Club ★★★★

Morfa Nefyn, Gwynedd, LL53 6DA
Nearest main town: Caernafon

The best course on the Llyn peninsula in North Wales is Nefyn and District, sitting in splendid isolation above the holiday town. Although it's a little off the beaten trail, and you won't find it in any lists of great places to play, Nefyn and District is assuredly a super course, the sort of place where you feel uplifted by the whole golf experience. There aren't many better scenic courses in the world and the club's boast is that no one plays here only once.

Cliff-top courses are not categorised as links in the truest meaning of the word, but it is undeniably of that character, with wild dunes and plenty of blind shots. Ten of the holes actually look out over the sea and the back nine is played on a peninsula no more than 274 metres wide. There's also the wind to cater for, and from this perch, it can be a nervy experience watching fronts coming in from the sea. You won't have anywhere to hide, the dunes not being large enough to provide any shelter.

Most people would label Nefyn and District a heathland course. The heather does not spill across the course in all directions, but it is patchy and relieves some holes of their stark, brutish character. You would not claim Nefyn and District has 18 great holes, particularly as the front nine is rather unimpressive. But it's on the back nine where the fun starts, particularly at the 12th, an eccentric par-5 that features two blind shots, a public footpath that leads to the delightful shoreline hamlet of Portdinlleaen and a public house sitting alongside the fairway. Players regularly stop off at the pub to collect their thoughts before a cracking finish, the highlight of which is the excellent 15th.

Nefyn and District will test every shot in your armoury and, as befits a course of its calibre, in each case you will be given fair reward for your effort.

Secretary:	Mr J. B. Owen	Tel: 01758 720966
		Fax: 01758 720476
Professional:	Mr J. Froom	Tel: 01758 720102
Playing:	Midweek: round £25.00; day £30.00. Weekend: round £30.00; day £35.00. Handicap certificate required.	

Facilities: Bar: 11am–11pm. Food: Lunch and dinner by arrangement. Bar snacks.

Comments: Stunning views, warm welcome ... Good condition ... Outstanding views and a nice day's golf ... Tough course ... For scenic beauty the course could be mentioned in the same breath as Cypress Point ... The old nine should be a listed treasure ... Simply the best location in all of golf ... Perched on cliffs with outstanding views ... Great do-or-die course ... Maintenance can't be matched.

Royal St David's Golf Club   ★★★★★

Harlech, Gwynedd, LL46 2UB
Nearest main town: Harlech

Between arriving at Royal St David's and teeing off, you will be hard pressed for someone not to tell you this is the toughest par-69 in the world. Of course, you won't believe it, and, until you reach the turn, will confidently dismiss the comments as humbug. Then it hits you, an astonishing stretch of holes, played against a backdrop of dunes the size of the *Titanic*, that eat away at your score and leave you yearning for the warmth and friendliness of the clubhouse.

This imbalance between the two nines may rancour with some players, but for the majority it's a great relief, allowing you to hone your game before the real test begins. Whether it's the toughest par-69 in the world is up for debate, and one can imagine it has been the subject of lengthy discussions in the bar at this historic and traditional club.

Set on flat terrain and overlooked by the medieval castle of Harlech (very imposing and somewhat eerie), Royal St David's is a true rival for Royal Porthcawl as the best course in Wales. It may not have the same feeling of space as Porthcawl, but what it lacks in length and openness, it more than makes up for in the intimacy it creates between the player and course. This is achieved, to some extent, by the visual cloak the dunes present all along the western extent of the course – unless you clamber over the back of the 16th tee, you can never glimpse the sea. There's also the local railway that rattles along in the shadow of the soot-coloured hills to the east.

Royal St David's feels like a natural stadium for golf, framed by the hills, the castle and the dunes, and the holes on the back nine mirror this effect, plunging into seemingly never-ending tunnels of sandhills. The 14th is a blind par-3 into a punchbowl green, then the 15th and 16th, resolute par-4s where the dunes funnel towards the green. The champagne has been well and truly drunk by the time you reach the 18th, a finish so flat you wish you'd packed up the hole before.

Although dunes protect the course, it does not mean you will escape strong winds, and on some drives you can be pushed to reach the fairways. But for the hardest par-69 in the world, what did you expect?

Secretary: Mr D. L. Morkill   Tel: 01766 780361
                                              Fax: 01766 781110
Professional: Mr J. Barnett   Tel: 01766 780857

Playing: Midweek: round n/a; day £30.00. Weekend: round n/a; day £35.00. Handicap certificate required.

Facilities: Bar: 11am–11pm. Food: Lunch and dinner from 11am–9pm. Bar snacks.

Comments: Not as interesting as most links but some super greens ... Excellent ... Some great individual holes – aura of a championship course ... Fantastic back nine ... Par-69 that plays to about 72 ... Different links that is a killer on the back nine ... Prevailing wind on the back nine makes it an absolute slog ... Weak par-3 finishing hole ... Super 15th and 16th – great holes anyday ... Back nine unbelievable.

Bull Bay Golf Club   ★★

Bull Bay Road, Amlwch, Isle of Anglesey, LL68 2YG
Nearest main town: Amlwch

Secretary: Mr I. Furlong   Tel: 01407 830960
                                             Fax: 01407 832612
Professional: Mr J. Burns   Tel: 01407 831188

Playing: Midweek: round £20.00; day £25.00. Weekend: round £20.00; day £25.00.

Facilities: Bar: 11am–11pm. Food: Lunch and dinner from 11am–9pm. Bar snacks.

Comments: Superbly natural course covered in gorse ... An awesome location in North Wales with views of the Isle of Man, Anglesey and Snowdonia ... You feel very alone up on this well-drained course.

Chirk Golf Club   ★

Chirk, Wrexham, Denbighshire, LL14 5AD
Nearest main town: Wrexham

Secretary:	Miss F. A. Barnes	Tel: 01691 774407
		Fax: 01691 773878
Professional:	Mr M. Maddison	

Playing: Midweek: round £15.00; day £22.00. Weekend: round £22.00; day £28.00.

Facilities: Bar: 11am–11pm. Food: Lunch and dinner from 11am–9pm. Bar snacks.

Comments: One of the longest par-5s in Europe (664 yards) ... Blessed setting overlooked by Chirk Castle ... New centre for all standards of player ... Basic layout, not always in good condition.

Conwy Golf Club   ★★★★

Conwy, LL32 8ER
Nearest main town: Conwy

Secretary:	Mr D. L. Brown	Tel: 01492 592423
		Fax: 01492 593363
Professional:	Mr J. P. Lees	Tel: 01492 593225

Playing: Midweek: round n/a; day £25.00. Weekend: round n/a; day £30.00. Handicap certificate required.

Facilities: Bar: 11am–11pm. Food: Lunch and dinner from 11am–9pm. Bar snacks.

Comments: Easy walking ... Pleasurable links terrain ... Superbly respectful pro ... Staff very good ... Very flat ... Natural course which oozes character ... A course for all seasons.

Holyhead Golf Club   ★★★

Trearddur Bay, Holyhead, Isle of Anglesey, LL65 2YG
Nearest main town: Holyhead

Secretary:	Mr J. A. Williams	Tel: 01407 763279
		Fax: 01407 763279
Professional:	Mr S. Elliott	Tel: 01407 762022

Playing: Midweek: round £17.00; day £22.00. Weekend: round £22.00; day £28.00. Handicap certificate required.

Facilities: Bar: 11am–11pm. Food: Lunch and dinner by arrangement. Bar snacks.

Comments: Very rugged links with some punishing rough in places ... A good test for all golfers ... Hilly with tight contoured fairways ... Thick heather and true greens ... Exciting in the summer.

Llandudno Golf Club ★★★

Hospital Road, Llandudno, Conwy, LL30 1HU
Nearest main town: Llandudno

Secretary: Mr G. Dean   Tel: 01492 876450
                                Fax: 01492 871570
Professional: Mr S. Boulden Tel: 01492 875195
                                Fax: 01492 875195

Playing: Midweek: round n/a; day £25.00. Weekend: round n/a; day £30.00. Handicap certificate required.

Facilities: Bar: 11am–11pm. Food: Lunch and dinner from 11am–9pm. Bar snacks.

Comments: Go when the gorse is blooming ... Part links, part parkland ... Nice welcome ... A little expensive for facilities ... Very varied and entertaining ... Enjoyed myself but once is enough.

Northop Country Park Golf Club ★★★

Northop, Chester, Flintshire, CH7 6WA
Nearest main town: Flint

Secretary: Mr D. Llewellyn   Tel: 01352 840440
                                  Fax: 01352 840445
Professional: Mr M. Pritchard

Playing: Midweek: round £30.00; day £45.00. Weekend: round £35.00; day £55.00. Handicap certificate required.

Facilities: Bar: 11am–11pm. Food: Bar snacks. Dinner by arrangement.

Comments: New facility, does everything right ... This and Carden Park have put the area on the map ... Opening holes a little tiresome but gets better ... An outstanding new service for golfers in North Wales.

Porthmadog Golf Club ★★★

Morfa Bychan, Porthmadog, Gwynedd, LL49 9UU
Nearest main town: Porthmadog

Secretary: Mrs A. Richardson   Tel: 01766 514124
                                       Fax: 01766 514638
Professional: Mr P. Bright   Tel: 01766 513828

Playing: Midweek: round £20.00; day £20.00. Weekend: round
                  £26.00; day £26.00. Handicap certificate required.

Facilities: Bar: 11am–11pm. Food: Lunch and dinner from
                  9am–9pm. Bar snacks.

Comments: Ideal mix of links and heathland ... Links/parkland with
                  great variety and food ... Sand dunes and more sand
                  dunes ... Good links in beautiful surroundings ...
                  Smashing.

Pwllheli Golf Club ★

Golf Road, Pwllheli, Gwynedd, LL53 5PS
Nearest main town: Pwllheli

Secretary: Mr E. Pritchard   Tel: 01758 701644
                                       Fax: 01758 701644
Professional: Mr I. R. Pilkington Tel: 01758 612520

Playing: Midweek: round £22.00; day £22.00. Weekend: round
                  £27.00; day £27.00.

Facilities: Bar: 11am–11pm. Food: Lunch and dinner from
                  11am–9pm. Bar snacks.

Comments: Another course with views of Cardigan Bay and
                  Snowdon ... Scenery rather overshadows the course ...
                  Poor condition ... Greens like shag carpets ... With
                  Cader Idris and Snowdon in the background this is very
                  evocative.

South Wales

Royal Porthcawl Golf Club ★★★★★

Rest Bay, Porthcawl, Mid Glamorgan, CF36 3UW
Nearest main town: Cardiff

Links lovers face an embarrassment of riches along the southern coast of Wales, but none is better than Royal Porthcawl. The most famous course in the Principality, visitors come back again and again, attracted by panoramic views of the Bristol Channel from every hole, and a unique mixture of classic links and heathland holes, played out on lush, springy turf.

The excellence of Royal Porthcawl could easily pass you by. Much as you might appreciate the spectacle of a musical and miss the nuances of the songs, so the raw beauty of this links might distract from the technical brilliance of its design. The first seven holes form a circle around the extremities of the site before spiralling inwards, thereby keeping the player constantly on his or her guard against the fluctuating directions of the wind. There are holes that reward accuracy, those that reward brute strength, penal holes and simple birdie holes.

As befits such a revered course, the opening three holes are as exciting as you will find anywhere and, at the 3rd, the player is asked to gamble on driving across rocks to an angled fairway. From there, you travel inland, rising to a heathland plateau where a simple stone wall marks the course boundaries. The strength of the course from here in, lies in the strength of the par-4s and par-5s, their character dictated by the ferocity of the wind. A mention should go to the 15th, a par-4 that is intimidating off the tee and has cracked the fragile concentration of many players.

Although Royal Porthcawl is not bestowed with the cachet from having staged an Open Championship (it has held Curtis and Walker Cups), it is undeniably a special course. The blandness and restrained feel of Porthcawl town, with its retirement bungalows spread in all directions, is not translated to the course or the club. Relaxing post-round in the warm wood-panelled bar, you are alive to the conversations of the lively, elderly membership, and a night spent in the dormy house can make this a never-to-be-forgotten golf experience.

Secretary: Mr F. Prescott

Professional: Mr P. Evans

Tel: 01656 782251
Fax: 01656 771687
Tel: 01656 773702

Playing: Midweek: round £35.00; day n/a. Weekend: round n/a; day n/a. Handicap certificate required.

Facilities: Bar: 11am–11pm. Food: Lunch and dinner from 11am–9pm. Bar snacks.

Comments: Very good course and friendly welcome ... Wonderful place to play and great reception ... Tough and testing golf ... As tough as any course ... Perhaps too many blind holes to be considered among the best ... Staying at the dormy house makes the visit ... Classic and unmastered by the so-called experts ... Perfect golf experience, superb atmosphere ... Sitting in the bar in the late afternoon with the sun streaming in is the best experience I've had in golf ... I could play this course every day for the rest of my life ... A complete delight.

Tenby Golf Club   ★★★★

The Burrows, Tenby, Pembrokeshire, SA70 7NP
Nearest main town: Tenby

Disciples of links golf regularly make the pilgrimage to south-west Wales to experience the outlandish delights of Tenby. There they immerse themselves in one of Britain's most muscular and eccentric links, fashioned over 100 years by the pounding of waves and the shifting coastal sands.

This rugged course, where players have been reduced to quivering wrecks, is a wonderful contrast to the dozy, tea-room atmosphere of the holiday town, situated just a few minutes' walk away. Indeed, holiday golfers who leave their game at the hotel, or are used to being cosseted at golf and country clubs, will be in for a rude awakening.

Tenby is as much a test of your patience as your game. The course, with three holes separated from the links terrain by a railway, calls for you to deal with sloping lies, irregular bounces, hogs-back fairways, blind drives and approaches, sentinel-like dunes and small, well-protected greens. As if that wasn't enough, there's an intimidating blind drive at the 1st, one of the toughest par-4s anywhere at the 3rd, and you will need your concentration at the 9th, where marksmen sound the crack of bullets on the shooting range.

If you drive well, most of the problems evaporate. When you stray off line, frequently you have a blind second shot over a dune. Tenby is certainly an acquired taste, and many consider the three railway holes (15th, 16th and 17th) to be a rather flat finish to an otherwise exhilarating round.

The course may not always be in perfect condition, but what can be said is that you won't have experienced anything like this before – and it's unbelievable value to boot.

Secretary:	Mr J. A. Pearson	Tel: 01834 842978
		Fax: 01834 842978
Professional:	Mr M. Hawkey	Tel: 01834 844447
		Fax: 01834 844447

Playing: Midweek: round £25.00; day £25.00. Weekend: round £30.00; day £30.00. Handicap certificate required.

Facilities: Bar: 11am–11pm. Food: Breakfast, lunch and dinner from 9am–9pm.

Comments: Welsh hospitality at its best ... Very tough, eccentric course that can test your patience ... A tortured piece of land that remains fresh in the eye years ahead ... A fine golf course where real golfers come to satisfy their minds ... Very, very tough ... A beast.

Ashburnham Golf Club ★★★★

Cliffe Terrace, Burry Port, Carmarthernshire, SA16 0HN
Nearest main town: Llanelli

Secretary:	Mr D. K. Williams	Tel: 01554 832269
		Fax: 01554 832269
Professional:	Mr R. A. Ryder	Tel: 01554 833846
		Fax: 01554 833846

Playing: Midweek: round £27.50; day £32.50. Weekend: round £32.50; day £40.00. Handicap certificate required.

Facilities: Bar: 11am–11pm. Food: Breakfast, lunch and dinner from 9am–9pm. Bar snacks.

Comments: Superb links ... Practice facilities being extended ... Great links that is playable all year round ... Hard-to-read greens ... Straightforward, but persistent wind makes life difficult ... Evocative course ... A memorable day.

Caerphilly Golf Club ★★

Pencapel, Mountain Road, Caerphilly, Mid Glamorgan, CF83 1HJ
Nearest main town: Cardiff

Secretary:	Mr R. J. Neill	Tel: 01222 863441
		Fax: 01222 863441
Professional:	Mr R. Barter	Tel: 01222 869104

Playing: Midweek: round £20.00; day n/a. Weekend: round n/a; day n/a. Handicap certificate required.

Facilities: Bar: 11am–11pm. Food: Lunch from 12pm–4pm. Dinner from 6pm–9pm.

Comments: Mountainous course with many par-5s ... Hard walking and poor facilities ... Undulating mountain course ... Par-73 and it feels like it.

Celtic Manor Hotel Golf & Country Club (Roman)   ★★★★

Coldrea Woods, Newport, Monmouthshire, NP6 1JC
Nearest main town: Newport

Secretary:	Mr D. Williams	Tel: 01633 413000
	(Golf Dir)	Fax: 01633 410284
Professional:	Mr S. Bowen	Tel: 01633 410268

Playing: Midweek: round £35.00; day n/a. Weekend: round £40.00; day n/a. Handicap certificate required.

Facilities: Bar: 11am–11pm. Food: Breakfast, lunch and dinner from 7am–10pm. Bar snacks.

Comments: Excellent course, fine condition and facilities ... Very nice, pleasant people and worth the trip ... Course can get boggy and it's a bit of a slog ... Great facilities, but course just drags on and on ... Shoot the designer ... Great, unbelievably tough course with many memorable holes.

Celtic Manor Hotel Golf & Country Club (Coldra)   ★★

Coldra Woods, Newport, Monmouthshire, NP6 1JQ
Nearest main town: Newport

Secretary:	Mr D. Williams	Tel: 01633 413000
	(Golf Dir)	Fax: 01633 410284
Professional:	Mr S. Bowen	Tel: 01633 410268

Playing: Midweek: round £10.00; day n/a. Weekend: round £15.00; day n/a. Handicap certificate required.

Facilities: Bar: 11am–11pm. Food: Breakfast, lunch and dinner from 7am–10pm. Bar snacks.

Comments: Too many par-3s on this tight course ... Facilities are probably second to none ... Very friendly staff.

Glamorganshire Golf Club

Lavernock Road, Penarth, South Glamorgan, CF64 5UP
Nearest main town: Cardiff

Secretary: Mr A. M. Reed-Gibbs Tel: 01222 701185
Fax: 01222 701185
Professional: Mr A. Kerr-Smith Tel: 01222 707401

Playing: Midweek: round n/a; day £28.00. Weekend: round n/a; day £30.00. Handicap certificate required.

Facilities: Bar: 11am–11pm. Food: Lunch and dinner from 11am–9pm. Bar snacks.

Comments: Rather expensive for what you get ... Reasonable facilities but course not up to much ... Friendly club that is always welcoming to visitors.

Monmouthshire Golf Club

Llanfoist, Abergavenny, Monmouthshire, NP7 9HE
Nearest main town: Abergavenny

Secretary: Mr R. Bradley Tel: 01873 852606
Fax: 01873 852606
Professional: Mr B. Edwards Tel: 01873 852532

Playing: Midweek: round £25.00; day £25.00. Weekend: round £30.00; day £30.00. Handicap certificate required.

Facilities: Bar: 11am–11pm. Food: Bar snacks.

Comments: Course running alongside the River Usk ... Parkland course in area devoid of good golf ... Better fish to fry elsewhere.

Morlais Castle Golf Club ★

Pant, Merthyr Tydfil, South Glamorgan, CF48 2UY
Nearest main town: Merthyr Tydfil

Secretary: Mr N. Powell   Tel: 01685 722822
                                Fax: 01685 388700
Professional: Mr H. Jarrett   Tel: 01685 388700

Playing: Midweek: round £14.00; day £14.00. Weekend: round £16.00; day £16.00. Handicap certificate required.

Facilities: Bar: 11am–11pm. Food: Lunch and dinner from 11am–9pm. Bar snacks.

Comments: The second nine has added much to this course ... Poorly designed and not worth a second helping ... Parkland course with views of the Bristol Channel.

Pennard Golf Club   ★★★★

2 Southgate Road, Swansea, West Glamorgan, SA3 2BT
Nearest main town: Swansea

Secretary: Mr E. M. Howell   Tel: 01792 233131
                                   Fax: 01792 234797
Professional: Mr M. V. Bennett   Tel: 01792 233451
                                       Fax: 01792 234886

Playing: Midweek: round £24.00; day £24.00. Weekend: round £30.00; day £30.00. Handicap certificate required.

Facilities: Bar: 11am–11pm. Food: Lunch and dinner from 11am–9pm. Bar snacks.

Comments: Rugged coastline frames a cracking, unusual links ... Steep hills force uneven lies ... Sloping lies, howling winds and chill factor make this tougher than any Scottish links ... Condition excellent ... A incredibly natural course with much charm ... It has everything.

Pontypridd Golf Club   ★

Ty Gwyn Road, Pontypridd, Mid Glamorgan, CF37 4DJ
Nearest main town: Pontypridd

Secretary: Mrs V. Hooley   Tel: 01443 409904
                                 Fax: 01443 491622
Professional: Mr W. Walters   Tel: 01443 491210

Playing: Midweek: round £20.00; day £20.00. Weekend: round £25.00; day £25.00. Handicap certificate required.

Facilities: Bar: 11am–11pm. Food: Lunch and dinner from 11am–9pm. Bar snacks.

Comments: Mature woodland at this fair value layout ... Classy golf in bleak area ... Views of Rhondda Valley excellent ... Not one to go out of your way for.

Pyle & Kenfig Golf Club ★★★★

Waun-y-Mer, Kenfig, Mid Glamorgan, CF33 4PU
Nearest main town: Porthcawl

Secretary: Mr S. D. Anthony   Tel: 01656 783093
     Fax: 01656 772822
Professional: Mr R. Evans   Tel: 01656 772446
     Fax: 01656 772446

Playing: Midweek: round £30.00; day £30.00. Weekend: round n/a; day n/a. Handicap certificate required.

Facilities: Bar: 11am–11pm. Food: Lunch from 11am–3pm. Dinner by arrangement.

Comments: An absolutely astonishing back nine ... People say it's an epic course – I'd agree ... All the trouble is off the tee ... If the greens were better protected this would be a monster ... Completely unknown outside Wales so let's keep it that way ... Unusually, first-class facilities for an established club ... This and Porthcawl just blow your mind.

Radyr Golf Club ★

Drysgol Road, Radyr, South Glamorgan, CF4 8BS
Nearest main town: Cardiff

Secretary: Mr A. M. Edwards   Tel: 01222 842408
     Fax: 01222 843914
Professional: Mr R. Butterworth   Tel: 01222 842476

Playing: Midweek: round £34.00; day £34.00. Weekend: round n/a; day n/a. Handicap certificate required.

Facilities: Bar: 11am–11pm. Food: Lunch and dinner from 11am–9pm. Bar snacks.

Comments: Always in good condition ... Small elevated greens make for some good shot-making ... Hillside, parkland course that gets windy ... Very variable condition.

Southerndown Golf Club   ★★★★

Ewenny, Brigend, Mid Glamorgan, CF32 0QP
Nearest main town: Bridgend

Secretary:	Mr A. J. Hughes	Tel: 01656 880476
		Fax: 01656 880317
Professional:	Mr D. G. McMonagle	Tel: 01656 880326

Playing: Midweek: round £25.00; day £25.00. Weekend: round £35.00; day £35.00. Handicap certificate required.

Facilities: Bar: 11am–11pm. Food: Lunch and dinner from 11am–9pm. Bar snacks.

Comments: Excellent large greens ... A very stiff test when the wind blows ... Very hilly and great views ... Vardon, Braid, Colt and Steel have all worked on this course ... Fairway mowers are the sheep ... Need to hit it low on this windy, exposed downland gem.

St David's City Golf Club   ★★

Whitesands Bay, St David's, Pembrokeshire
Nearest main town: St David's

Secretary:	Mr C. W. J. Snushall	Tel: 01437 720312
		Fax: 01437 720312
Professional:	None.	

Playing: Midweek: round n/a; day £12.00. Weekend: round n/a; day £12.00.

Facilities: Bar: Hotel bar next door.

Comments: No clubhouse or bar but changing facilities ... Superb views and greens ... Never busy ... Greens exceptional ... Basic golf where the course is the star ... Unusual, remote course ... Didn't want to leave ... Back-to-basics golf.

St Mellons Golf Club   ★★

St Mellons, Cardiff, South Glamorgan, CF3 8XS
Nearest main town: Cardiff

Secretary:	Mrs K. Newling	Tel: 01633 680408
		Fax: 01633 681219
Professional:	Mr B. Thomas	Tel: 01633 680101

Playing: Midweek: round £32.00; day £32.00. Weekend: round n/a; day n/a. Handicap certificate required.

Facilities: Bar: 11am–11pm. Food: Lunch and dinner from 11am–9pm. Bar snacks.

Comments: Demanding course with a tough finish ... Pleasant parkland course with good greens ... Varied selection of par-3s ... Careful at the 12th.

St Pierre Hotel Golf Club ★★★★

St Pierre Park, Chepstow, Monmouthshire, NP6 6YA
Nearest main town: Chepstow

Secretary: Mr T. J. Cleary   Tel: 01291 625261
                                    Fax: 01291 629975
Professional: Mr C. Dunn   Tel: 01291 635205

Playing: Midweek: round £30.00; day n/a. Weekend: round £30.00; day n/a.

Facilities: Bar: 11am–11pm. Food: Breakfast, lunch and dinner from 7am–10pm. Bar snacks.

Comments: Food and drink just great ... Everything you would expect from a resort course ... Well presented ... Great hospitality.

The Newport Golf Club ★★★

Great Oak, Newport, Monmouthshire, NP1 9FX
Nearest main town: Newport

Secretary: Mr J. V. Dinsdale   Tel: 01633 892643
                                    Fax: 01633 896676
Professional: Mr P. M. Mayo   Tel: 01633 893271

Playing: Midweek: round n/a; day £30.00. Weekend: round n/a; day £40.00. Handicap certificate required.

Facilities: Bar: 11am–11pm. Food: Lunch and dinner from 11am–9pm. Bar snacks.

Comments: Better than both nearby St Pierre and Celtic Manor ... Quality in buckets ... Greens in outstanding condition ... Warm welcome ... Club couldn't have been more helpful ... Fast, true greens.

The Rolls of Monmouth   ★★★

The Hendre, Monmouth, Monmouthshire, NP5 4HG
Nearest main town: Monmouth

Secretary: Mrs S. J. Orton   Tel: 01600 715353
                                          Fax: 01600 713115
Professional: None.

Playing: Midweek: round n/a; day £32.00. Weekend: round n/a;
                    day £37.00.

Facilities: Bar: 11am–11pm. Food: Lunch and dinner from
                    11am–9pm. Bar snacks.

Comments: Beautiful vistas ... Luxurious feel to this course ... Very
                    good all round ... Peaceful, remote location with lovely
                    mansion as centrepiece ... Greens just too fast for me
                    ... Highlight is the 18th ... Natural parkland golf as it
                    should be.

West Monmouthshire Golf Club   ★

Golf Road, Pond Road, Nantyglo, Monmouthshire, NP3 4QT
Nearest main town: Winchestown

Secretary: Mr S. E. Williams   Tel: 01495 310233
                                          Fax: 01495 311361
Professional: None.

Playing: Midweek: round £15.00; day £15.00. Weekend: round
                    £15.00; day n/a.

Facilities: Bar: 11am–11pm. Food: Bar snacks.

Comments: Weekend play on Sundays only ... Course designed
                    around coal tips, mountain climbs and valleys ... One
                    to steer clear of.

IRELAND

Munster

Ballybunion Golf Club (Old) ★★★★★

Sandhill Road, Ballybunion, County Kerry
Nearest main town: Limerick

Ballybunion, literally translated as town of the sapling, is a small resort village on the southern side of the Shannon estuary. It is rightly on the itinerary for those mega-rich Americans who come on short golfing tours to these islands. They take in Turnberry, Gleneagles, St Andrews and then Ballybunion Old. Not surprisingly, the price of playing here has gone through the roof, and anyone wanting to pick up some commemorative merchandise of their visit to Ballybunion will have to dig deep to afford the prices in the pro shop.

Ballybunion's remoteness and the sheer size of its dunes make it a honey-pot for all golfers. The dunes at Turnberry and St Andrews are bumps by comparison. Unlike, say, Royal Birkdale, where the dunes tend to flank the fairways, at Ballybunion, these often run perpendicular to the line of play. You are driving over them, into them, up them, and onto them. In the words of Christy O'Connor Snr, 'When the wind blows, anyone who breaks 70 here is playing better than he is able to play.'

It is difficult to score well at Ballybunion, simply because the distractions (shiny beaches, crumbling cliffs etc.) are so engaging. As early as the 1st tee you stand looking straight at a graveyard, hardly the uplifting encouragement you need at the start of the round.

By comparison with many other great links, it is a modest opening after the 1st, but things start to get better at the 7th, a par-4 laid out along the shore with a small plateau green clinging to the dunes above the Atlantic. The 10th, another par-4, doglegs its way left, back to the very edge of the ocean, and the 11th has the twin threat of sandhills on the left and the Atlantic to the right.

Some talk of playing Ballybunion as if their life has been changed completely by the experience. Don't listen to the hype: take the course for what it's really worth, an excellent links but one that is surely bettered elsewhere.

Secretary: Mr J. McKenna   Tel: 068 27146
                                         Fax: 068 27387
Professional: Mr B. O'Callaghan   Tel: 068 27842

Playing: Midweek: round £35.00; day £80.00. Weekend: round £35.00; day £80.00. Handicap certificate required.

Facilities: Bar: 10.30am–11pm. Food: Lunch and dinner from 10am–9pm. Bar snacks.

Comments: Day fee is round on each course … What an experience … Spectacularly beautiful, terrifically enjoyable … Super course when the wind blows … Absolute must for all golfers with stunning views and unique holes … An absolute masterpiece, Tom Watson is right.

Lahinch Golf Club   ★★★★★

Lahinch, County Clare
Nearest main town: Ennis

The small town of Lahinch overlooks Liscannor Bay and the Cliffs of Moher, and its fabric is inextricably interwoven with the life of the golf club – hence its nickname of the Irish St Andrews. It's traditional but very fair, imposing and rewarding, and so natural you'll even see goats milling around the course. They will tell you the weather – if the goats come off the dunes and are sheltering by the clubhouse, don't bother going out: the heavens are about to open.

The Scots introduced golf to Lahinch in 1893, but it was in 1928 that Dr Alister Mackenzie, who had recently completed work in Cypress Point and was soon after to collaborate with Bobby Jones on Augusta, revised the links. Mackenzie was not allowed to touch two holes, the 5th and the 6th. The former, known as Klondyke, is a long par-4 with a second shot that has to clear a mound very much in the fashion of the 16th hole at Southport and Ainsdale. The 6th, 'Dell', is a blind par-3, an anachronism that is not without charm.

The toughest holes at Lahinch are at the end. After the short par-4 13th where a birdie is up for grabs, it just gets better and better. The par-5 14th plays to a landing area that serves the 15th as well, before running up to a green guarded on both sides by treacherous hills and impenetrable rough. You'll need to land the ball on the front of the green at the short par-3 16th before facing up to two cracking finishing holes, with the 18th hole playing across the 5th fairway.

The course has been subject to modifications, but the many faces of Lahinch are the product of the wind off the Atlantic that whistles through the dunes and the huge rocks and the squalls that rush in on many occasions. Members will say you never really can work out the nature of this links, but the bottom line is that if you keep it straight and are familiar with bump-and-run shots, then you cannot go too far wrong.

Secretary:	Mr A. Reardon	Tel: 065 81003
		Fax: 065 81592
Professional:	Mr R. McCavery	Tel: 065 81408

Playing: Midweek: round £45.00; day £55.00. Weekend: round £45.00; day n/a. Handicap certificate required.

Facilities: Bar: 10.30am–11pm. Food: Breakfast, lunch and dinner from 9am–9pm. Bar snacks.

Comments: True golfer's course ... Classic links made even more enjoyable by the friendly atmosphere ... The whole Irish experience is tasted on the par-3 6th ... Great old-fashioned links with very springy turf ... The village and course as a unit are completely committed to golf ... A must for all links lovers ... Wonderful links with peculiar par-3 ... Great welcome, facilities and course ... Intriguing, immensely enjoyable links and very friendly ... Devilish course with best bunkering ever seen ... Remarkable course on choice piece of land ... Will never forget it.

Old Head Golf Club   ★★★★★

Kinsale, County Cork
Nearest main town: Kinsale

After seeing this course for the first time, an American journalist wrote: 'Golfing angels will congregate here and legends will be born.' Gushing it may be, but it is true you will be hard pushed to find a more dramatic course to play golf than Old Head of Kinsale. Indeed, it is probably one of the most exciting courses opened in modern times, tales of its grandeur passing lips in clubhouses across Britain and Ireland and the world each day.

The course sits on a huge rocky peninsula on the south coast of Ireland, its two loops of nine occupying a bulge of land that by rights should have been cut off from the mainland. Golfers cannot help but be faced with stunning views of 300-foot cliffs, especially as most of the greens are perched right on top of them. Such is the scenery that this promontory was included in the Inventory of Outstanding Landscapes in Ireland.

Old Head was opened for play in June 1997. It has five par-5s, five par-3s and eight par-4s, a very modern balance of holes on what is a site fashioned through the centuries. From the back tees, it weighs in at a hefty 7,100 yards and has already been mentioned in the same breath as Pebble Beach. Like that famed American course, you will be walking a cliff-top tightrope and in places, such is the prevailing nature of the wind, you will be sending tee shots out across the Atlantic in order to find the fairway when the ball lands. There are few hazards along the fairways at Old Head, as, basically, the wind is the only hazard you need. Indeed, such is the strength of the wind and the inclement weather that affects this place, the course is closed for the winter.

Old Head is destined to become a classic and for golfers travelling to the area to play Fota Island, Cork and Lee Valley, is likely to become the one you play first or last.

Secretary: Mr J. O'Brien   Tel: 021 778444
                                                Fax: 021 778022

Professional: None.

Playing: Midweek: round £90.00; day £150.00. Weekend: round £90.00; day £150.00. Handicap certificate required.

Facilities: Bar: 10.30am–11pm. Food: Breakfast, lunch and dinner from 9am–9pm. Bar snacks.

Comments: Unbelievable location ... Destined to be a classic ... You feel on the edge of the world ... Most exciting course to play in the world at the moment ... In places you simply hit the ball out to sea ... I've just played the best course in the world ... Gobsmacked ... Course shut half the year and on some days is simply unplayable ... The most amazing experience ... A little haphazard but no complaints about the scenery ... Play it now before everyone finds out.

Tralee Golf Club   ★★★★★

West Barrow, Ardfert, County Kerry
Nearest main town: Tralee

Tralee is home to the festival known the world over as the 'Rose of Tralee'. This is a curious event in these politically correct times, where young women from all over the country and the globe come to show off their beauty and, well, their Irishness. If there was to be a swimsuit section, they could do worse than film it on the beach below the 15th tee at the town's golf course, a stunning expanse of sand where the swirling emerald tide gushes through narrow channels to fill inland lagoons.

Tralee Golf Club (or Barrow to those in the know) would certainly win prizes for its natural beauty. It's a youngster compared to most of the other great links courses of the south west of Ireland. Designed by Arnold Palmer, the course is as individual as they come, a links laid out against some of the most majestic and rugged coastline on the island. It has just about everything – holes practically dropping off into the ocean, deep valleys, flat, downhill, uphill, sidehill holes, tumultuous dunes, views to make you feel lucky that you are alive and a changeable wind to let you know that this a golf course and you have a battle on your hands.

Some rate it too difficult, but that's just because the occasional visitor does not know it that well. Yes, there are some idiosyncratic holes, but where would we be if every course followed a formula? One thing is for sure, the back nine is a roller-coaster ride tempered with some of the finest views afforded from any golf course anywhere.

There are many memorable holes at Tralee but most name the 12th as the favourite and the toughest. It's a par-4 with a driving area the size of an airstrip between tall, wild grass on the right and rocks on the left. The second shot is played to an elevated green situated in a crater on the dune. On the left of the green is a huge abyss where balls will disappear forever. Then there's the view from the 17th green, in all directions surf crashing against the shore. The band has packed up and left by the 18th, a rather mundane par-4 by comparison to what's gone before, but you've still got the clubhouse to look forward to, one of the newest and best in the area, with views towards the cliff and the beach.

Secretary:	Mr M. O'Brian	Tel: 066 36379
		Fax: 066 36008
Professional:	None.	
Playing:	Midweek: round £35.00; day n/a. Weekend: round £35.00; day n/a. Handicap certificate required.	
Facilities:	Bar: 10.30am–11pm. Food: Lunch and dinner from 10am–11pm. Bar snacks.	
Comments:	Visually stunning ... Very exciting ... Best back nine in Ireland ... Memorable holes ... What views, what greens, what a privilege to play there ... Best ever welcome ... Arrived at a busy time and was immediately dispatched to the 1st tee ... Lunch and drinks were sent out by buggy ... Palmer really worked his magic here.	

Adare Manor Golf Club   ★★★★

Adare, County Limerick
Nearest main town: Limerick

Secretary: Mr M. Palne   Tel: 061 396204
Professional: None.

Playing: Midweek: round £15.00; day n/a. Weekend: round £20.00; day n/a. Handicap certificate required.

Facilities: Bar: 10.30am–11pm. Food: Bar snacks.

Comments: A Robert Trent Jones classic ... Huge moulding gives this a very un-Irish feel ... Not what you go to Ireland for ... Not your typical Irish course ... Very American, but who cares? ... Very hard going, like the K-Club ... Give the course two more years and it will be out of this world ... Superb new course with good bunkers and plenty of water ... Greens soft spikes only.

Ballybunion Golf Club (Cashen)   ★★★★★

Sandhill Road, Ballybunion, County Kerry
Nearest main town: Limerick

Secretary: Mr J. McKenna   Tel: 068 27146
                                        Fax: 068 27387
Professional: Mr B. O'Callaghan   Tel: 068 27842

Playing: Midweek: round £60.00; day £80.00. Weekend: round £60.00; day £80.00. Handicap certificate required.

Facilities: Bar: 10.30am–11pm. Food: Lunch and dinner from 10am–9pm. Bar snacks.

Comments: Day fee is round on each course ... Great job by Robert Trent Jones ... Even though it was designed by an American, there is a magically Irish feel to this course ... Old Course knocks it into a cocked hat ... Enjoyed it but was thinking about the Old Course ... More difficult than the Old ... A lot bleaker than the Old Course but just as enjoyable ... Amazing that this new course should feel so ancient.

Ballykisteen Golf & Country Club   ★★★★

Monard, County Tipperary
Nearest main town: Tipperary

Secretary: Mrs J. Ryan   Tel: 062 33333
                                        Fax: 062 33711
Professional: Mr D. Reddan

Playing: Midweek: round £20.00; day n/a. Weekend: round £25.00; day n/a.

Facilities: Bar: 10.30am–11pm. Food: Lunch and dinner from 11am–9pm. Bar snacks.

Comments: Warm, Irish welcome ... Welcome, people, food and course top class ... Water in play on ten holes ... Great par-3 15th ... .Seemingly unnatural course that rewards all types of shot ... 15th is the most difficult par-3 in the country according to Des Smyth ... Modern course in timeless landscape ... In ten years time everyone will be talking about this course ... Young greens but fast ... Go as soon as possible.

Beaufort Golf Club ★★★★

Churchtown, Beaufort, County Kerry
Nearest main town: Killarney

Secretary: Mr C. Kelly   Tel: 064 44440
Fax: 064 44752

Professional: Mr H. Duggan

Playing: Midweek: round £25.00; day £35.00. Weekend: round £33.00; day £46.00.

Facilities: Bar: 10.30am–11pm. Food: Lunch and dinner from 10am–9pm. Bar snacks.

Comments: Superb setting with the McGillicuddy Reeks forming an impressive backdrop ... Historic course with ruins, natural hazards, deep bunkers, impressive foliage and multi-tiered greens ... Blind shots make this so difficult.

Castletroy Golf Club ★★★

Castletroy, Limerick, County Limerick
Nearest main town: Limerick

Secretary: Mr L. Hayes   Tel: 061 335261
Fax: 061 335373

Professional: None.

Playing: Midweek: round £22.00; day n/a. Weekend: round £25.00; day n/a.

Facilities: Bar: 10.30am–11pm. Food: Lunch and dinner from 10am–9pm.

Comments: Very short course that can be very flattering on your score ... Don't play it to improve your game, just for fun ... Cheap and cheerful.

Charleville Golf Club

Smiths Road, Charleville, County Cork
Nearest main town: Charleville

Secretary:	Mr M. Keane	Tel: 063 81257
		Fax: 063 81274
Professional:	None.	

Playing: Midweek: round £15.00; day £18.00. Weekend: round £20.00; day £25.00.

Facilities: Bar: 11am–11pm. Food: Lunch and dinner from 11am–9pm. Bar snacks.

Comments: Busy parkland ... Short but really nice ... Not particularly well regarded in Cork.

Clonmel Golf Club ★

Lyreanearla, Mountain Road, Clonmel, County Tipperary
Nearest main town: Clonmel

Secretary:	Mrs A. Myles-Keating	Tel: 052 24050
		Fax: 052 24050
Professional:	Mr R. Hayes	Tel: 052 24050

Playing: Midweek: round £18.00; day n/a. Weekend: round £20.00; day n/a. Handicap certificate required.

Facilities: Bar: 10.30am–11pm. Food: Bar snacks.

Comments: Open, bland course ... Very short on length and interest ... Gives you the freedom to open your shoulders off the tee ... A real driver's course with room for error ... Inland course of little standing.

Cork Golf Club

Little Island, Cork, County Cork
Nearest main town: Cork

Secretary:	Mr M. Sands	Tel: 021 353451
		Fax: 021 353410

Professional: Mr P. Hickey   Tel: 021 353421

Playing: Midweek: round £40.00; day £40.00. Weekend: round
                  £45.00; day n/a. Handicap certificate required.

Facilities: Bar: 10.30am–11pm. Food: Breakfast, lunch and
                  dinner from 9am–9pm. Bar snacks.

Comments: Excellent condition and plenty of birdie chances ...
                  Touched by the hand of Alister Mackenzie ... Great
                  club with course to match ... Not very exhilarating, but
                  a fair technical challenge ... Prime condition ... Play
                  here on the way to the Old Head of Kinsale further
                  south.

County Tipperary Golf & Country Club   ★★★★

Dundrum House Hotel, Dundrum, Cashel, County Tipperary
Nearest main town: Cashel

Secretary: Mr W. Crowe   Tel: 062 71116
                                        Fax: 062 71366

Professional: None.

Playing: Midweek: round £20.00; day n/a. Weekend: round
                  £24.00; day n/a.

Facilities: Bar: 10.30am–11pm. Food: Breakfast, lunch and
                  dinner from 7am–10pm. Bar snacks.

Comments: Back nine is where course really impresses ... Good use
                  of water on some holes ... Unique Irish course designed
                  by Philip Walton ... You can feel the American influ-
                  ences here ... Nice use of man-made hazards ... Hotel,
                  converted from 18th-century manor, marks this a quality
                  weekend getaway destination.

Dingle Golf Club   ★★★★

Ballyougheragh, Tralee, County Kerry
Nearest main town: Tralee

Secretary: Mr T. O'Shea   Tel: 066 56408
                                        Fax: 066 56409

Professional: Mr D. O'Connor   Tel: 066 56225

Playing: Midweek: round n/a; day £25.00. Weekend: round n/a;
                  day £35.00.

Facilities: Bar: 11am–11pm. Food: Lunch and dinner from 10am–6pm. Bar snacks.

Comments: Magical setting overlooking Dingle Bay ... New links that's so exciting ... Wind wreaks havoc here ... Keep the ball as low as you can ... Links that simply teases you at every turn ... Evocative ... Preferred it to more prestigious courses in the area ... Very welcoming ... Very sandy and difficult ... Love this place ... A natural course with fine character.

Dooks Golf Club ★★★★

Glenbeigh, County Kerry
Nearest main town: Kerry

Secretary: Mr M. Shanahan   Tel: 066 9768205
                                 Fax: 066 9768476

Professional: None.

Playing: Midweek: round £25.00; day £35.00. Weekend: round £25.00; day £35.00. Handicap certificate required.

Facilities: Bar: 10.30am–11pm. Food: Lunch and dinner from 12pm–9pm. Bar snacks.

Comments: Not to be missed ... Tough links with friendly welcome and good food ... Always easy to get a game, lovely scenery and friendly members ... Gem of a course with interesting holes and warm welcome.

Dromoland Castle Golf Club ★★★

Newmarket-on-Fergus, County Clare
Nearest main town: Limerick

Secretary: Mr J. O'Halloran   Tel: 061 368444
                                    Fax: 061 368498
Professional: Mr P. Murphy   Tel: 061 368951

Playing: Midweek: round £28.00; day n/a. Weekend: round £33.00; day n/a. Handicap certificate required.

Facilities: Bar: 10.30pm–11pm. Food: Lunch and dinner from 10.30am–9pm. Bar snacks.

Comments: Set in the grounds of a magnificent castle ... Subtle greens with hard-to-read breaks ... Lack of length countered by blind tee shots and sculpted greens ... Not given the recognition it deserves ... Played badly but eyes were open to the quality of the course ... Rolling fairways ... Greens a pleasure to putt on.

Dungarven Golf Club ★★

Knocknagranagh, Dungarvan, County Waterford
Nearest main town: Waterford

Secretary:	Mr T. Whelan	Tel: 058 44707
		Fax: 058 44113
Professional:	Mr D. Hayes	Tel: 058 44707

Playing: Midweek: round £17.00; day £25.00. Weekend: round £22.00; day £30.00. Handicap certificate required.

Facilities: Bar: 10.30am–11pm. Food: Lunch and dinner from 12pm–9pm. Bar snacks.

Comments: Excellent variety of holes on a course that is improving all the time ... Comeragh Mountains provide the backdrop ... Weak course where all the hazards are man-made ... Average standard on not-too-difficult course.

Ennis Golf Club ★

Drumbiggle Road, Bodyke, County Clare
Nearest main town: Ennis

Secretary:	Mr J. Normoyle	Tel: 065 24074
		Fax: 065 41848
Professional:	Mr M. Ward	Tel: 065 20690

Playing: Midweek: round £18.00; day n/a. Weekend: round £18.00; day n/a. Handicap certificate required.

Facilities: Bar: 10.30am–11pm. Food: Bar snacks.

Comments: Basic course with few features ... Course can get heavy underfoot ... Enniscrone yes, Ennis no ... Very picturesque ... Part mature woodland, part downland ... Cheerful, straightforward layout ... Good for friendly and family golf.

Faithlegg House Golf Club   ★★★

Faithlegg House, Faithlegg, County Waterford
Nearest main town: Waterford

Secretary: Mr V. McGreevy   Tel: 051 382241
Professional: Mr T. Higgins   Tel: 051 382688

Playing: Prices on application.

Facilities: Bar: 11am–11pm. Food: Lunch from 12pm–5pm. Dinner by arrangement.

Comments: Green fees on application ... Mature trees give this course an established feel ... Not always in top condition but I always return ... A little tricked up with hazards not visible from the tee ... Be on your guard, this course will catch you.

Kenmare Golf Club   ★★★

Kenmare, County Kerry
Nearest main town: Killarney

Secretary: Mr M. MacGearailt   Tel: 064 41291
                                       Fax: 064 42061
Professional: None.

Playing: Midweek: round £16.00; day £26.00. Weekend: round £16.00; day £26.00. Handicap certificate required.

Facilities: Bar: 10.30am–11pm. Food: Bar snacks.

Comments: Not a difficult course but overall craic makes it a pleasant walk ... Expanded to 18 holes five years ago ... Par-3 17th a fun hole ... Nine holes in the valley very charming ... Small course with a lot going for it ... Open course, very enjoyable for the higher handicapper.

Killarney Golf Club (Killeen)   ★★★★

Mahoney's Point, Killarney, County Kerry
Nearest main town: Killarney

Secretary: Mr T. Prendergast   Tel: 064 31034
                                       Fax: 064 33065
Professional: Mr T. Coveney   Tel: 064 31615

Playing: Midweek: round £2.00; day n/a. Weekend: round £38.00; day n/a. Handicap certificate required.

Facilities: Bar: 10.30am–11pm. Food: Lunch and dinner from 10am–9pm. Bar snacks.

Comments: Lovely surroundings to a very special course ... From the back tees fairways looks very narrow ... An amazing challenge with trouble everywhere ... Wonderful, scenic course, not overlong for amateurs ... Great setting with course in superb condition ... Epitome of the idyllic – great courses, great people and great food and drink.

Killarney Golf Club (Mahoneys Point) ★★★★

Mahoneys Point, Killarney, County Kerry
Nearest main town: Killarney

Secretary: Mr T. Prendergast   Tel: 064 31034
                                      Fax: 064 33065
Professional: Mr T. Coveney   Tel: 064 31615

Playing: Midweek: round £38.00; day n/a. Weekend: round £38.00; day n/a. Handicap certificate required.

Facilities: Bar: 10.30am–11pm. Food: Lunch and dinner from 10am–9pm. Bar snacks.

Comments: Course in exceptional condition with great views everywhere ... Finishes with the toughest of tough par-3s ... Great finish ... Doesn't compare to the Killeen ... Play them both in the same day – an awesome, life-changing experience.

Killeline Golf Club ★

Newcastle West, County Limerick
Nearest main town: Limerick

Secretary: Mr J. McCoy   Tel: 069 61600
                                      Fax: 069 77428
Professional: To be appointed.

Playing: Midweek: round £12.00; day n/a. Weekend: round £12.00; day n/a.

Facilities: Bar: 10.30am–11pm. Food: Breakfast, lunch and dinner from 9am–9pm. Bar snacks.

Comments: Basic layout set in the Golden Vale ... Simple course but there is a premium on accuracy ... Reasonable value for parkland course.

Killorglin Golf Club   ★★★

Steelroe, Killorglin, County Kerry
Nearest main town: Killarney

Secretary: Mr B. Dodd   Tel: 066 61979
                                      Fax: 066 61437

Professional: None.

Playing: Midweek: round £14.00; day n/a. Weekend: round £16.00; day n/a.

Facilities: Bar: 10.30am–11pm. Food: Bar snacks

Comments: Played it when first opened – great ... Fairly easy despite small greens ... Overlooking Dingle Bay, this is cheap and cheerful ... Homely place where staff will arrange anything for you ... Great welcome at this testing, enjoyable course.

Lahinch Golf Club (Castle)   ★★★★

Lahinch, County Clare
Nearest main town: Ennis

Secretary: Mr A. Reardon   Tel: 065 81003
                                      Fax: 065 81592

Professional: Mr R. McCavery   Tel: 065 81408

Playing: Midweek: round £25.00; day £25.00. Weekend: round £25.00; day n/a. Handicap certificate required.

Facilities: Bar: 10.30am–11pm. Food: Breakfast, lunch and dinner from 9am–9pm. Bar snacks.

Comments: Classic links track which is worth a visit in its own right ... Loved it ... Perfect partner to the Old Course ... Underrated with holes that would not be out of place on the Old ... Shorter and easier, but a nice test.

Lee Valley Golf & Country Club ★★★

Clashanure, Ovens, Kinsale, County Cork
Nearest main town: Cork

Secretary:	Mr J. Reilly (Manager)	Tel: 021 331721
		Fax: 021 331695
Professional:	Mr J. Savage	Tel: 021 331758

Playing: Midweek: round £27.00; day n/a. Weekend: round £29.00; day n/a.

Facilities: Bar: 10.30am–11pm. Food: Breakfast, lunch and dinner from 9am–9pm. Bar snacks.

Comments: New course designed by Christy O'Connor Jr ... Very busy ... A course that caters for every standard of player ... Not much substance ... Take your time over every shot – you will have to ... Crowded course, not what I wanted from golf in Ireland ... Hilly, parkland course ... Unspectacular site for unspectacular design ... Facilities second to none ... State-of-the-art facilities better than the course.

Limerick County Golf & Country Club ★★★

Ballyneety, County Limerick
Nearest main town: Limerick

Secretary:	Mr A. Fallow	Tel: 061 351881
		Fax: 061 351384
Professional:	Mr P. Murphy	Tel: 061 351874

Playing: Midweek: round £20.00; day £30.00. Weekend: round £25.00; day £35.00.

Facilities: Bar: 10.30am–11pm. Food: Lunch and dinner from 10am–9pm.

Comments: The bar is out of this world ... A Des Smyth design, fairly unusual for a modern course ... Blind drives and deep bunkers give an old-style feel to a new course ... Unusual clubhouse ... Great venue for matchplay golf.

Limerick Golf Club ★

Limerick, County Limerick
Nearest main town: Limerick

Secretary: Mr D. McDonogh   Tel: 061 415146
                                  Fax: 061 415146
Professional: To be appointed.   Tel: 061 412492

Playing: Midweek: round £22.50; day n/a. Weekend: round n/a; day n/a. Handicap certificate required.

Facilities: Bar: 10.30am–11pm. Food: Lunch and dinner from 10am–9pm.

Comments: Parkland course with friendly, large membership ... Fair value for traditional parkland layout ... If you're in the area play Limerick County, not this one.

Mallow Golf Club   ★★

Ballyellis, Mallow, County Cork
Nearest main town: Mallow

Secretary: Mrs I. Howell   Tel: 022 21145
                                 Fax: 022 42501
Professional: Mr S. Conway

Playing: Midweek: round £20.00; day n/a. Weekend: round £25.00; day n/a.

Facilities: Bar: 10.30am–11pm. Food: Breakfast, lunch and dinner from 11am–9pm. Bar snacks.

Comments: Tree-lined parkland beauty ... Nice condition for this friendly club ... Nothing spectacular, but good honest golf.

Monkstown Golf Club   ★

Parkgarriffe, Monkstown, County Cork
Nearest main town: Cork

Secretary: Mr J. Long   Tel: 021 841376
                              Fax: 021 841376
Professional: Mr B. Murphy   Tel: 021 841686

Playing: Midweek: round £23.00; day £23.00. Weekend: round £26.00; day n/a. Handicap certificate required.

Facilities: Bar: 10.30am–11pm. Food: Lunch and dinner from 12pm–9pm.

Comments: Scenic views of Cork Harbour ... Bunkers absolutely
everywhere ... Bizarre bunkering ... Parkland course
where accuracy is your watchword ... Fair value on this
testing track.

Muskerry Golf Club   ★

Carrigrohane, County Cork
Nearest main town: Blarney

Secretary:	Mr J. J. Moynihan	Tel: 021 385297
		Fax: 021 385297
Professional:	Mr W. M. Lehane	Tel: 021 381445

Playing: Midweek: round £23.00; day n/a. Weekend: round n/a;
day n/a.

Facilities: Bar: 10.30am–11pm. Food: Bar snacks.

Comments: Epitome of golf in Ireland ... Good value course, good
craic ... Great welcome ... Course is so-so but the bar
is always buzzing ... 16th and 17th across the river are
the best holes.

Parknasilla Golf Club   ★★★

Parknasilla, Sneem, County Kerry
Nearest main town: Sneem

Secretary:	Mr M. Walsh	Tel: 064 45122
		Fax: 064 45323
Professional:	Mr C. McCarthy	

Playing: Midweek: round n/a; day £15.00. Weekend: round n/a;
day £15.00.

Facilities: Bar: 10.30am–11pm. Food: Breakfast, lunch and
dinner from 9am–9pm. Bar snacks.

Comments: Best nine-hole course ever played ... Location, location,
location ... Unique nine-hole course of beauty and tranquillity ... Overlooking Kenmare Bay.

Shannon Golf Club   ★★★

Shannon, County Clare
Nearest main town: Shannon

Secretary:	Mr M. Corry	Tel: 061 471849
		Fax: 061 471507
Professional:	Mr A. Pyke	Tel: 061 471551

Playing: Midweek: round £22.00; day £22.00. Weekend: round £27.00; day £27.00. Handicap certificate required.

Facilities: Bar: 10.30am–11pm. Food: Breakfast, lunch and dinner from 9am–9pm. Bar snacks.

Comments: A mix of links and parkland ... Highlight is the 216-yard par-3 over the estuary ... Very tight course with character ... Water hazards the primary defence ... Rough can get high ... Pop off the plane and onto the course ... Tight, but you are lost without the driver ... Site of Greg Norman's famous 370-yard drive. ... Front nine a hellish challenge.

Tramore Golf Club ★★★★

Newtown Hill, Tramore, County Waterford
Nearest main town: Waterford

Secretary:	Mr J. Cox	Tel: 051 386170
		Fax: 051 390961
Professional:	Mr D. Kiely	Tel: 051 871395

Playing: Midweek: round £25.00; day £37.00. Weekend: round £30.00; day n/a. Handicap certificate required.

Facilities: Bar: 10.30am–11pm. Food: Breakfast, lunch and dinner from 9am–9pm. Bar snacks.

Comments: Great experience both on and off the course ... Stormy weather has been known ... Very exposed and cold ... Welcoming club with well-groomed course ... Fair test for club golfer ... Lovely set-up at this club with warm, friendly members.

Waterford Castle Golf Club ★★

The Island, Waterford, County Waterford
Nearest main town: Watreford

Secretary:	Mr D. Brennan	Tel: 051 871633
		Fax: 051 871634
Professional:	None.	

Playing: Midweek: round £25.00; day n/a. Weekend: round £29.00; day n/a.

Facilities: Bar: 10.30am–11pm. Food: Bar snacks.

Comments: Des Smyth design ... On-site hotel a real treat, albeit expensive ... Large greens ... Unremarkable land on which to build a course ... Course sits on island in the River Suir ... A flat, featureless course ... Wide open – get your driver out ... Clever design ... With such flat, boring land it's a credit to Smyth for his design.

Waterford Golf Club ★★

Newrath, Waterford, County Waterford
Nearest main town: Waterford

Secretary: Mr J. Condon   Tel: 051 876748
    Fax: 051 853405

Professional: None.   Tel: 051 856568

Playing: Midweek: round £22.00; day n/a. Weekend: round £25.00; day n/a.

Facilities: Bar: 10.30am–11pm. Food: Lunch and dinner from 12pm–9pm. Bar snacks.

Comments: Fairly dour parkland course ... Had to wait until the 18th for the best hole ... Overshadowed by the other Waterford (Castle) ... Pleasant enough, but I like a challenge ... Humdrum parkland course ... Fine day out and the company is excellent.

Waterville Golf Club ★★★★

Ring of Kerry, Waterville, County Kerry
Nearest main town: Waterville

Secretary: Mr N. Cronin   Tel: 066 74102
    Fax: 066 74482

Professional: Mr L. Higgins

Playing: Midweek: round £60.00; day n/a. Weekend: round £60.00; day n/a. Handicap certificate required.

Facilities: Bar: 10.30am–11pm. Food: Lunch and dinner from 10am–9pm. Bar snacks.

Comments: One of the greatest courses in the world ... The best links in the world ... Remote, wild and big ... Fantastic greens ... Pro shop rips off the tourist but otherwise an exceptionally good course ... Remote but worth the trip for some holes of great beauty and thought ... Back nine are as good as it gets ... Some breathtaking holes ... Overpriced, overrated, overplayed and overpopulated with slow players ... Needs course rangers ... Long, cagey course ... Back nine a slog.

West Waterford Golf Club   ★★★

Dungarvan, County Waterford
Nearest main town: Waterford

Secretary: Mr A. A. Spratt   Tel: 058 43216
Fax: 058 44343

Professional: None.

Playing: Midweek: round £20.00; day n/a. Weekend: round £25.00; day n/a.

Facilities: Bar: 10.30am–11pm. Food: Lunch and dinner from 10am–9pm. Bar snacks.

Comments: Green fees on application ... Excellent greens for what is a young course ... Most natural course ... Contrasting nines ... Set by the Brickey River ... Panoramic views of County Waterford ... Great Irish welcome.

Leinster

Mount Juliet Golf Club

Kilkenny, Thomastown, County Kilkenny
Nearest main town: Kilkenny

Mount Juliet is blessed with some of the finest natural scenery Ireland has to offer: the outcroppings of the Kilkenny countryside, ancient trees, gullies, copses of trees and the furious rushing of the River Nore which is rich in salmon and trout. It is one of the best parkland courses in the country and was designed by none other than Jack Nicklaus.

That's not to say that it has been without criticism. Many say you could transplant this course to any country in the world and it would not look out of place. They claim the excessive moulding, shifting and manipulation of the landscape is completely out of place with the feel and look of this corner of Ireland. In short, Mount Juliet is an artificial course with no soul.

Whether you take this view or not, you cannot fault its condition. One journalist noted that the fairways are made from the same material as the carpets laid down when Prince Charles attends movie premiers, and that, even in the dead of winter, is hard to argue with. There are regiments of maintenance workers grooming the course and you can see golfers almost embarrassed to take a divot out of the fairways.

It is also very fair, some might say easy. Off the tee there is little trouble with wide, generous fairways, and even the greens are large. The majestic oak and lime trees that pepper the landscape rarely affect the line of shots into the greens. Nicklaus designs have become more lenient, but it seems there has been a policy that Mount Juliet should be fun, and you should not walk off the course hanging your head like a tired dog.

Water is the main form of defence at Mount Juliet, fronting the par-3 3rd and the par-4 13th. It also protects the 18th, a climatic finish that sums up everything about this modern course.

Secretary:	Mrs K. McCann	Tel: 056 24455
	(Golf Dir)	Fax: 056 73019
Professional:	Mr M. Reid	Tel: 056 730063
Playing:	Midweek: round £70.00; day n/a. Weekend: round £75.00; day n/a. Handicap certificate required.	

Facilities: Bar: 10.30am–11pm. Food: Breakfast, lunch and dinner from 9am–9pm. Bar snacks.

Comments: What every golf course should aspire to ... Best parkland course in Europe ... One of the best new courses in Ireland ... A Nicklaus cracker ... Doesn't necessarily fit into the landscape but good nonetheless ... Vast contoured greens ... One of Jack's best ... Didn't want to go home ... Basic Nicklaus fare, very unnatural ... Cracking par-3 3rd.

Portmarnock Golf Club (Old)   ★★★★★

Portmarnock, County Dublin
Nearest main town: Dublin

Few courses are blessed with the natural magnificence of Portmarnock. Set on a long tongue of links land between the Irish Sea and an inland tidal bay, Portmarnock is magnificently cut off from the world, a private playground for golfers in search of hidden delights. The holes run through dune grasses and are completely at the mercy of the wind, which rush in from the sea quickly changing the moods and toughness of the challenge.

Portmarnock is relatively flat and devoid of any blind shots, but that does not mean the course is monotonous or boring. Instead, you will find a collection of holes that are very exciting, ranging from short holes that require great thought and clever execution of shots, to long holes where brute strength and a daredevil game plan will pay dividends.

Never is this more clearly evident than at the 6th, one of the best holes on the front nine but long at 586 yards. Along its dimpled fairways and valleys, it can be three woods to reach the green, so big hitters are at an advantage. But immediately at the 7th, the emphasis changes with a short hole played into a dell, where you really need to get a feel for the shot.

This delicate balance continues around the turn with more good examples at the 14th, a shortish par-4 with a second shot to a long plateau green among the dunes, and the 15th, a brutish par-3 where, depending on the wind, you will have to set the ball off over the out-of-bounds line and bring it back in on the wind. From there, it is a cracking finish, with the 17th a penal par-4 where you'll do well to stay out of the bunkers and the 18th a fine hole, although it has lost some of its eccentricity since the home green was moved from hard by the clubhouse.

On a fine day there are few better places in Ireland to play golf than at Portmarnock. And with the new Portmarnock Links nearby, you don't need much more encouragement.

Secretary:	Mr J. J. Quigley	Tel: 01 846 2968
		Fax: 01 846 2601
Professional:	Mr J. Purcell	Tel: 01 846 2634

Playing: Midweek: round £70.00; day n/a. Weekend: round £90.00; day n/a. Handicap certificate required.

Facilities: Bar: 10.30am–11pm. Food: Lunch and dinner from 11am–9pm. Bar snacks.

Comments: Brilliant course and an outstanding pro shop ... Classic links that does not suffer fools gladly ... Not a patch on County Down or Sligo ... Fair links unlike many of the heralded ones in Ireland ... Had the time of my life ... Who could criticise this outstanding piece of natural golfing terrain? ... Expected a lot but nothing prepared me for this ... Quite simply the best course in the British Isles.

Carlow Golf Club ★★★

Deer Park, Dublin Road, Carlow, County Carlow
Nearest main town: Carlow

Secretary:	Mrs M. Meaney	Tel: 0503 31695
		Fax: 0503 40065
Professional:	Mr A. Gilbert	Tel: 0503 41745

Playing: Midweek: round £22.00; day n/a. Weekend: round £27.00; day n/a.

Facilities: Bar: 9.30am–11pm. Food: Breakfast, lunch and dinner from 9.30am–10pm. Bar snacks.

Comments: 16th and 17th are outstanding holes ... Always on my list to play ... Parkland with the best greeens in Ireland ... Excellent value with panoramic view from the 8th tee ... All the challenges laid out fairly in front of you ... Well-thought-out layout with subtle protection to good scoring – liked it a lot ... Finishing hole is a par-5 falling all the way down to the clubhouse.

Castlewarden Golf & Country Club ★

Straffan, County Kildare
Nearest main town: Dublin

Secretary: Mr J. Ferriter   Tel: 01 458 9254
                                 Fax: 01 458 8972
Professional: Mr G. Egan   Tel: 01 458 8219

Playing: Midweek: round £20.00; day n/a. Weekend: round £20.00; day n/a.

Facilities: Bar: 10.30am–11pm. Food: Lunch and dinner from 12pm–9pm.

Comments: New course with views of the Wicklow mountains ... Under ten years old with the best yet to come ... Nice welcome at this attractive, basic course.

Charlesland Golf Club   ★★★

Greystones, County Wicklow
Nearest main town: Dublin

Secretary: Mr L. Evans   Tel: 01 287 4350
             (Golf Centre Manager)   Fax: 01 287 4360
Professional: Mr P. Heeney

Playing: Midweek: round £26.00; day £40.00. Weekend: round £33.00; day £50.00.

Facilities: Bar: 10.30am–11pm. Food: Bar snacks.

Comments: Water hazards form course defence ... Not overly impressed ... Setting can't be faulted ... Best views from the 13th ... Located in the shadow of Sugarloaf Mountain ... Club with friendly attitude.

Clontarf Golf Club   ★

Donnycarney House, Dublin, County Dublin
Nearest main town: Dublin

Secretary: Mr A. Hall   Tel: 01 833 1892
                                   Fax: 01 833 1933
Professional: Mr J. Craddock   Tel: 01 833 1877

Playing: Midweek: round £26.00; day n/a. Weekend: round £35.00; day n/a. Handicap certificate required.

Facilities: Bar: 10.30am–11pm. Food: Bar snacks.

Comments: Parkland course in Dublin suburbs ... Nearest course to Dublin ... In poor condition ... A little overused ... Clubhouse the star ... 12th played over a quarry ... Watch out for the trains rattling by.

County Louth Golf Club ★★★★

Baltray, Drogheda, County Louth
Nearest main town: Drogheda

Secretary:	Mr M. Delany	Tel: 041 9822327
		Fax: 041 9822969
Professional:	Mr P. McGuirk	Tel: 041 982444

Playing: Midweek: round £45.00; day £45.00. Weekend: round £55.00; day £55.00.

Facilities: Bar: 10.30am–11pm. Food: Lunch and dinner from 10am–9pm. Bar snacks.

Comments: One of the best in Ireland ... Classic and very enjoyable ... Food always good ... A refined course, not as wild as some other renowned courses ... Difficult to get on due to competitions.

Courtown Golf Club ★★★

Kiltennel, Gorey, County Wexford
Nearest main town: Gorey

Secretary:	Mr D. Cleery	Tel: 055 25166
		Fax: 055 25553
Professional:	Mr J. Coone	Tel: 055 25166

Playing: Midweek: round £18.00; day n/a. Weekend: round £23.00; day n/a.

Facilities: Bar: 10.30am–11pm. Food: Lunch and dinner from 10am–9pm.

Comments: Friendly, quality golf ... Venue for learners ... Very few doglegs ... Nice alternative to nearby 'super courses' like the European ... Cheap and cheerful holiday golf ... Needs toughening up ... Parkland course that deserves praise.

Deer Park Golf Club   ★★

Deer Park Hotel, Howth, County Dublin
Nearest main town: Dublin

Secretary: Mr J. P. Doran   Tel: 01 8322624
                                            Fax: 01 8392405

Professional: None.

Playing: Midweek: round £9.40; day n/a. Weekend: round
                    £11.50; day n/a.

Facilities: Bar: 10.30am–11pm. Food: Breakfast, lunch and
                    dinner from 7am–10pm. Bar snacks.

Comments: Huge golf complex with fine facilities ... Great value ... A
                    kind of hypermarket for all your golfing needs ... Subtle
                    course ... Very busy course – was it worth the effort? ...
                    Don't listen to the snobs, this is a great facility for the high-
                    handicapper ... Boasts itself as Ireland's largest golf
                    complex ... Felt very welcome and enjoyed every minute
                    ... Nice views from fairways of so-so course.

Delvin Castle Golf Club   ★

Clonyn, Delvin, County Westmeath
Nearest main town: Mullingar

Secretary: Mr P. Murphy   Tel: 044 64315
Professional: Mr D. Keenaghan

Playing: Midweek: round £14.00; day n/a. Weekend: round
                    £16.00; day n/a. Handicap certificate required.

Facilities: Bar: 10.30am–11pm. Food: Bar snacks.

Comments: Basic course near Clonyn Castle ... Unmemorable ...
                    Suitable for beginners ... New facility for beginners but
                    not for those seeking new experiences ... New club that
                    tries hard.

Druid's Glen Golf Club   ★★★★

Newtownmountkennedy, Greystones, County Wicklow
Nearest main town: Newtownmountkennedy

Secretary: Mr D. Flinn   Tel: 01 287 3600
                                           Fax: 01 287 3699

Professional: Mr E. Darcy

Playing: Midweek: round £80.00; day n/a. Weekend: round £80.00; day n/a.

Facilities: Bar: 11am–11pm. Food: Breakfast, lunch and dinner from 9am–11pm. Bar snacks

Comments: Complete luxury ... Like Mount Juliet for comfort, but course not as good ... Condition out of this world ... Too expensive and exclusive ... Doesn't feel like Irish golf ... Who wants this when you can have some of the great Dublin courses nearby ... Not much of a craic here ... Generous fairways and greens – too easy ... Condition first class ... Never seen fairways and greens so good ... Watch out for Amen Corner.

Dundalk Golf Club   ★★★

Blackrock, Dundalk, County Louth
Nearest main town: Dundalk

Secretary: Mr J. Carroll   Tel: 042 21731
                                        Fax: 042 22022
Professional: Mr J. Cassidy   Tel: 042 22102

Playing: Midweek: round £19.50; day n/a. Weekend: round £23.50; day n/a.

Facilities: Bar: 10.30am–11pm. Food: Lunch and dinner from 12pm–9pm. Bar snacks.

Comments: Not as good as nearby County Down but a cracker ... Mountains of Mourne form a marvellous canvas for shots ... Forget the bump-and-run of nearby County Down, you need to hit them high here ... Get to the turn in good shape and you should score well ... Nice welcome ... This and Greenore give excellent, good value golf.

Edmondstown Golf Club   ★

Rathfarnham, Dublin, County Dublin
Nearest main town: Dublin

Secretary: Mr S. Davies   Tel: 01 493 1082
                                        Fax: 01 493 3152
Professional: Mr A. Crofton   Tel: 01 494 1049

Playing: Midweek: round £25.00; day n/a. Weekend: round £30.00; day n/a.

Facilities: Bar: 10.30am–11pm. Food: Lunch and dinner from 12pm–9pm. Bar snacks.

Comments: Nothing special about this parkland course … Overpriced … Pleasant enough … Convenient if you're staying in Dublin … Better courses to be found nearby.

Glasson Golf & Country Club   ★★★★

Glasson, Athlone, County Westmeath
Nearest main town: Athlone

Secretary: Mrs F. Reed   Tel: 0902 85120
                                         Fax: 0902 85444

Professional: None.

Playing: Midweek: round £27.00; day n/a. Weekend: round £32.00; day n/a. Handicap certificate required.

Facilities: Bar: 10.30am–11pm. Food: Breakfast, lunch and dinner from 9am–9pm. Bar snacks.

Comments: Most enjoyable … Remarkable location … Great addition to Ireland's courses … A little hilly but scenery takes your mind off it … Worth the drive … Set in the heart of Ireland, this is a picture … Situated on a peninsula bordering Lough Ree – magnificent … What do you expect from Christy O'Connor Jr? … The course on everyone's lips … Tee and green situated in a lake at the 15th.

Greenore Golf Club   ★★

Greenore, County Louth
Nearest main town: Dundalk

Secretary: Mrs R. Daly   Tel: 042 73212
                                         Fax: 042 73678

Professional: None.

Playing: Midweek: round £14.00; day n/a. Weekend: round £20.00; day n/a.

Facilities: Bar: 10.30am–11pm. Food: Lunch and dinner from 12pm–9pm. Bar snacks.

Comments: Part links, part woodland ... Variety in buckets – links, woods, a railway line and blind greens ... A new challenge at every turn ... Had a ball ... Will go back as soon as possible.

Headfort Golf Club   ★★★

Kells, County Meath
Nearest main town: Dublin

Secretary:	Mrs E. Carroll	Tel: 046 40146
		Fax: 046 49282
Professional:	Mr B. McGovern	Tel: 046 40639

Playing: Midweek: round £18.00; day n/a. Weekend: round £22.00; day n/a. Handicap certificate required.

Facilities: Bar: 10.30am–11pm. Food: Lunch and dinner from 10am–9pm. Bar snacks.

Comments: Beautiful parkland, hundreds of mature trees ... Value ... Excellent greens and fairways ... Excellent parkland course ... Greens fast and fair ... Easy to get a game, never overcrowded ... One of the top parkland courses in Ireland.

Hermitage Golf Club   ★★★

Lucan, County Dublin
Nearest main town: Dublin

Secretary:	Mr T. Stelman	Tel: 01 626 8491
	(Manager)	Fax: 01 626 8491
Professional:	Mr S. Burn	Tel: 01 626 8072

Playing: Midweek: round £32.00; day n/a. Weekend: round n/a; day n/a.

Facilities: Bar: 10.30am–11pm. Food: Lunch and dinner from 12.30pm–9pm. Bar snacks.

Comments: Nicely laid out, in good condition with good facilities ... Pretty inland course with unusual features ... Run-of-the-mill parkland track ... A few steep climbs ... Patience required with a few blind shots ... 10th a fine par-3 ... Seemingly simple course but danger lurks everywhere.

Hollywood Lakes Golf Club   ★★

Ballyboughal, County Dublin
Nearest main town: Dublin

Secretary: Mr A. Brogan   Tel: 01 843 3406
                                      Fax: 01 843 3002

Professional: None.

Playing: Prices on application.

Facilities: Bar: 11am–11pm. Food: Lunch from 12pm–4pm.
                  Dinner by arrangement.

Comments: Green fees on application … Very long parkland course
                  built to high specifications … Modern course with water
                  everywhere … Fun course with water and 600+ yard
                  par-5 … Dreary new design … Average condition for
                  new course … Modern club with fair facilities.

Kilkea Castle Golf Club   ★

Carlow, Castle Dermot, County Kildare
Nearest main town: Carlow

Secretary: Mrs K. Nolan   Tel: 0503 45156
                                      Fax: 0503 45505

Professional: None.

Playing: Midweek: round £25.00; day n/a. Weekend: round
                  £25.00; day n/a.

Facilities: Bar: 10.30am–11pm. Food: Lunch from 12pm–2pm.
                  Dinner from 6pm–9pm.

Comments: 12th-century castle dominates this magical parkland
                  course … Natural and in immaculate condition on visit
                  … Clubhouse a perfect 19th … Course does not match
                  the opulence of the surroundings … Two man-made
                  lakes and stream are primary defence of this layout.

Kilkenny Golf Club   ★★★

Glendine, Kilkenny, County Kilkenny
Nearest main town: Kilkenny

Secretary: Mr S. O'Neill   Tel: 056 65400
                                      Fax: 056 65400

Professional: Mr N. Leahy   Tel: 056 61730

Playing: Midweek: round £20.00; day n/a. Weekend: round £22.00; day n/a. Handicap certificate required.

Facilities: Bar: 10.30am–11pm. Food: Lunch and dinner from 10am–9pm.

Comments: Lovely mature parkland that is a tough test ... Tree-lined course, well established ... Pleasant day's golf on fairly easy track.

Killeen Golf Club ★★

Killeenbeg, Kill, County Kildare
Nearest main town: Sallins

Secretary: Mr P. Carey   Tel: 045 866003
                                       Fax: 045 875881

Professional: None.

Playing: Midweek: round £17.00; day n/a. Weekend: round £20.00; day n/a.

Facilities: Bar: 10.30am–11pm. Food: Lunch and dinner from 10am–9pm. Bar snacks.

Comments: Tight driving course, a pleasure to walk and play ... Short course, fairly tight ... Some holes designed around lakes ... Little of interest at this parkland venue.

Knockanally Golf Club ★★

Donadea, North Kildare, County Kildare
Nearest main town: Dublin

Secretary: Mr N. Lyons   Tel: 045 869322
                                       Fax: 045 869322

Professional: Mr M. Darcy

Playing: Midweek: round £20.00; day n/a. Weekend: round £25.00; day n/a.

Facilities: Bar: 10.30am–11pm. Food: Bar snacks. Dinner by arrangement.

Comments: One of the toughest opening holes in all of golf ... Clubhouse magnificent ... Undulating course that tails off after the opening hole ... Popular parkland course, can get busy.

Luttrellstown Castle Golf Club   ★★★

Clonsilla, County Dublin
Nearest main town: Dublin

Secretary:	Mr J. McColgan	Tel: 01 808 9988
	(Manager)	Fax: 01 808 9989
Professional:	Mr G. Campbell	

Playing: Midweek: round £40.00; day n/a. Weekend: round £45.00; day n/a.

Facilities: Bar: 10.30am–11pm. Food: Lunch and dinner from 12pm–9pm. Bar snacks.

Comments: Excellent fairways and greens on a well-designed, tough-but-fair course ... Beautiful and challenging ... The day I win the lotto is the day I join this great course ... Interesting, tough holes ... Excellent clubhouse and brilliant food ... Unknown designer means this course is underrated ... Lots of water fun, not so good for the traditionalist ... Loved it ... Always find time to play it ... One of the best newer courses in Ireland.

Malahide Golf Club   ★★

Beechwood, The Grange, Malahide, County Dublin
Nearest main town: Dublin

Secretary:	Mr T. Gallagher	Tel: 01 846 1611
		Fax: 01 846 1270
Professional:	Mr D. Barton	Tel: 01 846 0002

Playing: Midweek: round £30.00; day n/a. Weekend: round £40.00; day n/a.

Facilities: Bar: 10.30am–11pm. Food: Lunch and dinner from 11am–9pm. Bar snacks.

Comments: Very popular, friendly course ... Not a classic design but kept in excellent shape ... For all the challenge from the tee and fairway, the greens are generally flat ... Very fair to the once-in-a-while player ... Scoring usually good here ... Facilities excellent at this popular Dublin parkland course ... Clever use of water hazards.

Mount Temple Golf Club ★★★

Mount Temple, Moate, County Westmeath
Nearest main town: Moate

Secretary: Mr M. Dolan   Tel: 0902 81841
                                    Fax: 0902 81957

Professional: None.

Playing: Midweek: round £15.00; day n/a. Weekend: round
£18.00; day n/a.

Facilities: Bar: 10am–11pm. Food: Bar snacks.

Comments: It's a beast but worth the pain ... Long and difficult
course ... Extremely natural layout ... Undulating fairways and hard, unwatered greens make this a test of
your imagination ... Shot-maker's course.

Mount Wolsley Golf Club ★★

Tullow, County Carlow
Nearest main town: Tullow

Secretary: Mr D. Morrissey   Tel: 0503 51674
                                      Fax: 0503 52123

Professional: Mr J. Bolger

Playing: Midweek: round £20.00; day n/a. Weekend: round
£25.00; day n/a.

Facilities: Bar: 11am–11pm. Food: Lunch and dinner from
11am–10pm. Bar snacks.

Comments: Very fun course ... New course in super condition ... A
dream to play ... Can't wait to go back.

Mountrath Golf Club

Knockanina, County Laois
Nearest main town: Portlaoise

Secretary: Mr J. Mulhare   Tel: 0502 32558
                                      Fax: 0502 32558

Professional: None.

Playing: Midweek: round £10.00; day n/a. Weekend: round
£10.00; day n/a.

Facilities: Bar: 10.30am–11pm. Food: Bar snacks.

Comments: Sheep the main hazard on this nine-hole course ... Fun course open to everyone ... A beginner's course.

Mullingar Golf Club   ★★

Belvedere, Mullingar, County Westmeath
Nearest main town: Mullingar

Secretary: Mrs A. Cully   Tel: 044 48366
                                     Fax: 044 41499
Professional: Mr J. Burns   Tel: 044 40085

Playing: Midweek: round £20.00; day n/a. Weekend: round £25.00; day n/a. Handicap certificate required.

Facilities: Bar: 10.30am–11pm. Food: Lunch and dinner from 12pm–9pm. Bar snacks.

Comments: Tactical short course ... Despite being less than 6,000 yards, this course has stood the test of time ... Tight course ... Greens cleverly protected ... Bunkering protects this short course ... Will remember it for the par-3s ... Always a warm welcome.

Old Conna Golf Club   ★

Ferndale Road, Bray, County Wicklow
Nearest main town: Dublin

Secretary: Mr D. Diviney   Tel: 01 282 6055
                                     Fax: 01 282 5611
Professional: Mr P. McDaid   Tel: 01 272 0022

Playing: Midweek: round £27.50; day n/a. Weekend: round n/a; day n/a. Handicap certificate required.

Facilities: Bar: 10.30am–11pm. Food: Lunch and dinner from 10am–9pm. Bar snacks.

Comments: New course near Dublin that has a bright future ... Time will tell whether this Hackett course will make it ... Three of the last four holes are 420+ yards ... Overly long new course ... New players don't need to cover 6,000+ yards.

Portmarnock Hotel and Golf Links ★★★★★

Portmarnock, Dublin, County Dublin
Nearest main town: Portmarnock

Secretary: Mrs M. Cassidy   Tel: 01 846 1800
                   (Golf Director)   Fax: 01 846 1077
Professional: None.

Playing: Midweek: round £55.00; day n/a. Weekend: round
                   £55.00; day n/a.

Facilities: Bar: 11am–11pm. Food: Breakfast, lunch and dinner
                   from 9am–11pm. Bar snacks

Comments: New links, a real credit to designers ... Was amazed to
                   find out it was only designed recently ... This course
                   completely devoured me ... Slow start but gets better ...
                   Better than the Old Course ... Golf this good is rare ...
                   So natural ... Have bored my friends rigid with tales of
                   this one ... Condition exceptional for a links ... Very
                   exposed ... In years to come will be one of the best in
                   Ireland ... A fresh look at links golf.

Powerscourt Golf Club ★★★

Enniskerry, Bray, County Wicklow
Nearest main town: Bray

Secretary: Mr B. Gibbons   Tel: 01 204 6033
Professional: Mr P. Thompson   Tel: 01 204 6033

Playing: Midweek: round £45.00; day n/a. Weekend: round
                   £55.00; day n/a.

Facilities: Bar: 9am–11pm. Food: Lunch and dinner from
                   12pm–9pm.

Comments: Wicklow mountains provide a stunning backdrop ...
                   Dublin golfers are becoming very spoilt ... Par-5 17th of
                   698 yards not quite what I'm used to ... Inventive course
                   but not much soul ... Felt very welcome ... Condition a
                   tribute to the club.

Rathsallagh Golf Club ★★★★

Dunlavin, County Wicklow
Nearest main town: Naas

Secretary: Mr M. Bermingham   Tel: 045 403316
                                       Fax: 045 403295

Professional: None.

Playing: Midweek: round £35.00; day n/a. Weekend: round
                   £45.00; day n/a.

Facilities: Bar: 10.30am–11pm. Food: Lunch and dinner from
                   12pm–9pm. Bar snacks.

Comments: Difficult, long course suitable for players of all abilities
                   ... Beautiful setting and good value ... So much variety
                   ... A bit of everything at this Peter McEvoy-designed
                   course ... Watch out for the 6th ... Hard as nails ...
                   Homely club ... Simple from the tee, but the trouble
                   starts when you start firing at the flags.

Rosslare Golf Club   ★★★

Rosslare Strand, Rosslare, County Wexford
Nearest main town: Wexford

Secretary: Mr J. F. Hall   Tel: 053 32203
                                          Fax: 053 32203

Professional: Mr A. Skerritt   Tel: 053 32238

Playing: Midweek: round n/a; day £22.00. Weekend: round n/a;
                   day £30.00.

Facilities: Bar: 10.30am–11pm. Food: Lunch from 10am–9pm.
                   Bar snacks.

Comments: Very pleasant links that lacks length ... Underrated due
                   to its length ... Great welcome at this old-style links ...
                   Very exposed – can spoil the fun ... Rough gets too high
                   on occasions ... Charming little course – will be back.

Royal Dublin Golf Club

North Bull Island, Dollymount, Dublin, County Dublin
Nearest main town: Dublin

Secretary: Mr J. Lambe   Tel: 01 833 1262
                                          Fax: 01 833 6504

Professional: Mr L. Owens   Tel: 01 833 6477

Playing: Midweek: round £60.00; day n/a. Weekend: round
                   £70.00; day n/a. Handicap certificate required.

Facilities: Bar: 10.30am–11pm. Food: Breakfast, lunch and dinner from 7am–10pm. Bar snacks.

Comments: Welcome atmosphere ... Superb links and great pro shop ... Past its best ... A stunning natural course with deep greenside bunkers ... Very busy with visitors from Dublin ... Hard-to-master course with blind drives.

Rush Golf Club   ★

Rush, County Dublin
Nearest main town: Dublin

Secretary: Mr B. J. Clear   Tel: 01 843 7548
                                         Fax: 01 843 8177

Professional: None.

Playing: Midweek: round £16.00; day n/a. Weekend: round n/a; day n/a.

Facilities: Bar: 10.30am–11pm. Food: Bar snacks.

Comments: Nine hole links with pot bunkers and undulating fairways ... Bunkers the main hazard at his neat little course ... Natural course in average condition ... Excellent fun and a bracing wind ... Good value for a unique golf experience.

St Helens Bay Golf Club   ★★

Rosslare Harbour, County Wexford
Nearest main town: Wexford

Secretary: Mr L. Byrne   Tel: 053 33234
                                         Fax: 053 33803

Professional: None.

Playing: Midweek: round £22.00; day n/a. Weekend: round £25.00; day n/a.

Facilities: Bar: 10.30am–11pm. Food: Lunch and dinner from 12pm–9pm. Bar snacks.

Comments: Part links, part parkland ... Sleeping giant of a course ... Course suffers from identity crisis – is it parkland, is it links? ... Course finishes on right note with some cracking closing holes ... Course with potential ... Condition leaves a lot to be desired ... Ideal matchplay venue.

St Margarets Golf & Country Club   ★★★★

St Margarets, Dublin, County Dublin
Nearest main town: Dublin

Secretary: Mr T. Judge   Tel: 01 864 0400
                   (Chief Exec)   Fax: 01 864 0289
Professional: Mr D. Loys-Moroney

Playing: Midweek: round £30.00; day £45.00. Weekend: round
                   £45.00; day £65.00.

Facilities: Bar: 10.30am–11pm. Food: Breakfast, lunch and
                   dinner from 9am–9pm. Bar snacks.

Comments: Good championship course, but will be outstanding in
                   10 years time ... Best greens I have ever putted on ...
                   Flat farmland transformed into a rolling, modern master-
                   piece ... No bump-and-run here, high iron shots
                   needed ... 8th and the 12th are excellent par-5s ...
                   Fairly straightforward with shallow bunkers and easy-to-
                   read greens ... Manufactured course, nothing you
                   wouldn't find at the K-Club ... Excellent facilities and
                   course for the average player.

The Black Bush Golf Club   ★★

Thomastown, Dunshaughlin, County Meath
Nearest main town: Dublin

Secretary: Mr M. Walsh   Tel: 01 825 0021
                   (Manager)   Fax: 01 825 0400
Professional: Mr S. O'Grady   Tel: 01 825 0793

Playing: Midweek: round £16.00; day n/a. Weekend: round
                   £22.00; day n/a.

Facilities: Bar: 10.30am–11pm. Food: Lunch and dinner from
                   10am–9pm. Bar snacks.

Comments: A young club with great potential – very friendly ...
                   Exciting 1st with drive over the lake ... Superb facilities ...
                   Par-4s cater for average player ... Plenty of short par-4s.

The European Club   ★★★★

Brittas Bay, Wicklow, County Wicklow
Nearest main town: Wicklow

Secretary:	Mr P. Ruddy	Tel: 0404 47415
		Fax: 0404 47449

Professional: None.

Playing: Midweek: round £45.00; day £65.00. Weekend: round £45.00; day £65.00.

Facilities: Bar: Wine bar open all day. Food: Breakfast, lunch and dinner from 9am–9pm. Bar snacks.

Comments: Each hole a classic ... Very difficult links ... What a place! ... Easy to get a game on a beautiful links ... Outstanding welcome, manager even joined us for lunch ... Very demanding and exciting ... 7th and 17th are great holes ... Tough course with excellent greens ... Wonderful charm and hospitality.

The Heath Golf Club ★

The Heath, Portlaoise, County Laois
Nearest main town: Portlaoise

Secretary:	To be appointed.	Tel: 0502 21074
Professional:	Mr E. Doyle	Tel: 0502 46622

Playing: Midweek: round £10.00; day n/a. Weekend: round £15.00; day n/a.

Facilities: Bar: 10.30am–11pm. Food: Lunch and dinner from 12pm–6pm.

Comments: Heather and gorse the main feature of this old course ... Old course a little ragged around the edges ... Very natural but very average.

The Island Golf Club ★★★★

Corballis, Donabate, Dublin
Nearest main town: Dublin

Secretary:	Mr J. Finn	Tel: 01 843 6104
		Fax: 01 843 6860
Professional:	Mr K. Kelleher	Tel: 01 843 5002

Playing: Midweek: round £40.00; day £60.00. Weekend: round £50.00; day n/a.

Facilities: Bar: 10.30am–11pm. Food: Lunch and dinner from 10am–9pm.

Comments: Good all-round facilities with best holes the 5th, 6th, 10th and 15th ... True links ... Best course in Dublin but needs to be more welcoming ... 1st, 3rd and the 7th are the best holes on the front nine ... Surrounded on three sides by water ... Imposing sandhills in places.

The K Club ★★★★

Kildare Hotel & Country Club, Straffan, County Kildare
Nearest main town: Dublin

Secretary:	Mr P. Crowe	Tel: 01 601 7300
		Fax: 01 601 7399
Professional:	Mr E. Jones	Tel: 01 601 7321

Playing: Midweek: round £130.00; day n/a. Weekend: round £130.00; day n/a.

Facilities: Bar: 10.30am–11pm. Food: Breakfast, lunch and dinner from 7am–10pm. Bar snacks.

Comments: Ideal Ryder Cup venue – superb ... Four hours of my life I'll never get back – dreadful ... I don't reckon Arnie would finish this long, punishing track ... Thinking man's course ... Superb ... Good if you are good, a nightmare if you are bad ... High-class professional approach here ... Fantastic condition ... No expense spared here.

Tullamore Golf Club ★★★

Brookfield, Tullamore, County Offaly
Nearest main town: Tullamore

Secretary:	Mr P. Burns	Tel: 0506 21439
		Fax: 0506 41806
Professional:	Mr D. McArdle	Tel: 0506 51757

Playing: Midweek: round £16.00; day £24.00. Weekend: round £20.00; day £30.00.

Facilities: Bar: 10.30am–11pm. Food: Lunch and dinner from 11am–9pm.

Comments: Pure golf and great 14th hole ... Classic course recently improved ... Generous course where good shots are always rewarded ... Nothing tricky about this warm, friendly club ... Best course for miles around.

Wicklow Golf Club   ★★

Dunbur Road, Wicklow, County Wicklow
Nearest main town: Wicklow

Secretary: Mr J. Kelly   Tel: 0404 67379
Professional: Mr D. Daly   Tel: 0404 66122

Playing: Midweek: round £20.00; day £20.00. Weekend: round
                  £20.00; day £20.00.

Facilities: Bar: 10.30am–11pm. Food: Lunch and dinner from
                  10am–10pm. Bar snacks.

Comments: Beautiful scenery on a thinking man's course ... Views of
                  Wicklow mountains best thing about this place ... Short
                  nine-holer that offers little but views ... Wouldn't rush
                  back ... There's better nine-holers elsewhere.

Woodbrook Golf Club   ★★★

Dublin Road, Bray, County Dublin
Nearest main town: Dublin

Secretary: Mr J. Melody   Tel: 01 282 4799
                                         Fax: 01 282 1950

Professional: Mr W. Kinsella

Playing: Midweek: round £45.00; day n/a. Weekend: round
                  £55.00; day n/a. Handicap certificate required.

Facilities: Bar: 10.30am–11pm. Food: Lunch and dinner from
                  11am–9pm. Bar snacks.

Comments: Club prides itself on condition of course ... Not a tradi-
                  tional links but a fun place to play ... 36 out, 36 home
                  – nicely balanced course ... A facile links ideal for
                  beginners ... Don't go out of your way.

Woodenbridge Golf Club   ★★★

Woodenbridge, Arklow, County Wicklow
Nearest main town: Arklow

Secretary: Mr H. Crummy   Tel: 0402 35202
                                         Fax: 0402 35202

Professional: None.

Playing: Midweek: round £27.00; day n/a. Weekend: round £35.00; day n/a.

Facilities: Bar: 11am–11pm. Food: Lunch from 11am–3pm. Dinner from 6pm–11pm. Bar snacks.

Comments: Can get very busy during the weekend ... Delightful course in the spring ... Pretty parkland which is very fair ... Setting and vegetation make this course ... Very popular ... Never have a bad round.

Ulster and Donegal

Ballyliffin Golf Club (Glashedy) ★★★★★

Inishowen, Ballyliffin, County Donegal
Nearest main town: Londonderry

Nick Faldo labelled the Old Course at Ballyliffin as 'the most natural course ever'. You could not say the same about its younger brother, the Glashedy, which, although running through a moonscape of dunes, has been levelled out somewhat to create a fair playing surface. If the work had not been done, and the fairways allowed to keep their sloping, rugged appearance, this would surely be the toughest course in Ireland. Much like Tralee, Portmarnock Links and The European, Glashedy is a 'new' links course, and is the northernmost course in Ireland, situated near Pollan Bay off Doagh Isle. Designed by Pat Ruddy and Tom Craddock on the landward side of the original links, the Glashedy Links exploits its exalted location to the full. The designers promised the club that they would build one of the world's finest and most adventurous links courses, and although such things are hugely subjective, to some extent they succeeded. It is a vigorous test of golf, the wind running the full range from strong to very strong, and the greenkeepers letting the rough grow. You'll need all the shots to survive here, particularly the low runner that keeps below the level of the dunes. Hit it above them and the wind will send your ball flying in all directions and probably into a scrape or bunker.

There is a tremendous sequence of holes on the back nine starting with the par-5 13th, a hole that they say reminds you of Ballybunion when you look ahead and Turnberry when you look behind because of the dominating presence of Glashedy Rock.

Secretary:	Mr K. O'Docherty	Tel: 077 76119
		Fax: 077 76672
Professional:	None.	
Playing:	Midweek: round £28.00; day n/a. Weekend: round £33.00; day n/a. Handicap certificate required.	
Facilities:	Bar: 10.30am–11pm. Food: Lunch and dinner from 12pm–9pm.	

Comments: Great value ... Don't go and play here and miss out on the Old Course ... Lunar landscape with dunes like ocean liners ... Everything you need for a challenge – wind, doglegs, subtle greens, deep bunkers and tangly rough ... Better than the Old ... 12th, 13th and 14th just can't be bettered ... Magnificent new course, thank you Ruddy and Craddock ... Not as natural as the Old ... Could while away the rest of my life here ... Glashedy Rock reminiscent of Turnberry ... New course that feels 100 years old.

Royal County Down Golf Club ★★★★★

Newcastle, County Down, BT33 0AN
Nearest main town: Belfast

Along with Royal Dornoch in the nether reaches of Scotland, Royal County Down is arguably the finest links, never to have held an Open Championship. Praise for this beautiful links, which is towered over by the spectacular range of the Mountains of Mourne, has come from far and wide.

Dai Rees felt it to be second only to Pine Valley as the toughest course in the world. Tom Watson, as qualified as anyone to comment on the merits of links courses, having won the Open on five different ones, commented after his 1989 visit that the first 11 holes were 'the finest consecutive holes of links golf' he had ever played.

County Down's charm lies in the old-fashioned flavour of both the terrain and the layout. A few other courses are blessed with a similar mix of rugged dunes ordained with a colourful blend of purple heather and yellow flowering gorse, but few combine them to such dramatic effect.

The fairways and greens are no less than you would expect from a championship seaside course, but the rough has a delightfully unkempt appearance which gives the feel of playing golf in the last century. Sea grasses grow from the lip of the bunkers in such thick tufts that it is better to land in the traps than to just clear them.

The huge spines of dunes which bisect the course have resulted in five blind tee shots which naturally are a target of criticism in these days of laser-measured yardage charts.

But at County Down they add to the drama. Take the 486-yard 9th where, following a blind tee shot, you walk to the top of the ridge to see the glory of one of golf's most photographed fairways unfold far below you, with the 2,300-foot peak of Slieve Donard in the distance overseeing proceedings. The short par-4 16th, driveable with a big blow from a hilltop, has also come in for criticism, but perhaps the only thing out of place at County Down is the small lake in the middle of the 17th fairway, which seems unnecessarily contrived.

Secretary: Mr P. E. Rolph   Tel: 013967 23314
                                             Fax: 013967 26281
Professional: Mr K. J. Whitson   Tel: 013967 22419

Playing: Midweek: round £65.00; day £95.00. Weekend: round £75.00; day n/a.

Facilities: Bar: 11am–11pm. Food: Lunch from 12pm–3pm. Bar snacks.

Comments: Weekend play only on Sunday from 1pm–2.30pm ... Best course in British Isles ... Deserving of its ultra-challenging reputation ... Inspiring setting ... The best first 11 holes on any course in the world, but a shame about the rest ... Stunning, breathtaking ... Hard to concentrate on your game in such surroundings ... Friendly, well-informed pro ... Best course I have ever played ... The course is a dream and the 9th hole is the pick of the bunch ... Maybe the best course in Ireland ... Not a bad hole here ... Breathtakingly beautiful, but don't take your eyes off the course ... Very narrow, very dangerous ... Too long, too hard, especially in the wind and rain – but I love it.

Royal Portrush Golf Club (Dunluce)   ★★★★★

Dunluce Road, Portrush, County Antrim, BT56 8JQ
Nearest main town: Portrush

Few approaches to a golf course stir the passions more than the road to Royal Portrush. Shortly after passing the ruins of Dunluce Castle, you turn a corner and there, spread before you, is an expanse of crumpled links, rolling out towards the shimmering sea. In the distance are the brooding headlands of Inishowen and, on a clear day, you can see the Scottish landmarks of the Paps of Jura. It is a marvellously evocative setting.

Royal Portrush held the Open Championship in 1951 (the only course in Ireland to do so), but as the demands on space for hospitality grew, so its viability as a venue fell. It is certainly a course worthy of the event, and players walking off the 18th breathe a heavy sigh of satisfaction after what is an incredibly imaginative experience.

Essentially it is a driving course. The curves of the fairways and slopes of the terrain are intimidating from the tee and, although there are very few bunkers, the wind is a constant factor, and the rough is untamed and unruly, gobbling up any loose shot. The opening holes run fairly straight away from the clubhouse and it is not until the turn that the course starts to show its teeth. The holes swing back and forth, doglegging around dunes and greens backing onto the sea, most spectacularly at the 5th. What strikes you is that, although this is the most difficult part of the course, there are very few greenside bunkers, the small putting surfaces protected purely by small hummocks and hills.

The 14th, named Calamity Corner, is Portrush's most famous hole, a par-3 which is played to an elevated green located on a spine of rising land. All along the right is a hideous drop into a valley of bushes and scrub and, on the left, dangerous rough clinging to the banks.

Secretary:	Miss W. Erskine	Tel: 01265 822311
		Fax: 01265 823139
Professional:	Mr D. A. Stevenson	Tel: 01265 823335

Playing: Midweek: round £60.00; day £85.00. Weekend: round £70.00; day £95.00. Handicap certificate required.

Facilities: Bar: 11am–11pm. Food: Lunch from 11am–3pm. Dinner by arrangement.

Comments: Magnificent links ... Great setting ... Grandiose ... Take the Open Championship there as soon as possible ... You need the heart of a lion for this one ... A must-play course with great views and wonderful company ... Must be played ... Gruelling ... Just magic ... An unbelievable experience for the overseas golfer.

Ardglass Golf Club   ★★★

Castle Place, Ardglass, County Down, BT30 7TP
Nearest main town: Downpatrick

Secretary:	Miss D. Polly	Tel: 01396 841219
		Fax: 01396 841841
Professional:	Mr P. Farrell	Tel: 01396 841022

Playing: Midweek: round £15.00; day £15.00. Weekend: round £21.00; day n/a.

Facilities: Bar: 11am–11pm. Food: Lunch and dinner from 12pm–9pm, except Monday.

Comments: A jaw-dropping opening hole, delicious food, most
             notably the steaks! ... Beautiful track by the sea ...
             Many blind drives will send you potty ... An historic
             course ... First four holes perched on the cliffs ... Par-3
             11th blows your socks off ... Very fair, the test of a great
             golf course.

Ballybofey & Stranorlar Golf Club   ★★★

Stranorlar, Ballybofey, County Donegal
Nearest main town: Stranorlar

Secretary: Mr A. Harkin   Tel: 074 31228
Professional: None.

Playing: Midweek: round n/a; day £15.00. Weekend: round n/a;
             day £15.00.

Facilities: Bar: 11am–11pm. Food: Lunch and dinner from
             12am–9pm. Bar snacks.

Comments: A gentle, fun course ... Intoxicating atmosphere in the
             clubhouse ... Impossible to leave bar until after
             midnight ... Warm welcome guaranteed ... Great
             welcome ... Parkland course more renowned for its
             welcome than quality of golf ... Good course with views
             of the Donegal Hills.

Ballycastle Golf Club   ★★★

Cushendall Road, Ballycastle, County Antrim, BT64 6QP
Nearest main town: Portrush

Secretary: Mr B J. Dillon   Tel: 012657 62536
                                          Fax: 012657 69909
Professional: Mr I. McLaughlin   Tel: 012657 62506

Playing: Midweek: round £18.00; day n/a. Weekend: round
             £25.00; day n/a.

Facilities: Bar: 11am–11pm. Food: Lunch from 12pm–2pm.
             Dinner by arrangement.

Comments: Three courses in one ... Mixed parkland/links ... Great
             character ... Parts played around ruins of 13th-century
             friary ... Thoughtful course of some standing.

Ballyliffin Golf Club (Old)   ★★★★

Inishowen, Ballyliffin, County Donegal
Nearest main town: Londonderry

Secretary: Mr K. O'Doherty   Tel: 077 76119
                                       Fax: 077 76672
Professional: None.

Playing: Midweek: round £19.00; day n/a. Weekend: round
                   £22.00; day n/a. Handicap certificate required.

Facilities: Bar: 10.30am–11pm. Food: Lunch and dinner from
                   12pm–9pm.

Comments: Natural links course set in magnificent scenery ... Faldo
                   calls it 'the most natural golf course ever' ... Watch out
                   for 'The Tank' ... So beautiful ... Shorter than you
                   would expect but so charming ... Never a flat lie on
                   these fairways ... Stark beauty to this golfscape ... I do
                   my best thinking out here ... Will never forget my time
                   here ... Just so beautiful ... A haven of tranquillity from
                   the modern world.

Balmoral Golf Club   ★★★

518 Lisburn Road, Belfast, County Belfast, BT9 6GX
Nearest main town: Belfast

Secretary: Mr R. C. McConkey   Tel: 01232 381514
                                         Fax: 01232 666759
Professional: Mr G. Bleakley   Tel: 01232 667747

Playing: Midweek: round £20.00; day n/a. Weekend: round
                   £30.00; day n/a.

Facilities: Bar: 11am–11pm. Food: Breakfast, lunch and dinner
                   from 9am–9pm. Bar snacks.

Comments: Good course near Belfast city centre ... Very beautiful ...
                   Relaxed clubhouse ... Excellent greens on visit ...
                   Impressive clubhouse ... Fairly short but with plenty of
                   natural hazards ... Tree-lined course with some potential.

Bangor Golf Club   ★★★

Broadway, Bangor, County Down, BT20 4RH
Nearest main town: Bangor

Secretary:	Mr D. J. Ryan	Tel: 01247 270922
		Fax: 01247 453394
Professional:	None.	

Playing: Midweek: round £20.00; day £30.00. Weekend: round £25.00; day n/a.

Facilities: Bar: 11am–11pm. Food: Bar snacks. Dinner by arrangement.

Comments: Good course for the beginner and more experienced player ... Remote course but fun to play ... Numerous doglegs ... Another James Braid triumph ... Natural golf for the purist.

Bundoran Golf Club ★★★

Bundoran, County Donegal
Nearest main town: Donegal

Secretary:	Mr J. McGagh	Tel: 072 41302
		Fax: 072 42014
Professional:	Mr D. Robinson	

Playing: Midweek: round £17.00; day £25.00. Weekend: round £20.00; day £30.00.

Facilities: Bar: 10.30am–11pm. Food: Bar snacks.

Comments: Venerable links ... Testing par-3s, especially the 5th ... Very popular venue ... Round went on forever ... Parkland/links ... A nice stop-off but too short ... Holes by the ocean hard to beat ... Basic facilities at this welcoming club.

Cairndhu Golf Club ★★★

192 Coast Road, Larne, County Antrim, BT40 2QC
Nearest main town: Larne

Secretary:	Mr N. Moore	Tel: 01574 583324
		Fax: 01574 583324
Professional:	Mr R. Walker	Tel: 01574 583417

Playing: Midweek: round £15.00; day £22.50. Weekend: round £24.00; day £36.00.

Facilities: Bar: 11am–11pm. Food: Lunch and dinner from 11am–9pm. Bar snacks.

Comments: Don't be intimidated by the scenery ... Built on the side of a hill ... Views to the Antrim Hills ... 3rd tee-shot is from way up high and has to carry 170 yards ... Small greens make this so tough.

Carrickfergus Golf Club   ★

35 North Road, Carrickfergus, County Antrim, BT38 8LP
Nearest main town: Belfast

Secretary: Mr B. J. Lee   Tel: 01960 363713
                                        Fax: 01960 363023
Professional: To be appointed.

Playing: Midweek: round £14.00; day £14.00. Weekend: round £20.00; day £20.00.

Facilities: Bar: 11am–11pm. Food: Lunch from 12pm–2.30pm. Dinner from 5pm–8.30pm.

Comments: Opening drive straight over a dam ... Very intimidating opening tee shot ... Basic layout with little for the advanced player ... Lots of parallel fairways make this quite boring.

Castlehume Golf Club   ★★

Castle Hume, Enniskillen, County Fermanagh, BT93 7ED
Nearest main town: Enniskillen

Secretary: Mrs H. Keenan   Tel: 01365 327077
                                        Fax: 01365 327076
Professional: Mr G. McShae

Playing: Midweek: round £12.00; day £12.00. Weekend: round £18.00; day £18.00.

Facilities: Bar: 11am–11pm. Food: Breakfast, lunch and dinner from 9am–9pm. Bar snacks.

Comments: Fairly bland piece of land ... Average course for the area ... Good value ... Nice club course but not one for the visitor ... Rolling fairways, water hazards and clever bunkering make this a nice afternoon stroll.

Castlerock Golf Club   ★★★★

Circular Road, Castlerock, County Londonderry, BT51 4TJ
Nearest main town: Coleraine

Secretary: Mr R. G. McBride   Tel: 01265 848314
                                        Fax: 01265 849440
Professional: Mr R. Kelly

Playing: Midweek: round £25.00; day £40.00. Weekend: round
                   £35.00; day n/a.

Facilities: Bar: 11am–11pm. Food: Breakfast, lunch and dinner
                   from 9am–9pm. Bar snacks.

Comments: So hard, even for the members ... Good par-3s ...
                   Pleasure to play ... Some unforgettable holes ... Does
                   the wind ever blow gently? ... Friendly bunch of
                   members ... White-knuckle stuff when the wind blows
                   ... Great course and good welcome.

Clandeboye Golf Club (Dufferin)   ★★★

Conlig, Newtownards, County Down, BT23 3PN
Nearest main town: Bangor

Secretary: Mr W. Donald   Tel: 01247 271767
                                        Fax: 01247 473711
Professional: Mr P. Gregory   Tel: 01247 271750

Playing: Midweek: round £25.00; day £35.00. Weekend: round
                   £30.00; day n/a.

Facilities: Bar: 11am–11pm. Food: Breakfast, lunch and dinner
                   from 9am–9pm. Bar snacks.

Comments: Elevated greens, blind drives, streams, ditches – always
                   something to watch out for ... Some long carries off the
                   tee ... Woodland and heathland ... Drive on the 4th a
                   terror ... High skill levels for this mature course.

Clandeboye Golf Club (Ava)   ★★★

Conlig, Newtownards, County Down, BT23 3PN
Nearest main town: Bangor

Secretary: Mr W. Donald   Tel: 01247 271767
                                        Fax: 01247 473711

Professional: Mr P. Gregory   Tel: 01247 271750

Playing: Midweek: round £20.00; day £35.00. Weekend: round £25.00; day n/a.

Facilities: Bar: 11am–11pm. Food: Breakfast, lunch and dinner from 9am–9pm. Bar snacks.

Comments: Short and good fun ... Par-5 second a beauty ... So much fun on this charming little course ... Views of Strangford Lough ... Keep your wits about you on this beguiling course.

County Cavan Golf Club   ★★

Arnmore House, Drumelis, Cavan, County Cavan
Nearest main town: Cavan

Secretary: Mr J. Sheridan   Tel: 049 315041
Professional: Mr K. Carroll   Tel: 049 31388

Playing: Midweek: round £12.00; day £12.00. Weekend: round £14.00; day £14.00.

Facilities: Bar: 10.30am–11pm. Food: Lunch and dinner from 10.30am–10pm. Bar snacks.

Comments: Parkland course ... Can get unplayable in winter ... Local knowledge helps ... Very cheap green fee ... Fair value for money for this unimaginative course.

Cruit Island Golf Club   ★★

Kincasslagh, Dunglow, County Donegal
Nearest main town: Donegal

Secretary: Mr D. Gallaway   Tel: 075 43296
Professional: None.

Playing: Midweek: round £10.00; day n/a. Weekend: round £12.00; day n/a.

Facilities: Bar: 11.30am–4pm. Food: Bar snacks.

Comments: Nine-hole course perched on the edge of the Atlantic Ocean ... The 6th hole over the cove defies belief ... With the Atlantic crashing against the rocks this is an evocative experience ... Not in great condition but this is golf back to its roots ... Don't let the fact it's half a course put you off ... A blinder.

Donegal Golf Club ★★★★

Murvagh, Laghey, County Donegal
Nearest main town: Donegal

Secretary: Mr J. Nixon   Tel: 073 34054
Fax: 073 34377

Professional: None.

Playing: Midweek: round £20.00; day n/a. Weekend: round £27.00; day n/a.

Facilities: Bar: 10.30am–11pm. Food: Lunch and dinner from 10am–9pm.

Comments: A sensational links ... Can't be bettered ... The match of any of Ireland's links legends ... Opened in 1960 but has an older feel to it ... A gruelling course ... Course goes on and on ... Blue Stack Mountains dominate the course ... 5th named the 'Valley of Tears' and rightly so ... Staggering ... Long course putting great pressure on the short game ... Longest course in Ireland ... Course that fires the imagination ... Pray your driver is working ... Drive badly and you're out with the washing ... A Goliath of a course, felt like David ... Exciting ... Exhilarating.

Dungannon Golf Club ★★★

34 Springfield Lane, Mullaghmore, Dungannon, County Tyrone
Nearest main town: Dungannon

Secretary: Mr L. R. P. Agnew   Tel: 01868 722098
Fax: 01868 727338

Professional: None.

Playing: Midweek: round n/a; day £20.00. Weekend: round n/a; day £25.00.

Facilities: Bar: 11am–11pm. Food: Lunch and dinner from 12pm–7pm. Bar snacks.

Comments: Hilly in places but good way to work off hospitality ... Always enjoy society days here ... Established course with a nice feel ... Standard scratch is three under par ... A proper club with progressive attitude.

Dunmurry Golf Club   ★★

91 Dunmurry Lane, Dunmurry, County Belfast, BT17 9JS
Nearest main town: Belfast

Secretary:	Mr I. D. McBride	Tel: 01232 610834
		Fax: 01232 602540
Professional:	Mr J. Dolan	Tel: 01232 621314

Playing: Midweek: round £17.00; day n/a. Weekend: round £26.50; day n/a. Handicap certificate required.

Facilities: Bar: 10.30am–11pm. Food: Lunch and dinner from 9am–9pm, except Mondays.

Comments: Nice club with a relaxed atmosphere ... Popular venue but course is suffering ... Opened in 1983 but has matured well ... Fair value at this open-to-all, friendly club.

Kilkeel Golf Club   ★★

Mourne Park, Kilkeel, County Down, BT34 4LB
Nearest main town: Kilkeel

Secretary:	Mr S. C. McBride	Tel: 016937 62296
		Fax: 016937 65095
Professional:	None.	

Playing: Midweek: round n/a; day £16.00. Weekend: round n/a; day £20.00.

Facilities: Bar: 11am–11pm. Food: Lunch and dinner from 12pm–8pm. Bar snacks.

Comments: An excellent test on a scenic course ... Kept in reasonable condition ... Beautiful views in every direction ... Parkland course at the foot of the Mourne Mountains ... Quite an English feel to this parkland course ... Inland gem with great potential ... Mature woodland lends this course a regal air.

Kirkistown Castle Golf Club   ★★★

142 Main Road, Newtownards, County Down, BT22 1JA
Nearest main town: Belfast

Secretary:	Mr G. Graham	Tel: 012477 71233
		Fax: 012477 71699

Professional: Mr J. Peden   Tel: 012477 71004

Playing: Midweek: round £13.00; day £13.00. Weekend: round £20.00; day £20.00.

Facilities: Bar: 11am–11pm. Food: Breakfast, lunch and dinner from 9am–9pm. Bar snacks.

Comments: A hidden gem that is worth taking the trouble to find ... Never gets wet underfoot ... Parkland/links with strategic bunkering ... Stunning location and excellent condition ... Drainage super ... Consistent, quality course.

Letterkenny Golf Club   ★

Barnhill, Letterkenny, County Donegal
Nearest main town: Letterkenny

Secretary: Mr I. Mackensie   Tel: 074 21150
Professional: None.

Playing: Midweek: round £12.00; day n/a. Weekend: round £15.00; day n/a.

Facilities: Bar: 10.30am–11pm. Food: Bar snacks.

Comments: Lovely new clubhouse but course prone to damp ground ... Well presented and enjoyable ... Beautiful 11th hole ... Two halves to this course, the plateau holes get the nod ... Not much variety ... Not in the top rank for Donegal ... Did not do much for my game.

Lisburn Golf Club

68 Eglantine Road, Lisburn, County Antrim, BT27 5RQ
Nearest main town: Lisburn

Secretary: Mr G. E. McVeigh   Tel: 01846 677216
                                        Fax: 01846 603608
Professional: Mr B. R. Campbell   Tel: 01846 677217

Playing: Midweek: round £25.00; day n/a. Weekend: round £25.00; day n/a.

Facilities: Bar: 11am–11pm. Food: Lunch and dinner from 11am–9pm. Bar snacks.

Comments: Well laid out with lots of bunkers ... Good pro shop ... Well maintained with picturesque holes ... Very tranquil ... Finishes with a wonderful par-3.

Lurgan Golf Club   ★★

The Demesne, Lurgan, County Armagh, BT67 9BN
Nearest main town: Lurgan

Secretary: Mrs G. Turkington   Tel: 01762 322087
                                        Fax: 01762 325306
Professional: Mr D. Paul   Tel: 01762 321068

Playing: Midweek: round £15.00; day n/a. Weekend: round
                 £20.00; day n/a.

Facilities: Bar: 11am–11pm. Food: Lunch and dinner by arrange-
                  ment.

Comments: Internal out-of-bounds is annoying ... Set by Lurgan
                 Lake ... Opportunity to open your shoulders on this flat
                 expanse of a golf course ... Not high quality but cheap
                 and cheerful.

Mahee Island Golf Club   ★★

Comber, Belfast, County Down, BT23 6ET
Nearest main town: Belfast

Secretary: Mr A. McCracken (Steward)   Tel: 01238 541234
Professional: None.

Playing: Midweek: round £10.00; day n/a. Weekend: round
                 £15.00; day n/a.

Facilities: Bar: 12pm–8pm. Food: Lunch and dinner from
                  12pm–3pm. Bar snacks.

Comments: Top-of-the-drawer nine-hole course on island in
                 Strangford Lough ... Idyllic location on an island ... Best
                 maintained nine-hole course in Ireland ... Bizarre but
                 beautiful ... Predominantly in good condition ... One
                 primarily for the enthusiast ... Poor off-course facilities.

Malone Golf Club   ★★★

240 Upper Malone Road, Dunmurry, County Belfast, BT17 9LB
Nearest main town: Belfast

Secretary: Mr J. N. S. Agate   Tel: 01232 612758
                                         Fax: 01232 431394
Professional: Mr M. McGee   Tel: 01232 614917
                                         Fax: 01232 614917

Playing: Midweek: round £33.00; day £33.00. Weekend: round £38.00; day £38.00.

Facilities: Bar: 11am–11pm. Food: Breakfast, lunch and dinner from 9am–9pm. Bar snacks.

Comments: One of the best parkland courses in the area ... In top condition, hardly a divot to be seen ... Rolling hills, water, sand – it has it all ... Magnificent clubhouse ... Very British course ... Opened in the 60s and still in fine nick.

Massereene Golf Club   ★★★

51 Lough Road, Antrim, County Antrim, BT41 4DQ
Nearest main town: Antrim

Secretary:	Mrs S. Greene	Tel: 01849 428096
		Fax: 01849 487661
Professional:	Mr J. Smyth	Tel: 01849 464074

Playing: Midweek: round £20.00; day n/a. Weekend: round £25.00; day n/a.

Facilities: Bar: 11am–11pm. Food: Lunch from 11am–9pm.

Comments: A well-manicured, attractive course, very pleasing to the eye ... Very underrated but they like it that way ... Course has been fiddled with over the years ... Sporting and stylish ... Will make a point of returning to this parkland course.

Narin & Portnoo Golf Club   ★★★

Narin, Portnoo, County Donegal
Nearest main town: Ardara

Secretary:	Mr E. Bonner	Tel: 075 45107
		Fax: 074 25185
Professional:	None.	

Playing: Midweek: round £13.00; day £13.00. Weekend: round £16.00; day £16.00. Handicap certificate required.

Facilities: Bar: 10.30am–11pm. Food: Bar snacks.

Comments: Terrific potential – remove the cattle and caravans at the start and finish, upgrade the clubhouse, a few new tees and you would have a great course ... Windswept links ... Great hospitality and places to stay ... Starts poorly but gets better ... Popular course ... Respected venue almost deserted outside summer ... Short course with ugly clubhouse ... Short course protected by tight fairways ... Wonderful scenery.

North West Golf Club ★

Lisfannon, Fahan, County Donegal
Nearest main town: Buncrana

Secretary:	Mr D. Coyle	Tel: 077 61027
		Fax: 077 63284
Professional:	Mr S. McBriarty	Tel: 077 61715

Playing: Midweek: round £15.00; day £15.00. Weekend: round £20.00; day £20.00.

Facilities: Bar: 10.30am–11pm. Food: Lunch and dinner from 12pm–9pm.

Comments: A second-string course in Donegal but has attractions in itself ... Flattish links near the Mouldy mountains ... Good atmosphere at this out-of-the-way club.

Nuremore Hotel & Golf Club ★★

Carrickmacross, Nuremore, County Monaghan
Nearest main town: Carrickmacross

Secretary:	Mr M. Cassidy	Tel: 042 61438
		Fax: 042 61853
Professional:	Mr M. Cassidy	Tel: 042 64016

Playing: Midweek: round £20.00; day £20.00. Weekend: round £25.00; day £25.00.

Facilities: Bar: 10.30am–11pm. Food: Breakfast, lunch and dinner from 9am–9pm. Bar snacks.

Comments: Scary tee shot on the 10th ... Hotel dominates this attractive parkland course ... Some short par-4s that make you think ... Picturesque drumlins and lakes ... Impressive finishing hole.

Portadown Golf Club   ★

192 Gilford Road, Portadown, County Armagh, BT63 5LF
Nearest main town: Portadown

Secretary: Mrs M. E. Holloway   Tel: 01762 355356
                                        Fax: 01762 355356
Professional: Mr P. Stevenson   Tel: 01762 334655
                                        Fax: 01762 361947

Playing: Midweek: round £17.00; day n/a. Weekend: round
                  £22.00; day n/a. Handicap certificate required.

Facilities: Bar: 11am–11pm. Food: Lunch and dinner from
                  11am–9pm, except Mondays.

Comments: Flattish, fun course in parkland setting ... River Bann
                  provides a nice natural framing for a few holes ... 9th
                  over the river is impressive ... Variety of doglegs and
                  straightaway holes.

Portsalon Golf Club   ★★★★

Portsalon, County Donegal
Nearest main town: Letterkenny

Secretary: Mr P. Doherty   Tel: 074 59459
                                        Fax: 074 59459
Professional: None.

Playing: Midweek: round £14.00; day £14.00. Weekend: round
                  £17.00; day £17.00.

Facilities: Bar: 10.30am–11pm. Food: Lunch and dinner from
                  12pm–9pm.

Comments: Try playing to your handicap here ... A course to play for
                  the rest of your life ... Better than nearby Rosapenna ...
                  Great names – the Ballymostocker Bay and Knockalla
                  mountains ... Basic club ... Learn all about the unpre-
                  dictability of links golf here ... In the summer the ball
                  kicks everywhere ... Charming people ... Made
                  welcome ... So unique ... Can't wait to return.

Portstewart Golf Club (Strand)   ★★★★

117 Strand Road, Portstewart, County Londonderry, BT55 7PG
Nearest main town: Portstewart

Secretary:	Mr M. Moss	Tel: 01265 833839
		Fax: 01265 834097
Professional:	Mr A. Hunter	Tel: 01265 832601

Playing: Midweek: round £45.00; day £65.00. Weekend: round £65.00; day n/a.

Facilities: Bar: 11am–11pm. Food: Breakfast, lunch and dinner from 9am–9pm. Bar snacks.

Comments: Exhilarating experience ... The pro seems to remember every visitor ... Beautiful nine holes out ... Staff and members top drawer ... Wonderful first nine holes designed by the club's members ... Very exciting to play ... First nine just a dream ... Very friendly pro and staff ... Cosy, friendly clubhouse ... Can I play this course everyday for the rest of my life? ... I could play this course every day ... Front nine simply golf heaven ... Could not believe the tee-shot at the 2nd ... Redesigned in 1990 with seven new holes.

Radisson Roe Park Golf Club   ★★★

Limavaddy, County Londonderry, BT49 9LB
Nearest main town: Limavaddy

Secretary:	Mr D. Brockerton	Tel: 015047 22212
		Fax: 015047 22313
Professional:	Mr S. Duffy	

Playing: Midweek: round £20.00; day £20.00. Weekend: round £20.00; day £20.00.

Facilities: Bar: 11am–11pm. Food: Breakfast, lunch and dinner from 9am–9pm. Bar snacks.

Comments: Very testing parkland course with excellent facilities at good prices ... Interesting layout with pleasant clubhouse ... Lough Foyle and the Inishowen peninsula form the backdrop ... Beautifully sculpted course with US-style features.

Rosapenna Hotel Golf Club   ★★★★

Redcastle, Moville, County Donegal
Nearest main town: Londonderry

Secretary: Mr F. Cassey   Tel: 074 55301
                                         Fax: 074 55128

Professional: Mr D. Patterson

Playing: Midweek: round £20.00; day n/a. Weekend: round
                  £25.00; day n/a. Handicap certificate required.

Facilities: Bar: 10.30am–11pm. Food: Breakfast, lunch and
                  dinner from 7am–10pm. Bar snacks.

Comments: A peaceful place to play with 18 holes of good standard
                  ... Laid out by Old Tom Morris ... This, Portsalon and
                  Ballyliffin should meet all your golfing needs in Donegal
                  ... Unknown links of substantial character ... Fairly
                  facile links without ruggedness of other Irish courses ...
                  A course to learn over time ... If you play here only on
                  holidays, you will never match your handicap ... Remote
                  links of tranquillity.

Royal Portrush Golf Club (Valley)   ★★★★

Dunluce Road, Portrush, County Antrim, BT56 8JQ
Nearest main town: Portrush

Secretary: Miss W. Erskine   Tel: 01265 822311
                                          Fax: 01265 823139

Professional: Mr D. A. Stevenson   Tel: 01265 823335

Playing: Midweek: round £24.00; day £34.00. Weekend: round
                  £32.00; day £42.00. Handicap certificate required.

Facilities: Bar: 11am–11pm. Food: Lunch (included in round fee)
                  from 11am–3pm. Dinner by arrangement.

Comments: A deserved respite after the Dunluce ... Bites hard when
                  you least expect it ... Wee sister to the Dunluce but top
                  of my list every time ... 'Feel' course ... Didn't even
                  consider playing it after the Dunluce ... A bit 'after the
                  Lord Mayor's show'.

Slieve Russell Golf Club   ★★★

Ballconnell, County Cavan
Nearest main town: Cavan

Secretary: Mr P. J. Creamer   Tel: 049 26458
                                          Fax: 049 26474

Professional: Mr L. McCool   Tel: 049 26444
                                      Fax: 049 26640

Playing: Midweek: round £30.00; day n/a. Weekend: round
                  £38.00; day n/a.

Facilities: Bar: 10.30am–11pm. Food: Lunch and dinner from
                  10.30am–9pm. Bar snacks.

Comments: Excellent new course ... Facilities and course first class
                  ... Very linksy feel to this parkland beauty with huge
                  contoured greens and deep greenside bunkers ...
                  Exciting par-3s and birdieable par-5s ... Had a memo-
                  rable weekend at the hotel and course – will return one
                  day.

The Belvoir Park Golf Club   ★★★★

Church Road, Newtownbreda, Belfast, County Belfast, BT8 4AN
Nearest main town: Belfast

Secretary: Mr K. H. Graham   Tel: 01232 491693
                                      Fax: 01232 646113
Professional: Mr G M. Kelly   Tel: 01232 646714

Playing: Midweek: round £33.00; day £33.00. Weekend: round
                  £38.00; day £38.00. Handicap certificate required.

Facilities: Bar: 11am–11pm. Food: Lunch and dinner from
                  11am–9pm. Bar snacks.

Comments: Best inland course in Northern Ireland ... Lush fairways
                  on this rejuvenated course ... Hilly in places ... Highly
                  rated ... Close to Belfast but an apparent oasis of calm
                  ... Nice pro shop and accommodating to visitors.

The Knock Club   ★★★

Summerfield, Dundonald, County Belfast, BT16 0QX
Nearest main town: Belfast

Secretary: Mr S. G. Managh   Tel: 01232 483251
                                      Fax: 01232 483251
Professional: Mr G. Fairweather   Tel: 01232 483825

Playing: Midweek: round £20.00; day n/a. Weekend: round
                  £25.00; day n/a.

Facilities: Bar: 11am–11pm. Food: Lunch and dinner from
                  11am–9pm. Bar snacks.

Comments: A tree-lined course that can get wet in winter ... Have a hearty breakfast before you go out ... Needs good drives ... Busy at weekends ... Most fairways tree-lined ... Watch your driving ... All the problems laid out clearly before you.

The Royal Belfast Golf Club   ★★

Holywood, Craigavad, County Down, BT19 0BP
Nearest main town: Belfast

Secretary: Mrs S. H. Morrison   Tel: 01232 428165
                                   Fax: 01232 421404
Professional: Mr S. Spence   Tel: 01232 428586

Playing: Midweek: round £30.00; day n/a. Weekend: round £40.00; day n/a. Handicap certificate required.

Facilities: Bar: 11am–11pm. Food: Lunch from 12pm–3pm. Dinner by arrangement.

Comments: Very exclusive club ... If you can get on, fairly cheap for an exclusive club ... Oldest established club in Ireland ... Course condition always good ... Not as windy as other links ... Protected by over 60 bunkers ... Simple off the tee, problems start around the greens.

Warrenpoint Golf Club   ★★

Lower Dromore Road, Warrenpoint, County Down, BT34 3LN
Nearest main town: Newry

Secretary: Mrs M. Trainor   Tel: 016937 52219
              (Manager)   Fax: 016937 52918
Professional: Mr N. Shaw   Tel: 016937 52371
                                   Fax: 016937 52371

Playing: Midweek: round £20.00; day n/a. Weekend: round £27.00; day n/a. Handicap certificate required.

Facilities: Bar: 11am–11pm. Food: Lunch and dinner from 12pm–9pm. Bar snacks.

Comments: Simply breathtaking scenery ... Very hilly parkland course ... Not very hard but you come here for the views not the golf ... If you're in the area you're probably coming to County Down, not here.

Connacht

County Sligo Golf Club ★★★★★

Rosses Point, County Sligo
Nearest main town: Sligo

The rich seams of golf that exist in south-west Ireland gradually disappear as you pass through Galway and up through County Roscommon. Eventually you reach the town of Sligo, from where it is a short drive to Rosses Point, a golf course that is undoubtedly the best in this part of the Republic. Dominated by the majestic mountain of Ben Bulben, from which the small villages, beaches and crofters' cottages take their character, Rosses Point is a treat to play.

It is a traditional links course, the standard perils of bunkers, heavy rough and wind dictating the course and pace of play. But its character is not built on that alone. The subtleties of the slightly undulating fairways and positions and angles of the green make it a real 'feel' course, harmonising your game with the rhythm of the land.

The poetry of William Yeats used to speak fondly of this part of the world (he is buried in nearby Drumcliff), and visitors do fall under its charm, many leaving with the impression of Rosses Point as the finest links in Ireland. Certainly, it is incredibly fair, far removed from the traditional image of a links with its harsh bounces and cruel kicks.

One of the course's most memorable holes is the 5th, with its astonishing view of Ben Bulben. A par-5 named 'The Jump', you drive from an elevated tee to a fairway that hugs the cliff line from where, if you're lucky, you could be faced with a long iron or, more realistically, a lay-up in front of the tiny green. The feeling of the hole shrinking, and getting more difficult as you walk each yard from the tee, is technically very strong. That could also be said of the 17th, a par-4 played down into a gully, before climbing spectacularly to a hidden green protected on all sides. The incline and green all slope back towards you and one can imagine professional players spinning the ball back down the slope.

You may prefer the gung-ho thrillers of Waterville or Tralee with their enormous dunes, but you can't fail to be impressed with Rosses Point.

Secretary: Mr R. G. Dunne   Tel: 071 77134
Fax: 071 77460
Professional: Mr L. Robinson   Tel: 071 77171

Playing: Midweek: round £32.00; day £48.00. Weekend: round £40.00; day £60.00. Handicap certificate required.

Facilities: Bar: 10.30am–11pm. Food: Lunch and dinner from 10am–9pm. Bar snacks.

Comments: Great stretch of golf in the middle of the round ... Ben Bulben lends this links a mystical feel ... So natural, so magical ... Played it every year on holiday for the last 20 years ... Good putting green and clubhouse ... Very natural, the wind is its defence ... Hilly and exhausting, where are the carts? ... Basic facilities ... Views of the Atlantic and the Bay of Drumcliff ... Exceptional.

Athlone Golf Club   ★★★

Hodson Bay, Athlone, County Roscommon
Nearest main town: Athlone

Secretary: Mr T. Corry   Tel: 0902 92073
                                            Fax: 0902 94080
Professional: Mr M. Quinn

Playing: Midweek: round £18.00; day n/a. Weekend: round £20.00; day n/a.

Facilities: Bar: 10.30am–11pm. Food: Breakfast, lunch and dinner from 9am–9pm. Bar snacks.

Comments: Warmth and hospitality through and through ... Overlooking Lough Ree ... Fun course with short par-5s ... Straightforward course where you can feel good about your game ... Bunkers provide major headache.

Connemara Golf Club   ★★★★

Ballyconnelly, County Galway
Nearest main town: Clifden

Secretary: Mr J. McLaughlin   Tel: 095 23502
                                            Fax: 095 23662
Professional: Mr H. O'Neill   Tel: 095 23502

Playing: Midweek: round £30.00; day £45.00. Weekend: round £30.00; day £45.00. Handicap certificate required.

Facilities: Bar: 10.30am–11pm. Food: Lunch and dinner from 10am–9pm.

Comments: Great location and excellent food ... Course in need of more rough ... Spectacular setting and true Irish weather ... Very challenging ... Stunning setting ... Should be on every golfer's 'must-play' list ... Romantic course that gets going on the back nine ... Rough and fairway bunkers will catch you soon enough ... Disappointing front nine ... A course of two halves ... Would be the best in Ireland if you judged it on the back nine.

Enniscrone Golf Club ★★★★

Ballina Road, Enniscrone, County Sligo
Nearest main town: Enniscrone

Secretary: To be appointed.   Tel: 096 36297
                                    Fax: 096 36657
Professional: Mr C. McGoldrick   Tel: 096 36666

Playing: Midweek: round £25.00; day n/a. Weekend: round £34.00; day n/a.

Facilities: Bar: 10.30am–11pm. Food: Lunch and dinner from 10am–9pm. Bar snacks.

Comments: Beautiful location with great variety of holes ... A natural links, play it two or three times to know it ... A gem for very little money to play and eat ... Best holes are on the back nine among the dunes ... Contrasting nines, but both have their own appeal.

Galway Bay Golf & Country Club ★★★

Renville, Oranmore, County Galway
Nearest main town: Galway

Secretary: Mr J. Cassidy   Tel: 091 790500
                                Fax: 091 792510
Professional: Mr E. O'Connor   Tel: 091 790503

Playing: Midweek: round £35.00; day £50.00. Weekend: round £40.00; day £60.00. Handicap certificate required.

Facilities: Bar: 10.30am–11pm. Food: Breakfast, lunch and dinner from 7am–10pm. Bar snacks.

Comments: If there was no wind it would be a doddle ... Wind can get horrific ... Play this with a hangover and you'll soon blow the cobwebs away ... Exhilarating experience which I'll never forget ... Overlooking the Atlantic and Galway Bay ... Ordinary land turned into something special by Christy O'Connor Jr.

Galway Golf Club   ★★★★

Blackrock, Galway, County Galway
Nearest main town: Galway

Secretary:	Mr P. Fahy	Tel: 091 522169
		Fax: 091 529783
Professional:	Mr D. Wallace	Tel: 091 523038

Playing: Midweek: round £18.00; day n/a. Weekend: round £23.00; day n/a. Handicap certificate required.

Facilities: Bar: 10.30am–11pm. Food: Lunch and dinner from 10am–9pm.

Comments: Views over Galway Bay ... Outdated course in need of spicing up ... Greens variable on visit ... Old course with an indefinable spirit and mystery ... Very tight and difficult ... Came away having ballooned over my handicap.

Gort Golf Club   ★

Castlequater, Gort, County Galway
Nearest main town: Galway

Secretary: Mr S. Devlin   Tel: 091 632244
Professional: None.

Playing: Midweek: round £12.00; day £12.00. Weekend: round £12.00; day £12.00.

Facilities: Bar: 10.30am–11pm. Food: Bar snacks.

Comments: An old club built on a new site ... Excellent greens and tight fairways ... Opened recently and excellent addition to region's quota of courses.

Loughrea Golf Club ★

Graigue, Loughrea, County Galway
Nearest main town: Galway

Secretary:	Mrs M. Hawkin	Tel: 091 841049
Professional:	None.	

Playing: Midweek: round £12.00; day n/a. Weekend: round £12.00; day n/a.

Facilities: Bar: 10.30am–11pm. Food: Breakfast, lunch and dinner from 9am–9pm. Bar snacks.

Comments: Very short and cheap course … Great value for money … Nothing special about the course … Parkland course extended to 18 holes in early 1990s.

Roscommon Golf Club ★

Moate Park, Roscommon, County Roscommon
Nearest main town: Roscommon

Secretary:	Mr B. Campbell	Tel: 0903 26382
		Fax: 0903 26043
Professional:	None.	

Playing: Midweek: round £15.00; day £15.00. Weekend: round £15.00; day £15.00.

Facilities: Bar: 10.30am–11pm. Food: Lunch and dinner from 12pm–6pm.

Comments: Recently extended to 18 holes … You're not missing anything if you drive past … The extra nine does not hide the course's weaknesses … Cheap and cheerful.

Strandhill Golf Club ★

Strandhill, County Sligo
Nearest main town: Sligo

Secretary:	Mrs S. Corcoran	Tel: 071 68188
		Fax: 071 68811
Professional:	None.	Tel: 071 68725

Playing: Midweek: round £15.00; day n/a. Weekend: round £20.00; day n/a. Handicap certificate required.

Facilities: Bar: 10.30am–11pm. Food: Lunch and dinner from 12pm–9pm. Bar snacks.

Comments: Underrated, can be very tough with some unusual par-3s ... Unknown links with views of mountains ... Some memorable, friendly times here ... Too short to test the advanced player.

Westport Golf Club ★★★★

Carrowholly, Westport, County Mayo
Nearest main town: Westport

Secretary: Mr P. Smyth   Tel: 098 28262
                (Manager)   Fax: 098 27217
Professional: Mr A. Mealia

Playing: Midweek: round £19.00; day n/a. Weekend: round £24.00; day n/a.

Facilities: Bar: 10.30am–11pm. Food: Lunch and dinner from 10am–9pm. Bar snacks.

Comments: Excellent back nine ... Impressive locker room in friendly, welcoming clubhouse ... Views make it ... Don't give up, it gets better on the back nine ... Views of Croagh Patrick ... Long, tough, scenic inland course ... Course doesn't look great until the back nine ... 12th and 15th just great golf holes.

Index of Courses

Leabharlann Chathair Phort Láirge

Telephone: 051 - 873506

OPENING HOURS

CENTRAL LIBRARY:

Tues., Thurs., Sat. : 11.00 a.m. - 1.00 p.m.; 2.30 p.m. - 5.30 p.m. (Children's same)

Weds., Fri. : 2.00 p.m. - 8.00 p.m. (Children's 2.00 p.m. - 5.30 p.m.; 7.00 p.m. - 8.00 p.m.)

BROWN'S ROAD:

Tues., Weds., Fri. : 10.00 a.m. - 1.00 p.m.; 2.00 p.m. - 6.00 p.m.

This book is due for return on or before the last date shown below

23 AUG 2000